Approaches to Teaching
the Works of Amitav Ghosh

Approaches to Teaching the Works of Amitav Ghosh

Edited by

Gaurav Desai

and

John Hawley

Modern Language Association of America
New York   2019

© 2019 by The Modern Language Association of America
All rights reserved
Printed in the United States of America

MLA and the MODERN LANGUAGE ASSOCIATION are trademarks owned by
the Modern Language Association of America. For information about obtaining
permission to reprint material from MLA book publications, send your request
by mail (see address below) or e-mail (permissions@mla.org).

Library of Congress Cataloging-in-Publication Data

Names: Desai, Gaurav Gajanan, editor. | Hawley, John C. (John Charles), 1947– editor.
Title: Approaches to teaching the works of Amitav Ghosh / edited
by Gaurav Desai and John Hawley.
Description: New York : Modern Language Association of America, 2019. |
Series: Approaches to teaching world literature ; 157 |
Includes bibliographical references and index.
Identifiers: LCCN 2018048483 (print) | LCCN 2018048615 (ebook) |
ISBN 9781603293983 (Epub) | ISBN 9781603293990 (Kindle) |
ISBN 9781603293976 (pbk. : alk. paper)
Subjects: LCSH: Ghosh, Amitav, 1956—Study and teaching.
Classification: LCC PR9499.3.G536 (ebook) |
LCC PR9499.3.G536 Z58 2019 (print) | DDC 823/.914—dc23
LC record available at https://lccn.loc.gov/2018048483

Approaches to Teaching World Literature 157
ISSN 1059-1133

Cover illustration of the paperback and electronic editions:
Thomas and William Daniell, *Gale off the Cape of Good Hope*, 1810.
Courtesy of Mystic Seaport Museum.

Published by The Modern Language Association of America
85 Broad Street, suite 500, New York, New York 10004-2434
www.mla.org

CONTENTS

ACKNOWLEDGMENTS

The editors would like to thank James Hatch, Erika Suffern, and Zahra Brown at the Modern Language Association for their help with and support of this volume. We would also like to thank the staff at the Mystic Seaport Museum for their assistance in finding a suitable cover image for the volume. In particular, thanks to Louisa Watrous, Carol Mowley, Maribeth Bielinski, and Paul O'Pecko.

For their patience with the sometimes slow pace in the making of an edited collection of this kind, we thank all our contributors. It has been a pleasure to work with you and to see this come to fruition.

Introduction

Gaurav Desai and John Hawley

Reflecting on what seemed then to be a "seismic upheaval" in the curricular offerings at the University of Delhi, Amitav Ghosh remembers the first appearance of his novel *The Shadow Lines* on the English syllabus as follows:

> I was pleased, of course, since it would certainly help the book find a wider audience, but there was also something a little chilling about the thought that thousands of undergraduates would be forced to read it in the early morning hours before their exams. . . . Would an enforced reading cause a generation of students to hate *The Shadow Lines* as I had once hated *The Return of the Native*? Would there be stock questions about the book's themes and characters? Would I myself be characterized with a critical catch-phrase ("post-colonial," "post-modern," post-who-knows-what else)? (Foreword 5)

Ghosh's later visits to the university campus seem to have alleviated his fears; he records being party to numerous illuminating conversations about the novel, even if some of them reflected matters that "had little to do with [his] intentions as a writer" (6).

We open this volume on approaches to teaching the works of Amitav Ghosh with a nod to that reflection on the author's part, because it well encapsulates some of the dominant concerns of our contributors. First, there is the question of the canon itself—a shift from the almost exclusive curricular focus on British and some American literature to literature written by Indians in the English language. Second, the actual scene of reading—with an implicit shift being signaled from readers who might pick up the novel for pleasure as opposed to a form of "enforced" reading in preparation for an examination. Third, what Ghosh perceives as the risks of such institutional settings and, in particular, of the protocols of reading that they engender—here coded as "stock questions" or "critical catch-phrases" such as "post-colonial" or "post-modern." And perhaps, fourth, the notion of finding a "wider audience," which raises the question of whom the writer projects as his primary audience in the first place.

The questions raised here are pertinent to the substance of Ghosh's oeuvre as well as to the political economy of its circulation. On the issue of canonicity and its explicit origin in colonialism and empire, for instance, we have in Ghosh a complex stance that consistently rejects the violence of colonialism and denounces the category of the Commonwealth on the one hand, but, on the other, celebrates a cosmopolitan literary space (as evident in the discussion of his grandfather's bookcase) and insists on writing in English, the language of the former colonizer.[1] The particular choices of critical remove and affiliation that he has made have not always pleased his readers. For instance, Ghosh famously withdrew his novel *The Glass Palace* from the competition for the Commonwealth Writers' Prize because he found the idea of Commonwealth literature objectionable. While many of his readers and critics applauded this decision, some were later critical of Ghosh's decision to accept the Dan David Prize awarded by Tel Aviv University in Israel (Chowdhury). Ghosh's positioning vis-à-vis the academy is similarly complicated. Despite his protests about being labeled a postcolonial writer, his writings engage in a productive dialogue with much of what gets disseminated as postcolonial theory. Furthermore, his scholarly training in anthropology and his published discussions and debates with scholars such as Dipesh Chakrabarty place him closer to the formal academy than many of his peers. Indeed, if one wanted to introduce students to one strand of postcolonial thought—say, a concern with the subaltern—one could do that as productively with a text such as Ghosh's *The Hungry Tide* as with a more academic account penned by a historian associated with the subaltern studies movement. Our aim in this book is to showcase many such crossover possibilities and to demonstrate that the inclusion of a writer's work in the formal context of a classroom need not, as originally feared by Ghosh, reduce it into mere fodder for preconceived methods, questions, or catchphrases.

Before turning to the pedagogical concerns of the volume it may be useful to remind readers of some key biographical markers. Born in Calcutta (now Kolkata) in 1956 to an upper-caste Hindu family, Ghosh attended the Doon School (a competitive secondary school founded in 1935 by moderate Indian nationalists); the prestigious St. Stephen's College and the Delhi School of Economics, both of the University of Delhi; and St. Edmund Hall, Oxford University, where he received a DPhil in social anthropology. In 1999 Ghosh joined the faculty at Queens College, City University of New York, as a distinguished professor in comparative literature before leaving the position to pursue a full-time career in writing. Now an American citizen, Ghosh is the author of thirteen major works: eight novels, three collections of nonfiction essays, a recent treatise on climate change, and one hybrid text that is poised somewhere between the genres of ethnohistory and travelogue.[2] His debut novel, *The Circle of Reason*, was awarded the Prix Médicis Étranger in 1990, and his next book, *The Shadow Lines*, received both the Ananda Puraskar award in Calcutta and the annual award of the Sahitya Akademi (the Indian National Academy of Letters). Since the publication of these early works, Ghosh has gone on to receive a number of international awards, including the Arthur C. Clarke Award for *The Calcutta Chromosome*, the Crossword Book Award for *The Hungry Tide* and *Sea of Poppies*, the Tagore Literature Award for *Sea of Poppies*, and the Myanmar National Literature Award for the Burmese translation of *The Glass Palace*. In 2014 the membership of the Modern Language Association elected Ghosh an honorary fellow of the association.

While he has cited the influence on his work of Western writers such as Marcel Proust, Gabriel García Márquez, and Ford Madox Ford, as well as Bengali writers such as Rabindranath Tagore and Hindi writers such as Phanishwar

Nath Renu, Ghosh's own oeuvre has increasingly influenced both emergent creative and critical writing in South Asia and its diaspora. His works have been translated in more than thirty languages, and he has a wide readership across the globe both within and beyond the academy.[3] While it was arguably the publication of Salman Rushdie's *Midnight's Children* in 1981 and its subsequent Booker Prize that first brought international attention to an emergent tradition of anglophone writing from the South Asian subcontinent, Ghosh's incremental work over the years has made him a central figure for readers, teachers, and critics. If anecdotal evidence were reliable, it would appear that, while Rushdie retains his status as the venerable literary giant in anglophone South Asian literature, it is Ghosh who tends to be more widely taught across a greater diversity of courses at both the undergraduate and graduate levels. Ghosh is also likelier to be taught in courses other than those strictly in English departments. His standing not only as a writer but also as a trained anthropologist means that more scholars in the social sciences engage with (and teach) his work, particularly his pathbreaking *In an Antique Land*, which provides an entirely new map for imagining cross-regional connections in the Indian Ocean in the *longue durée*. The interest in Ghosh's work among scholars beyond literary studies may be noted, for instance, in an interview with him published in the journal *Cultural Anthropology* ("Anthropology and Fiction") and more recently in two special roundtables published in the interdisciplinary *Journal of Asian Studies* (J. Thomas) and the official journal of the American Historical Association, *The American Historical Review* ("AHR Roundtable"). The roundtable in *Asian Studies* is concerned with Ghosh's book on climate change, *The Great Derangement: Climate Change and the Unthinkable*, which brings into focus Ghosh's long-standing interest in environmental issues. The historians' roundtable is on the implications of rethinking the history of the opium trade through fiction and focuses on the *Ibis* trilogy.

More so than many contemporary writers, Ghosh's developing oeuvre, in its variety of genres and locales, reflects his biography and his insistent desire to recoup the histories of otherwise overlooked peoples. In "The Ghosts of Mrs. Gandhi" (1986), he reflects on 1984, a momentous year for India: there was separatist violence in Punjab, including a military attack on the Sikh temple in Amritsar; the assassination of Prime Minister Indira Gandhi, which was followed by riots; and the gas disaster in Bhopal. Many people's lives were irrevocably shaken by these events, and it seems Ghosh's was one of them. "Looking back," Ghosh writes, "I see that the experiences of that period were profoundly important to my development as a writer" (47).[4] Already he was identifying writing as his real life, distinct from his teaching and research. But the subjects he would choose to address and the style he would employ were still in flux. The events of 1984 seem to have solidified his thinking in both regards.

The riots were directed principally against Sikh men, and as their ramifications unfolded "it was not just grief I felt," he writes. "Rather, it was a sense of something slipping loose, of a mooring coming untied somewhere within" (47). More than 2,500 died in Delhi alone. "Like many other members of my generation," writes Ghosh, "I grew up believing that mass slaughter of the kind that accompanied the Partition of India and Pakistan, in 1947, could never happen again. But that morning, in the city of Delhi, the violence had reached the same level of intensity. . . . How do you explain to someone who has spent a lifetime cocooned in privilege that a potentially terminal rent has appeared in the wrapping?" (52–53).

He had been writing *The Circle of Reason,* and its style was very much in a Rushdean vein of imaginative seriocomic storytelling—a flight of fancy that had only the loosest ties to actual historical events. But 1984 changed all that: it is as though the next novel, *The Shadow Lines,* were written by someone else entirely. Here the style is, if anything, more sophisticated—but less fantastic. The history of Partition is very real indeed, but its broad strokes are used to paint a backdrop against which the personal struggle of the young protagonist and his family gets the spotlight.[5]

The settings of Ghosh's novels signal his persistent interest in the historic frangibility of national borders and serve as metaphors for his experimentation with generic borders as well. He has noted that he does not consider the genres in which he writes to be completely distinct from one another. Critics have noted, for example, the generically indeterminable *In an Antique Land,* which reflects the author's training as an anthropologist while serving as both a personal memoir and an imagined history of Indian Ocean cosmopolitanism, with a strong novelistic overlay. *The Calcutta Chromosome* is one of the earliest of those few writings that could be categorized both as science fiction and as medical history from a subaltern point of view. The shifting landmasses and multiple ocean swells of the Sundarbans in *The Hungry Tide* metaphorically repeat the protean generic constraints against which the author struggles, moving from an ecological treatise to a class-crossing romance. The *Ibis* trilogy (*Sea of Poppies; River of Smoke; Flood of Fire*), with its wide historical and geographic sweep and its epic cast of international characters, is notably as interested in teaching readers the history of words as it is in portraying and condemning the opium trade: the first volume ends with a chrestomathy, an extended glossary of terms that are often entirely foreign to even the most cosmopolitan of readers; its postmodern disorientation of readers' understanding of the appropriate role of diegesis in interpreting the book's generic status is compounded by the author's subsequent identification of himself in his lively blog as the Chrestomather (portrayed in the books as Neel, an imagined character). In that blog (which, along with Ghosh's carefully curated Web site, may be seen as generic experimentations in their own right), words are described as migrant indentured laborers, rendering Ghosh's experimentation with the Laskari language of his characters and his Kreol communication between many characters as another blurring of boundaries that the author embraces both thematically and structurally.

In an Antique Land is perhaps Ghosh's greatest experiment with genre, bringing together travelogue, fieldwork notes, and the experiences of an ethnographer with the historical quest for an older narrative pieced together from scraps of documents found in a medieval synagogue in Egypt. *The Calcutta Chromosome* engages with the genre of science fiction with magical, mystical, and supernatural elements. *The Glass Palace, The Hungry Tide,* and the *Ibis* trilogy have seen Ghosh return in a more disciplined way to the genre of historical fiction, but here too the incorporation of folk and subaltern knowledges, the insistence on syncretic belief systems and practices, and his own field trips in pursuit of his narratives (for example, his accompanying a cetologist studying the Irrawaddy dolphin) lend a note of descriptive detail that is often lacking among many of his contemporaries. To be sure, some have argued that it is precisely such a scholarly approach to writing—whether incorporating historical materials, scientific expertise, or field research—that risks compromising the purely literary aspects of Ghosh's prose, and this is a debate well worth having in the classroom. In this connection, it is intriguing to note that, despite his commercial success and his appeal to a large range of readers, Ghosh's work is rarely taught in creative writing workshops. We have not yet been able to get a convincing explanation for this from colleagues in creative writing other than general remarks on Ghosh being more of a "scholar's writer" than a "writer's writer." This too is a conversation worth pursuing in the classroom, especially one in which there are both students who primarily take the class as critics and those who aspire to be creative writers themselves.

As suggested earlier, the themes that Ghosh engages have preoccupied and resonated with parallel developments in what has come to be labeled postcolonial studies, and the essays in this volume situate his work in that broad framework. As Anshuman Mondal has perceptively noted,

> In all his major works, and in his essays and journalism, Ghosh meditates upon a core set of issues but each time he does so from a new perspective: the troubled (and troubling) legacy of colonial knowledge and discourse on formerly colonized societies, peoples and ideas; the ambivalent relationship to modernity of the so-called "developing" or "Third" world; the formation and reformation of identities in colonial and post-colonial societies; the question of agency for those previously seen as objects but not subjects of history; the recovery of lost or suppressed histories; an engagement with cultural multiplicity and difference; and an insistent critique of Eurocentrism in general. (*Amitav Ghosh* 2)

To this we might add that Ghosh's work has, increasingly over time, also been invested in matters of translocation, displacement, and movement; oceanic spaces (which, after the publication of Paul Gilroy's *The Black Atlantic: Modernity and Double Consciousness* in 1993, have increasingly become a central preoccupation in the humanities); environmental concerns and the human interface with the environment; and gender and sexuality.

In regard to environmental issues, *The Circle of Reason,* for instance, involves the lives of Indian migrants to a fictional Gulf state that is involved in oil extraction, and Ghosh's early essay on petrofiction is often cited by scholars looking at fictional representations of extractive industries ("Petrofiction"). *The Glass Palace* likewise is concerned with the deforestation in Burma, and *The Hungry Tide* takes environmental degradation, conservation, and risk as its central theme. But, while such issues have been important to Ghosh since the outset of his career, they have become increasingly central to both his fictional narratives (an engagement with botany and plants is one of the central narratives in the *Ibis* trilogy) and his nonfiction. *The Great Derangement* is among these latter texts that interrogate the role of fiction and the humanities in general in addressing the challenges of climate change.

The representation of gender and sexuality, and of women in particular, in Ghosh's fiction has been long debated by critics, but there has been a renewed attention and focus on this theme, particularly since the publication of the *Ibis* trilogy. The figure of the subaltern woman Deeti has been discussed most, but the novels offer a rich array of sexualities that are only now beginning to be considered by critics (see, for instance, Leverton; Elangbam; and Jayaraman).

Approaches to Teaching the Works of Amitav Ghosh addresses all of these themes, and while individual instructors may read from it selectively as per their own classroom interests and needs, the volume is structured so as to engage with Ghosh's work from multiple angles. As is standard practice with the *Approaches* series, the book is divided into two parts. Given the information overload now afforded by the Internet and the ease with which scholars can access online databases, the first part, "Materials," is relatively short. Rather than providing a comprehensive list of secondary sources, there are signposts for resources both primary and secondary that would be most useful to students and teachers of Ghosh's texts.

The second part of the book consists of four interrelated sections. The first section, titled "Contexts and Histories," consists of essays that help frame Ghosh's works in a larger historical and institutional context. Albeena Shakil starts off the discussion by returning to the institutional moment with which this introduction began, the inclusion of *The Shadow Lines* in the University of Delhi curriculum and the relation of that novel and Ghosh's fictional work as a whole to the tradition of the Indian-English novel in India. The three essays that follow focus on the broad historical sweep of Ghosh's writings, with Debjani Ganguly focusing on the scale of the historical novel in the *Ibis* trilogy, Vedita Cowaloosur engaging with the social and political contingencies of languages and linguistic hybridities in the trilogy, and Ned Bertz showcasing how Ghosh's Indian Ocean–inspired writings can be productively introduced to students taking courses not only in literature but also in history.

The second section, "Teaching between Ethics and Politics," includes essays that are more focused on getting students engaged with close readings of individual texts to draw out their most compelling themes: thus we have an essay on reading the politics of colonial subjectivity and choice in *The Glass Palace* (Ambreen Hai), an essay that invites students to read between the lines of Ghosh's nonfiction essays for political and activist positions (Kanika Batra), an essay that examines Ghosh's treatment of alternative rationalities in *The Circle of Reason* (Yumna Siddiqi), an engagement with the politics of postcolonial feminism through a reading of *The Hungry Tide* (Suchitra Mathur), an essay that asks students to read *Flood of Fire* as a way of rethinking the narration of empire (Vincent van Bever Donker), and an essay on reading intimacies in *Sea of Poppies* (Smita Das). What holds these essays together is the centrality of ethics in Ghosh's writings. As Ghosh put it in an interview with Chitra Sankaran, "writing is fundamentally ethical. And it's something that writers feel discomfort with because they don't want to think of themselves as being moralizers. . . . I don't think I'm in a position to be telling people what they should be doing, as a rule. But I'm very drawn to ethical predicaments . . ." ("Diasporic Predicaments" 13). It is such predicaments that this section tracks.

The third section, "Transgressing the Limits: Genres and Forms," shifts the discussion of the politics of boundaries and the transgressions that they sometimes engender from questions of theme to those of form. The section includes essays on teaching the very idea of genre to students by focusing on the Bakhtinian notion of the chronotope (Arnapurna Rath), on transnationalism in *The Circle of Reason* (Robbie B. H. Goh), and two essays on *The Shadow Lines*: one interested in it as an experiment in postcolonial formalism (John J. Su) and the other on how the novel reworks a family tale and bildungsroman into a geopolitical statement (Hilary Thompson).

The final section, "Scenes of Instruction," contains essays that speak to specific courses or institutional contexts. Roopika Risam suggests ways to teach the *Ibis* trilogy using some of the tools of the digital humanities. Ben Holgate interrogates the much-debated category of magical realism in the context of a classroom discussion of *The Calcutta Chromosome*. Russell Berman discusses the appeal of *The Hungry Tide* to students beyond the literature major in a course in the core curriculum. Jonathan Steinwand shows how *The Hungry Tide* might be used to introduce students to competing ideas of environmentalism. Adele Holoch asks us to consider some of the rewards of foregrounding the humor of *In an Antique Land* in a general education class, while Alan Johnson discusses some of the challenges of preparing students who are about to embark on a full-semester single-author course on Ghosh's works. Sneharika Roy asks what the most appropriate way of introducing Ghosh's work in a world literature class on the epic form might be. In the final essay in the section, Emily Stone describes the challenges and privileges of teaching a novel such as *River of Smoke* to students who are not native English speakers but who happen to be residents of the geographies that the novel emplots.

Scholars of literature know that every act of reading is at once an act of re-reading and that every act of rereading is at once an act of reading with a difference. The same is true of pedagogy and the work done in the classroom. No matter how many times we teach the same material, the actual pedagogical moment is unique, the experience different, the results varied. We hope that the essays gathered here will help inspire new approaches to teaching Ghosh and will allow for new conversations and innovations in the classroom. For students, we hope that reading Ghosh is never experienced as something "enforced" for the purposes of taking an exam; and we hope that this volume will assure Ghosh and other contemporary writers that the academy does indeed allow and encourage critical engagements beyond "stock questions about the book's themes and characters."

NOTES

[1] On Ghosh's grandfather's library, see Ghosh, "March of the Novel" [*Kunapipi*].

[2] *The Circle of Reason* (Hamish Hamilton, 1986); *The Shadow Lines* (Bloomsbury, 1988); *In an Antique Land: History in the Guise of a Traveller's Tale* (Granta, 1992); *The Calcutta Chromosome: A Novel of Fevers, Delirium, and Discovery* (Picador, 1996); *Dancing in Cambodia: At Large in Burma* (Ravi Dayal, 1998); *The Glass Palace* (Harper-Collins, 2000); *The Imam and the Indian: Prose Pieces* (Ravi Dayal / Permanent Black, 2002); *The Hungry Tide* (HarperCollins, 2004); *Incendiary Circumstances: A Chronicle of the Turmoil of Our Times* (Houghton Mifflin, 2005); *Sea of Poppies* (Farrar, Strauss and Giroux, 2008); *River of Smoke* (Farrar, Strauss and Giroux, 2011); *Flood of Fire* (Farrar, Strauss and Giroux, 2015).

[3] A comprehensive list of all translations of Ghosh's works does not seem to exist. In a personal e-mail communication with the editors, Ghosh indicated that the novels had been translated in about twenty languages while some of the essays and nonfiction had been translated in up to thirty.

[4] Quotations from "The Ghosts of Mrs. Gandhi" are from the version found in *The Imam and the Indian*.

[5] The previous two paragraphs draw upon Hawley, pp. 1–5.

Part One

MATERIALS

Critical response to living writers generally ripens over time, responding to the most recent book by attempting to fit it into an established or emerging set of topics and themes. At the same time, sudden popularity and a larger reading public often lead to a reassessment of an author's earlier works that may not initially have made much of an impact. Both of these dynamics have been true in the case of Amitav Ghosh. Bill Buford, editor of *Granta*, gave Ghosh an advance that enabled the writing of *In an Antique Land* (1992), but the book was not reviewed by many critics. Those few reviews were generally dismissive, because the work could not be defined by a particular genre's or academic discipline's criteria, and the sales were abysmal. Decades later, this is no longer the case for Ghosh. Each volume of the *Ibis* trilogy—*Sea of Poppies* (2008), *River of Smoke* (2011), and *Flood of Fire* (2015)—has been widely reviewed. Each has been accompanied by published and televised interviews with Ghosh and has been a success story for anglophone Indian fiction. Indeed, the *Guardian*'s reviewer writes of the *Ibis* trilogy that "the ground it has covered is almost immeasurable" (Clark). Ghosh's recent books sell fifty thousand copies easily; *River of Smoke* (shortlisted for the Man Asian Literary Prize) surpassed sixty thousand in its first year, and this has helped with sales of his earlier books. In 2015 his entire body of work was shortlisted for the Man Booker International Prize (awarded that year to the Hungarian novelist László Krasznahorkai).

Celebrity culture has no doubt played a role in this success: one might point to Ghosh's controversial 2001 dismissal of the Commonwealth Writers' Prize as having an effect on his career similar to the fatwa against Salman Rushdie, on a minor scale; his stand against the "Commonwealth" category provided a boost to his public profile and arguably increased his popularity among readers and critics alike. When *Sea of Poppies* was shortlisted for the Man Booker Prize in 2008, the award committee noted that in that year Ghosh's cumulative book sales had exceeded three million books worldwide and he had been translated in thirty-three languages.

This retrospective assessment of early work, though, is by no means complete in the case of this author. In particular, *The Circle of Reason* (1986) has received little attention. P. Saxena's 2015 essay is one of several that compare the novelist's style with that of the South American magical realists. Yumna Siddiqi uses the novel to discuss postcolonial rationality, which is becoming an important motif in other analyses of Ghosh's corpus (*Anxieties*). Much more work needs to be done on this novel, especially as an early indication of Ghosh's interest in the Indian Ocean world of commerce; along these lines, Claire Chambers discusses the book's treatment of the "oil encounter" ("Representations" 33). Frank Schulze-Engler speaks of a "global ecumene" and compares Ghosh's considerations of modernity in *Circle of Reason* with those in *In an Antique Land* (34–36, 39–41). P. B. Mehta points out Ghosh's early interest in a new way of cosmopolitanism and provocatively argues for a cosmopolitanism of distance rather than of hybridization. The fact that Mehta's article was published in a social science journal suggests the interdisciplinary nature of Ghosh's body of work and, of course, his own training in anthropology.

Ghosh is also, of course, a prolific essayist and commentator. One of his earliest books, *In an Antique Land*, is something of an extended essay, situated somewhere between travel writing and history, with some emphasis on memory and nostalgia. It has garnered far more attention in recent years than when it was first published in 1992.[1] Neelam Srivastava shows the connections between the book and Ghosh's doctoral thesis. Javed Majeed focuses on nationalism, which others deal with in much greater detail in Ghosh's later works. Christi Ann Merrill offers suggestive connections between humor and the portrayal of subaltern consciousness, and Samir Dayal discusses subalternity and "the emergence of the fragile subject" in Ghosh's writings.

Ghosh's four collections of nonfiction published over the years—*Dancing in Cambodia: At Large in Burma* (1998), *Countdown* (1999), *The Imam and the Indian: Prose Pieces* (2002), and *Incendiary Circumstances: A Chronicle of the Turmoil of Our Times* (2005)—have helped in the structural composition of a number of monographs of the writer's body of work[2] and in edited collections of articles by various hands.[3] Nonetheless, his collected essays need more sharply focused attention. His long-established concern for the environment, displayed to such striking novelistic effect in *The Hungry Tide*, becomes the central focus in *The Great Derangement: Climate Change and the Unthinkable* (2016).

Interviews with Ghosh have also been central in the monographs, and others have been published as separate pieces in various venues.[4] It is not surprising that many of the interviews focus primarily on the most recently published novel or have evolved into investigations into the recurring thematic tropes over the corpus.

To date, the most attention has been paid to *The Shadow Lines* (1988) and *The Glass Palace* (2000). The historical issues in both have by now established themselves in the minds of critics as being central to Ghosh's body of work. For *The Shadow Lines*, those topics include nationalism;[5] the Partition, borders, and the complexities of cartography;[6] and identity.[7] Many other essays are more comprehensive, dealing with topics like cosmopolitanism and its reinterpretation.[8] In 2011 Sandip Ain published a very helpful set of essays on various topics associated with *The Shadow Lines*.

With growing international attention to environmental concerns and the effects of global warming, *The Hungry Tide* is drawing more critical assessment and inviting consideration of its endangered setting, the Sundarbans.[9] These essays build on the work of others who refer to Ghosh's work as part of their broader discussion of ecocriticism.[10] Other critics approach the novel from a variety of perspectives: aesthetics (Giles; Jaising), subalternity (Gopinath), the plight of refugees, relations between men and women, and the ethics of action and inaction.[11] Ghosh has become a preeminent example for those writers who wish to find literary examples of the sources and extensions of globalization, and *The Hungry Tide* offers an opportunity for such discussions.[12]

The setting and history of *The Glass Palace* (2000) may be unfamiliar to most students, and their engagement with the novel could be enriched with some reference to the history of the royal family of Burma (Shah). Perhaps because Burma is an infrequent setting for anglophone fiction, several critics offer an orientation to similar works: Michael Prusse compares the novel with J. G. Farrell's *The Singapore Grip* to discuss migration, and Christopher Rollason compares the novel with George Orwell's *Burmese Days* as studies in transcultural communication ("'In Our Translated World'"; "Empire"). M. A. Sonia approaches the book from the viewpoint of fragmented identities, and N. Sukanya and S. Sobana similarly use a lens of the "displacement of nation" (120). These essays join others that provide less focused analysis.[13] Jaspal K. Singh discusses the diaspora in Burma.

Since it is science fiction, *The Calcutta Chromosome* (1995) is, as many note, unusual in literature commonly categorized as postcolonial. Uppinder Mehan and Carolyn Marcille demonstrate the genre's potential for postcolonial analysis, and they are echoed by others.[14] Christopher A. Shinn specifically addresses the limitations of Western science, as do Sanjit Mishra and Nagendra Kumar as well as Bodhisattva Chattopadhyay. Suchitra Mathur offers one of the first essays on the question of feminism in Ghosh's work. Barbara Romanik's essay is a bit of an outlier, using the novel to discuss the broader topic of the colonial city and its transformations.

Those who plan to teach parts of the *Ibis* trilogy would do well to read Travis W. Hanes III and Frank Sanello on the Opium Wars as historical background. *Sea of Poppies* (2008) has been written about by numerous scholars, sometimes with the tentative air of critics approaching what they know to be the first part of a proposed trilogy.[15] Omendra Kumar Singh discusses Ghosh's attempt at reinventing caste in the novel; Barnali Sarkar analyzes the role of sati. *River of Smoke* (2011) has received attention from Kanika Batra and Catherine Delmas. Binayak Roy discusses its portrayal of the Orient "from within" ("Exploring the Orient" 1, 14–20). *Flood of Fire* (2015) has not yet played a central role in individual articles, but essays considering the entire *Ibis* trilogy are inevitable (R. Sarkar; Lionnet, "World Literature").

Ghosh's work in general, but most particularly the *Ibis* trilogy and its chrestomathy, has called critics' attention to the author's fascination with words, with etymology. Supriya Chaudhuri, Vedita Cowaloosur, Sharmani Patricia Gabriel, Lise Guilhamon, and R. S. Gupta and Kapil Kapoor focus on this. Stephanie Han looks especially at *Sea of Poppies*, and Tapashi Mazumdar and John Skinner do the same for *The Glass Palace*.

So far, Ghosh's fascination with the Indian Ocean world has received the most concentrated focus by Gaurav Desai (*Commerce with the Universe*). The topic also plays into the work of Françoise Lionnet ("World Literature") and Leslie Elizabeth Eckel.[16] One suspects that future research will more fully develop critical perspectives in this area.

As noted above, the unusual *In an Antique Land* prompted questions about the genre in which Ghosh had chosen to write, but his historical novels raise similar questions. If one were to engage the issue in the classroom and regard the historical novel as a form, one might review the work of Desai ("Old World Orders"), Jenniefer Dkhar, Greg Forter, Anna Guttman, John Marx, Hamish Dalley, A. Tadie, and Hilary Thompson ("Before After"). Ananya Jahanara Kabir raises similar questions in her analysis of *The Shadow Lines. The Calcutta Chromosome*, which seems to straddle different forms, may prompt students to consider questions of genre as well as the expectations they have brought to the reading of the text. As it incorporates actual historical characters and events, a device also used by E. L. Doctorow in *Ragtime* and Philip Roth in *The Plot against America*, students will wonder: is this a history, a pure science fiction fable, or what? Other generic questions arise because of what some consider Ghosh's violation of the norms of realistic fiction. Some critics have considered the extent to which Ghosh's work typifies some version of postmodernism.[17] P. Pradeep and R. Poli Reddy apply similar questions to *The Shadow Lines* and M. Sreelatha to *Sea of Poppies*. Others ask a narrower but related question: is Ghosh a magical realist? Those who deal with this question, at least in passing, are Lois Parkinson Zamora and Wendy B. Faris in *Magical Realism*, along with Faris's *Ordinary Enchantments* and "Scheherazade's Children"; Eva Aldea; Maggie Ann Bowers; and Ato Quayson.

Theo D'Haen ("Antique Lands," "'Global Literature,'" and "Magical Realism"), Christopher Warnes, and Stephen Slemon pose the question more broadly, in terms of postcolonial literature in general; Saxena, more narrowly, focuses on *The Circle of Reason*. Anshuman A. Mondal ("Allegories of Identity"); Gousia Sultana; Vinay Lal; Bishnupriya Ghosh; and Gauri Viswanathan ("Beyond Orientalism") consider whether postcolonial is an appropriate designation for Ghosh's work. Murari Prasad asks the question of *In an Antique Land*, while Shital Pravinchandra considers *The Calcutta Chromosome*. John J. Su combines the two questions (magical realist/postcolonial) in speaking of the "aesthetic turn" in such writing ("Amitav Ghosh"); Jaising and Giles do something similar with *The Hungry Tide*.

Questions of gender and sexuality in Ghosh's works have received little attention, though some have looked more broadly at the treatment of homosexuality in Indian novels (Elangbam); Uma Jayaraman has studied the varieties of masculinity in *Sea of Poppies*, and Ania Spyra considers the masculinization of the notion of cosmopolitanism in *The Glass Palace*. Ian Almond and J. Edward Mallot have analyzed postcolonial melancholy in the novels. Much more work in this area is needed.

The Hungry Tide and perhaps *The Calcutta Chromosome* seem to cry out for studies of posthumanism, and some work has been done by Helen Tiffin, Neel Ahuja, and Shameem Black ("Post-Humanitarianism"). Subaltern studies has been the lens used by others.[18]

Finally, having established himself as one of the major living Indian writers, notably different from Salman Rushdie, Arundhati Roy, and Kamila Shamsie, Ghosh merits comparative studies that suggest his influence on a younger generation—for example, on writers such as Chetan Bhagat and Vivek Shanbhag—or perhaps more directly on writers beyond South Asia. His global reach as an author and public intellectual includes a robust online presence. The blog that he has curated on his Web site (amitavghosh.com) since April 2011 suggests the endurance of his various interests, and most notably his concern with climate change and the "great derangement" that he describes in detail in his 2016 book by that name. Calling himself the Chrestomather, Ghosh engages readers of his blog in a wide-ranging discussion of subjects dealing specifically with South Asian history, such as the psychological effects of the Partition, and more broadly with contemporary culture, such as the impact of smartphones. He recommends various books he has been reading and includes columns by others that he has found to be of potential relevance to his readers. Direct engagement with the author through this blog can be another avenue for students seeking to involve themselves in his work.

NOTES

[1] See Belliappa; Kamath; Chew; R. G. Davis; L. Gandhi; Desai, "Old World Orders"; Chambers, "Anthropology"; Gunning; U. Dutta.

[2] See Bhatt and Nityanandam; B. Bose; Hawley, *Amitav Ghosh*; and Mondal, *Amitav Ghosh*.

[3] See Khair, *Amitav Ghosh*; Choudhury; Sankaran; Jha; and Ghosh and Bhattacharya.

[4] See A. Ghosh, "Amitav Ghosh in Interview"; A. Ghosh, "Interview" by Sen; A. Ghosh, "Interview" by Aldama; Chambers, "Absolute Essentialness of Conversations"; A. Ghosh, "'Postcolonial' Describes You as a Negative"; Reddy; Vescovi, "Amitav Ghosh"; Zanganeh; A. Ghosh, "Networks"; A. Ghosh, "Between the Walls"; A. Ghosh, "Diasporic Predicaments"; A. Ghosh, "Anthropology."

[5] See Majumdar; A. Roy, "*Microstoria*"; Sharma; Sujala Singh, "Routes"; and Sirohi.

[6] See Barat; Dora-Laskey; Fu; Harrington; Kokila; Smith; Wassef; B. Roy, "Mapping the Transnation"; R. Roy; Simon; and A. Sen, "Crossing Boundaries."

[7] See Lint; Martos Hueso; and Sushila Singh.

[8] See Rao; Radhakrishnan, "Derivative Discourses"; A. N. Kaul; Bagchi; Bharali; Butt; Chambers, "'[A]cross the Border'"; Vinita Chandra; Chatterjee Sriwastav; A. De, "Mapping the Imaginary Lines"; Dedebas; Eleftheriou, "Bodies like Rivers"; M. Ghosh; James and Shepherd; Kapadia; S. Kaul, "Separation Anxiety"; Lauret, "Excavating Memories"; Mane and Shinde; Mee; and A. Sen, "Child Narrators."

[9] See Dutta Sharma; Gurr; Kaur; Murphy; Pirzadeh; Prabhu; Roos and Hunt; Sumati; Szeman; Weik; Dengel-Janic; Rath and Malshe; L. White; and Mallick.

[10] See Ramachandra Guha; Huggan and Tiffin; Nixon, "Environmentalism" and *Slow Violence*; M. Sen; Steinwand, "Teaching Environmental Justice Poetry" and "What the Whales Would Tell Us."

[11] See Ambethkar and Raj; Amelya and Al-Hafizh; Anand; Bartosch, "Good Dose"; Chakraborty; Cottier; R. Das; S. Das; A. De, "For the Right"; P. Devi; Fletcher; Goh; Griffiths; Gupta; Hanquart-Turner; Hicks; Huttunen, "Language"; Kaur; Khuraijam and Singh; Kumar and Prasad; Meyer; Pablo Mukherjee; Nayar, "Postcolonial Uncanny";

Pulugurtha; Ratnaker and Srinivas; K. Singh; Jai Singh; Tomsky; Vescovi, "Fear and Ethics"; and Zagade.

[12] Radhakrishnan, "Globalization"; Grewal; Bhat; Black, "Cosmopolitanism at Home"; Reis; and Nixon, "Anthropocene."

[13] Bhautoo-Dewnarain; Glasgow and Fletcher; Guejalatchoumy and Aruna; Kadam; Khuraijam and Acharjee; and Maharaj.

[14] Bruschi; Chambers, "Network of Stories" and "Postcolonial Science Fiction"; Fendt; Lee; S. Banerjee; Nayar, "Informational Economy"; Nelson; Rath; Thrall; and Vescovi, "Emplotting the Postcolonial."

[15] Acharjee and Khuraijam; Agrawal; Ambethkar and Sunalini; Arora; K. Davis; Delmas; Dhar; Eswaran; Gangopadhyay; Hawley, "Gateway"; Jayaraman; Jouzaee and Jamili; Kalpakli; Lauret, "Re-mapping the Indian Ocean"; Leverton; Luo; Rema; Stasi; and Baumgarten.

[16] Those interested in pursuing this area in their teaching might review the work of Alpers; Bertz; Hofmeyr; B. J. Mehta; Metcalf; Pearson; Simpson and Kresse; and Vink.

[17] See Bhattacharjee; Bindhu and Sachithanand; Chenniappan and Suresh; Dar; M. De; Freedman; and Malathi.

[18] See Bhattacharya; Burton; Choudhary and Sharma (for *The Calcutta Chromosome*); Cabaret; McClintock; Mujumdar, "Modernity's Others"; Pandey (the disconnect with the nation-state in *The Hungry Tide*); Paranjape; Pillai (in *The Glass Palace*); A. Roy, "Ordinary People" (subalternity and its relation to various cosmopolitanisms); Sujala Singh, "Who Can Save the Subaltern?" (in *The Circle of Reason*); Telwani; Vescovi, "Voicing Unspoken Histories."

Part Two

APPROACHES

Ghosh, *The Shadow Lines*, and the Indian-English Novel

Albeena Shakil

> Every word I write about those events of 1964 is the
> product of a struggle with silence. . . . The enemy of
> silence is speech.
>
> —Amitav Ghosh, *The Shadow Lines*

The turn of the century saw the inclusion of Amitav Ghosh's second novel, *The Shadow Lines*, in undergraduate syllabi across several universities in India. This was part of an uneven process to include Indian Writing in English (IWE) and translations within English studies courses, starting in metropolitan universities at the end of the 1990s and continuing till today in provincial as well as open and distance-learning universities across India. The preceding decades, starting with the dazzling entry made by Salman Rushdie's *Midnight's Children* in 1981, had witnessed the emergence of a string of Indian-English novelists like Anita Desai, Vikram Seth, Rohinton Mistry, Vikram Chandra, Arundhati Roy, and others who were propelled into the international spotlight in quick succession. Among them was Ghosh, who emerged as a consensus figure within Indian academia. The reasons for this lay in two momentous debates that were being waged in India at that time: one pertaining to the strained relationship between the English language and *bhashas*[1] (what later became infamous as the "authenticity" debate), and another pertaining to the felt need to move away from an exclusive focus on Anglo-American literature and liberal humanism in the English studies curriculum.

The strain between English and the *bhashas* was an outcome of dramatic changes in the fortunes of the Indian-English[2] novel during the 1980s and 1990s. Until that time, the durability of this literature had been in doubt. At best, the Indian-English novel was considered a minor stream of Indian literature and subjacent to *bhasha* literatures. It was also positioned as a minor contributor to anglophone literatures from across the world. The "big three" English novelists of the 1930s—R. K. Narayan, Mulk Raj Anand, and Raja Rao, who had cemented the respectability of the English novel in India—continued to dominate the scene several decades later. Recalling the prevailing mood during this period of "slump," Meenakshi Mukherjee, a foremost scholar of the Indian-English novel, wondered in the preface to *The Twice Born Fiction* whether the "entire enterprise was grinding to a halt." However, suddenly the Indian-English novel started receiving global recognition, with its writers becoming overnight sensations. The equation with the *bhashas* soon got reversed. Within a couple of years, writers were left deliberating whether it was worthwhile writing in any language other than English in India.

Passionate debates ensued. Questions were raised over whether writers who lived and wrote from abroad could be considered Indian. And exactly which readership did they address, Indian or Western? Did they write back to India from elsewhere, or did they represent India to the world? Weren't they casting disingenuous backward glances at India? Were they elites who wrote in English, or did the predetermined elitism of the English language afford them undeserved preeminence? What was so remarkable or worthy in their writings? And, while world literary history was full of writers who were read in translation—Cervantes, Balzac, Tolstoy, García Márquez, and others—why was it that only Indian-English writers got to represent India to the world? During these years, the relevance of postmodernism, postcolonial theory, hybridity, mimicry, exile, etc., was also a matter of fierce and polarized debate in India.

In 1993 Meenakshi Mukherjee wrote her influential essay "The Anxiety of Indianness: Our Novels in English," drawing a distinction between the first and second generations of Indian-English novelists as well as between English and *bhasha* novelists. She demarcated postglobalization Indian-English writers by their anxiety of writing national allegories with a tendency toward "homogenisation of reality, an essentialising of India, a certain flattening out of the complicated and conflicting contours, the ambiguous and shifting relations that exist between individuals and groups in a plural community" (2608). Among all English novelists, however, she singled out Ghosh for praise, more particularly his novel *The Shadow Lines*:

> The novel betrays no anxiety because it attempts to prove nothing and interrogates rather than defines the concept of a totalising India. The novel speculates tentatively on the varieties of human freedom and the bonds across space and time to explore personal relationships. India is neither a metaphor nor a philosophical idea. . . . As in the works of the

best Indian language writers today, words like "marginality" and "hybridity" seem irrelevant here and segmenting the world into first and third
regions a rather absurd activity. (2611)

Subsequently, she continued to argue that postcolonial discourses by migrant
intellectuals were shaped by their desire to belong to an international community and that "concerns like social injustices, erosion of democracy, and threat
of fundamentalism" were more central to local contexts than race, hybridity, or
mimicry (*Elusive Terrain* 187–88). Her opinion was symptomatic of a wider
opinion among literary critics in India who were poised at the interface of
the English-*bhasha* debate and who would also demarcate Ghosh from the
rest. For instance, Tabish Khair, who characterized Indian-English writers as
babus—essentially privileged, elite, Western, urban, English-educated bourgeois subjects—also made an exception for Ghosh (*Babu Fictions*).

In the ensuing years, a fierce debate over the "authenticity" of Indian-English
writing emerged in India. While "Indian-English," in its hyphenated avatar,
found greater acceptance within the multilingual terrain of Indian languages,[3]
it continued to cause deep unease. Fuel was added to the fire by Rushdie in
1997, when he infamously wrote that "[t]he prose writing—both fiction and
non-fiction—created in this period [post-independence] by Indian writers
working in English is proving to be a stronger and more important body of work
than most of what has been produced in the 16 'official' languages of India"
("Damme" 355).[4] This was the same year when a bilingual Marathi and English
novelist, Kiran Nagarkar, came up with his masterpiece, *Cuckold*, arguably
among the finest novels written in English in India. However, he faced the
brunt of the English-*bhasha* debate wherein he was abandoned by the Marathi
literary establishment for turning renegade in writing in English and not quite
embraced by the English establishment either. In the same year, Roy's *The God
of Small Things* made a dramatic entry on the literary scene. While the novel
was notable for its popularity in the United States, in India it upset the Syrian
Christian community and generated polarized opinions over its sexual frank-
ness and its derision of communists (who were particularly relevant in view
of the 1998 formation of a Hindu right-wing union government led by the
Bharatiya Janata Party). Some questioned whether Roy could write about the
authentic Dalit experience, and whether her novel connected with the global
dystopia following the collapse of the Soviet Union while remaining unmindful
of local concerns over secularism.

In the year 2000, Vikram Chandra wrote a sharply critical piece in the *Boston Review*, titled "The Cult of Authenticity: India's Cultural Commissars Worship 'Indianness' Instead of Art," recalling his 1998 encounter with Mukherjee
in New Delhi. He criticized scholars like Mukherjee for suggesting that Indian-
English writers wrote with "anxiety" while regional writers wrote in some sort
of "Eden of innocence." In early 2001 Rajeswari Sunder Rajan wrote a two-part
rejoinder to Chandra in *The Hindu* daily, "Writing in English in India, Again"

and "Dealing with Anxieties," accusing Chandra of sustained sexism and of fraudulently equating the left-liberal articulation of "Indian-ness" with the "authenticity" of cultural fascists. Chandra's two-part retort, "Arty Goddesses," reiterated his view that the left and the right in India indeed shared common readings of art and culture. Before this controversy could die down, V. S. Naipaul, a freshly anointed Nobel laureate, again made dismissive insinuations about *bhasha* writers in his inaugural address to the 2002 Indian Council for Cultural Relations Conference in Neemrana, a major literary event inaugurated by the prime minister of India (Saccidānandan et al.). The theme of the multilingual conference was ironically borrowed from the title of Timothy Brennan's 1997 book, *At Home in the World: Cosmopolitanism Now*, which wasn't particularly generous in characterizing the proliferating breed of globally visible writers as "third-world cosmopolitans."

The debate over reformulating English studies curricula in universities, driven mainly by the twin impulses of postcolonial theory and feminism, was taking shape in the same years in India. Since undergraduate teaching in India does not allow professors the freedom to frame courses (except recently in some select universities), the process of syllabus change has always carried considerable import. The story began unfolding with Gauri Viswanathan's *Masks of Conquest: Literary Study and British Rule in India* (1989). Important edited and authored volumes proposing changes in course content, syllabi, and theoretical paradigms appeared in quick succession: Rajeswari Sunder Rajan (ed.), *The Lie of the Land: English Literary Studies in India* (1992); Svati Joshi (ed.), *Rethinking English: Essays in Literature, Language, History* (1991); G. N. Devy, *After Amnesia: Tradition and Change in Indian Literary Criticism* (1992) and *In Another Tongue: Essays on Indian English Literature* (1993); and Susie Tharu (ed.), *Subject to Change: Teaching of Literature in the Nineties* (1998). Other volumes, like R. S. Gupta and Kapil Kapoor's (eds.) *English in India: Issues and Problems* (1991) and Kapoor's *Language, Linguistics, and Literature: The Indian Perspective* (1994), made a case for the inclusion of ancient Indian classical texts in the syllabi. As a result of these deliberations, Indian Writing in English (IWE) as well as translations, alongside literary texts from around the world, started finding a place within undergraduate curricula of English studies. Several Indian-English writers were included in different courses, but from among his generation, Ghosh emerged as a near-consensus choice. The reasons for this lay in Ghosh's different trajectory as an English writer.

Though Ghosh won the French Prix Médicis Étranger for his first novel, *The Circle of Reason*, his 1989 Sahitya Akademi Award for *The Shadow Lines* from India's National Academy of Letters preceded it. Thus, unlike many English writers of his generation who became known in India through international awards and prizes, he first earned his reputation in India and slowly acquired an international one. The fact that in 2001 Ghosh declined his nomination for a regional Commonwealth Writers' Prize also earned him praise within India, particularly from the *bhasha* camp. And, when the authenticity debate turned into a full-fledged controversy, Ghosh escaped getting caught in the cross fire while remaining mindful of prevailing sensitivities. *The Shadow Lines* additionally provided scope for discussing the great national debate of those years between secularism and communalism, one still pertinent within classrooms. And, though other stalwart Indian-English novelists of the same generation were taught within English studies classrooms, they were generally reserved for postgraduate teaching, where faculty members were at greater liberty to frame their own courses without being constrained by prevalent institutional or political opinions. In fact, some writers taught at the undergraduate level ran into political trouble, as in the case of Rohinton Mistry, whose 1991 novel, *Such a Long Journey*, was removed from the Mumbai University syllabus after it offended the grandson of Shiv Sena founder Bal Thackeray in 2010. Hence, undergraduate syllabi remain sites of intense contestations in India. The fact that Ghosh's novel has managed to sustain across syllabi over the years speaks volumes, not just about the relevance of the themes he dealt with, but also the manner of his dealing—through argumentative, tentative, and evolving narrators and characters who form opinions only with the benefit of experience.

This is not to suggest that Ghosh encapsulates some better "essence" or sense of India. Rather, in crucial matters of basic approach and style, Ghosh does not conform to the more distinctive novelistic traditions of India. It is useful to recall that scholars have indicated that novels in India have often relied upon the twin impulses of history and epics (Mukherjee, "Epic"), with strict demarcation between history, legend, epics, and myths being virtually impossible, be it in the colonial vernacular novels of Bakim Chandra and Devaki Nadan Khatri or in the postcolonial/postmodern novels of Rushdie, Roy, and even the popular Amish Tripathi. However, despite being a master of the historical novel, Ghosh is unique in that he writes history sans epics. In fact, his historical novels fit more into the Lukácsian framework of "critical realism" and "types," wherein individual characters share independent, psychological inner lives with other developing characters while being organically linked to the momentum of sociohistorical change (Lukács, *Historical Novel* and *Studies*). Yet, unlike the Lukácsian framework, which mainly credits novelists for their accurate depiction of individuals in evolving histories, the main strength of Ghosh's historical novels lies in the power of allegory. Nowhere has this been more evident than in his *Ibis* trilogy about the nineteenth-century Anglo-Chinese Opium Wars. In an interview, Ghosh provides the key to reading the first novel: "oil is the opium of today" ("Addicted to Empire"). Published in 2008, the year of the global economic crisis, with both India and China bucking the trend—when mounting opposition to the Iraq War and the optimism of the campaign slogan "yes, we can" were propelling Barack Obama to the presidency of the United States and India was politically split down the middle over the Indo-US nuclear deal interpreted as a gateway to a new strategic partnership with the United States—the first novel of the trilogy, *Sea of Poppies*, in addition to providing potent insights into the historical dynamics between the British Empire, India, and China, also evoked contemporary reality. The main shortcoming of the trilogy lies in the same aspect—that, after setting up this expectation, Ghosh retreats from the allegorical to mainly the historical, sociological, and anthropological terrains.

Ghosh has also been interestingly located in the pre- and postglobalization intellectual churning in India. The year 1981, which saw a turnaround in the fortunes of the Indian-English novel with the publication of *Midnight's Children*, coincided with the appearance of the influential Subaltern Studies Group in 1982. Much like the Indian-English novel, subaltern studies also generated initial controversies over whether it was a metropolitan discourse initiated by migrant intellectuals. Despite different disciplinary and thematic concerns, the main contribution of the school lay in its fundamental reformulation and reconceptualization of modernity as different from prevalent linear Western models based on Enlightenment thought. Ghosh was a contributor to the *Subaltern Studies* series, and the founding statement by Ranajit Guha to volume one of *Subaltern Studies* is pertinent to understanding Ghosh. Yet Ghosh represented both convergence as well as divergence with the Subaltern Studies project. For instance, in *The Shadow Lines*, he constantly deals with binaries— silence and speech, imagination and "precise" imagination, freedom and bonds, boundaries and shadow lines, self and other, home and away—to paradoxically construct a nonbinary vision of the world where India and East Pakistan (now Bangladesh) or East and West and First and Third Worlds do not necessarily find themselves on opposite sides. Despite contesting conceptions of modernity and progress in his writings, his commitment to core Enlightenment values like democracy, secularism, equality, and liberalism remains unquestionable. In his entire body of work, his sharpest critiques and skepticism are perhaps reserved for nation and nationalism, a line of thought that links up better with the early-twentieth-century stalwart Rabindranath Tagore. If the political scientist Benedict Anderson's nation was an "imagined community," Ghosh's world did not necessarily consist of nations or communities, but was a place where strangers could meet in ruins to find affinity and love. Moreover, his treatment of migration in his work was not only about the anxieties of East and West, or colonial and postcolonial anxieties, but was mainly a battle with amnesia involving memories of forgotten historical traditions, of lateral as well as reverse migration.

Of late, Ghosh has been dividing his time equally between India and the West. It is not a coincidence that *The Shadow Lines* has slowly slipped from the Indian Writing in English course in the undergraduate syllabus of the University of Delhi into the course on Partition literature. Given political animosities, South Asian literature still remains outside the ambit of undergraduate teaching in India, and South Asia is still perceived as a concept existing elsewhere rather than within the region. However, Ghosh's novel would remain a leading candidate for inclusion in any such course if it were to be formulated in the future, given the dramatic improvement in social diversity in higher education institutions in India, especially since statutory changes made in admission policy in 2006.[5]

Undergraduate classrooms in India are experiencing unprecedented social and linguistic diversity, with students who aspire to be on the cutting edge of global thought, livelihood, and culture working alongside first-generation learners, and those who have some "taste" in literature learning with those who have never read for leisure before. In such a context, *English* and *literature* within "English literature" courses are often poised in a tenuous relation. Given the voice and language of Ghosh's narrator, *The Shadow Lines* remains a more accessible text for undergraduate students. While this exceptional novel can be discussed for its diverse literary and thematic merits, it is also important to keep the contours of the overall evolving context in view in order to understand why the writer and his novel gained initial acceptability within Indian academia and have managed to sustain it for nearly two decades.

NOTES

[1] The word *bhasha* literally means "language." It was recoined by G. N. Devy in the 1990s to denote the acceptance of Indian English as an Indian language while still maintaining its distinction from other Indian languages.

[2] The nomenclature for Indian-English writing has evolved over time from Anglo-Indian literature to Indo-Anglian literature, Indo-English literature, anglophone literature, Indian Writing in English, and finally Indian-English writing. Literatures in other Indian languages have been variously labeled vernacular literature, literature in Indian languages, regional language literatures, and *bhasha* literatures.

[3] By 1999 Aijaz Ahmad, in his book *In Theory: Classes, Nations, Literatures*, noted, "English is simply one of India's own languages now" (77).

[4] Rushdie reiterated the same damaging position in his introduction to a collection of writings coedited with Elizabeth West in 1997, *The Vintage Book of Indian Writing, 1947–1997*. Since 2002, however, Rushdie has revised his opinion, calling for better translations.

[5] Publicly funded higher education institutions in India are mandated to follow a reservation policy in student admissions. Fifteen percent of all admitted students must be Scheduled Castes (Dalits) and 7.5 percent Scheduled Tribes (Adivasis). Another 3 percent of seats are reserved for disabled students in admissions from across all designated social categories of students. In 2006, a law was promulgated in the Indian Parliament to include another 27 percent reservation in admissions for Other Backward Classes (a designation comprising socially, educationally, or economically disadvantaged castes). This move was a watershed in expanding socially diverse representation in higher education institutions. This system of admissions has significant similarities and differences with affirmative action policies practiced in the United States.

Opium and Indian Ocean Worlds:
The Scale of the Historical Novel in
Ghosh's *Ibis* Trilogy

Debjani Ganguly

If the "sea is History," as the Nobel laureate Derek Walcott famously declared, the ocean is an archive (*Selected Poems* 137). At least that is the overwhelming sense one is left with after exhausting the voluminous novels that make up Amitav Ghosh's Indian Ocean trilogy, popularly known as the *Ibis* trilogy. The last of these, *Flood of Fire*, published in June 2015, is more than six hundred pages long. Each of the novels is appended with a list of primary sources that aided the author in his creation of microhistorical worlds of men and women entangled in British maritime trading adventures. Together, these total no fewer than five hundred sources, enough to write an extended historical tract on the period between 1820 and 1840, during which the First Opium War took place. Populated with fine-grained historical vignettes of lives in motion across the myriad bodies of water that make up the eastern expanse of the Indian Ocean during the period of British maritime expansion, the *Ibis* novels veritably overflow with archival *jouissance*. I hesitate to say archival *overload*, because the live pleasure, or fever if you will, of the archive is so very palpable in these novels. Sources range from historical records maintained by Commissioner Lin Xexu's office to paintings by the Anglo-Macanese artist George Chinnery. One revels in the authorial play with obscure documents, historical tracts, quaint lexicons, and botanical sketches that miraculously conjure characters, places, battles, journeys, discoveries, addictions, loves, lives, and deaths during the infamous era of opium trade between British India and China. What might this mode of crafting tell us about the purchase of the historical novel in the twenty-first century? How might these novels help us make unique inroads into debates on global literary world making in our era?

What follows is my experience of teaching the first two novels of the trilogy as advanced seminars with a focus on these two key questions and, of course, on the trilogy's magnificent retrieval of the now lost worlds of colonial-era Indian Ocean trade routes. I end with some reflections on *Flood of Fire*.[1] In undertaking a close textual analysis of *Sea of Poppies* and *River of Smoke*, we read them together rather than sequentially in order to be able to organize our seminar discussions around the following themes: thalassography and microhistory, the scale of the Indo-Chinese opium trade, the allegorical entwining of colonial-era indenture and natural histories, global history and the historical novel, and Ghosh's dazzling linguistic experimentation and its implications for thinking Anglo-globalism.

The Oceanic Turn

In teaching *Sea of Poppies* and *River of Smoke* in both honors and graduate seminars in largely anglophone Western universities, I find it useful to begin by encouraging students to think about the genres these works embed: the classic historical novel, for sure, and other sea-inspired novelistic and poetic genres, but also thalassography, a branch of oceanic writing that focuses on smaller bodies of water that are populated with habitations intimately connected with oceanic routes, such as bays, estuaries, rivers, gulfs, and deltas (Miller). After all, much of the action in Ghosh's novels has these smaller aqueous bodies as their backdrop: the Hooghly River, the Bay of Bengal, the Arabian Sea, the Pearl River Delta, and the Hong Kong Bay. The sea or the ocean has featured as a setting in any number of classic literary texts, from Samuel Taylor Coleridge's *The Rime of the Ancient Mariner*, Herman Melville's *Moby-Dick*, and Jules Verne's *Twenty Thousand Leagues under the Sea* to Ernest Hemingway's *The Old Man and the Sea*, Joseph Conrad's *Lord Jim*, and Derek Walcott's *Omeros*. These works are often familiar to advanced students, and we spend a few minutes in the very first seminar sharing our perceptions about them. Before we proceed to analyze Ghosh's novels in considerable detail, the students and I discuss the implications of moving from the theme of the ocean in literature to the ocean as both a material force in and a conceptual frame for literary history. This is a challenge of a different order and scale, and one that is critical to understanding the import of the *Ibis* trilogy. Works like the *Ibis* trilogy open toward conceptual frameworks that can be deployed retroactively to aid understanding of how past systems of globalism have impacted the making and refashioning of literary worlds, such as, for instance, the late eighteenth- to nineteenth-century Franco-British maritime world system. This world system, we note right away, had more than the Atlantic at its heart.

The connections between cartography, cognitive mapping, and aesthetic representation are particularly complex in oceanic literary studies. The Atlantic has featured as a major paradigm since the publication of Paul Gilroy's pathbreaking *The Black Atlantic*. The making of Euro-America on the back of the slave trade provides a powerful and sobering counterpoint to the triumphant theatricality of Franco-British maritime domination in the same era, while simultaneously connecting literary discourses and literary themes previously understood as territorially and culturally distinct. Atlantic studies has revolutionized the way we study the emergence of modern French, British, and American literatures today. In postcolonial and world literary studies, the phrase "Black Atlantic" has reconceptualized the Atlantic Seaboard as the site of the emergence of capitalist modernity as a transnational system. The African slave trade, the American plantation economies, and the industrial world of Europe are seen as inextricably linked, a phenomenon that the students are historically attuned to.

They are less aware of an equally resonant oceanic world—the Indian Ocean—that lay at the heart of the European maritime expansion from Africa and the Middle East to South and Southeast Asia, a world that Ghosh's *Ibis* novels bring powerfully to the fore. Indian Ocean literary worlds have been disconcertingly absent in conceptions of modern European and world literatures since the eighteenth century. The history of the slave trade was followed by the history of indentured labor (commonly known as the "coolie" trade) from India and Malaya to outposts of the British and French Empires, primarily to the Mascarenhas Archipelago and the Caribbean. The Indian Ocean trade routes served as the primary conduit for this transportation.[2] Indians, Chinese, Africans, and Arabs commingled in zones that continued to experience the dark memories of the slave trade. Frederick Douglass, the author of the novella *The Heroic Slave*, wrote in 1871 about his distress at the grim reality of the "coolie" trade (Foner 55). A century later the Mauritian poet Khal Torabully articulated a transnational poetics of "coolitude," drawing on the pan-African negritude movement of the 1930s and arguing for the centrality of the sea voyage—as both destructive and creative force—in the recovering of the "coolie's" identity and story. The opium trade between British India and China is equally crucial to foregrounding the importance of the Indian Ocean in the making of capitalist modernity. Opium was Britain's solution to the imbalance of trade with China. The British import of Chinese tea, silks, and porcelain in exchange for silver had drained British resources. Aware of the Chinese addiction to opium, the East India Company forced peasants in eastern India to turn to the cultivation of opium. By the beginning of the nineteenth century the British had used the port of Calcutta and the waters of the eastern Indian Ocean to send more than four thousand crates of opium through third-party traders to Canton. This consignment quadrupled in the years leading up to the Chinese crackdown on this trade in the 1830s and the First Opium War. The war led to the victory of the British imperial military forces in 1842 and the handover of Hong Kong to the Crown.

Ghosh's *Ibis* novels are an indispensable countermemory to the absence of archival evidence of Sino-Indian-British lives affected by the opium trade from Calcutta to Canton. During the seminar we discuss the implications of this historical amnesia after I give a short account of how the opium trade became the largest source of British imperial trade revenue for nearly 150 years, from the late eighteenth to the early twentieth century, and was also the cause of the infamous Opium Wars between British India and China in the mid-nineteenth century. I also share excerpts from an interview wherein Ghosh expresses his outrage at the lack of historical focus on the opium trade in accounts of British imperialism on the subcontinent. In his words:

> There is very little historical work on the opium trade, which is a bizarre thing because the opium trade played such a large part in our economy until the 1920s. People quite often ask me why is there so little awareness

of the Opium War in India. I don't know the answer. In the case of Asia, the Opium War was a world historical event that changed the continent. Yet the calamity of the war and of the trade remains hidden. ("Networks"; see also A. Ghosh, "Between the Walls")

It is this lost history that Ghosh attempts to retrieve through his imaginative foray in the novels. An excerpt from *Sea of Poppies* captures this monumental history of the opium trade in just one sentence: "In eastern India opium was the exclusive monopoly of the British, produced and packaged entirely under the supervision of the East India Company; except for a small group of Parsis, few native-born Indians had access to the trade or its profits" (85).[3] The three novels give flesh to the various agents mentioned in this quote: the East India Company (represented by the Burnhams, the Jardines, and the Mathiesons), the rural peasants displaced and impoverished by the opium cultivation on the Gangetic plane (Deeti and her kin), and the affluent Parsi businessmen in the opium trade (Bahram Modi and his entourage aboard *Anahita*). *Ibis*, the eponymous schooner owned by the Burnhams in the novels, is a slave ship before being transformed into a vehicle for transferring indentured labor to sugar plantations in the Mascarenhas. It subsequently becomes an indispensable vehicle for the opium trade between eastern India and southern China.

The interconnectedness between the Atlantic slave trade and the movement of labor on Indian Ocean trade routes, and the consequent entanglement of literatures of slavery and indenture, is brought to the fore in our first seminar discussion on the trilogy, as is the world of colonial-era Afro-Asian, Arabic, and Indo-Chinese trade routes via the Indian Ocean and the transcontinental cultural complexes these have generated across three centuries. The students read excerpts from works by Gaurav Desai (*Commerce*), Isabel Hofmeyr ("Black Atlantic" and "Print Cultures"), Engseng Ho, Sanjay Subrahmanyam, Sunil Amrith, and Nile Green, among others. They become aware of the need for a renewed and vigorous attentiveness to the interconnected print and literary public spheres of the Indian Ocean world from the eighteenth to the mid-twentieth century. European imperial incursions in this region can be seen as generating renewed cultural mixing with pre-European worlds. Literature during this period is broadly understood to cover diverse genres in multiple languages, including Gujarati, Hindi, Swahili, Arabic, English, and French. Itinerant travelers, such as pilgrims, sailors, soldiers, traders, merchants, and administrators, have left records of their experiences. Records also exist of prisoners in the penal settlements of Robben Island and the Andamans. The genres range from travel writing, folktales, letters, poems, and testimonies to short stories and novels. Many of these exist in special collections primarily in South Africa, the United States, the United Kingdom, India, Mauritius, and Madagascar. Extant texts on the Zanzibari Gujaratis, such as Gunvantrai Acharya's *Dariyalal*, exist alongside Mia Couto's *Voices Made Night* and Zuleikha Mayat's weekly columns from Durban in *Indian Views*. Cynthia Salvadori's three-volume publication

We Came in Dhows records the movement of Indian traders across the Indian Ocean between the west coast of India and Kenya and their eventual settlement in East Africa during the colonial era. Memorabilia, photographs, travel narratives, diaries, and memoirs feature in this collection and offer a powerful tableau of Indo-British-African cultural connections. Scripts of theatrical performances in the colonial era by Asians and Indians in East Africa also abound in the special archives. Other scarcely studied works include Bahadur Tejani's novel *Day after Tomorrow* and Peter Nazareth's *In a Brown Mantle*. Not an insignificant proportion of this literature finds inflection in the works of many contemporary novelists apart from Ghosh. These include Abdulrazak Gurnah, M. G. Vassanji, J. M. G. Le Clézio, and Shenaz Patel.

In short, the students learn to see how they can posit the Indian Ocean as a powerful archive through which to understand modern literary world making and to trace lines of intersection with Atlantic perspectives to which they are much more attuned. They also begin to appreciate how the ocean might function less as a thematic than a conceptual frame for a new kind of literary history.

Thalassography and Microhistory

Much like Deeti in *Sea of Poppies*, who sees an apparition of the ship *Ibis* from her landlocked hut in Ghazipur and is filled with fear about what it entails—the journeying into an unknown world of black waters—the students experience considerable trepidation as they dip their feet into the *Ibis* world. Despite their readiness to learn about a world from a relatively unknown past, a world they have mostly not encountered in their literary and humanistic training, their disorientation is quite serious. They encounter a facet of the global that resists easy translation. The hybrid languages of oceanic mobility in the early nineteenth century, we soon collectively realize, are completely lost to generations who have grown up in the age of air travel.

This becomes an opportune moment in the seminar to turn to the linguistic experimentation in the novels and their revival of the many lost idiolects of nineteenth-century Asian maritime worlds. The trilogy's language weave is truly astonishing, ranging from sea-trading argot like Laskari and Cantonese pidgin to Baboo English and Butler English, not to mention the generous sprinkling of various regional Indian tongues such as Hindi, Gujarati, Bhojpuri, and Bengali. We make it a point to be attentive to the nuances of the speech-acts of all the major characters in every seminar. But at this relatively early stage of our discussion we focus on Ghosh's use of Laskari, the extinct idiolect of the lascars, the laboring Afro-Asian underclass on board these ships, and of Cantonese pidgin, spoken only by those integral to the Canton trading system in southern China in the first half of the nineteenth century. In Ghosh's words, it is "a Sino-Portuguese-English pidgin that came to be associated with the South China Coast. This marvellous expressive dialect once flourished in many corners of the Indian Ocean but like Laskari did not outlast the age of sail" ("Of Fanas and Forecastles" 58). The entanglement of these tongues with specific bodies of water is brought to the fore through characters like Jodu, Serang Ali, Ah Fatt, and Bahram Modi and his Cantonese mistress. We spend a few minutes in class reading aloud excerpts where exchanges occur in Cantonese pidgin. A group of four to five students offer to make a list of about a hundred Laskari words that appear in the novels. I share with them the story of Ghosh's discovery of a Laskari dictionary in a library at Harvard that really provided him with the impetus to make generous use of this now-extinct vocabulary in his trilogy. Compiled by Lieutenant Thomas Roebuck in 1881, *A Laskari Dictionary; or, Anglo-Indian Vocabulary of Nautical Terms and Phrases in English and Hindustani*, was a major inspiration for the novelist, as was Henry Yule and Arthur C. Burnell's *Hobson-Jobson: A Glossary of Colloquial Anglo-Indian Words and Phrases*. The students also research the glossary developed by Ghosh and posted on his official website. Entitled "The *Ibis Chrestomathy*," the glossary has a narrative about Neel Rattan Haldar, the disgraced Raja of Raskhali, as the reborn lexicographer who makes it his mission to document every possible word used by girmitiyas, lascars, and their Anglo-Indian masters during their oceanic journeys in the colonial era. These are words that Neel predicted would make their way into the first major lexicographic project undertaken on behalf of the English language, namely the *Oxford English Dictionary*, but which Neel calls the Oracle. In the 1840s the *OED* was nowhere on the horizon. We see this new Neel as the painstaking lexicographer of a global English before the era of globalization in the final novel of the trilogy, *Flood of Fire*. Ghosh's brilliant lexicographic excavation in the trilogy bears significant purchase on contemporary engagement with the idea of English as a world language in the era of globalization, an observation that invariably leads to an invigorating seminar discussion.

While the students begin to familiarize themselves with the use of Cantonese pidgin in the Pearl River Delta as depicted in *River of Smoke*, and with Laskari as used in *Sea of Poppies*, I also introduce them to the idea of thalassography and its relevance to the setting, characters, plot movements, and the language deployed in the *Ibis* novels. The idea of human habitations that grow around smaller bodies of water—thalassography—is central to these novels. These generate their own microhistories that are often lost when we scale up our mostly terrestrial pedagogic models to nations and continents. We explore ways in which we might study these novels as fictional thalassographies of eastern Indian Ocean worlds stretching from Mauritius and India to southern China and Hong Kong. We decide to zoom in, *Google Earth*–like, on the various bodies of water that serve as myriad scenes of action and that constitute the many nodes in the oceanic network of the *Ibis* trilogy. This is where the class breaks up into four groups and each chooses to undertake an intensive study of a water-borne locale or a network of movements on water:

> Group A decides to focus on the Hooghly River stretching from the
> Botanic Gardens on the one end to Kidderpore and Garden Reach on

the other. *Sea of Poppies* is rich in its depiction of the lives of Jodu, Paulette, and the Burnhams on the banks of the Hooghly. Each stands as the exemplar of the world of lascars, naturalists, and colonial free traders, respectively.

Group B researches another stretch in the Bay of Bengal from the river estuaries to the Great Nicobar Islands, where the convicts and the girmitiyas make their escape from the *Ibis*.

Group C explores the habitation of foreign traders, local agents, and boat people in Fanqui Town on the Pearl River Delta in Canton, as depicted in *River of Smoke*.

Group D explores the links between Calcutta and Canton through the correspondence of Paulette and Robin Chinnery in *River of Smoke* and also through the character of Neel.

Much of this group work is undertaken outside class hours after we have an in-class discussion about some of the common topics that each group will cover:

the significance of the locale or network for maritime opium trade routes;

the representation of lascars, girmitiyas, and convicts;

the individuated presence and centrality to the action of the various ships, such as the *Ibis*, *Redruth*, and *Anahita*;

the collusion between British traders and the Indian feudal and merchant class;

the mix of languages and cultures in each locale;

the entanglement of natural history and trade history during maritime colonialism; and

the clash between British and Chinese trading cultures.

These topics could vary in significance for each group: in some they are central, in others peripheral. In presenting their findings to the rest of the groups, I encourage the students to make generous use of data visualization techniques and other digital resources, such as a geographic information system, in order to bring to life the various thalassographic worlds in the novels.[4] For this they seek assistance from the Scholars' Lab and other digital media units available at the University of Virginia. They also research the architecture of the various ships and generate fine-grained visual graphics of each. This enables them to imagine the long and arduous journeys of the travelers aboard these vessels across the waters of the Indian Ocean. Such research and shared learning is painstaking at first but invariably spectacular in its presentation, not to mention insightful, for all groups. I have found that the students are pretty adept at getting their geographical and historical coordinates right. Once the various dots on the trade routes are connected, the seminar group as a whole begins to appreciate the scale of colonial maritime operations on the Indian Ocean and Ghosh's craft in bringing this world to life 150 years later through meticulous

historical, archival, and philological research. This becomes an opportune moment to steer the discussion toward the genre of the historical novel and its
transformation in the era of global history. The question of scale becomes critical in appreciating these novels as historical fiction. The novelist's ingenuity in
weaving the private lives of individuals with large historical forces across a truly
global terrain, from Baltimore and Bombay to Calcutta, Mauritius, Macau,
Canton, and Hong Kong, offers a challenge to the literary scholar. The trilogy
compels us to reexamine the remit of the historical novel as it has featured in
modern European literary scholarship and to reevaluate its provenance for our
global times.

The Ibis *Trilogy and the Historical Novel*

The start of this essay mentions the overwhelming presence in the novel of historical detail, of Ghosh's painstaking archival work, of his authorial pleasure in
mining the lost history of the opium trade. In a recent interview he distinguishes
his historical labor from that of the professional historian in these terms:

> If I may put it like this: history is like a river, and the historian is writing
> about the ways the river flows and the currents and crosscurrents in the
> river. But, within this river, there are also fish, and the fish can swim in
> many different directions. So, I am looking at it from the fish's point of
> view and which direction the fish swims in. So, history is the water in
> which it swims, and it is important for me to know the flow of the water.
> But in the end I am interested in the fish. ("Between the Walls")

The apposite aqueous metaphor aside, the words of the author convey a complementary relation between history and fiction rather than an antinomian one.
In other words, for the historical novelist the epistemological claims of the past
are as relevant as they are for the historian, except that the former works with
both invented and documented sources and has to carefully navigate the tension between imaginative re-creation and historical claims. Further, as Ghosh's
statement attests, such novelistic work oscillates between the depiction of the
everyday world of actors and the macrohistorical forces at work.

There is no dearth of scholarly sources to illuminate these tensions. In steer-
ing the seminar discussions around the relation between the historical and the
novelistic imagination and between historical writing and literary genres, the
students are taken through a brief tutorial on theories of the historical novel,
beginning with Georg Lukács's seminal book *The Historical Novel* and his discussion of Walter Scott as the first modern practitioner of the genre. We also
briefly revisit the scholarly writings of James Chandler on literary historicism,
Katie Trumpener on national character and realist tropes, and Catherine Gallagher on fictionality and probability. Gallagher's essay "The Rise of Fictionality" offers an especially compelling account of the complex relation between

real-life referents and their fictional depiction in the modern novel: "Because a general referent was indicated through a particular, but explicitly non-referential, fictional individual, the novel could be judged generally true even though all of its particulars are merely imaginary" (342). Extrapolated into our seminar discussions about the referential force of the historical novel, this statement acquires particular significance since so many of Ghosh's characters in the trilogy—Burnham, Bahram Modi, Jodu, Neel, Paulette, Bhyro Singh, Deeti— appear precisely with such allegorical force, representing real historical forces in the era of the opium trade. In another essay, Gallagher discusses the appearance of Napoleon as a character in three different texts ("What Would Napoleon Do?"). This again offers a site for productive discussion since Napoleon does appear as himself in an episode in *River of Smoke*, when Bahram Modi and Zadig Bey go to meet him in Saint Helena. We also discuss the portrayal of the real-life Commissioner Lin, the upright official who put a temporary halt to the opium trade from Canton, in *River of Smoke*. The seminar discussions subsequently explore postcolonial and global perspectives on historicism, fictional probability, realism, and the historical novel with Ian Baucom's work on actuarial typification and melancholic singularity in the context of the Atlantic slave trade; Ann Rigney's work on typification, invented exemplars, and realism; and Hamish Dalley's work on allegorical realism in the postcolonial historical novel. Much of this scholarly corpus deploys Lukács's theorization as the starting point while going beyond its foundational Marxist (and Eurocentric) premises.

The historical novel for Lukács, we might remember, is not just a novel with a historical setting but one that captures the emergence of a modern historical consciousness after the French Revolution—one that generates an awareness of a new social order at the conjunction of the early industrial revolution, the emergence of a nationalist sensibility, and the consolidation of the nation-state in Europe in the early nineteenth century. In other words, this is a temporal consciousness that is seen to emerge alongside capitalism, the rise of nationalism, and an enlightened rationality. For Lukács, Walter Scott's novels represent this modern genre. The valorization of realism as the most apposite mode of self-apprehension of the modern historical subject occurs in tandem with Lukács's theorization of the genre. Lukács also highlights the mode of characterization typical of the historical novel—one that veers between the historical typification of competing forces (mercantile capitalism and feudalism in Scott's *Waverly*, for instance) and a middle-ground character that mediates this dialectic. Postcolonial and global reformulations of Lukács's thesis take nineteenth-century imperialism into account, thus thoroughly fracturing his conjunction of capitalism, reason, progress, and realism. Through a postcolonial lens, historical realism appears complicit with imperialism, a key reason for the wholesale rejection of the provenance of realism and mimesis in postcolonial criticism and the neglect of the historical novel in postcolonial theory (Rigney; Dalley). Hence also the valorization in postcolonial studies of magical realism and a range of antimimetic, antirealist writers like Salman Rushdie, Tayeb Salih, Chinua Achebe, Gabriel García Márquez, and the rest.

Ghosh's historical novels, set exactly during the period of the publication of Scott's novels and the maritime imperial adventures of the British, urge us to attend seriously to this genre again. Their archival realism, key to Ghosh's craft, functions less to highlight a progressive and reason-centered historical world trajectory than to excavate an alternative account of British imperial activities on the Indian Ocean and to testify against the venality of the British Empire. The novels also offer a more global history of the workings of the British Empire and give flesh to the historian Thomas Metcalf's thesis in his book *Imperial Connections* that India was at the heart of the web of empire in every way, including that of the Indian Ocean world, and it constituted "a nodal point from which peoples, ideas, goods and institutions—everything that enables an empire to exist—radiated outward . . . the ties of empire ran not only to London but also to Calcutta, Bombay and Madras" (1). Metcalf especially highlights the importance of ports like Calcutta and Bombay (now Mumbai) in the British governance of Indian Ocean worlds from Africa in the west to Malaya in the east.

The last novel in the trilogy, *Flood of Fire*, offers a compelling novelistic (and allegorical) rendering of these historical facts. The opium trade was justified by East India Company officials in the name of the free market (a point powerfully depicted through the operations of the Canton Chamber of Commerce in *River of Smoke*), and the First Opium War was seen as the battle of freedom over Manchu tyranny. The words of Burnham in *Flood of Fire* rallying his ship's troops to attack the Chinese navy exemplify the casting of the destructive imperial mission in the rhetoric of liberty and progress:

> [On you] will fall the task of freeing a quarter of mankind from tyranny; of bestowing on the people of China that gift of liberty that the British Empire has already conferred on those parts of the globe it has conquered and subjugated. . . . It is you, gentlemen who will give to the Chinese the gifts that Britain has granted to the countless millions who glory in the rule of our gracious monarch, secure in the knowledge that there is no greater freedom, no greater cause for pride, than to be subjects of the British Empire. (436)[5]

The military and the administrative machinery of the British East India Company as it prepared for the First Opium War had at its core a large contingent of Indian personnel. Characters like Bhyro Singh, Kesri Singh, and Maddow Colver are exemplars in the novel. HMS *Cornwallis*, the warship on which the 1842 Treaty of Nanjing was signed to ratify China's defeat in the First Opium War, was built in the Bombay Dockyard by a Parsi shipbuilder, Wadia, in 1813. In *River of Smoke*, Wadia's compatriot Bahram Modi, a Parsi opium trader in Canton, commits suicide at the prospect of losing his livelihood because of the Chinese embargo on the trade in 1839, which saw the destruction of more than twenty thousand chests of opium. His widow, Shireen Modi, appears in *Flood of Fire* as the avenger of Bahram's death and an allegory of those Parsi trading communities who benefited from the large compensation the East India Company sought from the Chinese emperor for its temporary loss of revenue from the trade embargo. The compensation also included the handing over of Hong Kong to the British and the auctioning off of its various portions to bidding traders. We see Shireen refuse her share of the Hong Kong land auction in *Flood of Fire* as she decides to wait for a spot on the slopes of the Peaceful Mountains. The novel ends with the establishment of an influential global trading partnership among Burnham, Zachary Reid, and Lenny Chan and their acquisition of prime real estate in Hong Kong. The success of mercantile capitalism over centuries-long feudal economies is here played out on a topological scale that is oceanic, one that far exceeds Scott's historical novelization of the same conflict (between England and Scotland) in *Waverly*. The historical novel in Scott's time, as James Chandler has argued, embeds a past onto a cultural space that is putatively national in its remit (94–154). In Ghosh's novels, this space-time configuration straddles the globe. Furthermore, far from illuminating a stadial view of historical development typical of the nineteenth-century historical novel, Ghosh succeeds in laying bare the imperial underside of the very emergence of this modern historical consciousness that invested so heavily in the idea of uneven development and in chronologies of "backward" and "advanced." The temporality in the *Ibis* novels, far from endorsing a progressive trajectory toward a mercantile modernity, repeatedly breaks the flow of capitalist time in its melancholic retrieval of lifeworlds washed away by rivers of smoke and floods of fire:

> How had it happened that when choosing the men and women who were to be torn from this subjugated plain, the hands of destiny had strayed so far inland, away from the busy coastlines, to alight on the people who were, of all, the most stubbornly rooted in the silt of the Ganga, in a soil that had to be sown with suffering to yield its crop of story and song? It was as if fate had thrust its fist through the living flesh of the land in order to tear away a piece of its stricken heart. (*Sea of Poppies* 399)

In offering a literary corpus that helps us rethink the historical novel and the purchase of modern literary historicism, not to mention the scope of modern literary historiography, in our global era, Ghosh's *Ibis* trilogy becomes indispensable reading for literary scholars in the twenty-first century.

NOTES

[1] I have taught these works in the United States, the United Kingdom, and Australia. The recent publication of *Flood of Fire* has meant that I haven't had the opportunity yet to teach this text. My comments on it toward the end of the essay are untested in a classroom.

[2] See C. Anderson; Bragard; Carter, *Servants* and *Voices*; and Carter and Torabully.

[3] This essay quotes the 2008 Penguin/Viking edition of *Sea of Poppies*.

[4] A geographic information system is designed to capture, store, manipulate, analyze, manage, and present all types of spatial or geographic data.

[5] This essay quotes the 2015 John Murray edition of *Flood of Fire*.

Language in the *Ibis* Trilogy

Vedita Cowaloosur

Amitav Ghosh's *Ibis* trilogy is a popular teaching text in universities across the world, especially with the growing academic interest in the Indian Ocean from disciplines across the social sciences and humanities. Though a work of fiction, Ghosh marries history with anthropology, sociology, and linguistics to trace the events in the 1830s leading to the first Anglo-Chinese war (also known as the Opium War) from the perspectives of Indian, British, Chinese, and diasporic and peripatetic participants across a large spectrum of class, race, and gender boundaries. The interest it evokes among scholars from such diverse fields is therefore not surprising.

One of the biggest challenges of teaching the trilogy, though, is its language. How does one teach novels that feature more than a dozen languages—ranging from recorded contemporary and ancient languages in their standardized forms, to pidgins and creoles that thrive in unformalized versions in specific parts of the world, to unrecorded (potentially nonexistent) languages that seem to be the product of the author's own imagination as he re-creates them for the purposes of his novels[1]—to students who often speak only one of these languages, sometimes as a second or third language at that? One of the recurrent criticisms of the *Ibis* trilogy (mostly in the anglophone world but also beyond) has attacked Ghosh's experimentations with language, which not only faithfully replicate "the social diversity of speech types . . . and different voices" through vivid dialogues given to characters, but also percolate his narrative and descriptive passages (Bakhtin, *Dialogic Imagination* 263).[2] Reviewing *Sea of Poppies* for the British newspaper *The Telegraph*, Sameer Rahim writes that the novel fails to strike a chord with readers because of its hybridity, its "pishpash language," which takes it beyond readers' grasp and imaginative reach "even with the help of the OED." Chris Patten—in another British newspaper, *The Financial Times*—thought that the merit of *River of Smoke* is lessened by Ghosh's "somewhat self-indulgent use of the period pidgin, creole and patois slang." As for *Flood of Fire*, the Indian publication *DNA* found that its far too "liberal use of Hindustani" might prove to be a hindrance to "foreign" readers—though Nirmalya Dutta does gloss over this seeming inconvenience by stating, "[B]ut it's not a problem that *Google* can't help you overcome."

To the invested reader, not just *Google* but the author too extends a helping hand. He may not attach an extensive glossary to each novel, but Ghosh does provide on his Web site a compendium of words and phrases from the different languages that figure in the novels. This compendium, which he calls "The *Ibis* Chrestomathy," has been up since the publication of *Sea of Poppies* and has been updated with each novel. Even considering that this facilitation has been made possible only because of the advances and spread of multimedia technology, Ghosh offers far more assistance than most Indian-English writers extend to their readers to aid them with the language of their novels. Indian-English writers have displayed a long-standing fascination with polyglot prose, usually without offering glossaries or accompanying translations in English of the other languages incorporated.[3] This prose, consisting of the code-mixing of English with indigenous Indian languages (or *bhashas*),[4] has led some transnational readers to regard code-mixed language as the fetish—and even selling point—of the multilingual Indian-English writer.[5]

Where the *Ibis* trilogy surpasses the other Indian-English writers (and even Ghosh's earlier writing) is in the way that it frightens and alienates not just anglophone readers, but also Indian readers who speak some of the *bhashas* included. As reflected in his chrestomathy, Ghosh's palette includes not only words and phrases from Indian and regional languages such as Hindi/Urdu, Bhojpuri, Bengali, Gujarati, Tamil, Malayalam, Arabic, and Persian, but also fragments from languages farther ashore, such as Malay, Cantonese, Mandarin, Portuguese, and French—words "who have sailed from eastern waters towards the chilly shores of the English language" (A. Ghosh, *"Ibis Chrestomathy"*). Significantly, he calls these words "girmitiyas," that is, indentured laborers, so that the very act of immigrating non-English and non-Indian words into his narrative encapsulates the stories of maritime contact and exchanges—for trade, migration, and conquest—that make up the trilogy.

To skirt the topic of language would therefore be to miss out on one of the most crucial aspects of the novels, as language is not just a stylistic device but also an important component of the narrative. It captures the challenge that Ghosh takes up of emerging from "the long intellectual shadow of the Age of European Empire" (S. Mohanty 92) by initiating a multitiered dialogue about the narratives of colonialism and inviting voices from India, China, and their diasporas to join in. These voices, which had been silenced in the Anglocentric narrative of history, emerge as Ghosh explores existent and adept networks among the colonies and the colonized. Standard British English, the language of the "mother country" (Fanon 18), is symbolically dethroned and made to share a stage with languages from the colonies, pidgins by itinerant communities, and the languages formed through interactions with different linguistic communities in diasporas. Ghosh even reverses any notion of so-called purity in Standard British English by illustrating how English itself is a dynamic language that has been shaped through contact with multiple languages. This is made very clear in "The *Ibis* Chrestomathy," which, despite all appearances, includes only words and phrases that have (had) a claim to naturalization within the English language and have already "found a place in an English dictionary, lexicon, or word-list." In this way, Ghosh blurs the artificial line between Standard English and these borrowed terms. The novels' deliberate polyglossia comes to mirror the various decenterings that Ghosh attempts in the narrative by highlighting the contribution of India, China, and their diasporas in the shaping of the world as we know it today.[6] Using the nineteenth-century setting to reflect on the present time, the trilogy also provides a range of competent deliberations on current and future linguistic mutations, commenting on the strengthening of links between India, China, and their Indian Ocean diasporas in the contemporary era.

Teaching language in the *Ibis* trilogy is therefore a particularly significant, if tricky, task, because the topic of language opens up opportunities to push the discussion beyond the realm of linguistics and questions of technique, to reflect on the politics of humanism that Ghosh is espousing by resisting Anglocentric narratives of English preeminence and unearthing forgotten stories of collaborations and friendship between countries currently perceived as cutthroat competitors for ascension to the status of global superpower.[7]

We know from various studies (ranging from Frantz Fanon to Gauri Viswanathan [*Masks of Conquest*]) that linguistic and cultural forces are seen as complicit in the colonial mission, so that the language of the colonizer often came to be regarded as the language of power and authority. Here is Fanon's analysis of the significance attached to the language of the colonizer (in this case, French):

> To speak a language is to take on a world, a culture. The Antilles hero who wants to be white will be the whiter as he gains greater mastery of the cultural tool that language is. . . . Historically we must understand that the Negro wants to speak French because it is the key that can open doors which were still barred to him fifty years ago. (38)

Since Fanon here reads language as the factor that confers stratified power, by extension of the same logic, speaking an imperfect or impure version of that language therefore means falling short of wielding that power. Fanon elaborates, citing the historical and proverbial case of the "Negro of the Antilles," a generalized representative of black men who have received European education and who feel closer to white men: "To speak pidgin to a Negro makes him angry, because he is himself a pidgin-nigger-talker. . . . [I]t is just this absence of wish, this lack of interest, this indifference, this automatic manner of classifying him, imprisoning him, primitivizing him, decivilizing him, that makes him angry" (32). "Impure" versions of languages, in the form of pidgins and hybrids, were therefore primarily perceived as the language of the "pidgin-nigger-talker"— attributed to uneducated black men both by white Europeans and by the "Antilles Negro"—and connoted a failure to match up to a certain standard of the language that wields power. There was nothing enviable in resorting to hybrids.

Ghosh reverses such an equation. Authority in the trilogy is not wielded by Standard English but by the invented, Indianized version that incorporates *bhashas*. He stages this within the narrative of *Sea of Poppies* through a speech accorded to a veteran of the East India Company, Mr. Doughty. Speaking in the very language about which he is preaching, Mr. Doughty educates Zachary Reid, an American newly arrived in India, on the necessity of using hybridized Indian English in order to ensure his hold over the natives:

This was India, where it didn't serve for a sahib to be taken for a clodpoll of a griffin: if he wasn't fly to what was going on, it'd be all dickey with him, mighty jildee. This was no Baltimore—this was a jungle here, with biscobras in the grass and wanderoos in the trees. If he, Zachary, wasn't to be diddled and taken for a flat, he would have to learn to gubbrow the natives with a word or two of the zubben. (49)[8]

Through Mr. Doughty and the other sahibs and memsahibs who resort to interlacing their English with *bhashas*, Ghosh makes the point that, historically, this Kiplingesque "zubben" prevailed as a tool of governance and a means of ensuring the perpetuation of one's authority over the ruled. Significantly, Mr. Doughty uses the word *gubbrow*, that is, "to frighten." It emerges that British imperial power to frighten rested not in being able to speak a pure variety of the colonial language—as Fanon posited that it does—but in speaking a hybridized variety of it.

While hybridized English would often be associated with the uneducated or used to elicit comedic value in early Indian-English writing, in the *Ibis* trilogy the joke is instead on Standard English. For instance, Neel, who has been instructed by a tutor from England, is ridiculed—rather than admired—for his mastery of the colonial tongue. This is how Mr. Doughty speaks of Neel's English: "'Wait till you hear the barnshoot bucking in English—like a bandar reading aloud from *The Times*.' He chuckled gleefully, twirling the knob of his cane. 'Now that'll be something else to look forward to this evening, apart from the chitchky—a spot of bandarbaiting'" (48). In a particular passage where English and chutnified English interact, Neel is at the receiving end of jokes:

> Mr. Doughty made a harrumphing sound when the boy was introduced: "Is this little Rascal your Upper-Roger, Raja Nil-Rotten?"
>
> "The upa-raja, yes," Neel nodded. "My sole issue and heir. The tender fruit of my loin, as your poets might say."
>
> "Ah! Your little green mango!" Mr. Doughty shot a wink in Zachary's direction. "And if I may be so bold as to ask—would you describe your loin as the stem or the branch?"
>
> Neel gave him a frosty glare. "Why, sir," he said coldly, "it is the tree itself." (107–08)

Despite making reference to English poets and imitating English poetic analogies, Neel's English emerges as having less currency than the hybrid that the British themselves prefer to speak, and Ghosh practically invites us to join Mr. Doughty in mocking Neel. The other character who is mocked for his insistence on English is Baboo Nobokrishna Panda, a clerk of a Calcutta-based British opium trader, who is so keen to purge his speech of "foreign influences" that he "preferred to be spoken to in English, and liked to be addressed by the anglice of his name, which was Nob Kissin Pander" (133).

Reviewing his loyalty to English in *Flood of Fire*, Neel recalls his disillusionment with the language at the moment when he realized that speaking the language of the mother country neither evoked awe nor made a kindred of a fellow speaker:

> I remembered my English tutor, Mr. Beaseley, and how he had guided and encouraged me in my reading; I thought of the pleasure and excitement with which I had read Daniel Defoe and Jonathan Swift, and the long hours I'd spent committing passages of Shakespeare to memory. But I remembered also the night I was taken to Alipore jail, and how I had tried to speak English with the British sergeant who was on duty there: my words made no more difference to him than the chattering of crows. (83)[9]

Never mind its comedic value or its lack of authority; speaking English in fact puts the speaker at a distinct disadvantage, as is apparent through Neel's humiliation by the speakers of hybrid, who accuse him of affectation. In Ghosh's trilogy, English is a language of which even its native speakers are suspicious and distrustful.

In contrast to this, Ghosh claims the following about the language preferred by nineteenth-century Chinese traders doing business with European merchants: "Even though many Chinese spoke English with ease and fluency, they would not negotiate in it. . . . In pidgin they reposed far greater trust, for the grammar was the same as that of Cantonese, while the words were mainly English, Portuguese and Hindustani . . ." (*River* 171).[10] The projection of this Chinese-European-Indian hybrid as a preferential trading language (even when doing business with Europeans) is quite telling. Ghosh seems to stake a claim regarding the increasing roles of China and India (then and perhaps now) through the integrality of Cantonese and Hindustani to this business language. It is meaningful that Ghosh demarcates this collaborative hybrid as the language that elicits "greater trust," suggesting that the collaboration of south-south powers is more reassuring than a system in which Anglocentric hegemons prevail.

What adds to the credentials of this language of south-south collaboration is that it also emerges as the language of friendship. Neel's relationship with Ah Fatt (a Cantonese prisoner of mixed Chinese and Indian parentage) and later with Compton (the Cantonese owner of an English-language printing press and a translator) and Zhong Lou-si (Compton's teacher and an attaché of Commissioner Lin)[11] develops through this very pidgin. Pidgin builds bridges. In a poignant passage in *Sea of Poppies*, Neel revels in the "venture of collaboration" that is his attempt at hybridizing, which he is initially forced to do in order to be able to communicate with Ah Fatt (175). Over these collaborative conversations, Neel learns about Ah Fatt's native Canton, which, Ghosh writes, Neel comes to accept as his own city. It is pidgin that enables Neel—who, earlier in the novel, would even refuse to mix with people of other races and convictions to guard against the contamination of his caste—to make connections between his and Ah Fatt's home and to envisage another place in the world as home. Neel's transformation is apparent in the fact that he, the aristocrat tutored by a British speaker in the English language, would, in *Flood of Fire*, express his greater comfort in a space defined by linguistic disarray:

> I must confess that I am overjoyed to be back in Canton's foreign enclave—that unique little outpost that we used to call Fanqui-town! It is strange perhaps, to say this about a place where cries of *"Gwailo!"*, *"Haak-gwai!"* and *"Accha!"* are a constant reminder of one's alienness—but nonetheless, it is true that stepping into Canton was like a homecoming for me. (18–19)

It is his knack for hybridization and linguistic experimentation that comes to Neel's rescue once he leaves behind his sheltered life in Calcutta. Not only will his livelihood be dependent on his ability to navigate among different languages, but Neel's very survival will depend on his capacity to hybridize, experiment with language, and readapt himself to different linguistic environments. While his prowess in English and *bhashas* secures him employment with Mr. Bahram Modi (a Gujarati-speaking Parsi opium trader), his ease with hybridizing and picking up the pidgin of Canton earns him the domestic solidarity with the locals and inhabitants that in turn enables him to preempt some of the calamities that befall his employer in *River of Smoke*; in *Flood of Fire*, his position as a translator and then as a spy is ensured because of his linguistic talents, which are solicited to aid the Chinese in their war effort.

When China is defeated in the Opium War, Compton says to Neel, "Maybe from now on we speak English again, jik-haih? I will need to practice" (533)—perhaps imagining that the victory of the British presages the end of the era of hybrids and looking forward to a time when the English language will acquire hegemonic status. However, as we gather from the narrative, Neel leaves Canton and ends up in Mauritius, which is another space defined through its linguistic diversity and its heteroglossia. The principal language of Mauritius is a French creole, which incorporates aspects of English, Bhojpuri, Mandarin, and several other Asian (and some African) languages. But the choice of Mauritius as the site to which the protagonists escape is an interesting one. Mauritius is both an Indian and a Chinese diaspora. In the present geopolitical context, in which it has become increasingly important to India and China to have a network of allies to support them in their march to superpower status, Mauritius becomes a representative of such an ally for both countries. Ghosh here seems to use language to express his views about the geopolitical clout of both countries.

That Neel specifically takes this step is significant. As mentioned above, Neel, one of the few recurrent characters in the trilogy, endures because of his language skills. He is also meaningfully styled as the compiler of the chrestomathy by Ghosh and thus arguably epitomizes the philosophy of the trilogy. His decision to leave the space where anglophone rule has prevailed and move to another linguistically experimental zone can be read as a comment on learning to look outside the anglophone world, toward new linguistic collaborations and chutnifications, for survival and continuing relevance in an increasingly multi-polar world.

How then does one teach language in the *Ibis* trilogy? One could promote readings that move beyond linguistic analysis to look at the dynamic between languages as reflecting the concerns addressed in the content—readings that view language not only as a medium but also as a subject of inquiry in itself. One could encourage students to look at the ways in which the language of the trilogy points toward the commonalities and similarities across south-south and Indian Ocean communities, while revising the anglophone and Anglocentric history of the region. To be put off by the use of so-called foreign words or phrases, or to view them as merely serving a decorative purpose, would be to lose out on the way Ghosh uses language to politicize the past, present, and future of Indian Ocean alliances.

NOTES

[1] While Ghosh might draw inspiration from the *Hobson-Jobson* (a thousand-page dictionary of Anglo-Indian terms used by the British in India, compiled by Henry Yule and Arthur C. Burnell and published in 1886) for pidgins such as that of the British colonials in India and the Laskari hybrid spoken by Asian seafarers, much of the argot that he reproduces is necessarily invented, since there is very little evidence of the way people actually spoke in India in the mid-nineteenth century. Before recordings were made in the very late nineteenth and early twentieth centuries, following George Abraham Grierson's *Linguistic Survey of India* (conducted between 1894 and 1928), there was little documentation of actual demotic speech in that era. I am grateful to Michael Titlestad and Sofia Kostelac for bringing this to my attention.

[2] Mikhail Bakhtin maintained that internal stratification of language should be a prerequisite of the novel in order to "orchestrate all its themes, the totality of the world of objects and ideas depicted and expressed in it" (*Dialogic Imagination* 263). But the trilogy's remarkable heteroglossic fluidity lies in Ghosh's use of hybridization techniques not just to imitate actual demotic speech but also to characterize his narrative, thus pushing Bakhtin's theory further.

[3] In another paper, "The Novels of Amitav Ghosh and the Integral Hegemony of Inglish," I survey the various ways in which this prose has been utilized across time by Indian-English writers. I refer to Rudyard Kipling, Jim Corbett, and R. K. Narayan from an earlier generation and to Salman Rushdie, Upamanyu Chatterjee, and Ghosh from current writing.

[4] *Bhasha* is the Hindi term for "language," but I will use it here to refer to indigenous Indian languages, such as Hindi, Urdu, Bengali, Marathi, Gujarati, Tamil, and Telugu, among others.

[5] For a longer discussion about the fetishizing process that "turns the literatures/cultures of the 'non-Western' world into saleable exotic objects," see Huggan (*Postcolonial Exotic* 10).

[6] One such notable example is the tale of the transformation of an uninhabited Hong Kong into the strategic and powerful business center that it is now, which runs across the three novels.

[7] I have previously explored how "[t]his decision to prime hybrids and chutneys over the English language not only points to Ghosh's resistance to Anglocentric narratives of English preeminence, but also joins Ghosh's other writings—especially *In an Antique Land*, *The Calcutta Chromosome*, and *Shadow Lines*, among others—to become a manifesto for a world that is less exclusivist, and more integral in its humanity" (12).

[8] This essay uses the 2008 Penguin/Viking edition of *Sea of Poppies*.

[9] This essay uses the 2015 John Murray edition of *Flood of Fire*.

[10] This essay uses the 2011 Hamish Hamilton–Penguin edition of *River of Smoke*.

[11] Lou-si has the task of screening trade and political activities in Canton by consulting journals published in various languages and by employing people with different linguistic abilities to source information from the foreigners living in the city.

Sailing across Antique Seas:
Ideas of Historicity in the Writings of Ghosh

Ned Bertz

This essay seeks to offer ideas about possible uses of Amitav Ghosh's writing to university instructors of historically themed courses. *In an Antique Land, The Hungry Tide*, and the *Ibis* trilogy all portray innovative, subversive, and controversial readings of Indian Ocean histories, especially when situated against conventional scholarship. In part, this is accomplished by Ghosh's presentation of stories and research that raise questions about fieldwork, sources, and their impact on the development of ideas about human difference. Tracing nostalgic ideals of premodern cosmopolitanism through encounters with European colonialism and the emergence of various, often chauvinistic nationalisms, Ghosh's Indian Ocean–centered work is augmented by *The Shadow Lines* and *The Glass Palace*, which through a focus on mobility also challenge the deployment of historiographical categories that are boxed by national borders. Threaded through all of Ghosh's work is a grappling with the power of history itself, revealed by unmasking the embeddedness of the past in the present and, in the process, offering students alternative readings of historicity that can be glimpsed while sailing across antique seas.

I have used Ghosh's writing in five different history courses taught at two institutions, the University of Hawai'i at Mānoa in the United States (a flagship public state research university) and Ambedkar University Delhi in India (a small public state university with a liberal arts focus). These courses included upper-level undergraduate and master's-level offerings on the interdisciplinary history of the Indian Ocean, capstone disciplinary courses on historical theory and methodology, and introductory surveys of world history since 1500. This essay will follow these three types of history classes—Indian Ocean, world history, and historiography—that, while overlapping, might be common to many universities around the world.

It is virtually obligatory for any scholarly monograph on the history of the Indian Ocean to invoke Ghosh as an inspiration, notably his pathbreaking *In an Antique Land*. Michael Pearson's *The Indian Ocean*, a comprehensive survey of the history of the region, calls it nothing less than "brilliant" (103). The reason *In an Antique Land* receives so much attention from historians is that Ghosh's hybrid book—fictional-nonfictional, historical-ethnographic, epoch-spanning—is not only set in the Indian Ocean area, but also goes beyond painstakingly re-creating this world's earlier eras to use the ocean and its history to think through an extensive array of themes. In a metaphorical way, the titular "antique land" can be seen as the spirit of an older Indian Ocean realm whose faint traces might still be recoverable today if we no longer view their manifestations as anachronistic.

We can break down possible classroom usages of *In an Antique Land* into two broad categories: historiography and historical content. Ghosh's work engages—if indirectly and almost covertly—with several historiographical debates and can be paired with readings that trace the contours of these issues.[1] Two of the most contested aspects of Indian Ocean scholarship might be thematized as time and space. Through temporal and spatial investigations, historians have sought to explore how to periodize chronologies of Indian Ocean history and define the boundaries of the maritime region as part of efforts to push back against the dominance of land-centric histories.

There are three central debates around the periodization of Indian Ocean history: 1) the impact of the arrival of Europeans in the early modern period; 2) how deepening imperialism across the long nineteenth century affected the region's cohesion; and 3) whether transoceanic connections continued into the twentieth century and beyond. *In an Antique Land* minces no words in its view on what the appearance of the Portuguese, who would soon be followed by other Europeans in the Indian Ocean, meant at the close of the fifteenth century: "Within a few years of that day [when Vasco da Gama arrived in India] the knell had been struck for the world that had brought Bomma, Ben Yiju and Ashu[2] together, and another had begun in which the crossing of their paths would seem so unlikely that its very possibility would all but disappear from human memory" (286).[3] Amplifying his nostalgia[4] for this lost world into disgust, Ghosh continues: "Soon, the remains of the civilization that had brought Ben Yiju to Mangalore were devoured by that unquenchable, demonic thirst that has raged ever since, for almost five hundred years, over the Indian Ocean, the Arabian Sea and the Persian Gulf" (288). Strong words, but ones that run counter to prevailing historiographical wisdom. Pearson argues that for the first 250 years after the arrival of da Gama, the overall impact of Europeans "on the Indian Ocean, its trade, its people, even its politics, was limited" (113). Engaging students with divergent historiographical perspectives can be rewarding— for example, asking them to reflect on how historians measure change over time and what is at stake in defining periods of history. Considering the role of violence in this story can also be productive. While Pearson mounts a counterfactual argument assessing whether the Portuguese might have done better business in the Indian Ocean if they had traded peacefully (142–44), Ghosh settles on mourning what was lost, suggesting that the earlier Indian Ocean world's greatest asset, cosmopolitanism, was its undoing: "As always, the determination of a small, united band of soldiers triumphed easily over the rich confusions that accompany a culture of accommodation and compromise" (288).

Despite its lamentation of loss, *In an Antique Land* goes on to illustrate cross-cultural interactions in the other two contested periods of history noted above, crafting a provocative comparison between the premodern Indian Ocean and the one Ghosh encounters in his late-twentieth-century fieldwork in Egypt. The implicit conclusion is both startling and unsettling: that the earlier Indian Ocean world was the more cosmopolitan one.[5] Whether or not students will agree with this assessment is uncertain, but the claim should spark reflection on our modern globalized world in addition to other aspects of Indian Ocean history and historiography: What historically "united" the region, and do similar or different elements continue to do so? Do "antique" traces of the past remain visible and viable today?

These questions could lead students into a discussion of how epistemologies of historical knowledge have been constructed in the modern world and what role imperialism has played in this process. *In an Antique Land*'s sections on Egyptology are rich in material to support such debates. Extending the idea further, students might be asked whether newly created epistemologies led to altered understandings of what constitutes human difference, including firmer boundaries drawn between religious groups and identities staked on territorialized notions of national characteristics. Regarding religion, students could analyze how the Islam practiced by the Egyptian village folk of Ghosh's anthropological fieldwork differs from that of earlier denizens of the Indian Ocean world. And the influence of national identities takes shape in the book on many occasions, whether in the locals' endless associations of the author with things stereotypically Indian and Hindu (for example, cow worship, lack of male circumcision practices, and cremation of the dead) or when the Egyptian villagers seek out Ghosh's approval of a diesel water pump that was manufactured in India: "placing both hands on the diesel motor, I fell to my knees and shut my eyes. When I looked up again [the owner was] anxiously awaiting the outcome of my silent communion with this product of my native soil" (73).

Adjoining temporal debates in recent oceanic history are spatial ones involving how to measure the boundaries of the Indian Ocean world. Markus P. M. Vink sums up the "new thalassology" on this point as follows: "mental remapping requires moving away from relative [*sic*] immobile, essentializing 'trait geographies' . . . towards 'process geographies' with various kinds of action, interaction, and motion . . . in which regions can be conceptualized as both dynamic and interconnected" (52). Sugata Bose's invocation of the Indian Ocean's "hundred horizons . . . of many hues and colors" (4) also moves in this direction and relies more on "the cognitive domain of mental processes" (5) than physical boundaries in sketching the scale of the transoceanic "interregional arena of human interaction" (3).

Inserting Ghosh's work into this scholarly conversation can illuminate dense historiographical concepts for students. Travel and imagination are central to the lives of *In an Antique Land*'s characters as they conceive of themselves within the boundaries of multiple horizons of their shared oceanic world. For many of the villagers whom Ghosh encountered in early 1980s Egypt,

> The area . . . had never been a rooted kind of place; at times it seemed to be possessed of all the busy restlessness of an airport's transit lounge. Indeed, a long history of travel was recorded in the very names of the area's "families". . . . That legacy of transience had not ended with their ancestors

either . . . some men had passports so thick they opened out like ink-blackened concertinas. (173–74)

While mobility could operate to connect residents of the Indian Ocean world across space, imagining the obstacles involved also could serve to divide, especially when mapped onto the borders of the modern world. In a memorable exchange with a humble weaver, Ghosh contemplated the villager's question, asking if one could ride on a donkey from Egypt to India. Citing visa regimes, regional wars, desert heat, and the snow leopards, hairy yaks, and high peaks of the Hindu Kush mountains, the author instead left the impression of "how far away my country was . . . and of the terrible fate that would befall one if one were to set out for it on a donkey" (173).

Asking students to unpack these episodes forces them to grapple with whether boundaries, including those drawn as national borders and erected in constructing human difference, are real or imagined. Ghosh gives the impression that transoceanic connections and the bridging of human empathy across difference were more easily achieved in the earlier Indian Ocean than in the modern world. Regarding the reconstruction of the life of a twelfth-century Jewish merchant through his correspondence, Ghosh writes, "In matters of business, Ben Yiju's networks appear to have been wholly indifferent to many of those boundaries that are today thought to mark social, religious and geographical divisions"; this indifference, he adds, even led to the possibility of forging "bonds of inseparable friendship and brotherhood" across chasms of dissimilarity that might seem insurmountable now (278–79). The most powerful modern counterstory that Ghosh offers to Ben Yiju's cosmopolitan world is drawn from his own childhood experience of witnessing a communal riot in Dhaka in the buildup to Bangladesh's war of liberation from West Pakistan in the mid-1960s. He writes, previewing issues probed more thoroughly in *The Shadow Lines*, "The stories of those riots are always the same: tales that grow out of an explosive barrier of symbols—of cities going up in flames because of a cow found dead or a pig in a mosque . . . of women disemboweled for wearing veils or vermillion, or men dismembered for the state of their foreskin" (210). While borders are illusory in many senses—as the title *The Shadow Lines* is meant to indicate— their associated symbols of difference, inscribed in boundaries of human existence, also can be the source of terrifying violence, forced migrations, and barriers to mobility and empathy, as Ghosh's work reminds students.

Moving on from historiographical issues, Ghosh's work is rich in sophisticated illustrations of matters of historical content relevant to students in classes on the Indian Ocean. *In an Antique Land* features an astonishing range of issues that such courses cover: slavery, ethnic and kin networks of business, merchants and trade, port cities, Islam, diaspora, cosmopolitanism, the spirit world, language, and more. *The Hungry Tide*, while largely contemporary, integrates the natural and social environment of the Bay of Bengal as a major component of its story. *The Glass Palace* links India to Southeast Asia through colonial-era connections that strain or rupture with the outbreak of global wars and national struggles for independence. The *Ibis* trilogy takes readers into the roiling nineteenth-century Indian Ocean world and features an exceptional re-creation of how people acted and thought, spoke and traveled, and lived and died. The historical research underpinning these books is voluminous and largely kept out of the view of the reader, unlike in *In an Antique Land*. Taken as a whole, the *Ibis* trilogy reverses the traditional gaze on major events in nineteenth-century world history—colonialism, intensified global interconnections, conflict between Europe and Asia and the reversal of power hierarchies—to detail how indigenous residents of the Indian Ocean, wealthy merchants and subaltern sailors alike, might have experienced these cataclysmic forces. This makes the trilogy useful in courses beyond those on the Indian Ocean, although relevant discussions on the history of the latter are numerous.

Sea of Poppies, the first book in the *Ibis* trilogy, follows the recruitment of indentured laborers from northern India to their intended destination, a plantation in Mauritius.[6] All three books in Ghosh's trilogy use commodities traded through intertwined economic networks to map new exchanges in Indian Ocean and world history. This begins with the trade in people and poppies, escalates into the British colonial monopoly on opium production and distribution, and eventually, in the second novel, *River of Smoke*, enmeshes Chinese goods like tea, silks, and porcelain into regional and global economies. This turn to the East bridges an artificial division in Indian Ocean courses that severs the South China Sea from the connected oceanic worlds to the west and is aided by Ghosh's artful depiction of the cosmopolitan port cities of Canton and Hong Kong in the latter two novels of the trilogy. *Flood of Fire*, the final installment, takes readers into mainland China, recognizing the links between maritime worlds and landed lives. The central drama in this novel involves Indian sepoys who fight for the British during the Opium Wars, which could serve to engage students' understandings of colonial, global, and Indian Ocean historiographies.

It is worth mentioning that a lot of the action in the three novels occurs while sailing on the water, whether on board the *Ibis*—the ship that takes the Indian indentured laborers from Calcutta to Mauritius and gives its name to the trilogy—or other Indian Ocean sailing vessels. Ghosh lovingly re-creates what life was like at sea for a motley range of people, from laborers fashioning themselves as *jahaj-bhais* and -*behens* ("ship-brothers" and "-sisters") to the mixed crews who run the ships. Readers are invited to envision a world that was becoming more hybridized in the nineteenth century through interactions among various groups of Euro-Americans and Asians. Nowhere does Ghosh pay more attention to this theme than in the realm of language. Littered throughout the trilogy is specific nineteenth-century vocabulary for items in use during that age, especially maritime technology. Moreover, the dialogue between characters reflects Ghosh's idea of how people from different regions would have communicated with one another in a world that was accelerating in its diversity. The distinguishing feature of this speech is an admixture of linguistic derivations, both etymological and grammatical, from the Sino-Portuguese-English pidgin of the South China Sea to the maritime language of the Indian Ocean, which draws and adapts words from Arabic, English, Hindi, Malay, Malayalam, Persian, Portuguese, Swahili, Urdu, and other languages.

Helping students make sense of this linguistic menagerie is a scholarly article by Ghosh ("Of Fanas and Forecastles") that obviously was produced as a result of his research into writing the *Ibis* trilogy. He introduces us to the rise of a unique language, Laskari, derived from the term *lascar*, essentially defined as a hired sailor indigenous to the Indian Ocean region. Grammars and dictionaries arose during the nineteenth century as Europeans increasingly needed to communicate with, and command, cosmopolitan crews at sea. Ghosh provocatively locates lascars in world historical perspective as the "first Asians and Africans to participate freely, and in substantial numbers, in a globalised workforce" (19). Interestingly, the term *lascar* eventually faded away, "drowning under the derogatory racial freightage that came to be loaded upon" the word (16). That a label with an ocean as a referent would disappear along with the age of sail is not surprising, although there is no doubt that this process also was propelled by the increasing imperial imperative to separate people based on perceptions of specific racial and national characteristics. Unpacking this term would assist students to understand Ghosh's position on the dissolution of older Indian Ocean cultures of belonging, replaced with impositions of hierarchies based on new notions of difference, notably involving conceptions of race, power, and modernity.

Negotiating modernity is a recurring theme in much of Ghosh's work, especially the more historical texts that spend time in the twentieth century. It is also a critical concept in understanding the historical discipline itself, in addition to unpacking the modern world that we live in. There is an episode in *The Glass Palace* when two brothers share their diverging perspectives on this issue: "'Look at us!' Arjun would say after a whisky or two, 'we're the first modern Indians; the first Indians to be truly free. We eat what we like, we drink what we like, we're the first Indians who're not weighed down by the past.' To Dinu this was profoundly offensive. 'It's not what you eat and drink that makes you modern; it's a way of looking at things'" (242–43).[7]

The Glass Palace is arguably Ghosh's most accessible historical novel and one in which ordinary individuals' lives illuminate important—yet sometimes opaque to students—processes in contemporary world history. The novel opens in 1885 with the British overthrow of the Burmese monarchy and concludes in the 1990s with a coda describing the rising movement in Myanmar led by pro-democracy activist Aung San Suu Kyi. The novel's linchpin themes—colonialism and nationalism—created massive changes in the nineteenth and twentieth centuries, and Ghosh's characters betray clear, if evolving, opinions on each that students can be asked to identify and analyze. The novel also spans a great expanse of territory and features European-Asian encounters across more than a century. Migrations occur on a massive scale: the images of Indian servants of empire and free migrants going to Burma and Malaya are later mirrored by refugees pouring over the eastern border into India while fleeing Japanese war-time expansion in Southeast Asia, where Ghosh adds in the presence of a Chinese diaspora. Echoing the orientation of the *Ibis* trilogy, *The Glass Palace* tells the story of world history through many familiar events—colonial conquest, nationalist struggles, world wars—from a non-European vantage point, thereby assisting instructors seeking to float world history surveys away from originally Eurocentric moorings.

At a more advanced level, *In an Antique Land* explores the impact of modernity on history itself, adding to the text's discourses on primary sources, methodologies of research, and ethics of fieldwork to make it a useful resource in disciplinary courses on historiographical theory and methods.[8] Ghosh's descriptions of historical and ethnographic fieldwork—investigating both the older world of Ben Yiju and Egyptian villages of the early 1980s—enable students to debate methodological and ethical issues, such as representations of individuals, responsibilities to sources and informants, and systems of citation and note-taking, among others. As part of this conversation, the story of the looting by Euro-American scholars of the Geniza of the Ben Ezra Synagogue in Cairo (80–95)—"the very site which held the greatest single collection of medieval documents ever discovered" (59)—opens students' eyes to the role of power in collecting historical evidence, while raising ethical issues concerning the proprietorship and appropriation of research information. Ghosh's meditation on the epistemological impact of the dispersal of Geniza documents also should provoke students to reflect about fixed categories of historical knowledge:

> In some profound sense, the Islamic high culture of [Egypt] had never really noticed, never found a place for the parallel history the Geniza represented, and its removal only confirmed a particular vision of the past. . . . It was as though the borders that were to divide Palestine several decades later had already been drawn, through time rather than territory, to allocate a choice of Histories. (95)

Other strategies of inventing and forgetting history are on display in *In an Antique Land*, forcing students to wrestle with the question of objectivity and the uses of history. When Ghosh visits what he suspects to be Bomma's community, the Tulu-speaking Magavira fisherfolk who live near Mangalore, he finds that the group—seeking to shed its low place in India's caste hierarchy—has distanced itself from its traditional guardianship of shrines dedicated to a deity, legendarily the spirit of a Muslim sailor who perished at sea, in favor of mimicking high-caste Hindu conventions.[9] This repeated theme—the scrubbing of intimately entangled pasts in order to present purified community histories—reaches a crescendo in the book when Ghosh, back in Egypt on a return trip eight years after his doctoral fieldwork, journeys to the tomb of Sidi Abu-Hasira, a nineteenth-century North African rabbi and mystic who came to be venerated as a saint by Jews and Muslims alike. In describing his struggle to explain to the guard at the tomb why he, nominally a Hindu Indian, wanted to visit, Ghosh muses:

> But then it struck me, suddenly, that there was nothing I could point to within his world that might give credence to my story—the remains of those small, indistinguishable, intertwined histories, Indian and Egyptian, Muslim and Jewish, Hindu and Muslim, had been partitioned long ago. . . . I had been caught straddling a border, unaware that the writing of History had predicated its own self-fulfillment. (339–40)

Later, in trying to learn more about Sidi Abu-Hasira, Ghosh is thwarted when searching library headings related to religion or Judaism: "that tomb, and others like it, had long ago been wished away from those shelves, in the process of shaping them to suit the patterns of the Western academy" (342). The author instead locates relevant material by using search terms like "anthropology" and "folklore." This is a practical lesson that could open a fruitful discussion with students about the politics of libraries and archives around the world, and how the imposition of ideas of modernity on categorizing historical knowledge has a practical dimension for budding and experienced researchers alike.

A final example of modernity's infiltration into history itself rests in Ghosh's famous conflicts with Imam Ibrahim in *In an Antique Land*, later spun off to compose part of a volume entitled *The Imam and the Indian*. While Ghosh, the outsider researching in Egypt, excitedly attempts to document the imam's traditional healing skills, the religious leader avoids the queries and instead draws attention to his ability to deliver medicines through syringe injections (192). This prompts the author to meditate on the "real and desperate seriousness" of the Egyptian villagers' "engagement with modernism," reflecting that the villagers have internalized the Western perception that their situation is "shamefully anachronistic, a warp upon time" (200). The lethal weight of modernity, combined with atavistic national pride, finally incites Ghosh into a shouting match with the imam—"delegates from two superseded civilizations" (236)—over whether Egypt or India is more technologically advanced, as measured especially through their countries' capability to manufacture weapons of mass destruction.

Having students debate the implications of the encounters between Imam Ibrahim and Ghosh could help to underscore many of the potential teaching lessons discussed above. At stake is what history writing might lose sight of, or even destroy, through its particular approaches. As Ghosh resignedly notes after their argument, both he and the imam had lost what they once shared, a cultural language in common that stitched together the diverse lives of residents of the Indian Ocean world: "We had acknowledged that it was no longer possible to speak, as Ben Yiju or his Slave, or any one of the thousands of travellers who had crossed the Indian Ocean in the Middle Ages might have done: of things that were right, or good, or willed by God; it would have been absurd for either of us to use those words" (237). Is this true? If so, how did this circumstance come about? Can this or other histories, including ones that linked those who sailed the "antique" seas of the Indian Ocean, be recovered and prove useful in the modern world? Is there a place for nostalgia in history writing, and what are the ethics involved in such a project? Like a lot of Ghosh's nondidactic writing, this essay helps identify topics and thematic frameworks in his work that instructors could use to productively engage students, leaving it ultimately up to them to make up their own minds about how to answer questions related to historicity and where those answers leave us in the modern world today.

NOTES

[1] For example, Markus P. M. Vink's historiographical essay or more recent Indian Ocean surveys like Edward A. Alpers's.

[2] These are three main figures in the book (in addition to Ghosh himself): Ben Yiju, a twelfth-century Jewish merchant from Tunisia; his slave and business agent, Bomma, from the Tulu-speaking fisherfolk community close to Mangalore, India; and Ashu, likely a Nair from the Malabar coast, India, who Ghosh speculates began her relationship with Ben Yiju as his slave and ended up obtaining manumission and becoming the mother of his children.

[3] This essay uses the 1992 Ravi Dayal edition of *In an Antique Land*.

[4] For a critique of nostalgia in Ghosh's writing, notably concerning *In an Antique Land*, see Desai's *Commerce with the Universe*, especially chapter two, and Viswanathan's "Beyond Orientalism."

[5] Cosmopolitanism is a theoretical concept that increasingly has been interrogated by Indian Ocean historians. A good discussion of its strengths and limitations can be found in Simpson and Kresse's introduction to *Struggling with History*.

[6] Building on vibrant scholarship on indentured servitude, recent Indian Ocean works trace British imperial webs of connections to link multiple nodes of the Indian Ocean in the nineteenth century. See especially Metcalf but also S. Bose.

[7] This essay uses the 2002 Random House edition of *The Glass Palace*.

[8] *In an Antique Land*'s discussions on modernity would nicely illustrate more theoretical texts like Chakrabarty's *Provincializing Europe*. And, for more on Ghosh's research methods in the book, see his article "The Slave of MS. H.6." in *Subaltern Studies*.

[9] To Ghosh's delight, the community was not entirely successful at shedding its past, for the old sea deity, while in "wholly altered guise," somehow had been installed in the newly built Hindu temple: "The past had avenged itself on the present: it had slipped the spirit of an Arab Muslim trader past the watchful eyes of Hindu zealots and installed it within the Sanskritic pantheon" (*In an Antique Land* 274).

Complicating Collusion and Resistance: Teaching Ghosh's *The Glass Palace*, Intersectional Reading, and the Ethics of Colonized Subjecthood

Ambreen Hai

Amitav Ghosh's *The Glass Palace* seems a daunting novel to assign in an undergraduate course. At almost five hundred pages, spanning four generations—a numerous cast of characters—from the 1880s to the 1990s, stretching geographically from India to Burma, Malaysia, and Singapore, and including Japan, Britain, and the United States, it can appear a formidable challenge to most college students. Yet it can also be a powerful reading experience and a highly rewarding pedagogical one. I have taught it in an introductory (intermediate-level) course titled The Empire Writes Back: Postcolonial Literature, which focuses on non-settler anglophone literature from Africa, the Caribbean, and South Asia. However, I can imagine teaching it in a variety of courses, from the intermediate to advanced levels, on literature and ethics; literature and history; the contemporary novel; imperialism and postcolonial retelling (paired with George Orwell's *Burmese Days*); globalization, nation, migration, and diaspora; or in a single-author course on Ghosh.

Rather than taking a single approach, I emphasize multiple aspects of the novel and the rich array of questions it poses (the mutually implicated histories of India and Burma under the British Empire, despite subsequent separate constructions of nationhood; the coexistence of multiple Indian diasporas, originating with the "coolie" indentured labor population in Burma and Malaysia and concluding with the professional class in Britain and the United States; postcolonial photography as an artistic mode of reflection and political action).

But I also focus, in response to the strong tug the novel exerts, on ethical dilemmas in postcolonial contexts: how is a colonized subject (whom we understand intersectionally as at once also gendered, classed, sexualized, racialized, etc.) to act rightly, given very particular constraints and conditions and in the absence of a coherent moral system or guide; how do we as readers conduct ourselves ethically in trying to understand various characters' choices or actions without either rushing to judge or abstaining from judgment; what ethical cues or guidance does the novel offer as it complicates and repeatedly shifts how we see and what we think we see? For me, this becomes an opportunity to demonstrate and engage in an ethical reading practice of *not* imposing a prefabricated grid upon the text and instead to challenge students to read openly, to respond to the text's own particularity and distinctiveness, and to address the questions that the text itself poses, in addition to ones that we bring to the text. I draw here on the intersectional feminist approach that understands human identity and experience not as constituted by a single socially constructed factor alone, such as gender, but as a condition in which any factor, such as gender, is always intersected by others—race, class, colonized status, nationality, age, sexuality, etc. Our understanding of various characters' ethical choices has to be informed, as the novel suggests, by an understanding of how their experiences and hence their perspectives are shaped by these mutually constitutive intersecting factors.

I teach at Smith College in Massachusetts, the largest liberal arts women's college in the United States. Since the course is open to all but first-year students, those who take it include English and comparative literature majors, but the majority are nonmajors with very different levels of literary-critical preparation and a diversity of interests and disciplinary trainings, from neuroscience or biology to history, political science, psychology, anthropology, women's studies, and American studies. The course also draws a number of international students from a range of postcolonial and other nations. Consequently, students' assumptions, reactions, and prior historical or cultural knowledge are highly heterogeneous, a resource of great benefit for our class discussions. It is a challenge for all to engage in conversation and to learn from each other. Though the course is officially a lecture course, with roughly twenty-five to thirty-five students, I emphasize discussion as a mode of engaged, active learning and assign specific tasks and responsibilities (working in pairs or small groups to answer specific questions, or choosing passages for close reading or textual evidence) to foster collaboration and class participation.

We arrive at *The Glass Palace* about two-thirds into the semester, so students have already been introduced to key postcolonial concepts, questions, and histories. In the first unit of the course (on Africa) we read Chinua Achebe, Ngũgĩ wa Thiong'o, Edward Said, Ama Ata Aidoo, Chimamanda Ngozi Adichie, and Tsitsi Dangarembga, coupled with selected chapters from John McLeod's *Beginning Postcolonialism*. Students have thus discussed issues of cultural invasion, orientalism, colonial historiography, writing as resistance (Achebe, *Things*

Fall Apart), colonial education (Ngũgĩ, *Decolonising the Mind*; Dangarembga, *Nervous Conditions*), and postcolonial feminism. We have also addressed the meta-issues of *how* we read, located as we are in the global North, changing paradigms and approaching our texts not as "Commonwealth literature" via the lens of liberal humanism, but as postcolonial literatures via the (self-)critical lenses of postcolonialism (McLeod 12–19, 38–41). In the second unit, on the Caribbean, we read essays, poems, and a novel to explore questions of hybridity, diasporic identity, nationhood, nation language, and the reimagining of lost histories (Stuart Hall, Kamau Brathwaite, Wilson Harris, Derek Walcott, and Michelle Cliff's *Abeng*). In the third unit, on South Asia, we usually read an early novel, such as Kamala Markandaya's *Nectar in a Sieve*, so that students are also familiar with the history of the British Raj. Yet none of this is a necessary precondition for teaching *The Glass Palace*, which enables readers unfamiliar with these contexts or frameworks to learn through its own modes of introduction, starting as it does with the key moment of British imperialist invasion and conquest of Mandalay in 1885, and the destruction of Burma's monarchy, as seen from the perspective of eleven-year-old Rajkumar, a Bengali-Indian itinerant orphan, who learns, as do we, the causes and consequences of this pivotal event.

I spend two and a half weeks (at least five eighty-minute class sessions) on *The Glass Palace*, spread over Thanksgiving break, to give time for reading and discussion. I begin our first session by asking students (who are expected to read through at least part one, "Mandalay") what clues the novel's opening provides about its concerns, genre, setting, and time. We discuss whether the novel is (like some that we have read) a bildungsroman, historical fiction, counterhistory, or family saga. Could it be all of those? How does not knowing the genre shape how we read? How does it induce us to open ourselves to the novel's guidance and reorient us beyond our expectations? How does it tell us what the novel will be about? We talk about why the British are in Burma and why Ghosh offers different perspectives (e.g., Queen Supayalat's view that a British timber company had violated the "kingdom's customs regulations" and refused to pay fines and that the British governor had decided to "humiliate" her husband, King Thebaw of Burma [19]; Matthew's comment that the British "want all the teak in Burma"; and Rajkumar's disbelief that there could be a "war over wood" [13]).[1]

I make sure students understand that the historical events described did in fact occur and that King Thebaw, Queen Supayalat, and their children were real people, as Ghosh notes in his afterword, though the other characters are fictional. I thus situate the novel both geographically and historically. We look carefully at the 1945 map provided by Ghosh and compare it with a modern map of the region. We notice the new boundaries and place names, and we reflect on the arbitrariness or historical contingencies of national borders and the postcolonial politics of renaming cities, towns, countries. I provide a thumbnail history and timeline of events for nineteenth- and twentieth-century Burma (now Myanmar). Even students familiar with the history of the Indian subcontinent are surprised to discover the forgotten imbrications of India and Burma:

the First Anglo-Burmese War of 1824–26, when the British conquered Assam, Manipur, and Arakan; 1852, when the British annexed Pegu and renamed it Lower Burma; 1885, when the British declared war on Mandalay and exiled King Thebaw and his family to India (in a chiasmic parallel to the earlier exile of the last Indian Mughal king, Bahadur Shah Zafar, to Rangoon); and the consequent large population of Indians (merchants, traders, workers, soldiers) in Burma.[2] I also use *PowerPoint* to show images easily available on the Web (the Glass Palace, the royal residence in Mandalay, the Burmese royal family, the British in Burma, occupying British soldiers, buildings, temples, marketplaces, etc.) to situate Ghosh's narrative and provide visual cues for contexts unfamiliar to most college students in the United States.

I then move to a class exercise that I have found useful in teaching most realist fiction, from Jane Austen on. Who are the main characters? I ask. Whose story is it? How can we tell? Whose perspectives are privileged? As students volunteer names, I put them on the board. I then ask each student to take five minutes to choose one character, find a passage that tells us something about that character, and prepare to talk about the significance of the passage. Each student is thus given time (so no one is caught unawares when called on) to take responsibility, to get right into the text, to exercise the skills of close reading rather than make distant generalizations, to learn to identify textual evidence and clues, and to ground observations in textual analysis. (I have my own list of key passages that I pull out later or in response to ones students bring up.) We talk about Rajkumar's history, his resourcefulness, resilience, enterprise, and intrepidity. We discuss Dolly and her passivity. Why is she called Dolly? I ask. Is she seen as a beautiful, serviceable doll by Queen Supayalat, by Rajkumar, or by Ghosh as well? Will she grow and change? Why does Ghosh present large historical events as experienced by marginal characters, like Rajkumar and Dolly, both orphans, one a street urchin, one a palace slave and servant? We discuss other characters and how Ghosh represents them: Saya John and Ma Cho as Rajkumar's culturally hybrid, surrogate parents, similarly bent on survival; the Burmese king and queen as victims of British imperialist greed, yet highly privileged, the Queen a brutal tyrant and the King willing to relinquish control. How does Ghosh invite both our condemnation of the Queen's horrific abuses of power and our sympathy for the royal family's shocking treatment by the British? We pause over a striking passage, where Ghosh remarks how Rajkumar, "a feral creature," cannot understand national belonging, "the invisible bonds linking people to one another through personifications of their commonality," or why the common people who had just looted the Glass Palace were now weeping over the humiliation and exile of the Burmese king and queen as they are marched through the streets of Mandalay (40). What kind of protagonist (and moral agent) is Rajkumar, who, "beyond the ties of blood, friendship and immediate reciprocity, . . . recognized no loyalties, no obligations and no limits on the compass of his right to provide for himself"? We connect this to his mother's dying injunction: "Stay alive, . . . hold on to your life" (12). To survive alone, with no family, as Rajkumar accordingly does, what values in his brutal world must he know and exercise?

I then ask what issues the novelist seems to call to our attention in part one. I point to the repetition of something odd. Why are there six thousand Indian soldiers (sepoys), themselves colonized, fighting for the British, helping them invade and colonize Burma? First we get a simple description of their presence (23) and then Saya John's comment on these mercenaries: "It always amazed me: Chinese peasants would never do this—allow themselves to be used to fight other people's wars with so little profit themselves" (26). "They're just tools," Rajkumar replies dismissively. "Without minds of their own. They count for nothing" (27). But clearly their presence does count, a lot. This allows me to establish how the novel lays the foundation for a central question it will explore, deepen, and complicate: what ethical choices colonized subjects can make— whether they are to be condemned (as Saya John clearly condemns Indians by comparison to the Chinese) for allowing themselves to become "tools" (especially "for little profit") or whether we must understand them differently.

In our second session we work through part two, "Ratnagiri," and how Ghosh extends his critical portrayal of British colonialism in India and Burma and his postcolonial revision of history, both highlighting forgotten elements and countering colonial versions. We discuss the new characters Uma Dey and the Collector, their arranged marriage, their gender and colonial politics. Is the Collector a casualty of Macaulay's infamous program? What agency does Ghosh attribute to this man who allows his colonial education to turn him into a British stooge? By contrast, how does Uma learn from Dolly to shift perspective, to question, alongside the Burmese queen, the adulation of the Victorian queen in whose imperial name many more "people have been killed" (97)? I point again to unexpected, odd features of the text that may not apparently fit within given rubrics or frameworks of what are taken to be postcolonial themes. Why does Ghosh spend so much time describing in detail the world of teak forests, its botany and topography, and the timber industry that depended on the arduous work of white and brown men to harness, with elephants, this invaluable resource? Entering openly into such puzzling moments allows us to see not just what we want to see, but what the novelist directs us to see—the gendered and racialized work of empire with its differential risks and benefits; the material economic resource that lies at the heart of political struggles and their cultural, linguistic, and psychological consequences—and hence to understand imperialism not as an abstraction.

We focus finally on the dramatic scene in which the Collector is summoned and informed by the Queen that her oldest daughter, the unmarried First Princess, is pregnant (128–30). Given how beautifully this scene reads, like a segment from a play, I ask student volunteers to read it aloud. Doing so allows the class to experience it as an embodied performance, to hear different voices, and to perceive and enjoy, as we are invited to do, the humor and the irony of the Queen's (admirable) female resistance to colonial hegemony, as represented by the Indian Mr. Dey. We note the multiple causes for the Collector's horror: the child will be illegitimate; the father is a servant and a Hindu; and he, the Collector, will be held responsible by the British government.

> "But what am I to report. What am I to tell the Government? . . . Your Highness, . . . consider the Princess's reputation, consider your standing in society."
> "Our standing? And what exactly is that, Collector-Sahib?" . . .
> "Your Highness, I beg you to reflect. Is it appropriate that a Princess of Burma should link herself to a household employee, a servant?"
> A tiny trilling laugh escaped the Queen's lips. "Collector Sahib, Sawant is less a servant than you. At least he has no delusions about his place in the world." (129)

Students whose interest has begun to flag suddenly find themselves in sympathy with the Queen, even as they are pushed to scrutinize their own reactions, both to the Queen and to Mr. Dey. We note how the Queen repeats his words, throwing them back at him; how she points out the horrible truth of his own servility and greater ignominy; and how she challenges his outrage, scorning his notions of morality, of gendered sexual and class snobbery, learned from his colonial masters. The scene thus also allows us to advance our discussion of the question of postcolonial ethics. The Collector admonishes the Queen for making "light of such a scandal." "'*Scandal?*' The Queen's eyes hardened as she repeated the English word. 'You have the insolence to come here and speak to us of *scandals*? There is no *scandal* in what my daughter has done. The *scandal* lies in what you have done to us; in the very circumstances to which you have reduced us; in our very presence here" (129). With the heavy repetition of the loaded word *scandal*, Ghosh makes clear how a particular bourgeois English cultural system is imposed on and repudiated by colonial subjects who are far more egalitarian in their own understanding of female sexual agency (Burmese women choose their husbands and keep their own names after marriage, we are told) and who upend British pretensions to moral superiority by pointing out the moral failures manifest in the government's own actions.

But, while rejecting the conventional morality that sacrifices some to the self-interest of others, Ghosh poses more difficult questions about ethical action. Several figures in part two collude with and profit from the opportunities provided by the British: Saya John, Rajkumar's "teacher" of economic opportunism and enterprise, who builds a business "ferrying supplies to teak camps" (58); Mr. Dey, who joins the Indian Civil Service to become the official in charge of the exiled Burmese royal family; Baburao, the "labor contractor" who deceives Indian peasants into migrating as indentured servants to Burma (106); and Rajkumar himself, who becomes a timber magnate by learning from Baburao to exploit the destitute. Given each one's complex history and intersectional subject position, each one presented with and inviting different degrees of empathy, these characters suggest a range rather than a binary opposition between collusion and resistance as responses to colonial subjecthood.

Students sometimes tend to regard colonized subjects as "good" "victims" of "bad" imperialism. *The Glass Palace* disallows such binary ethical categories, showing how different colonized subjects make different choices in extremely constrained circumstances, demanding that we understand each choice in its contextualized specificity, and illuminating the impossibility of simplistic judgments of choices made by individuals under the differing conditions imposed by imperialism. It asks us to enter imaginatively and empathetically into and complicate the difficult, divergent choices made by its central characters, illustrating Dominic Rainsford and Tim Woods's point that literature can become "an arena in which readers can address their moral sympathies and limits through the staged ethical concerns of the characters, and implicitly, the author," because "literary texts have a thickness—a density of human experience beyond finite ideas—that facilitates ethical thought in a way that texts that do not aspire to literariness cannot" (15). Among the older generation, we are asked to contrast Rajkumar, the opportunistic street urchin turned entrepreneur and trader in indentured labor, and Uma, the Collector's wife turned anticolonial Gandhian activist. But in neither case do we have a clear hero or villain, endorsement or condemnation. What are we to make of their arguments, conflicts, and astounding embrace (symbolic and literal) at the novel's end? Among the younger generation, we are drawn into the contrast and rivalry between Dinu and Arjun, the former clearly opposed to fascism and totalitarianism, the latter first an officer of the British army who later turns "traitor" to his former masters when he joins the Indian National Army (INA) in World War II, which is being helped by the Japanese, yet another imperial force (130). All these choices are complicated, and each demands careful thinking and empathetic understanding. The novel also resists dichotomies among the choices made by other characters, particularly women: Dolly, who survives by finding ways "to stay alive" (384); Alison, who fights and then shoots herself before she can be captured by the Japanese (393); and Manju, who cannot endure privation even for her baby's sake and commits suicide on the infamous 1942 march after the Japanese invade Burma (408).

Rather than draw on a particular ethical system, I understand ethics broadly as asking questions about how one should live, how one should live among and with others, how one should shape oneself and one's actions. "As articulated in the recent revival of ethical criticism, ethics connotes not behavioral codes, dogma, or a singular idea of the good but instead illuminates how literary works grapple with problems that pervade a world of competing values," notes Shameem Black (*Fiction* 3). "The word *ethical* is used in common speech to refer both to the field in which criteria are applied or practical judgment enacted and to the positive valence put on certain acts," observes Michael Lambek; like him, I use "*ethical* in the broader sense, referring to the field of action or practical judgment rather than to what is specifically right or good" (9). In this course,

I cannot get into debates in moral philosophy or literary theoretical poststructuralist or Marxist critiques of the presumed universal subject,[3] but I can help students distinguish between conventional or religious morality and ethics (the larger secular enterprise of thinking about how we make judgments); between "particular rules" and "the general field of inquiry" (Harpham 397). I introduce the three main moral philosophical modes of ethical reasoning—the Kantian deontological (universalist) categorical imperative, consequentialist or teleological utilitarianism, and Aristotelian character or virtue ethics—with arguments for their strengths and weaknesses. I find useful Lambek's anthropological focus on "ordinary ethics," the understanding that "ethics is part of the human condition; human beings cannot avoid being subject to ethics, speaking and acting with ethical consequences, evaluating our actions and those of others, . . . intrinsic to speech and action" (1). This resonates with Zygmunt Bauman's key insights on postmodern ethics: "We are . . . ineluctably—*existentially*—moral beings: that is, we are faced with the challenge of the Other, which is the challenge of responsibility for the Other, a condition of *being-for*," and hence it is precisely the lack of a given system of rules or codes that creates the challenge of being truly ethical: "facing the ambivalence of good and evil (and thus, so to speak, 'taking responsibility for one's own responsibility') is the meaning of being moral"; thus "it is possible to give up on the idea of a grand narrative idea of a single ethical code, without giving up on the idea of moral responsibility as a regulative ideal" (1–2, 6). Without necessarily assigning readings from the host of scholars who have addressed how to relink literature and ethics, I draw upon the work of Martha Nussbaum, Wayne Booth (*Company*), James Phelan (*Narrative*; "Sethe's Choice"), and others, reminding students that literature does not tell us *what* to do, but puts us in highly concretized contexts and affective situations that prompt us to think about *how* to make ethical choices.

In the recent ethical turn in the humanities, "the decentering of the subject has brought about a recentering of the ethical" (Garber et al. ix). But which subject? What about the colonized subject, or the gendered, racialized, classed subject? Much current discussion around ethics seems geared toward privileged subjects (how those typically referred to as "we" treat the less fortunate or make "ourselves" better). Lawrence Buell observes that, while the French philosopher Emmanuel Levinas's emphasis on alterity, or otherness of the "Other," can offer a powerful alternative to the entanglements of recent debates, its ethical call seems also more applicable to "the privileged or the oppressor" (9). Ghosh, however, asks us to think about how differently *oppressed* subjects are to act rightly, or what *right* in their contexts could even mean. As we read *The Glass Palace*, I want students to think about both the particularities of ethical choices made in specific social, political, and historical contexts by specifically situated characters within the novel they are reading and how we as readers can be ethical ourselves as we assess those choices.

Thus I also want to place the question of ethics and ethical choice within the frameworks of (relative or unequal) power, imperialism, and globalization.

Should a promise by the oppressed to the oppressor be kept if breaking it might mean fighting off the oppressor—a question Arjun must face (286–87, 360, 387–88)? Should Arjun shoot Kishan Singh, his devoted military attendant, for deserting the INA in a state of extreme exigency, when he has himself deserted the British army in order to prove his own commitment to the INA (450–53)? Should Uma expose Rajkumar's infidelity to Dolly and violation of an indentured woman in his charge, or should she suppress her outrage and accede to the woman's request to maintain silence for the sake of her son Ilongo's future (205)? I am interested in exploring how ethics, as Gita Rajan puts it, "in our contemporary globalized frame, means conducting oneself responsibly in one's areas of interaction, wherein stated or subtle principles of justice undergirding one's actions are open to negotiations" (125). Some dilemmas, in their contexts, may be irresolvable, impossible to agree on. Class discussion then becomes an ideal arena for making, listening to, and responding to different arguments. *The Glass Palace* repeatedly presents us with moral dilemmas created by conflicting or competing ethical claims and asks us to understand how those dilemmas are informed and complicated by a character's intersectional gendered, colonized, classed status. Indeed, according to Geoffrey Harpham, "ethical choice is never a matter of selecting the right over the wrong, the good over the evil . . . a choice is 'ethical' insofar as *both* options available for choosing embody principles that can be considered worthy. . . . [E]very (moral) choice in an ethical situation chooses against other alternatives with comparable claims" (396, 398). While some choices are easier to adjudicate (most of us agree that, despite his circumstances, Rajkumar can choose not to rape a helpless indentured woman on his ship, though we are asked to understand that he does his imperfect best afterward toward moral repair by secretly supporting her and their son), other choices are ineluctably ambiguous, to be determined by individual conscience, not consequence (when some Indian officers desert the British army and join the INA).[4]

By our third session we are ready to take on more fully key questions of ethics at the heart of this novel. I ask students to prepare for the third and fourth sessions (on parts three and four of the novel) by focusing on the furious disagreement between Uma and Rajkumar that causes their big rift (214–15) and the three-sided debate between Uma, Arjun, and Dinu before Neel and Manju's wedding (253–56).[5] The very form of the novel is dialogic, I remind the class; *The Glass Palace* is constructed out of dialogue, difference, debate, the concatenation of multiple voices and perspectives. How do we discern whose position has more worth? How does Ghosh guide us to understand each perspective? Does he prompt us toward seeing one position as preferable to another? Does Uma's class privilege negate her points that Rajkumar has abused his power to his benefit or that the British Empire is using Indian soldiers to subjugate other colonized peoples? Does Rajkumar's early economic disprivilege and need to support his family entitle him to ignore "the atrocities of the Empire" in which he has become complicit (214)? How do we balance Uma's class privilege and gender disprivilege with Rajkumar's relative gender privilege and class disprivilege? How do we compare Arjun's self-interested careerism in joining the British Indian army; Uma's anti-imperialist support for the Indian National Congress and demands that India be promised independence in return for fighting in World War II for the British; and Dinu's argument that India would be far worse off if Indians refused to fight with the British, and Hitler, Mussolini, and Japan won (254–55, 266)? The novel asks us to combine empathy with discernment, to make up our own minds only after we work through each point of view. Yet we also note how, through their thoughtful and more informed responses, Ghosh nudges us toward Uma's and Dinu's positions and discourages easy abstention from judgment. "We need a way to distinguish between rash judging—not judging well—and the kind of judging that lies at the heart of what it means to be a self-respecting human subject in a community of other equally self-respecting subjects," "that critical thinking we call judging," argues Jean Elshtain; to refrain from judging (well) is a "cop-out, a way to stop forming and expressing moral judgments altogether" (176, 178, 182).

In our final sessions, as the novel moves into the experiences of this extended family in India, Burma, and Malaya during World War II, we focus on the insistent question it poses: why should Indians fight for the British in an imperialist war, subject as they are to British colonization and racism? We discuss, with student-selected passages, Arjun's growing realization that he has been a tool, "a toy, a manufactured thing, a weapon" (326), who wonders whether he can ever become his own person and reclaim autonomy (372); how Arjun and Hardy, among others, after much debate, switch allegiances (377–78); and why Arjun, maintaining a paradoxical sense of personal loyalty despite his switch to Indian nationalism, saves his British CO, Bucky, from being captured by the Japanese (381). In a useful exercise we compare Dinu and Arjun's last conversation (445–47) with their earlier debate before the wedding (254–56). Both have changed their positions by the end, because both have opened themselves, listened to others, and changed their minds. Listening to Arjun, Dinu begins to "doubt his own absolute condemnation" of those colonized subjects who joined the Japanese to fight the British (447). He recognizes other claims, that for "them imperialism and Fascism were twin evils, one being a derivative of the other" (413). Ethics and politics are "inseparable," though not the same (Parker 4). Dinu's final empathy for Arjun and shift away from certitude becomes an exemplum for Ghosh's readers. Students often assume that literature has a message or moral to impart. *The Glass Palace* offers no single doctrine but an ethics of reading (literature and life) that asks that we encounter diverse points of view, listen to each story, decide for ourselves, and yet be open to changing our minds.

In our last session we discuss the ending. Why does it matter, I ask, that the final sentence reveals that the nameless narrator is no disconnected being, but none other than Jaya's son, Dolly and Rajkumar's great-grandson and Uma's great-nephew? Why does Ghosh end with the bizarre yet unforgettable image of the aged Rajkumar and Uma in bed, their dentures locked together? Perhaps the answer to both questions is the same: the narrator and concluding image serve to highlight the inextricability of seemingly different histories, the hidden interconnections that bind people together despite their overt disagreements, and the situatedness of historiography and storytelling. We discuss the significance of Dinu's photography as a mode of expression, reassertion of freedom, preservation of history, and reconnection, for his photos literally enable Jaya to identify him and to find him again to complete their stories for each other.

We turn finally to Ghosh's now-famous letter to the Commonwealth Writers prize committee, explaining his decision to withdraw *The Glass Palace* from the contest ("Conscientious Objector"). Having read the novel through, we can discuss the significance and logic of Ghosh's action and argument. At one point, he notes that "the ways in which we remember the past are not determined solely by the brute facts of time: they are also open to choice, reflection and judgment." I point out how here again Ghosh calls for us to be ethical, as readers and inheritors of history. Judgment is key to the conscientious objector, to the writer, and to the reader. We conclude with Ghosh's resonant reminder at the end of the novel, when Dinu denounces Myanmar's military dictators as "worse than the colonialists" and his wife rebukes him: "[they] use the past to justify the present . . . but it's just as bad to use the present to justify the past" (462). This warning against amnesia and nostalgia becomes an injunction toward an ethics of remembrance and the exercise of judgment in context, reaffirming what the novel argues as a whole.

In interviews Ghosh has emphasized his interest as a novelist in exploring the specific predicament of an individual placed within a particular historic location, rather than in retelling larger historical events per se ("Diasporic Predicaments" 1–2). Approaching the novel by asking students to think about the ethics of colonized subjecthood allows them to complicate their responses: to get beyond the binaries of good-bad, collusion-resistance; to emphasize the importance of historical, political, and social contexts to understanding individual actions; to learn both to withhold easy judgment and to arrive at informed, nuanced judgments. It seems an appropriate approach to a novel that urges us as readers to become more empathetic, ethically attuned subjects by asking us to exercise careful judgment, to understand the complexity of history and of ethical choices made by constrained colonial subjects in their historical moments, to recognize their agency as well as the lack of clarity imposed by conditions of imperialism, and to both understand and interrogate a multiplicity of responses by various individuals who must act within the confined circumstances in which they are placed.

NOTES

[1] This essay uses the 2001 Random House edition of *The Glass Palace*.

[2] See Myint-U, Shah, and Cunningham.

[3] For those interested, see Adamson et al., including Parker's introduction (1–18); Davis and Womack; and Rainsford and Woods. For undergraduates I assign Rachels's very

useful and accessible piece on the difference between (and merits and demerits of) cultural and moral relativism.

[4] On moral repair, see Walker.

[5] By this point in our reading, the number of new characters can become confusing for many students, so I hand out a family tree that shows the connections among the main characters over the generations. I also have a meta-conversation with the class about the reading. Since many students, especially in this age of social media and short attention spans, are not habituated to the discipline of reading long novels, I invite them to share strategies, such as allotting oneself uninterrupted stretches of time to read, making notes, marking passages, etc. Many attest to the pleasures of curling up on a couch for hours and justifying that as homework. After the first class, I also hand out guiding questions ahead of each class to enable students to prepare for class discussions, alerting them to particular issues in the reading and soliciting evidence to help focus our conversations.

Citizen-Writer:
Teaching Ghosh's Ethnographies of Conflict

Kanika Batra

While Amitav Ghosh's fiction is widely taught in the Euro-American and post-colonial academy, his ethnographic pieces have less pedagogic circulation. Other than *In an Antique Land*, few of Ghosh's nonfictional texts are taught extensively, though they are sometimes used to supplement analysis of his fiction. Following this predictable trend, I first included Ghosh's writing in a graduate-level course on postcolonial literatures at a southwestern institution in the United States. This course is described in the university's catalog as "Concentrated studies in postcolonial theory and global literature, treating in various semesters poetry, prose, drama, film, popular culture, and major authors." In keeping with this mandate, and with my training in comparative rather than region-specific postcolonial studies, the first iteration of the course in 2009 included a selection of literature from India, Africa, and the Caribbean.

The reading schedule placed Ghosh's canonical novel *The Shadow Lines* in juxtaposition to Aijaz Ahmad's essay "The Politics of Literary Postcoloniality" and Ella Shohat's "Notes on the Post-Colonial." Ahmad's and Shohat's valuable, though somewhat dated, critiques contest the term *postcolonial*, in particular its elision of class, the celebration of diasporic hybridity, and the flattening of space and time. My purpose was to ensure that students connected the contestations over the heuristic postcolonial with the literature we were reading. Ghosh's writing, in particular the clarity and lucidity of his prose, the cosmopolitanism of the characters and the author, and the centrality of diasporic experience, facilitates an easy connection with the diasporic postcolonialism that Ahmad and Shohat critique. I also attempted to balance Ghosh's Indian-English novel with Mahasweta Devi's short stories in translation, particularly "Puran, Pirtha, and Pterodactyl" from *Imaginary Maps*. In the second iteration of the same course a few years later, I substituted for *The Shadow Lines* Ghosh's then relatively recent work *The Hungry Tide*. The theoretical context provided by Ahmad and Shohat was supplemented with Robert Marzec's introduction to the 2009 special issue of *Modern Fiction Studies* on ecocriticism, "Speaking before the Environment: Modern Fiction and the Ecological." In retrospect, I was providing students a palatable introduction to postcolonial studies, largely through fiction, some nonfiction, and theory. This fulfilled the mandate of the course description in the university catalog but did not completely fulfill my goal of situating postcolonial studies as an interdisciplinary mode of analysis.

In a recent graduate course on comparative literature, my aim was to test the limits of comparativism by pushing the boundaries of the generic course catalog description: "[t]heory and practice of the study of comparative literature, with emphasis on themes and motifs." To this end, I stated that the course content included "anthropological and sociological writing on globalization and urbanization" to "make connections between comparative work in literature and other disciplines."[1] The first few class meetings introduced comparative literary methods through the work of Susan Bassnett, David Damrosch, Emily Apter, Haun Saussy, Djelal Kadir, and the American Comparative Literature Association's *State of the Discipline* reports published in 2006 (Saussy) and 2014 (Heise et al.). The 2014 report, which is available online and contains brief exegesis of theoretical concepts, was especially useful. It was sometimes unavoidable that my training as a postcolonialist would influence the discussions. Adding to this were redefinitions of comparative literature that unmoored the field from its origins in European and American contexts (Bassnett; Spivak, *Death*; Lionnet, "Cultivating Mere Gardens").[2] My students brought with them different interests in British, American, and world literatures, making this class a little different from previous seminars on postcolonial literature, where students working primarily in American literature sought to apply postcolonial theory to the Americas. Our class discussions this time were less focused on the postcoloniality of Ghosh's essays or the situations they described.

Reading various accounts of the discipline, students found Bassnett's ideas in *Comparative Literature: An Introduction* easily comprehensible and Apter's writing in *Against World Literature* dense but extremely useful. Apter's work provided us with key concepts that resonated through the course. Her ideas— "untranslatables," "terrestrial humanism," "planetary dysphoria," "dispossessive collectivism"—were used and debated by students in their weekly online discussions and on-site exchanges. We read three of Ghosh's essays: "The Testimony of My Grandfather's Bookcase," "The Ghosts of Mrs. Gandhi," and the longer *Countdown*.[3] The first piece complemented Orhan Pamuk's Nobel lecture, "My Father's Suitcase," to indicate the multiple European and non-European literary influences on these two important writers of our times; the latter two describe urban dystopian scenarios fueled by interethnic and international violence. These works culminated our discussion of urban studies and literature as an instance of new definitions of comparative literature relevant for the twenty-first century.

I believe we need to expand literary training beyond the existing novelistic and critical canon that stands in for comparative and postcolonial literature. Among others, Jahan Ramazani (*Hybrid*) and Helen Gilbert and Joanne Tompkins (*Post-Colonial Drama*) have pointed out the neglect of postcolonial poetry and drama. To add to these critiques, postcolonial nonfiction reluctantly finds its way onto syllabi and exam lists despite the work of Veena Das, Mahmood Mamdani, David Scott, Deborah A. Thomas, and others, who usefully indicate how social science research can be combined with literary and cultural analysis.[4] The value of disciplinary crossings is exemplified by students' engagement with the course and with Ghosh's nonfictional writings.[5] I am not arguing for the abandoning of literary training in such an endeavor. In fact, an emphasis on form, style, voice, method, and reliability allowed us to think of tentative answers to the following questions: What are the global frames of understanding civil conflict (anti-Sikh, anti-Muslim, anti-black violence) and low-intensity hostilities (between India and Pakistan or the United States and Cuba)? Can we think of Ghosh's accounts as contributing to or subverting quasi-ethnographic reportage of non-Western civil and political violence in Euro-American print and electronic media? In short, then, if advanced literary training enables students to become better writers and thinkers, the daily valences of such training can and must include awareness of genres that are not merely journalistic, activist, or literary but a combination of all these. These are all valuable to those aspiring to use their degrees in academic and extra-academic contexts.

First, a short description of the essays under consideration: initially published in *The New Yorker* in 1995, "The Ghosts of Mrs. Gandhi" describes events in Delhi in the immediate aftermath of the assassination of Prime Minister Indira Gandhi by her Sikh bodyguards in November 1984. The gap of almost a decade between the riots and the writing of the essay allows Ghosh to reflect on the impact of the events on his life and his development as a writer. The essay can easily serve as an introduction to Ghosh's novel *The Shadow Lines*, but since our focus in the course was not on fiction, and we had just finished discussing Abdou-Maliq Simone's ethnographic account of four African cities, we talked about Ghosh's reliance on cartographic strategies to describe the insidious spread of violence across Delhi within a few hours of Gandhi's death. The author recounts how he was a resident of Delhi at the time; he had just finished teaching a class at the university and was making his way across the central and south sides of the city in a bus when the mobs began to search for Sikh targets. In the carefully delineated accounts of the various class-stratified residential areas in the city, what emerges is a map of terror and resistance. Where, on the one hand, there is "a calculated attempt to terrorize the people . . . evident in the common tendency among the assailants to burn alive Sikhs on public roads," there is also a peace march across the burning city streets by activists. When the rioters confront the marchers, all the women in the group "stepped out and surrounded the men; their saris and kameezes became [a] thin, fluttering barrier, a wall around us . . . to face the approaching men, challenging them, daring them to attack." The conundrum faced by the writer was whether to write about this event and, in so doing, convert it into an aesthetic phenomenon. He chose not to for many years, until the Hindu-Muslim violence of the 1990s forced him to remember and respond to what he witnessed.

Prior to our discussion of "The Ghosts of Mrs. Gandhi" we had read Arjun Appadurai's *Fear of Small Numbers*, subtitled *An Essay on the Geography of Anger*, which provided a global perspective on terror in the context of the 9/11 attacks. Appadurai's is a comparative analysis of the majoritarian fear of "minorities" arising out of an "anxiety of incompleteness and unacceptable levels of uncertainity" and often leading to "ethnocide" (9). Appadurai mentions how the Sikhs in India were turned into a minority: "the massive unleashing of state and popular violence against Sikhs in 1984 . . . produced the Sikhs as a cultural and political minority, whose own small terrorist component acquired a general sacrality after this event" (46). While reflecting on his memories of and response to the violence, Ghosh asks:

> When I now read descriptions of troubled parts of the world, in which violence appears primordial and inevitable, a fate to which masses of people are largely resigned, I find myself asking: Is that all there was to it? Or is it possible that the authors of these descriptions failed to find a form—or a style or a voice of a plot—that could accommodate both violence and the civilized, willed response to it? ("Ghosts")

Here the citizen-writer's mapping of state-sponsored violence in the heart of the nation's capital and the activist response to it yielded a diverse set of responses somewhat typical of eager graduate students at a university in the United States. Some students asked for clarifications about the context, others compared it with anti-Muslim sentiment in the United States following the 9/11 attacks, and a few connected it to recent news reports about police brutality against African Americans and the public response to these acts.

In their online discussions students commented on the construction of racial, ethnic, and religious minorities. Recounting a discussion with her partner, a student wrote:

> We talked about . . . the recent debate over the status of the many children who arrived at the border of the United States this summer. From a social psychological perspective—which aligns well with Appadurai's argument—the perceived threat to the "national ethnos," in combination with the general public uncertainty about the status of the children and the effect of their numbers on the hegemony of the majority, caused many people to react with extreme prejudice. . . . Despite the fact that we pay lip service to the values of diversity, equality, and multiculturalism, black Americans (like certain other racial or religious groups) are not part of the "national ethnos." Further, our treatment of black Americans as a population to be targeted for criminality directly clashes with the diversity-equality-multiculturalism rhetoric. For police officers—especially white, middle-class police officers who may be carrying their own baggage of racism or racial guilt—black Americans present a great deal of social uncertainty.

Another student used the example of an Indian man in Alabama assaulted by a police officer, which led to severe injuries. She pointed to the similarities and differences between African American and Indian American persecution:

> [A] new kind of violence is emerging (arising from the same old fear of cultural difference), particularly in America. I don't know what to call it.

Some people like to gloss over it as "police brutality." As a student of literature and an immigrant, I see it as a multilayered, multifaceted exhibition
of power, cruelty, racism, and an uncanny translation of Apter's "untranslatables" to real life.

   After Eric Garner and Michael Brown, we now have Sureshbhai Patel.
The reason that I am riled up is not only the fact that Patel is an Indian
(wow, nationalism!), but also because this man faced what he faced
because of his color and because he lacked knowledge of English and a
"cultural sameness" that could have saved him!

Notice the breathless quality of both samples, almost as if the writers are rushing to get the words out. As heartening as the comparative analysis of the various
kinds of intrastate violence against minorities is, the writing also demonstrates
intelligent connections between the construction of race and ethnicity and the
languages and geographies of multiculturalism. These two students continued the
dialogue in their comments on each other's discussion posts.

   Building on interdisciplinarity and geography, the next few classes, titled
"Translating Cities: Urban Studies and Comparative Literature," included
Simone's detailed ethnographies of Douala, Winterveld, Dakar, and Jeddah in
For the City Yet to Come: Changing Life in Four African Cities. We talked
about whether the "failed city" paradigm applied to African cities is also relevant
to Delhi, a city torn by violence in 1984 and even today, over three decades later,
marked by targeted incidents against women and minorities. If the state is in-
effective or unwilling to contain various forms of violence in the national capital,
as was the case in 1984, what then remains of its credibility? Ghosh writes that
"in New Delhi—and much of North India—hours followed without a response"
to the violence against Sikhs ("Ghosts"). We concluded that, as in the case of
the African cities described by Simone, the idea of failure is complicated by the
dense web of supportive social connections. Ghosh describes how neighbors
risked their lives to save their Sikh friends and community members; activists
marched, endangering their lives amid the violence; and members of a citizens'
commission gave up years of their lives in efforts to rehabilitate victims of violence.[6] Such resilience echoes Simone's idea of the "city yet to come." Ghosh's
auto-ethnographic account provides an effective though not a complete rejoinder
to those who would posit that violence is "primordial" and "inevitable" in "trou-
bled parts of the world," often synonymous with Asia, Africa, and Latin America
("Ghosts").

   The last section of the course, which I had titled "Planetarity," included
Gayatri Spivak's *Death of a Discipline*, Rob Nixon's and Bruce Clarke's essays on
the Anthropocene, and Ghosh's tract *Countdown*, published in the aftermath
of India's nuclear tests in 1998. Spivak's work calls for a revitalization of comparative literature as a discipline through the methods of language training and
interdisciplinarity found in area studies. This is not an easy text to read, but

students heroically grappled with it to write some of the smartest, most engaging, and funniest responses of the semester. Here is an example:

> Just when I'm commending myself for finally making sense of Spivak, politics creeps up its head again. It won't let comparative literature cross borders. And all this while we were looking at "depoliticization" of comparative literature. Spivak rightly points out the effects of globalization in the form of "satellite dishes" (17) in Nepal but laments, "[t]he everyday cultural detail, condition and effect of sedimented cultural idiom, does not come up into satellite country" (17). Hello, Apter! There she is with her "untranslatables" at the back of my mind. Hoping that comparative literature will eventually be able to cross borders, I move on to "collectivities". . . . The ideas that I could clearly grasp were the ones where Spivak talks about joining the forces of area studies and comparative literature to make the crossing of borders feasible.

Here is another from a student who was scheduled to present in class that day:

> Spivak is concerned by a "multicultural" comparative literature that focuses primarily on European and Euro-American cultures to the exclusion of other cultures and languages forced to the edge (if not over) of extinction by the spread of globalization and commercialization. European and Euro-American comparative literature has for too long been studying its own navel (or the navels of its nearest neighbors), taking what it finds to be indicative of the "universality" of European and American experience.

Spivak's call allowed me to talk about the nuclear race in the subcontinent—a brief area studies analysis, so to speak—before delving into Ghosh's writing. The author himself provides a detailed background to the politics of the nuclear bomb, its strategic importance (or lack of it) for India, and the heavy militarization of the border between India and Pakistan.[7] This work directly reflects Ghosh's training as an anthropologist since it is based on field visits and interviews he conducted in Khetolai, Pokhran, New Delhi, Calcutta, and Islamabad. The rigorous research modeled here was also expected from the students, who were by this stage planning their final projects. It also exemplified the direct connections between urban studies, anthropology, and literature that I had emphasized through the semester. Ghosh sketches a dystopian scenario of a nuclear fallout involving New Delhi as a flashpoint, much as it was the node of interethnic violence in the previous essay: "On a hot and humid August day, I drove around New Delhi with an old friend, Kanti Bajpai, trying to assess the damage the city would sustain in the event of a nuclear explosion" (*Countdown* 71). In the ensuing pages, Ghosh wonders "how the people of Delhi—or any other Indian or Pakistani city—would respond to a catastrophe of this kind" (79).

Students had prepared for the class by reading Nixon's and Clarke's questioning of the hubristic promotion of the Anthropocene as a fashionably interdisciplinary catchall concept explaining the mutual impact of humans on Earth. Nixon points out how the concept often fails to account for the politics of geography, development, distribution, and availability of resources: "We may all be in the Anthropocene but we're not all in it in the same way." Clarke participated in the discussion in our last class meeting, providing an Earth systems perspective on the Anthropocene that the students engaged with, challenged, and nuanced with a social historical perspective we collectively endorsed.

In their online discussions students connected the Anthropocene, urbanisms, and planetarity to come up with commentary on the globality of the nuclear race and the locality of its immediate impact. One student wrote that

> [b]oth Pakistan and India viewed the development of nuclear weapons not only as a political maneuver but also as politically meaningful. Symbolically and politically, [weapons] raise the nation to the height of world power despite the dangers and harms caused by their production. By viewing them as global chess pieces, we overlook the impact of their development on cities like Pokhran or Los Alamos, New Mexico, whose residents experienced (and still experience today) many of the toxic effects of nuclear weapons testing.

One especially diligent student connected all the threads from the course in her last response, titled "Actors and Agency: Human-Centeredness and Canon-Centeredness":

> Earlier in the semester, we discussed the Western domination in defining literature, genre, period, etc. In some ways, the field of comparative literature strives to rethink these definitions or at least allow for a multiplicity of definitions through strategic comparison (thinking here of Emily Apter's untranslatability). The notion of the Anthropocene seems to be similarly dominating or accommodating of dominance in a system that is far more complicated than human-centrality. . . . Just as the Western notion of canonicity asserts dominance in attempts to define genre and period in literatures of other cultures that do not necessarily fit, so too [have] global power relations affected the ways in which India engages with the world.

The response was a good reminder of the literary qualities of Ghosh's writing, in particular the ability to position himself as an insider-outsider, citizen-writer, ethnographer-fabulist. Toward the end of "The Ghosts of Mrs. Gandhi," the writer questions his own involvement in the victim-relief and peace-building efforts undertaken by teachers, activists, and politicians. He admits to slipping back into his own writerly routine while others continued to work for years to rehabilitate those impacted by the violence and to produce a report indicting those responsible for it. In the last few paragraphs of *Countdown* he describes experiencing a strange satisfaction in India's nuclear tests on learning of "the tone of chastisement adopted by many Western countries, the finger-wagging by many who were themselves content to live under nuclear umbrellas. . . . I remember thinking at the time . . . perhaps India's nuclear tests had served a worthwhile purpose after all, by waking the world from this willed slumber" (81). In the final indictment of ethnic and national violence we see the complex perspective adopted by a writer whose audience is both Indian and international, whose writing carries local and global authority, and who is aware of his responsibility to imaginary and real-world scenarios. Beyond the obvious pleasure of teaching such writing is my hope that the student-citizen-writers who successfully engage with it will use academic and public forums to shoulder some of this responsibility.

NOTES

[1] The multimodality of the course facilitated some of my goals. This was a hybrid course, which typically involves a mix of on-site and synchronous online pedagogy using *Skype* audio, video, and chat. However, since there were no online students registered for the class that semester, after the first four class meetings, the on-site students requested to meet in person every week. I readily agreed. We used the online portal *Blackboard Learn* for at least as much interaction as the weekly on-site meetings. Students commented on one another's discussion posts prior to the class meeting and continued their conversations when we met in person.

[2] Bassnett's and Spivak's works have been read as making a case for postcolonial studies as the most recent avatar of comparative literature.

[3] This essay uses the versions of "The Testimony of My Grandfather's Bookcase" and "The Ghosts of Mrs. Gandhi" found on Ghosh's Web site.

[4] Arjun Appadurai is an exception in this regard, since *Modernity at Large*, and in particular the much-anthologized essay "Disjuncture and Difference in the Global Cultural Economy," is often included in postcolonial syllabi and exam lists.

[5] A brief description of the composition of the class is in order here. This was a graduate-level methods course, which is a requirement for MA and PhD students intending to opt for the comparative literature, globalization, and translation (CLGT) specialization. Of the seven students in the course, two were international (from India and Saudi Arabia) and five American; all were women. Three were potential CLGT specialists; others enrolled because the course seemed appealing and of interest to them. Students had period- and area-specific interests in classics, medieval studies, postcolonial studies, American studies, and linguistics. The common set of readings we discussed illustrated methods of analysis that each student applied to her specialization.

[6] See, in particular, Veena Das's detailed ethnography of women survivors of Partition and the 1984 anti-Sikh riots.

[7] For a similar contextualization see Anand Patwardhan's landmark antinuclear documentary *Jang aur Aman / War and Peace* (2002), which was banned in India by the Hindu nationalist government.

The Tensions of Postcolonial Modernity: Enlightenment Rationality, Migration, and Gender in *The Circle of Reason*

Yumna Siddiqi

Amitav Ghosh's first novel, *The Circle of Reason*, published in India in 1986, is a particularly apt text for courses on postcolonial and world literature because it engages in a lively way with many of the tensions of postcolonial modernity. As the title suggests, the novel explores the vagaries of Enlightenment rationality outside North America's and Europe's borders. While the novel focuses largely on India, it also addresses the connected histories of South Asia, the Middle East, and North Africa, and the themes it foregrounds—colonial knowledge, anticolonial thought, modernization and development, state power, repression, internal displacement and migration, labor, and social stratification—are common to many postcolonial societies. Like all of Ghosh's fiction, the novel is rich in ethnographic and historical details about trade and economy, cultural and social practices, arts and crafts, science and the environment, and town and village life, among other topics. Ghosh uses rich descriptions in his fiction to create a sense of verisimilitude as he conjures times, places, and circumstances that seem far removed from the experiences of his anglophone Indian and international readers. At the same time, the novel requires students to see the connections between apparently distant worlds. As Keya Ganguly puts it, "the entire novel proffers readings of the connections, at various levels, between local circumstances, 'our' historical conjuncture, and larger narratives about the logic of capital and 'other' subjects of History" (187).

Set in the decades after Indian independence, the novel centers on the experiences of Alu, an orphan, who finds himself caught up in a feud between his foster father, an eccentric schoolteacher, and Bhudeb Roy, the principal of the school, who is also a police informant. Falsely identified as a dangerous insurgent by Bhudeb Roy, Alu is forced to flee his village and travels to a Gulf State. He is pursued by a whimsical police detective, Jyoti Das, who is more interested in tracking birds than in tailing people. Das eventually joins Alu and his companions in their subsequent flight to Algeria. *The Circle of Reason* invites readers to inhabit the worlds of villagers in Bengal, students in Calcutta, a middle-class policeman, and Indian migrants in the Gulf and Algeria in the 1960s and 1970s. From the point of view of students, these unfamiliar worlds and moments can be challenging to investigate and interpret. To give those unacquainted with the cultural landscape at least some orientation to the historical and social forces that fashion the world depicted in *The Circle of Reason*, I show a two-hour film, Arnaud Mandagaran's *India: The Turmoils of a Century*, which uses documentary footage to present a fairly good overview of twentieth-century India. I outline briefly the history of British colonialism, the Indian independence struggle, and India's post-independence trajectory, including the 1971 war with Pakistan that led to the creation of Bangladesh. Students also find helpful some contextualization of social classes and caste and gender dynamics that are presented in the novel.

I also ask the students to consider what knowledge and beliefs they bring to their interpretation of *The Circle of Reason*. In the first pages of the novel, Ghosh satirizes the pseudoscience of phrenology and the hazards of investigating human beings according to its principles when Alu's uncle, Balaram, rushes for his Claws—huge calipers with which he proposes to measure the bizarre lumps on the boy's head. Balaram, an aficionado of phrenology, hopes to determine what organs and qualities the protuberances on Alu's head correspond to. This moment serves as a useful allegory for the hazards of interpretation in general and for "considering the 'native' as object for enthusiastic information retrieval," as Gayatri Spivak puts it ("Three Women's Texts" 243). Spivak astutely addresses the question of imperialism and the kinds of violence—material, psychological and emotional, and epistemic—that it involves. She emphasizes that this violent history shapes the conditions of cultural interpretation, and she warns, "To consider the Third World as distant cultures, exploited but with rich intact literary heritages waiting to be recovered, interpreted, and curricularized in English translation[,] fosters the emergence of 'the Third World' as a signifier that allows us to forget that 'worlding,' even as it expands the empire of the literary discipline" (243). The mode that Spivak describes as "information retrieval" obscures the global historical lines that link readers to the trajectory of imperialism. This fact is evident in the very language of *The Circle of Reason*: the novel was written in English, placing it in the category of the literary fiction of an elite shaped by institutions that have British colonial roots, which is worth pointing out to students. Which social, economic, and political forces have fashioned them as readers of Third World texts in the First World academy? How can they better gain knowledge of the historical ties that bind them to the unfamiliar worlds of *The Circle of Reason*?

One way to avoid falling into the mode of "information retrieval" in regard to the Third World when teaching a text such as *The Circle of Reason* is to focus on the tensions that the novel explores and the questions that it raises. In classes, I tend to focus on four problematics treated in the novel: the nature of Enlightenment rationality, as signaled by the title, and of modernity more broadly; the logic of police and governmental rationality, as suggested by the novel's playful use of the detective plot;[1] various dimensions of migration, especially labor migration; and gender constructions and postcolonial feminism. All of these problematics cut across distinctions of First and Third World and bring home Spivak's point about the mutual, differential "worlding" of postcolonial geopolitical spaces.

Modernity and The Circle of Reason

I introduce the problematic of modernity and Enlightenment rationality by pointing to the title and the idea of reason. I outline some of the ideas associated with the European Enlightenment, especially the notion that man (with its masculinist, Eurocentric connotation) can free himself from superstition, ignorance, and error and, through the exercise of the universal faculty of reason, can achieve moral, material, and political progress.[2] A familiarity with the discourse of the Enlightenment helps students make sense of the characterization of Balaram, from his participation in the college's Society for the Dissemination of Science and Rationalism among the People of Hindoostan, or the Rationalists for short, to his setting up of the School of Pure Reason and the School of Practical Reason, titles that playfully invoke Kant's critiques. After a brief discussion of the novel's allusions to the European Enlightenment, I explore the term *modernity* and its cognates *modernization* and *modernism*.[3] I ask students what they understand modernity to be, try to locate the period historically in relation to capitalism and imperialism, and discuss the centrality of the ideas of progress and reason in the Western discourse of modernity. A few words on Hegel's view of history as the progressive instantiation of reason are often helpful to students here. I also ask students to reflect on how they understand history and remind them that the idea of history as having a progressive trajectory, with the West ahead of the rest, is a historically and culturally particular one, though so ideologically embedded is it that students tend to take it for granted. The motif of the circle in the book's title works against the notion that the course of history is linear and progressive, following the movement of reason. I ask students to consider: what is the significance of the European Enlightenment and the European discourse of modernity in colonized societies such as that of India? The project of modern nationhood pivots on the ideals of progress and development in postcolonial societies. Indeed, Indian social reformers such as Raja Ram Mohan Roy saw them as vital to the amelioration of Indian society, and nationalists such as Jawaharlal Nehru embraced the ideals of Enlightenment thinkers as key to the emergence of a modern nation, freed from superstition and ignorance—and the chains of the British (Nehru 17). Anticolonial nationalists, who saw colonial powers as thwarting the progress of India's people, assumed the mantle of true development. In *The Circle of Reason*, Balaram represents this embrace of Enlightenment principles. This was not a view shared by all Indian nationalists, though, and it's worth pointing out to students M. K. Gandhi's view, in his 1910 essay *Hind Swaraj*, that Western modernity—which he argues promotes material rather than spiritual development—is damaging to Indian society.

In addition to discussing different views of what Western modernity signified to Indian nationalists, I sketch briefly for students the more recent debate about whether there is "a singular modernity," determined by the global forces of colonialism and capitalism, or whether different parts of the world experience "alternative modernities," defined by the interplay of local and global forces upon places with specific histories and cultures (Jameson, *Singular Modernity*). I ask students, How are modernity and the modern portrayed in *The Circle of Reason*? Balaram's campaign as a student to promote clean underwear and his later efforts to disinfect the village of Lalpukur are driven by his commitment to the modern, scientific discoveries of Pasteur (his most treasured book is *The Life of Pasteur*), and his Schools of Pure Reason and Practical Reason are a vernacular implementation of Kant's philosophy. Is Balaram's enthusiasm for modern science portrayed as absurd or admirable? Is his obsession with cleanliness and purification "modern" and Western, or "traditional" and Indian, or both? To what extent does the desire of people who live in postcolonial societies to enjoy the perceived benefits of modernization that are part of the vision of Western modernity have to be taken at face value? Balaram's embrace of phrenology, a pseudoscience long debunked in the West, is clearly misguided and ludicrous; is Enlightenment rationality inevitably belated as well as hybridized in a colonial milieu? Are there domains of knowledge and practice that the novel portrays as part of a global, shared history? The novel depicts weaving, Alu's passion, as having such a global history (55–58); it is presented as a figure for human experience, one that disavows divisions—of mind and body, of countries, of history, of reason itself (42–43).[4] One can also discuss the craft of weaving in relation to the writing of the novel and its form. *The Circle of Reason* weaves together many different historical, personal, and social strands into a complex pattern, like the intricate *jamdani* cloth that Alu weaves.

Enlightenment Rationality and Police

While *The Circle of Reason* represents certain aspects of Enlightenment rationality and Western modernity positively, it presents a far more negative portrayal of another legacy of Enlightenment rationality: the police and state power. I point out to students that the etymology of the term *police* shows a link between the state's regulation of conduct to promote individual well-being and social progress and the repressive aspects of state power. In Europe, from the Middle Ages until the eighteenth century, *police* referred to the administration of the population to promote the public good and happiness through specialized knowledges and practices—what we would understand as public policy. It was only during the late eighteenth and early nineteenth century that *police* acquired the meaning we are familiar with now: "the maintenance of order and the prevention of dangers" (Pasquino). This distinction between administration and repression is questionable even in so-called liberal democratic Western societies. In the colonial context, the rational administration of the population was primarily aimed at the maintenance of colonial power and the extraction of profit, often with little knowledge of local custom. And postcolonial nations in

South Asia maintained the "overdeveloped" repressive institutions of colonial states—the police and the army—more or less unchanged in their structure and mode of operation (Alavi).

In *The Circle of Reason*, Ghosh underscores the repressive aspects of the state. On several occasions in the novel, those who have superior force, usually the police, smash seemingly modern, enlightened projects. The chapter "Signs of the Times," in which a military plane crashes in the village during the 1971 war, shows the workings of political power and police in a thoroughly modern way. The augurs in the village interpret this event variously as an ill omen, a sign of the times, or an ordinary happenstance of *kalyug*, or a doomed era, but Balaram believes that it should be interpreted rationally. In fact, it is Bhudeb Roy who has the most practical, rational view of this crash: he takes possession of the plane and sells off its parts to the villagers piecemeal. The novel touches on the multiple meanings of modernity in this episode. A warplane, an emblem of modern technological development, is transformed into modern building mate-rials for the village: the metal sheets of the fuselage are used as a roof, the wings are used as a bridge, and the glass, rubber, nuts, and bolts are used for construction. Two days later, two jeeps arrive with uniformed men who unerr-ingly go to the villagers who have bought the scraps from the plane and recover the "government property," evidently aided by Bhudeb Roy. The scraps of the modern that literally fall out of the sky and are incorporated by the villagers into their habitat are quickly wrested away from them by the "blue-uniforms" of the state, though not before the village's police informant has made his profit (96–97).

Balaram's attempts to promote modern and rational principles that may be applied in everyday life in India are repeatedly thwarted by the brute forces of unreason. During his student days in Calcutta, his campaign to introduce clean underwear is violently foiled when his antagonists try to inspect *his* underwear and he jumps off a balustrade and breaks his legs. Years later, as India and Pakistan go to war and refugees stream into the village and set up temporary homes, Balaram establishes the School of Pure Reason and the School of Prac-tical Reason to meet their needs. There, students are to be taught reading, writ-ing, arithmetic, and the history of science and technology; they are also to learn weaving from Alu and tailoring from Parboti Devi, Balaram's wife. Balaram also champions "Reason Militant" and tries to battle germs by dousing the vil-lage with carbolic acid (117–18). While his grandiloquent scheme to bring Schools of Reason to the village is gently lampooned, his program of education and hygiene represents a reinterpretation of Enlightenment rationality to serve the needs of a postcolonial society. This utopian project is destroyed when Bhudeb Roy convinces the police that Balaram and his household are engaged in an insurgent plot. Balaram barricades himself behind barrels of carbolic acid. In fact, a young man who lives in the compound has been making and sell-ing bombs, and when the police send a warning flare, it triggers an explosion. Everyone dies except Alu, who is away at the time. This episode brings home the point that enlightened attempts by individuals to bring about social improvement are vulnerable to the violence of the police.

A third example of how an enlightened, utopian project is destroyed by the brute force of the police takes place in the Persian Gulf town of al-Ghazira, where Alu has traveled after being pursued by the police (chs. 14–15). Alu identifies money as a pernicious germ in his community and moves to eliminate its use within the Souk, where migrants live. Alu's utopian vision bears fruit: removed from the predations of middlemen in the Souk, the community prospers. When Alu and his friends enter the town to spend the money they have saved, they are ambushed by police employed by oilmen who have established themselves in al-Ghazira. This instance of another kind of modernity propelled by oil, arms, and technology, and dependent on the labor of migrants, is worth exploring. Once again, this version of modernity is shown in its repressive aspect.

The kind of rationality associated with Enlightenment principles and modernity is not only linked in *The Circle of Reason* with the repressive action of the police. It is critiqued at a more fundamental level. Self-serving and greedy Bhudeb Roy articulates this rationality in his vision of progress: "Look at Europe, look at America, look at Tokyo: straight lines, that's the secret. Everything is in straight lines. The roads are straight, the houses are straight, the cars are straight (except for the wheels). They even walk straight. That's what we need: straight lines" (99). Bhudeb Roy associates straight lines with the modern and the prosperous. The village, by contrast, is a place with "unrepaired cycles" resting against a banyan tree, "the rickety shed of the pharmacy," "ponds mildewed with water-hyacinth and darkened by leaning coconut palms"—a place of disorderly rural beauty (6). In lampooning a world of "straight lines," Ghosh hints at the oppressive qualities of a concretized reason that, in its linear, forward movement, is inimical to difference. It is to counter this that he also elaborates the concept of reason through the figure of the circle and the process of weaving. The brief overview by Lambert Zuidervaart in the *Stanford Encyclopedia of Philosophy* of Theodor Adorno and Max Horkheimer's argument in *The Dialectic of Enlightenment*—that the logic of domination that inheres in the myths of Enlightenment underpins the turn to fascism in Europe—gives students a broader context for the critique of Enlightenment rationality in *The Circle of Reason*. This is also a point of departure to round off a discussion of what the discourse of Enlightenment rationality and Western modernity means for postcolonial societies. Is a model of progress and development that has at its core the domination of nature damaging for postcolonial societies? Who benefits from this model of development? In what ways and to what extent is the imposition of the discourse of Western modernity and Enlightenment rationality a kind of "epistemic violence," as Spivak argues in "Can the Subaltern Speak"?

A consideration of the novel's formal structure and genre is also an effective way of exploring the significance of Enlightenment rationality and the police. *The Circle of Reason* has elements of detective and police fiction. It is partially the narrative of a police chase: Jyoti Das is investigating a supposed insurgent plot and pursues Alu across the country and to the Gulf because he is a suspect. Classical detective fiction tends to endorse the police activity and rationality of the state. Here, the narrative of police and detection is turned inside out—Alu is falsely identified as an insurgent, and Jyoti Das turns out to be more interested in studying birds than in chasing down a suspect. At the end of the novel, Das joins Alu and his companions in their migratory flight. The novel is also a picaresque, following Das's meandering investigation and Alu's aimless flight. The narrative has a circling, perambulatory quality, moving between past and present, the city and the country, and from character to character in a highly associative way. It disavows the rationality of police and of "straight lines" in its form as well as in its content.

The final part of the novel also rehearses a debate about modernity. Alu and his companions, now joined by Jyoti Das, find themselves in a small town in Algeria. Here, the expatriate Indian community recruits them to participate in a performance of a classical play, *Chitrangada*, but while they are practicing, Kulfi, who plays the main character, suddenly dies of a heart attack. In the face of the gibes about the scientific, "modern" Dr. Mishra, Dr. Verma tries to perform religious last rites, using tap water instead of holy Ganga water and broken furniture for a funeral pyre. The episode dramatizes the complexities of religious consciousness in India through the tension between the narrowly doctrinal view of the secular, rationalist, left-speaking Dr. Mishra and Dr. Verma's view of religion as a historically contingent cultural practice that expresses deeply felt sentiments. This part of the novel serves well in the classroom as a springboard for discussing Enlightenment rationality, secularism, and religion in postcolonial cultures.

Migrants, Refugees, and The Circle of Reason

A third problematic that I explore in the novel concerns the circumstances of subaltern and middle-class travelers, migrants, and refugees. Ghosh explores the experiences of migrants, travelers, and refugees in many of his works, including the *Ibis* trilogy, *The Hungry Tide, In an Antique Land*, and *The Shadow Lines*. To give students a sense of the scale and nature of international migration, one can point them to the UN Population Division's reports on international migrants. According to a UN wall chart, 243 million people were international migrants in 2015. That same year, more than a million refugees and migrants entered Europe, and thousands died on the journey. I discuss some of the causes of migration: postcolonial underdevelopment, religious persecution, civil war fueled by arms from the United States and other arms-exporting countries, climate change. The picture is complex and hard to do justice to briefly, but an open discussion of what the causes of migration are in the novel can ground such a discussion. The logic of "police"—the tendency to identify an opponent as politically dangerous or criminal so as to legitimate repression—that leads the state to construct Alu as a terrorist forces him to flee first Lalpukur and eventually the country. Although Alu is first an internal migrant in the face of political persecution by the state, the novel has a much briefer account of his experiences as a refugee in India, and the narrative itself focuses on his voyage to the Gulf, his life and work there, and his subsequent flight to Algeria. It's worth stressing, though, that international migrants are often first internal migrants who are displaced by violence from their homes, as is Alu.

Ghosh's narrative in *The Circle of Reason* of Alu's experiences as a refugee from the state and as a migrant is rich material for a discussion of several different aspects of migration: the journey, community and family, labor, and social and political marginality. In class, I emphasize the different trajectories of subaltern and elite migration. Alu's voyage on the *Mariamma* in chapter 9 is a key phase of the difficult journeys that subaltern migrants undertake to find new homes. The description that most poignantly brings home their precarious status is Karthamma's attempts to hold back the birth of her child until she signs forms. Her perplexed companions finally realize that she believes she will in this way assure her newborn birthrights, and one of them rips a page out of Alu's copy of *The Life of Pasteur* and has her sign on the bottom, after which she goes into labor. Here, a text that signifies the possibilities of Enlightenment doubles as a template for the inscription of a state rationality that assures a migrant a legitimate identity. Alu's and his companions' experiences as workers in al-Ghazira constitute a fictional portrait of the circumstances of the millions of low-wage Asian workers in the Gulf Cooperation Council (GCC) countries who build and sustain the high-tech, oil-fueled development of these countries. Alu's accident and Rakesh's death on the construction site of the Star point to how precarious their lives are and how limited their political rights. As American universities open campuses in GCC countries, critics are highlighting the harsh and dangerous conditions in which migrants live and work. In the face of these difficult conditions, Alu and his companions on the boat manage to build communities and unconventional families that sustain them.

Finally, I address the different trajectories of migration sketched at the end of the novel. While poor, supposedly unskilled migrants lack the credentials, money, and social networks to join wealthy diasporas and, when they do immigrate to the West, are relegated to an underground, illegal status, middle-class migrants are in a better position to obtain jobs and legal status in the West. We see this dichotomy in the last paragraphs of the novel, where Jyoti Das faces Gibraltar with a sense of hope, expecting to join his uncle in Düsseldorf, while Alu, Zindi, and little Boss wait for the ship that is to carry them home, though it is not clear where home is or where hope lies. I conclude the class by circling back to the larger question that the novel raises, that of what kind of home and future postcolonial societies seek to build and what forces they contend with.

Gender, Postcolonial Feminism, *and* The Circle of Reason

In the course of our analysis of *The Circle of Reason*, I foreground the constructions of gender and sexuality and introduce students to postcolonial feminism.[5] I begin by asking students how they think women from the Third World are represented in popular media. I then introduce them to Chandra Mohanty's criticism, in her essay "Under Western Eyes," that Western feminists also make problematic assumptions about so-called Third World women. Mohanty argues that Western scholars tend to construct a generalized category of the "Third World woman" who is a victim of male violence and of family structures, weak, disempowered by colonial processes, oppressed by religious ideologies, and in need of opportunities of "development" along certain (economic) lines. This essentialist view of women from the Third World, a view that fails to recognize the social and historical specificities of their lives and identities, denies them agency and the power of resistance. Next, I ask students how they think women, men, gender, and sexuality are portrayed in *The Circle of Reason*. I focus especially on the fully developed characterization of Zindi and ask students to consider all the ways in which the portrait of Zindi contravenes many of the stereotypes of Third World women as submissive, silent, weak, and oppressed. Third World women have been constructed as chaste, respectable, demure bearers of authentic tradition, both in their home countries and in immigrant communities. Zindi, by contrast, is a large-bodied, rough-tongued, tough Indian migrant whose burka only makes her more imposing. Once they reach al-Ghazira, Alu; Karthamma and her newborn baby, Boss; Kulfi; the Professor; and Rakesh live with Zindi in her compound. She finds them work through her connections, charges them a small rent, and cooks for them. She is a big-hearted den mother who bullies, cajoles, and wheels and deals to keep her adopted family afloat. The characterization of Zindi also offers an opportunity to discuss Western stereotypes of Muslim women and of veiling. Marnia Lazreg's essay "Women and Difference: The Perils of Writing as a Woman on Women in Algeria" is useful for making sense of how many Muslim women across the world are perceived. Lazreg argues that Western feminist scholars who write about women from North Africa and the Middle East, like social scientists in general, give "religion a privileged explanatory power" (83). When they focus on Islam in particular, they hold a view of the religion and gender that lacks nuance. As Lazreg puts it, "Because language produces the reality it names, 'Islamic Women' must by necessity be made to conform to the configuration of meanings associated with the concept of Islam. The label affirms what ought to be seen as problematical" (87–88). In these discussions, Lazreg adds, scholars are especially preoccupied with the practice of veiling, which is again treated in a culturally and historically reductive way. The upshot of these missteps in Western feminist scholarship on women in North Africa and the Middle East is that difference is essentialized. For students who are completely unfamiliar with debates about women, gender, and Islam, Leila Ahmed provides an excellent introduction in the film *Women and Islam* (Jamal).

The Circle of Reason conveys with rich ethnographic detail a sense of place and of history in its portrayal of both rural and urban milieus in postcolonial India in the 1960s and 1970s. At the same time, the questions it raises about the nature of postcolonial modernity make it contemporary and global in its scope. I have discussed briefly how the novel portrays different dimensions of postcolonial modernity. It playfully lampoons the ways in which the Enlightenment discourse of reason is taken up in postcolonial India and points to both the repressive and emancipatory aspects of postcolonial rationality. The novel suggests that the modernity of postcolonial societies may be different from those of Europe and North America, but at the same time, for many postcolonial people, the desire to be modern in a European and North American way is powerful. It shows the postcolonial state to have inherited the logic and the apparatuses of police. The novel critiques these by turning the formal conventions of police fiction on their head, so that the policeman joins the fugitive in flight. The novel portrays the displacements and migrations that are so crucial to contemporary postcolonial experience and serves as a springboard for the discussion of global movements of people. It presents complex constructions of gender and kinship that challenge Western stereotypes of Third World women. In its form, in its themes, and in the problematics with which it engages, *The Circle of Reason* foregrounds the ways in which geopolitics and history bind postcolonial subjects in a singular, yet differentiated, modernity.

NOTES

[1] This essay draws upon "Police and Postcolonial Rationality in Amitav Ghosh's 'The Circle of Reason'" in my book *Anxieties of Empire and the Fiction of Intrigue*, which examines how colonial and postcolonial fiction about detection and espionage portrays threats to the social and political order (140–66). In the first part of the book I focus on how writers such as Arthur Conan Doyle and John Buchan represent threats to imperial rule. In the latter part of the book, I argue that postcolonial writers such as Amitav Ghosh, Arundhati Roy, Salman Rushdie, and Michael Ondaatje use the genre of intrigue to reflect upon the anxieties of the postcolonial state and make both the repressive and emancipatory aspects of postcolonial political sovereignty visible.

[2] Roy Porter provides a quick if Eurocentric overview in his book *The Enlightenment*.

[3] Frederick Cooper's chapter "Modernity," in his book *Colonialism in Question: Theory, Knowledge, History*, nicely rehearses the political and cultural implications of the term.

[4] This essay uses the 1987 Abacus edition of *The Circle of Reason*.

[5] Chris Weedon's article on postcolonial feminism provides a quick overview of this field.

The Problematic of Fokir's Death:
Exploring the Limits of Postcolonial Feminism

Suchitra Mathur

In my experience, teaching an upper-level course on feminist theory is as much about unlearning as it is about learning. Students usually come into such a course with preconceptions regarding feminism as a mode of analysis focusing on *woman* defined in essentialist terms, with the woman-man binary as the predominant frame of reference. In addition, their approach to theory is often based on understanding it as a set of ideas that need to be assimilated and applied rather than interpreted and interrogated. To embark on a study of theoretical texts with such unexamined baggage invites the danger of conceptual oversimplification. The pedagogical challenge posed by such reductionist reading may be met by interspersing theoretical texts with literary works. The idea here is to provide an open terrain for engagement with the issues raised by theory through the multiple interpretations that are possible for a literary text. The pedagogical strategy of multiple rereadings of the same set of texts in the light of new insights emerging from iterative in-class discussions enables learning along with unlearning. This results in a participative process wherein students embark on an exciting journey of discovery to develop an understanding of feminism that is complex and dynamic rather than dogmatic. In this essay, I will attempt to trace this pedagogical process as it unfolds in my course through repeated readings of Amitav Ghosh's *The Hungry Tide* in conjunction with three foundational theoretical texts of postcolonial feminism: Chandra Talpade Mohanty's "Under Western Eyes: Feminist Scholarship and Colonial Discourses" and Gayatri Chakravorty Spivak's "Three Women's Texts and a Critique of Imperialism" and "Can the Subaltern Speak?" In the first cycle of readings, putting *The Hungry Tide* in conversation with these three theoretical texts challenges students' preconceptions regarding feminism through postcolonial feminism's engagement with the power inequalities that splinter the category *woman*. As this leads to a more nuanced reading of the novel that foregrounds intersectional axes of oppression, the focus converges on Fokir's death and its implications for the postcolonial feminist category of the gendered subaltern. The literary text thus takes us back to uncover and unlearn the gender bias in the theoretical texts' exclusive focus on the female subaltern as the site for political intervention.

I introduce postcolonial feminism toward the latter half of my course on feminist theory after we have completed an overview of mainstream Anglo-American feminism. In our first discussion of the three articles, therefore, our focus is on how they define postcolonial feminism in contradistinction to Western feminism. Mohanty's "Under Western Eyes" does so in terms of feminist theory and its mode of analysis, foregrounding the strategies adopted by Western feminists to represent the Third World woman as a special case of the universal "oppression of women." The articulation of this "third-world difference" not only homogenizes Third World women into a unified category but also places them in the position of "object" with respect to Western feminists, who are the "subjects" creating this knowledge about the "other" (351–52). Spivak's "Three Women's Texts and a Critique of Imperialism" offers a similar argument through an analysis of *Jane Eyre*, the paradigmatic text of Western feminist individualism, wherein Jane's subject position is consolidated through the subjugation of Bertha, the woman from the colonies. Spivak's analysis of Jean Rhys's *Wide Sargasso Sea*, a rewrite of *Jane Eyre* from Bertha's perspective, further reveals how the politics of imperialism constructs women in the colonies in multiple ways as overdetermined by racial hierarchies. In both cases, the category *woman*—the purported unified constituency of feminism—is revealed to be divided by colonial ideology into First World and Third World women who have a distinctly hierarchical relationship. By highlighting the global power structures that divide women along racial or ethnic lines drawn by material historical processes, postcolonial feminism thus challenges the dominant feminist idea of global sisterhood based on an essentialist definition of *woman* as a singular identity.

I deliberately invoke intersectional feminism here, for this is an opportune teaching moment to forge connections among different feminist theories. The proliferation of multiple feminisms—differentiated variably on the basis of their theoretical underpinnings, their ideological positioning, their historical and locational specificity, or a combination of these—often leads to confusion and the danger of politically paralyzing dispersion. One way of dealing with this problem is by highlighting overlaps and connections. Reading postcolonial feminism in terms of intersectional feminism (seen to be concerned primarily with the intersection of race and gender within the Anglo-American context) enables fruitful cross-pollination between antiracist and anti-imperialist feminisms.

After this introduction to the theoretical texts, when students are asked to read *The Hungry Tide*, they are quick to see the novel as exemplifying the tenets of postcolonial feminism. Focusing on the female characters, especially Piya and Nilima, students argue that the substantial narrative space occupied by these two strong and independent Third World women (as defined by their ethnic origins) establishes the postcolonial feminist credentials of this text. Piya is an American of Bengali origin, a cetologist by profession, who has come to the Sundarban region to carry out fieldwork. Nilima, a generation older, moved to the Sundarbans from Calcutta with her husband and now heads the Badabon Trust, an NGO running various social programs in the area. Since these women are portrayed neither as undifferentiated representatives of a homogenous category nor as victims without voice or agency, they clearly challenge the colonialist representational politics of hegemonic Western feminism as outlined by Mohanty and Spivak and consequently embody a postcolonial feminist perspective.

To make students see the essentialist underpinning of such an understanding of postcolonial feminism in terms of the East-West binary, I steer the discussion toward the two other female characters in the novel, Kusum and Moyna. While the four women are similar in their resilience and determination to make a better life for themselves, they clearly do not inhabit a level playing field. The success achieved by Nilima and Piya in their respective enterprises is not merely a result of their inner resources as individuals; it is achieved on the basis of their class/caste privilege, which gives them direct access to powerful social and financial resources. It is Piya's uncle, "who's a big wheel in the government" (12),[1] who enables her initial access to the Sundarbans for her fieldwork, while it is her access to international funding that finances her conservation plans in the Sundarbans. Similarly, Nilima calls upon friends and relatives in Calcutta to provide government backing and financial support for her plans with the Badabon Trust. As lower-class, lower-caste women, Kusum and Moyna lack any such inherited resources and have to forge their own alliances to provide them with the necessary support in their struggles.

This difference in access to resources creates a fundamental difference in their struggles as well. While Nilima and Piya are engaged primarily in their individual struggles to forge an identity for themselves (their work with the trust and river dolphins, respectively, being an avenue for their self-expression), Kusum and Moyna are part of a collective fight for basic survival. For Moyna, this collective is defined by her nuclear family; her focus is on ensuring economic stability and a viable future for her son and husband as well as for herself. For Kusum, who loses her family as a young girl and becomes a displaced refugee in the process, the collective is the community that helps her to survive, and it is for the continued survival of this community that she fights.

To understand this difference between the two sets of women in terms of postcolonial feminist theory, we turn back to Spivak, where I draw students' attention to the following passage:

> The broad strokes of my presuppositions are that what is at stake, for feminist individualism in the age of imperialism, is precisely the making of human beings, the constitution and "interpellation" of the subject not only as individual but as "individualist." . . . As the female individualist, not-quite/not-male, articulates herself in shifting relationship to what is at stake, the "native female" as such (within discourse, as a signifier) is excluded from any share in this emerging norm. ("Three Women's Texts" 244–45)

Seen in this light, the caste-class privilege enjoyed by Nilima and Piya appears to be consolidated by an ideological position that corresponds closely to Spivak's "female individualist." This recognition provides an opportunity to engage students in an interpretative, nonliteral reading of theory. Spivak, after all, is talking about imperialist texts from nineteenth-century Britain, while Ghosh's novel is a twentieth-century Indian novel. So how can *The Hungry Tide* be seen as paralleling *Jane Eyre*? This takes us to an examination of the historical context of the novel. While *The Hungry Tide* is certainly not a nineteenth-century text, it is nonetheless situated in the extended age of imperialism, which includes the present historical moment. The novel makes this extension explicit by positing parallels between the colonialist establishment of Lusibari (the Sundarban island where Nilima lives) by Sir Daniel Hamilton and the postcolonial establishment of the Badabon Trust on the island, both of which are accomplished through an appropriation of material resources (land) as well as the operation of an epistemic violence that imposes its own knowledge economy on the local inhabitants. Imperialism then cannot be understood restrictively as a nineteenth-century phenomenon defined in terms of an East-West binary; instead, imperialism needs to be understood as a socioeconomic-political project defined by specific relations of production that continues to structure contemporary reality even within the bounds of a single nation-state. Such an extended understanding of imperialism, provided by a discussion of the literary text, allows students to extract Spivak's argument from its historical specificity. Students are able to appreciate how Nilima and Piya occupy the position of feminist individualists in the age of imperialism who, furthermore, are engaged in "the imperialist project cathected as civil-society-through-social-mission" (Spivak, "Three Women's Texts" 244), as evidenced in their activities related to the Badabon Trust. As such, the discursive position they occupy as a signifier in the novel is definitely not that of the "native female"; this latter position is occupied only by Kusum and Moyna, who may be seen as being "excluded from any share in this emerging norm" of feminist individualism.

Having learned to interpret theory, instead of accepting it unreflectively, students are able to do the same with Mohanty's essay by mapping her claims about "Third World women" and "Western feminists" onto the two sets of female characters in Ghosh's novel. Mohanty's insistence, for example, that *Third World woman* should not be seen as a homogeneous category is evident in the differences between Moyna and Kusum. Though their lack of access to resources marks them both as Third World, their attempts to create their own communities are significantly different. Moyna's chosen path for consolidating the position of her family is through meritocracy as defined by individual educational accomplishments and the subsequent climbing of the professional ladder within the given system. In other words, Moyna attempts to rise above her Third World status through an embrace of modernity and a corresponding disassociation from her "native" moorings. Not only does she literally move away from her native island to Lusibari, home to the modern, Badabon Trust–run medical and educational services, but she also actively distances herself from the local ways of life as represented by her husband, Fokir, while aligning herself with Nilima, who acts as her benefactress. Kusum, on the other hand, forges alliances with fellow refugees to create a community rooted in the local environment in defiance of external (national as well as global) pressures. This difference between the two characters exemplifies Mohanty's theory of postcolonial feminism, as not only recognizing the heterogeneity of Third World women but also rejecting the disempowering representation of Third World women as victims by highlighting movements of resistance by Third World women (Mohanty 352).

Similarly, Nilima and Piya may be interpreted as representations of Mohanty's Western feminist despite their nonwhite/non-Western identity in terms of ethnic origin. According to Mohanty, Western feminists "codify Others as non-Western and hence themselves as (implicitly) Western" through "images constructed from adding the 'third world difference' to 'sexual difference' . . . predicated upon (and hence obviously bring into sharper focus) assumptions about Western women as secular, liberated, and having control over their own lives" (334, 353). This subject-object relationship between the Western feminist and the Third World woman is evident in Nilima's first encounter with local women soon after her move to the Sundarban region:

> These women were easily identifiable because of their borderless white saris and their lack of adornment: no bangles or vermillion. . . . Making inquiries, she learnt that in the tide country girls were brought up on the assumption that if they married, they would be widowed in their twenties . . . [so] when the menfolk went fishing it was the custom for their wives to change into the garments of widowhood. . . .
>
> There was an enormity in these acts that appalled Nilima. She knew that for her mother, her sisters, her friends, the deliberate shedding of these symbols of marriage would have been unthinkable. . . .
>
> What to make of these women and their plight? . . . It was thus . . . that Nilima had her epiphany. It did not matter what they were; what mattered was that they should not remain what they were. (80–81)

Piya's proposal to Nilima for her conservation project, which concludes the novel, echoes the same sentiments with mild variations: "You know a lot about the people who live here. . . . If I was to take on a project here, I'd want it to be under the sponsorship of the Badabon Trust, so it could be done in consultation with the fishermen who live in these parts. And the Trust would benefit too of course. We'd share the funding" (397). "We" here is clearly distanced from "the people who live here," and the divide is defined by an epistemological power dynamic that allows the former to control and shape the representation of the latter, who are seen to have no independent agency. Through such rereading of specific passages from the novel in conjunction with Mohanty's essay, students are able to further refine their understanding of the binary underpinning postcolonial feminism as referring not to the literal locational difference between the West and the Third World, but to a positional difference that is better expressed as metropolitan versus native, wherein the two terms are indicative of differential access to epistemological power rather than any essential ethnic identification.

This unlearning of essentialist identity politics also leads students to a reevaluation of the feminist politics embodied by the novel itself. The narrative concludes with Piya and Nilima joining hands to consolidate their social and financial resources and including Moyna in their distribution of largesse. However, Moyna's position in this global sisterhood is clearly that of a second-class citizen, "almost the same, but not quite"—an oft-quoted truism of postcolonial theory, a slight modification of Homi Bhabha's "almost, but not quite" ("Of Mimicry and Man" 91), which foregrounds the workings of colonial discourse that claim to create the native in the colonizer's image but at the same time to assert a necessary difference.[2] Though seemingly interpellated as a "female individualist" through her embrace of modernity, Moyna remains circumscribed by caste-class hierarchies that continue to privilege the two metropolitan women who control the terms of her access to this hegemonic position—they can fire Moyna at any time if she does not conform to their dictates. This possibility is affirmed by a recollection of Nilima's firm refusal to help Kusum in any way during her struggle to protect her newfound community from government forces since it would endanger the position of Nilima's NGO. The help provided by metropolitan women to their native counterparts is clearly contingent upon the latter continuing to act as what Spivak might call "good women" who do not destabilize the existing power structure that ensures the former's privileged position (see "Can the Subaltern Speak?" 101–03). And the novel itself consolidates this power structure through the narrative fate it decrees for the three female characters who are alive at the end. While Piya and Nilima are shown to be happily discussing their plans for the future at the conclusion of the novel, Moyna is nowhere to be seen. She has already exited the book, at the moment when she realizes that Fokir is dead, making her a widow. In an ironic twist, the woman who steadfastly distanced herself from the traditions of the fishing community is ultimately claimed by those traditions through the self-fulfilling prophecy of widowhood. Moyna thus leaves the book as an embodiment of Mohanty's Third World woman—silenced and appropriated as an object for representational manipulation by Piya, who invokes her as the beneficiary of her conservation project. From this perspective, students reinterpret the feminist politics of the novel as a reinscription of the dominant "Western feminist" paradigm rather than an embodiment of postcolonial feminism.

The process of iterative discussions described so far completes one cycle of unlearning/learning with respect to postcolonial feminist theory. Through progressive interrogation of literary and theoretical texts, students are able to recognize and challenge their earlier essentialist definitions of *woman* as the unified subject of feminism and of the East-West binary as it structures postcolonialism. Using *The Hungry Tide* as the linchpin text for this pedagogical strategy, however, provides the opportunity to initiate a second cycle of unlearning/learning with respect to a more fundamental assumption regarding women as the exclusive constituency of feminism. This emerges directly from the discussion of the novel's ending that concluded the first cycle. Having discussed the text's silencing of Moyna as the Third World woman, I draw students' attention to the process whereby Piya is finally interpellated as the "Western feminist." While

Moyna's exit from the novel is not necessary for Piya's emergence as a narratorial focus, Fokir's death is essential for Piya's reestablishment as the subject of the narrative. Progressively through the novel, and especially in the couple of chapters preceding his death, Fokir, who becomes Piya's self-appointed protector, emerges as a significant actor on the novelistic scene. His death, however, clears the stage for Piya's triumphal emergence as the feminist individualist with the independent resources to establish her home in Lusibari. How is this centrality of Fokir's death to be understood within a postcolonial feminist framework?

To understand Fokir's death, we return to Spivak's essays, since in both "Three Women's Texts" and "Can the Subaltern Speak?" she clinches her central argument through a scene of death. Antoinette's self-immolation as Bertha, Spivak argues, "act[s] out the transformation of her 'self' into that fictive Other, set[ting] fire to the house and kill[ing] herself, so that Jane Eyre can become the feminist individualist heroine of British fiction" ("Three Women's Texts" 251). In the case of Bhuvaneswari Bhaduri, Spivak reads her decision to commit suicide at a time when she was menstruating as "an unemphatic, ad hoc, subaltern rewriting of the social text of sati-suicide as much as the hegemonic account of the blazing, fighting, familial Durga" ("Can the Subaltern Speak?" 104). This postcolonial feminist reading of the act, however, does not gain purchase within the dominant epistemological framework, making Spivak claim that "the subaltern as female cannot be heard or read" (104). For Spivak, then, the representations of these subaltern deaths enact a scene of epistemic violence wherein the dominant discursive frameworks consolidate themselves through a deliberate silencing, through misrepresentation, of subaltern speech.[3] Acknowledging and deconstructing such representations to foreground the imperialist politics that structure them is, according to Spivak, the primary task of postcolonial feminism.

When students revisit Fokir's death with this understanding of Spivak in mind, they recognize the similarity in the narrative pattern here and the trajectory of Bertha's death in *Jane Eyre*; in both cases, the death of the subaltern enables the triumphal emergence of the feminist individualist. The parallel with Bhuvaneswari Bhaduri's suicide is a little more complex; in both cases, the act is caught between two seemingly oppositional discursive formulations that do not allow the voice of the gendered subaltern to be heard. In the case of Bhaduri, as mentioned above, these two formulations are the colonialist "save the victim" and the nativist "good wife" discourses, respectively. In the case of Fokir, the two dominant interpretive frameworks may be understood as the patriarchal "good husband" and the colonialist "native informant" ("Can the Subaltern Speak?" 103). The novel invokes both: Piya tells Kanai that Fokir had "said Moyna's name and Tutul's before the breath faded on his lips" (392), while Nilima is pleased to "have a memorial for Fokir, on earth as well as in the heavens" (399), since it is the preservation of his knowledge in the satellites of the global positioning system that has allowed Piya to get funding for her project, which is to be named after Fokir. Significantly, both these formulations represent Fokir as a passive object. Not only is his use of his knowledge (evident in the way in which he helps Piya survive the fury of the cyclone) denied, his role as provider and protector (of Tutul and Piya) is also suppressed. This undermining of his agency parallels the discursive silencing of Bhaduri, making Fokir occupy the position of gendered subaltern within the novel.

To help students understand the gender politics of Fokir's position, I bring in the concept of colonialist patriarchy, which is part of the hegemonic epistemology of imperialism. It is this patriarchal formulation that emasculates the native man by defining both "good husband" and "native informant" in ways that preclude any expression of autonomous agency. Based on their earlier unlearning of East-West essentialism, students are quick to recognize that this emasculation, while fully applicable to Fokir, does not impact Kanai. While Fokir is a good husband in his emotional dependence on Moyna and Tutul, Kanai is a good husband as the efficient caretaker of his company; while Fokir's knowledge as a native informant is captured by satellites, making him redundant, Kanai is fully in control of his insider knowledge, packaging his privileged access to Nirmal's story in his own terms. But this difference between the representation of Fokir and Kanai, when seen through the lens of colonialist patriarchy, does not merely deconstruct the essentialist East-West binary of postcolonialism; it also questions the more fundamental woman-man binary of feminism. Not only does colonialist patriarchy effeminize Fokir while masculinizing Kanai, but, as seen above with respect to Fokir, its discursive framework is invoked in the novel by the two metropolitan female characters. The significance of this gendering becomes clearer when Piya tells Nilima, "[I]t'll be good to have him [Kanai] home" (399). For Nilima and Piya, therefore, while Fokir and Moyna function as the self-consolidating other, Kanai is an integral part of the self. Thus, within the dynamics of imperialism, the metropolitan self that wields epistemic power is also implicitly masculinized, while the native other who is silenced is feminized.

To resolve the problematic of Fokir's death, therefore, students need to unlearn the fundamental assumption that feminism is premised upon the woman-man binary wherein both terms denote an essential nonreducible identity. This unlearning also facilitates a redefinition of students' approach to theory, encouraging them to interrogate rather than simply accept its conceptual formulations. The three essays of postcolonial feminism discussed here all implicitly subscribe to an essentialist definition of gender. "Under Western Eyes," though defining Western feminists in terms of their epistemological position, represents them almost exclusively through female scholars, while the constant invocation of Third World women also preserves this gendered exclusivity. "Three Women's Texts and a Critique of Imperialism" invokes women in the title itself, while "Can the Subaltern Speak?" genders the subaltern as woman through the choice of examples, from sati to Bhuvaneswari Bhaduri. With their newfound understanding of the complex gendered dynamics of masculinity and femininity within the framework of imperialism through their reading of Fokir's death in *The Hungry Tide*, students are able to recognize and critique the implicit sexist frame of reference that reinscribes an essentialist woman-man binary at the heart of these texts of postcolonial feminism. At the same time, their unlearning also puts them in a better position to appreciate the implication of the essays' intersectional analysis of patriarchy and imperialism—that within the framework of colonialist patriarchal discourse there is no straightforward mapping of metropolitan/native onto men/women and masculinity/femininity.

What then do students finally take from these discussions of postcolonial feminism? Fokir's death, I argue, places postcolonial feminism at a crossroads. As a self-proclaimed mode of intersectional analysis, should postcolonial feminism use this lens to look only at women to understand how colonialist and patriarchal discourses overlap in structuring their lived realities? Or should it develop an intersectional standpoint that recognizes colonialist patriarchy as a complex system of domination that shapes all of us and posits postcolonial feminism as an alternative, liberating epistemological framework enabling broad-based alliances across gender, class, caste, and ethnicity? I leave students with these questions while pointing out that the position from which we choose to answer these questions—the position of instructor, student, or academic—also needs to be analyzed in terms of its own epistemological power dynamics. For me, teaching this course using such an open-ended pedagogical strategy acts as a powerful reminder that there is ultimately no innocent or objective approach to any text; we can only unlearn our privileges by acknowledging the power they confer upon us, while learning to negotiate a way of reading that allows all voices—in texts and in the classroom—to be heard and addressed.

NOTES

[1] This essay uses the 2004 Ravi Dayal edition of *The Hungry Tide*.

[2] Postcolonial feminism intervenes in postcolonial theory by interrogating its analysis from a specifically gendered perspective such that colonial and patriarchal discourses are seen to intersect in the creation of the ambivalent figure of the gendered native.

[3] In an interview, Spivak clarified her assertion that the subaltern cannot speak: "By 'speaking' I was obviously talking about a transaction between the speaker and the listener" ("Subaltern Talk" 289). As such, the subaltern "utterance" does not "fulfill itself in a speech act"; in other words, the subaltern voice has no impact on the dominant epistemological framework.

Flood of Fire, Empire, and the Ethics of Literary Memory

Vincent van Bever Donker

The finale to a magnificent trilogy, *Flood of Fire* brings to conclusion a story stretching to 1,600 pages and nearly a million words. Its breadth of narrative reach makes the trilogy an excellent complement to a course on postcolonial literature. It engages with several prominent postcolonial themes, particularly the ethics of historical narrative and, in *Flood of Fire*, eco- or green postcolonialism. As it is the final installment in a trilogy, it is of course ideal if students are able to read all three books. However, with its numerous reiterations of previous events, *Flood of Fire* could be taught largely as a stand-alone text, although reference to the earlier novels and some extracts from them would allow a more nuanced analysis.

The story of the *Ibis* trilogy is a story of concealment, transformation, and recognition of the broader history of the British Empire. Amitav Ghosh's oeuvre repeatedly delivers carefully crafted narratives with meticulously timed revelations driving narrative tensions and climaxes. The books in the trilogy—and *Flood of Fire* in particular—are no different. In opening this narrative structure to students, a helpful starting point is Terence Cave's *Recognitions: A Study in Poetics*, specifically extracts from the chapters "Anagnorisis in Antiquity" and "Transition." This provides an important framework for grasping the nuances of recognition and how it has developed over the centuries from the initial nominal recognition advocated by Aristotle (most famously Oedipus's recognition of his true identity and therefore that of his wife/mother) through to recognitions of spiritual identity, hidden states of affairs, and the movement of concealment and revelation of narrative itself. Deploying this range of uses as an "elaborate paradefinition" (Cave 222) allows for multiple points of entry into the narrative of *Flood of Fire* and the broader postcolonial concerns that it addresses.

Beginning with individual characters, the first two novels detail—and *Flood of Fire* recaps—the dislodging of Deeti, Kalua, Jodu, Paulette, Zachary, and Neel from their community-centered lives as they are swept up in the transnational currents of empire. The first four characters conceal their identities in order to seek out a better life, while Neel—who later also disguises himself—at first discovers a new sense of self through the adversity that he suffers. Their lives intersect aboard the *Ibis*, a schooner that has itself been transformed from a slave ship into a regular trading vessel and is present throughout the trilogy as a crucible of transformation. The conclusion of *Sea of Poppies*, with its rapid, climactic sequence of recognitions, sees these characters cut adrift and going their own way to prosper as best they can. It is in *Flood of Fire* that their individual paths begin to cross once more, drawn as if by a confluence of historical currents to the beginning of the First Opium War. Each character has passed through several incarnations of him- or herself when all but Deeti, Paulette, and Zachary meet again on the *Ibis* and flee to freedom.

The most enlightening comparison of the characters' transformations can be made between Neel and Zachary. Neel is first introduced as a *zamindar*, wealthy and indulgent, but he undergoes a significant transformation through his imprisonment for fraud and subsequent deportation. Escaping from the *Ibis* with several others, he passes through a number of roles. Becoming Ah Neel and living in Canton, he works as a scribe for a wealthy Indian merchant, a translator, and eventually an advisor and translator for the Chinese as they prepare to defend themselves against the British. Zachary's transformation is more unsettling. From assisting the convicts to escape the *Ibis*, Zachary goes on to become a manipulative and cruel individual whose only aim is profit, although there is a suggestion of hope toward the end. Nevertheless, two scenes worth putting alongside each other in this regard are Zachary's confrontation with the first mate Crowle in his cabin in *Sea of Poppies* and Zachary's confrontation with Captain Mee in the same cabin in *Flood of Fire*. The parallels between the scenes are striking and serve to emphasize the dramatic reversal of roles, with Zachary having become the exploiter of hidden secrets and thus akin to Crowle.

Such character transformations within the novel, apart from driving the narrative, cast a revealing light on the British Empire. Through Zachary, we gain a personalized glimpse into the ruthless underpinnings of the quest for profit, complementing the self-righteous, hypocritical claims of the British merchants who assist with the attack on China. The fact that the merchants' claims can be read as hypocritical, of course, is indicative of the perspective occupied in the novel. That is, the narrative of (primarily) Neel, with his proximity to the Chinese, sets up the contrast that allows the hypocrisy to emerge as such. This leads to the work that Ghosh is doing in his text on history and historiography. Before venturing into that more metanarrative analysis, it is worthwhile to have students spend some time analyzing the connections that develop between characters. Apart from the occasional sympathetic British or American character, the only real connections that emerge between characters in the novel are among the colonized and the invaded. Thus Kalua has a moment of recognition when he realizes that Kesri Singh is Deeti's brother and therefore his brother-in-law (although not legally). This prompts him to remain close to Singh during battles, with the result that he saves his life and ultimately helps him escape. More significantly, Neel, Jodu, and Serang Ali all begin to work for the Chinese, aiding them in their resistance of the British. *Flood of Fire* thus serves as a prime example of the networks and assistance shared among the colonized, detailed in, for instance, Elleke Boehmer's *Empire, the National, and the Postcolonial*.

Yet the picture of empire developed in the novel and the series more generally is anything but a simple antagonism between good and evil. Students might be tempted to view empire in such romantic terms, yet a crucial complication is the realization that, on an individual level, the British Empire was, to use Gayatri Spivak's phrase, an "enabling violation" (*Critique* 217 n33). Thus Seth

Bahram is able to prosper as a trader of opium, and Zachary, successfully passing as white, becomes similarly wealthy. Of course, in both cases, their material prosperity is exceptionally fragile. Indeed, Bahram's ventures culminate in his death. Yet there is a resurrection of hope as his wife, Shireen, travels to China to claim his part of the wealth reaped from the British invasion of China. We consequently have a complex situation of individuals making the most of the circumstances in which they find themselves, of lives being ruined and lives prospering within the networks of empire, even as the violence and hypocritical deeds of empire are revealed as such.

It is with this more nuanced engagement with the British Empire in mind that students would benefit most from turning to the overarching thematic concern: history. Questions of history are prominent throughout Ghosh's oeuvre. *In an Antique Land* was Ghosh's first explicit foray into historiography, excavating the story of "the slave of MS. H.6." (17)[1] through both narrative imagination and academically rigorous historical and sociological research. The combination of fiction and research in that work serves to demonstrate the limits of historiography by revealing its narrative structure and the elision of subaltern voices within it, even as its disciplinary resources are deployed to establish a frame that is subsequently filled in through narrative. "There are silences that you cannot hope to fill by research alone," Ghosh has commented ("Networks" 32). This simultaneous use and critique of history—following the double gesture outlined by Dipesh Chakrabarty in *Provincializing Europe: Postcolonial Thought and Historical Difference* (Mondal, *Amitav Ghosh*)—can be observed in many of Ghosh's novels, up until the *Ibis* trilogy.

A good entry point into these debates around historiography for students, in addition to Chakrabarty's book, is Ghosh's own discussion with Chakrabarty on this project. Yet the particular benefit of teaching *Flood of Fire* rather than, say, *The Hungry Tide* or *In an Antique Land* is the further nuancing of the engagement with history that unfolds within it. There are several axes of the novel's engagement. Certainly there is a work of historical excavation in the *Ibis* trilogy. The story of lower-caste characters like Deeti, Kalua, Jodu, and Kesri Singh (the first and last of whom are primary focalizers in the novels) has clear connections to the heavy lifting undertaken in Ghosh's other works. Through their narratives, the particular realities of lives not recorded in the (colonial) archive, yet powerfully affected by the currents of empire, are given an existence that broadens our historical understanding.

While these characters confront the silences of history, seeking, in Ghosh's words, "not to become imprisoned by the archive" ("Networks" 31), any reader of the trilogy is also immediately confronted by the breadth of historical sources that Ghosh draws on for the novels, giving rise to an indicative list in the epilogue that stretches to several pages. Ghosh makes extensive use of real texts—speeches, diaries, journals, treaties, and so forth—that were written during the events leading up to and during the First Opium War. It quickly becomes apparent that there is more at work than pressing against the limits of history:

there is not only a questing beyond the archive, but also the recovery of a lost or forgotten archive—specifically the archive of the historical Neel upon whom the character is based.

The vital postcolonial project of, to put it simply, attempting to reach toward the subaltern of history (despite its impossibility, as famously outlined by Spivak in works such as *A Critique of Postcolonial Reason*) here intersects with the interplay between memory and history—a distinction developed particularly in the works of Maurice Halbwachs and Pierre Nora. Memory, within this line of inquiry, differs from history in forming an active part in present lived experience and identity formation. History can be visualized through the storehouse of texts, the library, accessed by but a few. Memory, in distinction, is historical recollection that is drawn upon by communities in developing their self-understanding; it has a present bearing on how communities and individuals within them understand themselves. The work done by a popular novel like *Flood of Fire* and its siblings in the trilogy is to shift the archive of the Opium Wars from history to memory. The use of military force to pry open the Chinese markets for the sale of opium in the name of free trade, leading to the establishment of Hong Kong as a British colony, is a part of colonialism that has largely been erased, often remaining unknown and untaught ("Networks" 34).

Ghosh's unique approach to this slightly different task of historical recovery can be illuminated for students by a comparison with Caryl Phillips's *Cambridge*. A novel that is a pastiche of historical sources, *Cambridge* nonetheless maintains a coherence of voice and perspective that is remarkable. Lars Eckstein's book *Re-membering the Black Atlantic: On the Poetics and Politics of Literary Memory* helpfully provides an extensive appendix showing, in parallel columns, the text of the novel and the respective historical sources cited and transformed. What the comparison reveals about *Flood of Fire* is mainly a difference in perspective and voice. Whereas Phillips deploys the historical material to reconstruct a fictional version of a white European character (who is circumscribed by her own unreliability and a brief testimony from the slave Cambridge), Ghosh presents the recovered archive through the point of view of primarily non-European characters. This completes the circle, linking back to the search for history beyond the archive: it is precisely because of this difference of perspective that Ghosh is able both to excavate and release into memory a forgotten archive and to reach beyond the limits of the archive to give voice to those who have fallen beyond its totalizing organization. Thus, for instance, through the travels of Kesri Singh on the campaign in China, we are given a view of the well-documented but elided events of the time as well as an exploration of what a colonial subject fighting for the British in China might have faced.

The axes of *Flood of Fire*'s engagement with history through its characters ultimately open into the broader debate of the ethics of literary memory. Eckstein's work, together with Richard Kearney's *On Stories*, can open up this debate for students in a productive manner, with further comparisons possible with Sam Durrant's *Postcolonial Narrative and the Work of Mourning*. The crux of this debate serves to turn the students from theoretical considerations back to a focus on character and narrative development. For it is precisely the meticulous craftedness of *Flood of Fire*, with its carefully developed characters and calibrated transformations and recognitions, that becomes the object of debate: What risks are involved in such a detailed representation of those elided by history? What is the role of narrative in the memory of historical violence? It is Ghosh's clear position within these debates that makes his work, and *Flood of Fire* in particular, a suitable ground for students to find their critical bearings within this important discussion in postcolonial studies.

NOTE

[1] This essay uses the 1992 Granta edition of *In an Antique Land*.

Intimate Alterities in Ghosh's *Sea of Poppies*

Smita Das

Cathleen Schine, in her review of Amitav Ghosh's *Sea of Poppies*, writes that "Ghosh's India could never fit on a map; it requires a globe, a spinning three-dimensional sphere extending in every direction at once, where every path circles back to its starting point." Schine's comment seems a fitting description of Ghosh's novel, as it erases rather than privileges national boundaries in order to construct alternative oceanic geographies that emphasize the complexities of a mobile borderscape. Eschewing a map in favor of the oceanic space, moreover, allows Ghosh to theorize emergent transnational and global formations and new spatial identities and affiliations. In this oceanic construct or frame, I ask undergraduate students in my Introduction to Colonial and Postcolonial Literatures course a series of questions regarding gender and sexuality, such as: How do gender and sexuality operate in this dynamic, chaotic, and multifaceted representation of British colonialism and imperial expansion? Why is Ghosh's narrative spurred by the vision of an illiterate, poppy-picking, domesticated, and oppressed Indian woman? How does Ghosh challenge binary norms such as homosexuality and heterosexuality, which have dominated identity politics and sexual theory? Do the characters seem like sexual nonconformists? If so, how does this contest the perception of East Indian migrants as heteronormative, passive, and docile? These questions inform the critical pedagogy I advance in my class, where gender and sexuality become the lens through which students can investigate the complexities of labor and transnational migration for the South Asian diaspora. Inquiry into Ghosh's representation of the history of transnational migration and empire building also facilitates arguments about whether or not the narrative seeks an emancipatory project that envisions the diasporic, nonnational space as a space of freedom from racial hierarchies, gender norms, and caste restrictions.

This essay asserts that using an interdisciplinary and transnational methodology in the classroom enhances discussions of gender, sex and sexuality, and nation. By focusing on the multiple ways in which Ghosh represents gender norms and the transgressions and transformations of his characters, students begin to understand migration and labor as gendered processes. In examining queerness, furthermore, students interrogate issues surrounding performance and the possibilities of transformational identities within diasporic movements. My emphasis on gender and sexuality, which still engages with history and narrative, also highlights the stakes of Ghosh's work in terms of Asian "coolie" labor and the intimate alterities between and among multiple diasporas. Through cognitive mapping exercises, close readings of specific passages, and critical analyses and interpretations that rely upon the deconstruction of multiple spaces in the text, students can grapple with the relation of gender and sexuality to multiple structures of domination, such as global economic structures and patriarchal nationalisms and their demands for heteronormativity.

My overall objective in the course is to encourage students to understand that gender and sex identities arise alongside and in conjunction with categories of race, class, nationality, family status, and citizenship. In *Sea of Poppies*, discussions of gender, sex, and sexuality often become marginalized or overshadowed by the novel's historical context and significance and by its representation of linguistic and cultural hybridity. Certainly, *Sea of Poppies*'s appeal in colonial and postcolonial studies is precisely because of its portrayal of histories that exist outside of an East-West or metropole-colony framework; its sprawling narrative depicts the polyglot and vibrant economic and political intricacies between India, the United States, China, and Britain by centralizing the economic significance of opium to empire building. *Sea of Poppies*, moreover, introduces students to linguistic diversity and allows students to negotiate cultural heteroglossia. Through the novel's representations of creolization and the violent mixture of new, hybrid linguistic and cultural forms, students can engage with linguistic histories of cultural interaction and assimilation. The text provides ample opportunities for undergraduates to examine how language can also operate in opposition to dominance, particularly when it comes to gendered forms of labor; linguistic fragmentation and the integration of multiple languages and meanings therefore confuse or destabilize hegemonic forces. For example, Deeti, who eventually becomes an indentured worker, prepares rotis, which are both midday meals and poppy products sold in the factory. Ghosh writes: "Deeti gave her daughter the job of sweeping the poppy petals into a heap while she busied herself in stoking the fire and heating a heavy iron tawa. Once this griddle was heated through, she sprinkled a handful of petals on it . . . the petals began to cling together so that . . . they looked exactly like the round wheat-flour rotis Deeti had packed for her husband's midday meal . . ." (6).[1] When students unpack the multiple linguistic meanings of *roti*, it becomes evident that poppy production and distribution for empire is advanced through female and domestic labor in the novel. A critical pedagogy centering on gender and sexuality, therefore, intervenes and enriches conversations about history and language in *Sea of Poppies* so that students analyze and interpret the myriad ways that power structures intersect and collide.

Because linguistic diversity can be challenging to students in the 100-level class, I stress close readings of passages with non-English words. Students can begin to understand that a word like *roti* not only has multiple meanings associated with it but also saturates specific spaces, like the kitchen where it is produced and the factory where it is consumed. Through linguistic devices, it becomes clear that Ghosh refuses to detach economic systems of exploitation, like the production and circulation of opium, and the labor demands of empire from issues of gender and sexuality.

Mapping Gender on Land, River, and Sea

The classroom dialogue on language and its relation to space projects in other directions as well. Ghosh has neatly divided his novel into three main sections, "Land," "River," and "Sea." Within these divisions, however, Ghosh fills his text with characters that occupy multiple spaces and have their own trajectories that will lead them to the Black Water, or Kala-Pani. It is important for students to recognize that even before the narrative begins Ghosh incorporates an image of the Indian Ocean and the South Asian, Asian, West African, and South African lands that border it. This image suggests that mapping operates as a key metaphor, and I ask students to keep this image or map, titled "The Journey of the *Ibis*," in mind as they read the novel. During one of the first classroom discussions on the novel, I ask them to work in small groups in order to deconstruct what this image tells us about the kind of text (the genre, narrative styles, themes) that we are about to read. What expectations does this map set up? And what do they feel is missing or absent from the map? Does Ghosh's map deterritorialize or create new understandings of territories? These questions can lead to historical context on the production of maps and their links to practices of colonization and the creation of territories. On another level, it helps them understand that location and dislocation will be important in the text and allows me to set up future deliberations on place and identity as they function in both national and diaspora space.

To help concretize students' understanding of place, space, and gender, I ask them to examine multiple spaces and identify how they are linked or positioned in the narrative. Students look at land and water, home and ship, home and field or factory, the shrine and ship, etc. In order to infer what kind of relation Ghosh sets up between these spaces, students are required to locate specific passages and provide close readings. For example, the text illustrates the shrine as a consecrated, timeless space of the past that houses the "family pantheon" and the ship as a futuristic "living being" (9). The shrine gestures toward traditional, ritualistic, and ancestral genealogy while the ship portends newness, destiny, and an indeterminable future. Since both spaces are maintained and envisioned by women, female bodies are not only responsible for venerating lineage but are also responsible for the propagation and creation of new beings.

An in-depth study of space leads to other kinds of analyses in the text, specifically the evolving, ambiguous, and tenuous relationships between the characters who occupy different spaces and are initially cocooned by caste, race, class, and gender classifications. In a cognitive mapping exercise on the board, I draw a circle and write "land" in it. Multiple spokes branch out from the circle. I connect this circle to another circle that encapsulates the word *water* and also draw lines coming out of the second circle. On each line, I write characters' names, such as Deeti, Kalua, Zachary, Paulette, etc. On the first circle, I ask students to connect Paulette and Jodu and, through close readings of passages, to explain the relationship that exists between the two characters and the significance of that relationship. The line between Jodu and Paulette becomes very important in the narrative, as it is one of many examples of kinship between characters based not on blood but on shared environment, empathy, or nurture. One passage that students can potentially choose describes their relationship as bonded through breast milk: "The sahib . . . was greatly relieved when Jodu's mother quietened the baby by putting her to her breast" (61). Jodu's mother acts as wet nurse to Paulette, calling her Putli as a way of "domesticating the girl's name" (61). In addition to this familial relationship, one that historically threatened the separation between natives and British in India and exposed the often sexualized and covert affairs between Indians and whites, Ghosh explicates the domestic spaces traversed by Jodu by way of his mother as well as the racialized, classed, and gendered transgressions of Paulette, who prefers to wear saris and eat "rice-and-dal kichri" and later masquerades as an Indian "coolie" woman (62). The many unusual pairings of characters depict transgressive affiliations between genders, classes, races, religions, and castes. It is useful for students to form groups and work on different pairings, like Raja Neel Rattan Halder and his cellmate, Aafat; or Zachary Reid and Paulette; or Deeti and Kalua; or Baboo Nob Kissin and Ma Taramony; in order to see how intimacies between these characters destabilize the modes of existence from which they are forced to leave or desire to escape.

"Coolies" and the History of South Asian Transnational Migrations

Alongside discussions on mapping, dislocation, and spatialization, I contextualize the ways that South Asian transnational migration has been represented in the late nineteenth and early twentieth centuries.[2] This background history is important for students who have been exposed mostly to American or British history that precludes nonmetropolitan locations like South Asia and Africa. Although the transnational migration of South Asians predates European colonial history, the largest dispersal was instigated by the British colonial administration during the post-emancipation period. The burgeoning demand for labor to fulfill the immediate needs of capital on the plantation economies in the island colonies, on railways, and in administration enabled unprecedented movements. In the Caribbean region, migration occurred between the 1830s and 1920, when more than 750,000 indentured laborers were shipped to work as "coolies," a label that homogenized the wide range of backgrounds the migrants came from. Students can see that Ghosh resists this homogenization by creating characters that stem from different backgrounds with regards to race, class, caste, ethnicity, gender, etc. In recognizing and realizing the intervention that Ghosh makes in official histories of transnational migration when he portrays characters as diverse as Deeti and Paulette, students come to understand how partial histories need to be supplemented. The information I provide from official histories of South Asian migration is supplemented by documents like ship records that detail passenger information, and I ask students to conduct a close reading of passenger lists. What kinds of information are revealed in these lists? Do they include names? If so, what kinds of names are included? Why do the records incorporate body marks of different contract laborers? And how does Ghosh represent the infliction of such marks through characters like Raja Neel?

It is important for students to recognize that the term *coolie* is contested, negated, or something appropriated, as in Khal Torabully's "coolitude." The comparative history between African enslavement and Asian indentureship also proves useful so that students understand the importance of the ship *Ibis* as well as Zachary Reid's position in the narrative as a mixed black character passing as white and one who is ultimately responsible for transporting con- tracted labor across national borders. This relation between Zachary and the "coolies" he transports alludes to racial hierarchies among Indians, whites, and blacks. It also illustrates that Indians, as Gaiutra Bahadur notes, "were at the bottom, below the English, the Scottish and the Irish as well as the African descendants of slaves sometimes assigned as 'drivers,' or foremen in the charge of work gangs" (xx). I emphasize to students that the designation of "coolie" was permanent and an inescapable marker of difference that kept Asian workers marginalized from the national sphere in the colonies they were transported to.

This exclusion was even more complicated for women, who emigrated "to escape the sexual and other abuses of the *zamindars*, the landlords, or to elude the punitive consequences of acts deemed by the Hindu orthodoxy as sexually or socially transgressive" (Pirbhai 7). Through Deeti, Paulette, Munia, Heeru, Sarju, Ratna, and Champa—the female characters transported by the *Ibis*—students perceive that indentureship was a double-edged sword for women: exploitative and abusive on one hand and escapist and liberatory on the other. In other words, indenture provided women with the means to escape oppressive conditions of existence, such as child marriage, widowhood, and caste discriminations, while endowing them with relative economic independence. Regardless of these lib- erties, women were vulnerable, often being assaulted, forced into prostitution, or both. The stories of the women on the *Ibis* attest to the multiple forms of abuse that led them toward a similar trajectory.

While teaching the history of indenture, I introduce visual media, like post- cards, to our discussion of labor, stressing that images of East Indian laborers operated as primary sources of knowledge for different interested parties, like Indian nationalist groups, British imperialists who wanted to justify a "humane" system of transportation after the abolition of slavery, and wealthy plantation owners who wanted to entice more people to migrate to places like Mauritius or the Caribbean islands. Images of "coolies" were important in cultural construc- tions of otherness, specifically in expressing cultural ideals of East Indian femi- ninity and docile East Indian masculinity. My students examine photographs of East Indian "coolies" and work in small groups to construct narratives that they believe the photographs delivered. Then they must present these narratives to the class in ways that show and articulate how these messages appear to conflict with, contradict, or support Ghosh's *Sea of Poppies*. It is important for students to understand that these images were saturated with meanings regarding the family formation, sexualities, work habits, and desirability of certain types of laboring bodies, and that they were part of the cultural discourse that presented South Asian or East Indian laborers as a natural solution to empire's labor shortage.

As Saloni Mathur notes, colonial postcards became commodities that were transnationally circulated, collected, and consumed by imperialists. Inseparable from gender constructs, the postcards reveal a "complicated sexual and political economy" (96) that traversed national borders. The postcards captured images of exotic women from the colonies, making visible differential and hierarchical constructions of womanhood. The objective for students is to understand how and why Indian women's bodies were often portrayed as located in interior spaces, in poses that suggest they were thinking or dreaming. Although the women are heavily adorned and immobile, the images indicate highly sexualized and exotic fantasies of the Indian other, specifically by making visible a single body part, such as a bared foot. Other postcards recast the "coolie" woman as traditional, domestic, and familial, even after she crosses the Black Water.

As the class progresses through the novel, we work on the second circle of our cognitive mapping exercise. This second circle, water, identifies the transformations and transfigurations that occur while the characters are on the *Ibis*. From previous close readings, students have seen that Deeti's flight from sati—ascension through a symbolic and literal death—provides her with new possibilities for survival. Like the other "coolies" and lascars aboard the *Ibis*, Deeti undergoes several kinds of border crossings, one of which is the creation of a new name and identity: Deeti becomes Aditi, the wife of Madhu from the Chamar caste, who is really Kalua, once an untouchable. Ghosh also depicts other identities as fluid, since his characters transgress conceptions of masculinity and femininity. Gender roles are illusionary as characters appropriate various languages, clothing, and attitudes. Paulette asks the mulatto Zachary Reid, "Are not all appearances deceptive, in the end?" (459). Reid himself disguises his "blackness," while Baboo Nob Kissin undergoes a transgendered change and appears "strangely womanish" (196) with his long hair and female attire and mannerisms. His transgendering is narrated as a reincarnation, a rebirth of a spiritual mother who uses his body as a vessel. These crossings and transgressions by the heterogeneous crew undo the imperial divisions that seek to impose rules and hierarchies based on color, class, and caste.

This second circle illustrates that the ship becomes a deterritorialized place and space that undermines normative social formations, allowing the migrants to strive toward a more human existence through a shared responsibility for the other, which Ghosh suggests can exist only in a borderless, decentered world. Paulette tells Deeti that "on a boat of pilgrims, no one can lose caste and everyone is the same" (328). Without caste restrictions, social hierarchies disappear and enable an alternative community of subjects. Paulette's assertion of liberation from borders, of equality across caste and linguistic differences, affects all the women on the ship. These shifts that allow Deeti to cut "herself loose from her moorings in the world" offer a new existence made possible by the *Ibis*, which becomes a space of rebirth and regeneration (217). Deeti often wonders if the passengers' "rebirth in the ship's womb had made them into a single family" (397) when thinking about the *Ibis* as a "great wooden *mai-bap*, an adoptive ancestor and parent of dynasties yet to come" (328).

I ask students to consider how we are to read or understand the transformations that transpire on the ship. Are they meant to deliver the "coolie" women to a new destiny, and are they engendered by a new and alternate genealogy outside of the British Empire and the oppressive nation-state? When the women see themselves as ship-sisters, *jahaj-behens*, Deeti thinks the possibilities, as "children of the ship," are thrilling (328). Ghosh states, "It was now that Deeti understood why the image of the vessel had been revealed to her that day, when she stood immersed in the Ganga: it was because her new self, her new life, had been gestating all this while in the belly of this creature" (328). The imagery of gestation and birth underlines Ghosh's investment in crafting new subjects with an alternative genealogy created by the mutable space of the ship, signaling that natural belonging is not rooted in the nation but in Deeti's alternative vision of a postnational natality or the birth of a new type of subject. Not just a biological process, an event that occurs in the belly of the ship, her rebirth becomes a human condition that delivers new subjects into existence. To explain this, I use Hannah Arendt's understanding of natality as fused with action: "Because they [the newborn] are initium, newcomers and beginners by virtue of birth, men take initiative, are prompted into action" (177). New beginnings formed by the birth of genuine political actors, moreover, affect all other life stories, and therefore Deeti's rebirth envisages an alternate ideology of communal belonging outside the nation. For the migrant women, their status as "coolies" bonds them to modernity, empowering them with access to lines of social mobility, agency, power, and liberation beyond nationalist demands of reproductive heteronormativity.

The complete loss of origins for Deeti and the other "coolies" is due to a fluidity of culture enabled by diasporic movement as these new subjects of subaltern history resist the rigidities of national boundaries. Even though Ghosh locates the opium trade as the capitalist logic for transnational circulations, the transcendence of his characters alludes to the boundless possibilities of his utopian oceanic space. The oceanic culture that Ghosh creates contains uncertain promises in its romantic liaisons and adventure only to be devastated by floggings, attempted rape, and drowning.

If *Sea of Poppies* begins with Deeti's envisioning of a new journey, a new state of being outside the nationalist confines of a heteropatriarchic, ritualistic family that demands progeny, ill gotten as it might be, the ending leaves the reader with the image of Deeti's gray eyes as Zachary gazes on her in her maternal form, pregnant with Kalua's child. I ask students to consider whether Deeti escapes the binds of Indian nationalism, one that enfigures women as culture-bearers and mothers. To what extent do they believe that Ghosh's novel perceives the space of the sea as emancipatory, progressive, and resistant to the social relations that dominate the nation?

In teaching *Sea of Poppies*, I attempt to further a critical pedagogy that empowers students to investigate and critique gender and sexual norms within multiple spaces, ranging from local to transnational. I maintain that advancing a conceptual apparatus that underscores gender and sexuality as crucial categories of analysis deepens students' understandings of South Asian labor migrations after the abolition of slavery. By paying careful attention to gender and sexual politics in the novel, through close readings and cognitive mapping exercises, students can analyze the significance of narrating the history of indenture through "coolie" women—figures that have historically been marginalized in discussions of South Asian migration.

NOTES

[1] This essay uses the 2008 Farrar, Straus and Giroux edition of *Sea of Poppies*.

[2] In addition to this history of female indentured workers, I require students to read selections from Gayatri Spivak's "Can the Subaltern Speak?," Chandra Mohanty's "Cartographies of Struggle: Third World Women and the Politics of Feminism," and James Clifford's "Diasporas." These secondary readings ground classroom discussions about the social and discursive category of the "Third World woman," existing academic discourses on women and global feminism, subaltern subjectivity, and the meanings associated with diasporas. They also provide students with terminology and give them a theoretical framework for engaging with the novel.

The Fiction of Ghosh and the Poetics of Literary Genres

Arnapurna Rath

The challenge that I have faced in my classrooms while teaching the concept of genre in relation to the novels of Amitav Ghosh is that Ghosh's writings constantly question the watertight division of genres and generic categories. The concept of genre studies emerges from a Western or, more precisely, a European, theoretical tradition classifying literature broadly into fiction, non-fiction, poetry, and drama.[1] The poetics of literary genres, as Aristotle would indicate, is an intricate philosophical quest in narratives.[2] Translating these philosophical problems in a classroom is fraught with dangers. In a literature class meant for graduate students, we still depend heavily on close reading of texts to discuss genres and generic divisions. The dilemma of negotiating Western theories of genre studies in relation to fictional writings from South Asia is a difficult one.

Nevertheless, the intersection between the larger generic categories of literature, history, cultural geography, and anthropology in Ghosh's fiction makes such categories invaluable resources for graduate-level teaching. In this essay I undertake a discussion of Ghosh's select fictional texts that I have introduced in the classroom with regard to generic and subgeneric distinctions. To supplement the close reading of texts, I assign interviews that help define the author's position and correspondences that clarify his insight into critical theories. I also use graphs that illustrate my ideas visually, and *PowerPoint* slides highlighting specific quotes from Ghosh's novels, as analytical tools for understanding the complex intersection of generic categories.

In order to go beyond the structural classification of genres on the one hand and elusive deconstruction on the other, I choose the Russian thinker Mikhail Bakhtin's "visualizations" of time-space through his study of the chronotopes as the basis of classroom discussions.[3] Bakhtin's study of the genre of novel from across world literature presents a new conceptual framework for my understanding of South Asian fiction, specifically Ghosh's writings. In order to explain the significance of generic distinctions based on time-space interrelationships, I interweave some of the freehand graphs that I designed for my doctoral research into classroom discussions. I discuss Ghosh's narratives as specifically connected to his creative perception of events arranged consciously in time and space. We read Ghosh as an extraordinary creative voice with sensitive insight into what Bakhtin called *fictional time* and *real time*. Taking into perspective the Bakhtinian chronotopic model,[4] which suggests that time-space interrelations have been fundamental aspects of classification of genres and subgenres, I discuss the arrangement of events in Ghosh's novels based on a conscious understanding of temporal and spatial matrices.

To explain the philosophy of events occurring at the intersection of time-space axes, Bakhtin's definition of the chronotope from "Forms of Time and of the Chronotope in the Novel" is particularly useful; Bakhtin notes, "[i]t can even be said that it is precisely the chronotope that defines genre and generic distinctions" (85). In order to visually illustrate this distribution of the events in "real time" in *The Shadow Lines*, I plot the novel's events on a time-space graph (fig. 1). While the temporal cluster is specified as the 1930s, 1960s, and 1980s in the novel, geographic places like India, Bangladesh, Sri Lanka, and England remain as "spaces" in my model. Linear time is represented in the horizontal X axis and multidimensional space is represented by the vertical Y axis. Each diamond represents a cluster of events happening around a particular time-space intersection in the novel at points in between the X and Y axes. These events are interrelated through the saga of the Datta-Chaudhuri and Tresawsen families. The interrelations are shown through skewed lines, and the narrator is placed at the novel's present moment, i.e., in the 1980s. The events are positioned from the past to the 1980s and the future remains an empty time axis.

The graph is specifically meant to draw students' attention toward complex arrangements of events in the novel and to indicate how the generic distinction between "real" and "fictional" is challenged by the text. It is designed to help students negotiate the intricate details in the novel and to encourage them to avoid oversimplification or pure summarization of the text. *The Shadow Lines* contains multiple thematic strands of freedom, memory, imagination, histories, and cultural imperialism. We study the novel as a realistic narrative that problematizes sociocultural constructs of freedom and explores the philosophical notions of internal and external freedom. An important point of classroom reference here is "Maps and Mirrors: Co-ordinates of Meaning in *The Shadow Lines*," in which Meenakshi Mukherjee hints at the dynamics of spaces in the novel: "space can be fluid even when held solidly within the concrete scaffold-

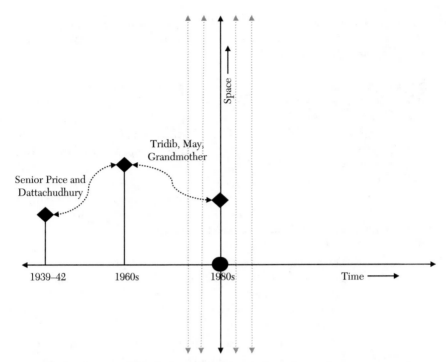

Figure 1. Plot of events in *The Shadow Lines*. There are three clusters of events corresponding to three time-space sets in the narrative: the 1930s, 1960s, and 1980s. The diagram positions the characters at different time-space intervals and places the narrator in the 1980s.

ing of a house or confined within the firm outlines etched as national boundaries on a map" (261). Mukherjee discusses time and space in the novel as both "illusory" and "concrete" (259).

We discuss *The Shadow Lines* through a plethora of images that overlap through a deliberate disarrangement of the temporal and spatial sequences in the text. In terms of its geographic reach, the novel spans two continents, Europe and Asia. The author populates real places like London, Calcutta, and Dhaka with the memories and nostalgia of his fictional characters.[5] Spaces emerge in the text as chronotopic motifs, combining the abstract terrains of the mind with concrete geopolitical markers of places.

In "Forms of Time," Bakhtin studied the growth of the novel by identifying various artistic chronotopes as the foundation of genres and subgenres. By "chronotopes," he implied the larger generic categories like romance, adventure, biography/autobiography, and the realistic novel. For instance, I discuss *The Shadow Lines* under this rubric as a realistic novel. Within these generic chronotopes, Bakhtin identifies a number of overlapping chronotopic motifs. A few examples of these motifs are chance, meeting and parting, and escape in the genre of Greek romance (92–100); the public square and friends in the biographical/autobiographical novel (123–40); fools, rogues, and clowns in the chivalric romance (152–53); and food and drink, sexual intercourse, death, folklore, rituals, and idyllic chronotope in the Rabelaisian realistic novel (170–241). The novel is a highly flexible genre, open to additions of new chronotopes and chronotopic motifs. Since Bakhtin's generic classifications can inform the temporal-spatial dialogues within the linguistic consciousness of Ghosh's novels, I discuss Ghosh's fiction in the graduate classroom with some of the generic categories that evolve from Bakhtin's typology.

In exploring the motifs that emerge from our classroom analysis, we discover a rich tapestry of overlapping themes within each novel. Ghosh's creative style can be seen as a conscious blend of cultural histories and literary techniques. For example, *The Circle of Reason*[6]—chosen less frequently for critical classroom discussion than most of Ghosh's works—blends adventure, scientific reason, and magical realism. As the title suggests, the text has reason as its core thematic vision. In the classroom, we explore the technique of magical realism within the larger genre of science fiction in the context of this novel. Students are urged to understand the theoretical framework of magical realism and science fiction and to identify passages from the book that correspond with these aspects. They observe the text as dealing with the intersection of places and spaces and as subverting the notion of the linearity of time. The novel begins in the small village of Lalpukur in Bengal in the early twentieth century and moves through Calcutta, Bangladesh, Kerala, and the Middle East to an imaginary place called al-Ghazira. The movement from the "real" to the "imaginary" is presented to students as slow but deliberate. Only rarely do we encounter a date, as when the birth year of the character Balaram is given as 1914 (39) and the publication date of Vallery-Radot's book *The Life of Pasteur*, which guides Balaram's and Alu's thoughts, as 1885 (28). Based on the historical events described in the novel, students are asked to discuss the era in which the text may be situated. The other chronotopic subgenre discussed through a close reading of *The Circle of Reason* is oral narratives. The novelist has deliberately used the elements of oral narratives in order to subvert the genre of the novel as a realistic fiction.

The novel moves through oral tales and is replete with statements like "it was generally reckoned" (2), "someone says" (214), "just a foolish story" (215), and "this was long ago" (260), constantly playing on the idea of storytelling. John Thieme has discussed the element of magical realism in this novel with reference to Gabriel García Márquez's style as a way of "narrativizing experience" (255). In the classroom we choose the motif of weaving as a mode of oral narrative and discuss the way oral tales get woven into cultures. The motif of weaving and its connection to the chronotopic vision of a "polylinguistic history"[7] is specifically discussed in this context. Bakhtin notes that "language, as a treasure house of images, is fundamentally chronotopic" ("Forms of Time" 251). Ghosh too presents the motif of weaving in the novel as a time-space event that signifies this historical consciousness where the past and the present are in a linguistic interplay. The character Balaram notes this process of weaving in the novel: "Weaving is hope, because it has no country, no continent. Weaving is Reason, which makes the world mad and makes it human" (58).

Students are encouraged to dwell on the interplay between philosophy and literature in *The Circle of Reason*. We discuss the three parts of the novel, titled "Sattwa," "Rajas," and "Tamas," indicating the engagement of the novelist with the depth of the three gunas (attributes in Hindu philosophy). The interweaving of philosophical insight into the fictional genre is discussed in this context. For instance, the interlude in the Chitrangada story where death in Tagore's play matches the death of the character Kulfi is discussed in detail. This symbolizes the idea that death is a crucial moment in the play of reason, realism, and romanticism and is important for the cyclical motion of time (414).

We also discuss Ghosh's conscious attempt to break away from generic distinctions and disciplinary categorizations through some of his interviews. I refer students to the interview with Neluka Silva and Alex Tickell in which Ghosh persistently opposes the idea of his novels being studied under the generic term "postcolonial" ("Amitav Ghosh in Interview" 171). He reiterates this idea in an interview with Frederick Luis Aldama, resisting all generic terms like "Third World," "postcolonial," and "Commonwealth" literatures ("Interview" 89). In addition to challenging the simplicity of these denominations, Ghosh's engagement with cultural histories and archival studies has led to the evolution of different subgenres as a technique in his novels and as the essence of his literary vision.

During one particular session, we discussed the porous boundaries between the larger disciplines of history and literature and the idea of interdisciplinary writings. The discussion was based on a series of e-mail correspondences between Ghosh and Dipesh Chakrabarty on the latter's book *Provincializing Europe*, where Ghosh acknowledges, "History is never more compelling than when it gives us insights into oneself and the ways in which one's own experience is constituted" (147). Discussing *The Glass Palace* as a journey of the individual that coincides with greater political and cultural changes is a natural extension of this idea. *The Glass Palace* starts with the story of eleven-year-old Rajkumar, an orphan from Chittagong who survived a killer fever that claimed his parents, brothers, and a sister. He is looking for an elderly matriarch shopkeeper, Ma Cho, in the streets of Mandalay. Rajkumar lives during a time of major social and political change, with the British spreading their colonial roots in Burma. He is one of the many faceless witnesses of the overthrow of King Thebaw and Queen Supayalat, the last of the ruling monarchy of Burma. We highlight the presence of a fictional character in real time through our discussions of the initial sections of *The Glass Palace*.

The story creates a quasi-historical account of the Burmese king and queen's life in exile at Ratnagiri with Dolly and Rajkumar, two fictional characters, as the chief protagonists. The novel covers an expanse of one hundred years and attempts to capture all the major moments of historical time that defined the sociocultural and individual lives of the entire Indian subcontinent: the economic depression of 1929 (306), World War II (311–12), the march of the Indian National Army (478), Indian and Burmese independence (480–81), the Burmese uprisings (536–39), the military regime in Myanmar (541), and Aung San Suu Kyi's protests (541–42).[8] These larger historical movements are woven with the narration of Rajkumar's and Dolly's family histories through three successive generations.

While teaching Ghosh's novels, I encourage students to observe the works cited and acknowledgments provided by the author. Some of the acknowledgments are detailed and reflect Ghosh's extensive field research. In the author's notes appended at the end of *The Glass Palace*, Ghosh acknowledges the "times and places" about which he started writing through second-hand and third-hand accounts, before they became a "wholly fictional world" (549). We discuss *The Glass Palace* as a conscious recording of these historical processes visible in the techniques of collating traces of history, information, rumor, and legend.

The lives of the royal family in the novel are tied to the chronotopic motif of the provincial town of Ratnagiri and to the precincts of "home," or Outram House, where they live in exile. In Outram House, neither time nor space goes through any significant change. There are occasional "moments" of disruption in the cyclical flow of everyday time (76). Two graduate students in one of my courses, titled Tropes of Time and Topography, designed a blog with review articles on South Asian novels, one of which presents an in-depth analysis of Ratnagiri as a trope of exile and isolation in *The Glass Palace* (Payel Mukherjee).

When we turn to *The Hungry Tide*, our discussion is based on text-intensive readings and *PowerPoint* presentations on the concept of ecopoetics and the chronotopic motif of the love idyll between Fokir, Tutul, and Piya. We discuss the ecosensitivity of this narrative. I find that students are particularly receptive toward the following quotation indicating the simple realities of everyday time in the novel: "Their chests were moving in unison as they slept and the rhythm of their breathing reminded her of the pair of dolphins she had been watching earlier. It calmed her to see them sleeping so peacefully—the contrast with her own state of mind could not have been more marked" (138).[9] The character of Fokir is often discussed by students with reference to the basic needs of sleep, food, and love.[10]

Studying genres through a discussion of chronotopes in the fiction of Ghosh significantly enriches the classroom. In the course of reading the novels, students are often able to add new motifs pertaining to gender roles, cultural narratives, and ecological themes. In so doing, they see how Ghosh creates a poetics of literary genres that cuts across boundaries of academic disciplines and thus new aesthetic experiences.

NOTES

I am grateful to Professor Milind Malshe for his guidance during my doctoral research on Ghosh's novels and Bakhtin's concept of the chronotope and, in particular, his help with my understanding of the theory of genres in Ghosh and Bakhtin.

[1] See Jacques Derrida's article "The Law of Genre," where he argues that texts participate in the formation of genres rather than being a priori categorized into one or the other genre (203).

[2] See Gérard Genette's *The Architext: An Introduction* for a historical survey of genres starting from ancient Greek civilization.

[3] I focus on two of Bakhtin's essays during my discussions on the narrative genres: "The Bildungsroman and Its Significance in the History of Realism (Toward a Historical Typology of the Novel)" in *Speech Genres* and "Forms of Time and of the Chronotope in the Novel" in *The Dialogic Imagination*.

[4] I use the word *model* here because the temporal-spatial study of South Asian novels in the context of chronotopes is limited. Chronotopes are far more dense than their treatment as mere technical categories would suggest. They are the philosophical core of narratives. In the classroom, however, I use a chronotopic "model" to explain narrative tropes.

[5] For an insight into individual thematic strands like nostalgia, see Gaurav Desai's article "Old World Orders: Amitav Ghosh and the Writing of Nostalgia."

[6] This essay uses the 1986 Hamish Hamilton edition of *The Circle of Reason*.

[7] Stephanie Jones, in her reading of this authorial commentary on the historical process of weaving in *The Circle of Reason*, suggests that "it is not just necessary to understand cotton, but to understand the polylinguistic history of cotton" (437).

[8] This essay uses the 2000 HarperCollins edition of *The Glass Palace*.

[9] This essay uses the 2004 HarperCollins edition of *The Hungry Tide*.

[10] See Arnapurna Rath and Milind Malshe, "Chronotopes of 'Places' and 'Non-Places': Ecopoetics of Amitav Ghosh's *The Hungry Tide*."

Imagining with Precision:
Postcolonial Formalism in *The Shadow Lines*

John J. Su

Amitav Ghosh's *The Shadow Lines* provides an important contribution to the postcolonial and global anglophone literature courses I teach. As with many institutions, mine has a diverse cultures general education requirement for undergraduates. Such courses serve the laudable and ambitious aims of training students to learn about cultures and values different from their own and to examine their own presuppositions and biases. In this context, students often come to literary texts with an expectation that they will acquire a privileged, insider view of other cultures. Such quasi-sociological readings are by no means illogical; formative authors within the postcolonial canon of texts can be read to endorse them. In one of his most cited statements, Chinua Achebe, for example, declares, "I would be quite satisfied if my novels (especially the ones I set in the past) did no more than teach my readers that their past—with all its imperfections—was not one long night of savagery from which the first Europeans acting on God's behalf delivered them" (*Hopes* 45). Postcolonial studies itself established its disciplinary credibility, for Robert J. C. Young, by focusing on depictions of "representative minority experience" rather than the aesthetic qualities of literary works (7).

The challenge is to engage students with literary forms whose salient features are conditioned by and respond to the historical, political, and cultural contexts in which such forms were produced. *The Shadow Lines*, as I introduce it to students, encourages them to develop techniques of a postcolonial formalism—a formalism distinct from the New Criticism that served to institutionalize norms of literary value in the postwar Anglo-American academies. The primary learning outcomes for students studying *The Shadow Lines* in my classroom are to identify the historical and cultural conditions that influenced the defining formal elements and techniques of Ghosh's novel (e.g., genre, narrator, narrative structure); to evaluate how such techniques complicate the interpretive lenses provided by prominent theories of reading contemporary anglophone literatures (e.g., Fredric Jameson's theory of Third World literature as national allegory ["Third-World Literature"]); and to formulate hypotheses for how formal techniques in *The Shadow Lines* are utilized to respond to feelings of historical determinism regarding civil unrest in postcolonial nations.

To begin to develop student proficiency with these outcomes, I first engage in a close reading of the novel's opening paragraphs, which draws readers' attention to literary form and its limits. The narrator highlights the novelistic quality of his story immediately after introducing the first character, his father's aunt Mayadebi. He notes that he always referred to her in conversation by another name, Mayathakuma (3).[1] The discrepancy between everyday lived experience and its representation in literary form is reinforced by an admission of the limits of the narrator's ability to imagine: trying to picture Mayadebi's son, Tridib, as a boy, the narrator acknowledges that ultimately he can picture his cousin only as looking like himself.

After inviting students to explore initial hypotheses for why Ghosh draws explicit attention to literary form and the limits of imagining, I turn their attention to Ghosh's own comments on the historical events that shaped the genesis of *The Shadow Lines*. In several of the essays that are collected in *Incendiary Circumstances: A Chronicle of the Turmoil of Our Times*, Ghosh discusses the significance of the 1984 assassination of Prime Minister Indira Gandhi and the civil violence that emerged in its wake. The assertion is intriguing because *The Shadow Lines* never directly refers to Gandhi's assassination, focusing instead on riots that occurred twenty years earlier in Calcutta and Dhaka in 1964. Civil violence, according to Ghosh, is often rapidly forgotten in historical records because such records tend to focus on the nation-state as the primary agent of history. In a passage that closely parallels a scene in *The Shadow Lines*, Ghosh describes his frustration at finding "dozens of books about the Indo-Chinese war of 1962" but "not a single book" on the 1964 riots (*Incendiary Circumstances* 46–47).

The challenge facing the novelist, then, is to create a literary form that is able to represent past events that appear absent from official and academic historical records. The privileging of the nation-state in historical records causes events in which nations are not the central actors to be rendered invisible, even when such events may have regional or international impact. *The Shadow Lines'* particular focus on 1964 rather than the more immediate political events enables Ghosh to emphasize the consequences of privileging the nation-state as the basis of collective experience: the inability for populations living in many postcolonial nations to envision the future. To develop their awareness of the challenge Ghosh identifies, I invite students to engage in a free-writing exercise on Ghosh's claim: "It is as though the events of the immediate past have made the future even more obscure than it is usually acknowledged to be. Now, close on two decades later, I find myself asking, Why is this so? Why was it that in the 1980s, history itself seemed to stumble and come to a standstill?" (*Incendiary Circumstances* 48).

Using their responses as a guide, I facilitate a classroom discussion of Ghosh's critique of Fredric Jameson's infamous argument about Third World literature as national allegory. In an interview with Frederick Luis Aldama (89) and in his correspondence with Dipesh Chakrabarty (Ghosh and Chakrabarty 147, 166), Ghosh takes pains to reject the idea that literary forms produced by postcolonial authors are preoccupied with representing the nation.[2] Privileging the nation as the hermeneutic through which the novel is read occludes the experiences of families whose lives and social networks cross the national boundaries produced by the Partition of India in 1947.

Central to the articulation of alternative modes of viewing human experience is the formal claim that the novel is a family memoir, privileging multiple voices and histories over a single protagonist's story of development. This is crucial to the overarching argument for the historicity of forms themselves, against the mode of formalist reading associated with New Criticism. Through a series of passages, I lead students to explore the consequences of reading *The Shadow Lines* as a family memoir. The family memoir not only provides an alternative mode of historical writing that crosses the national lines produced by Partition, but it also refuses to privilege a unitary historical narrative, creating more multilateral histories through the events told by the characters. These comments help establish the significance of Ghosh's claims regarding the genre of *The Shadow Lines* as family memoir. Form provides a mode of critiquing the propensity to read nationalism as the defining hermeneutic for all human experience. More significantly, the articulation of literary form is seen to be crucial to recovering historical dimensions of experiences that are effaced by defining history in national terms. The genre of family memoir, in this context, privileges gaps and misunderstandings in personal memories by emphasizing how the central event around which the novel's plot turns—the murder of Tridib during the 1964 riots—can only be told indirectly, through the accounts of Tridib's younger brother, Robi, and an English love interest, May Price.

This recognition enables students to return to the opening paragraphs of the novel with greater insight. The emphasis on the limits of the narrator's ability to provide an interpretive lens creates the conditions under which readers are expected to read against a unifying historical narrative. The key passages used to discuss this occur in the context of the narrator's childhood memories of Tridib's injunction "to use my imagination with precision" (24). Such a declaration establishes the task of the imagination and its limits, a task contextualized both by the identification of Tridib as an archaeologist (who, the narrator asserts, is totally uninterested in "fairylands") and by the contrast to the memories of Tridib's younger sister, Ila. The family memoir, in other words, enables Ghosh to provide readers the opportunity to view alternative modes of remembering the past and their consequences.

The contrast with Ila is of particular importance, clarifying the significance of the novel's title. In the scene immediately following Tridib's injunction to imagine precisely, the novel traces the different ways in which the narrator and Ila experience London and the past more generally. Whereas the narrator is able to re-create through his imagination the experiences of the city described to him by Tridib and others, Ila experiences the present "like an airlock in a canal, shut away from the tidewaters of the past and the future by steel floodgates" (30). The difference leads to their conflicting definitions of freedom: Ila's declaration that she is free because she has separated herself from her past and from locality versus the narrator's declaration that freedom requires imagining the past, arguing that "if we didn't try ourselves, we would never be free of other people's inventions" (31).

The primary inventions with which the novel is concerned are revealed to be the shadow lines of nation: national boundaries drawn by political actors far removed from the families in the novel, boundaries that separate them and distort their experiences of the past—most notably the narrator's grandmother, who finds herself in the curious situation of visiting the city of her birth, Dhaka, as a foreigner, estranged by the national boundaries created by Partition.

After my minilecture on the narrator's efforts to imagine the past he never personally experienced, I assign students to small groups in which they explore the different portrayals of how other characters (Robi, May, the narrator's grandmother) remember or imagine the past. The grandmother's experience is particularly illuminating, and her refusal to believe that the Dhaka she visits in 1964 is in fact the city of her birth sets up a significant contrast to the narrator's experience of traveling to London in his twenties. When confronted with the discrepancies between the past and the present, the narrator notes that he did not expect stasis. In order to help students fully appreciate the contrast between the narrator's imaginative reconstructions (56) and his grandmother's memories (191), I invite students to focus on the former.

To contextualize the narrative voices, I draw a contrast to the opening of Salman Rushdie's *Midnight's Children*. Like *The Shadow Lines*, Rushdie's novel emphasizes the inescapability of form in representing contemporary India. Rushdie utilizes a number of narrative devices also used in *The Shadow Lines*, challenging the narrator's perspective through characters (Padma) and through the narrator's own admissions of error (regarding the date of Mahatma Gandhi's assassination). However, the central difference appears in the ways in which Rushdie's novel aligns its narrative with the history of contemporary India. Saleem's story is portrayed as literally India's story; born at the precise moment of independence, Saleem repeatedly emphasizes how his life mirrors the nation's. As Saleem declares in the first paragraph, "I had been mysteriously handcuffed to history, my destinies indissolubly chained to those of my country" (3). In contrast to Ghosh, then, Rushdie's critique of official histories of India does not challenge but reinforces the primacy of the nation-state in understanding the experiences of the past.[3]

The third formal dimension to which I draw students' attention is the nonlinear temporality of the narrative, its resistance to the teleological presumptions of historical narratives. After reminding students that in the two previous classes we focused on the formal elements of genre and narrator, I explore with them the implications of the novel's resistance to linear time. This resistance is necessary to develop the idea of imagining precisely. I emphasize to my students that any comprehensive interpretation of *The Shadow Lines* needs to account for the fact that its central episode—the murder of Tridib—is not depicted until the end of the novel. The event seems to exist outside of time, haunting the characters more than two decades later and informing their actions, yet the narrator himself cannot fully describe the event. The significance of this recognition invites explicit contrast: while the narrator can reproduce the memories and experiences of his relatives in London in the midst of World War II, he apparently cannot do so for this one particular experience closer in both time and space. This event defies his imagination.

I indicate to students that, on the basis of the analysis we have developed over the first two days, we have an initial interpretation: historical accounts in which the nation is the central focus have historically been highly linear and teleological; hence Ghosh might take a deliberately antiteleological narrative structure. I emphasize, however, that the narrative structure of the family memoir historically has also been relatively linear, and that in any case such an argument does not fully account for the curious ending in which the narrator and May spend the night with each other after she finally recounts to him the story of Tridib's death. Indeed, the novel pointedly ends not with the recollection of trauma—that May's entire adult life has been defined by guilt for placing Tridib in danger—but rather with what the narrator describes in the last words of the novel as a "final redemptive mystery" (246).

To arrive at a more satisfactory interpretation, I suggest to students that we need to read Ghosh's novel in the light of a tradition of postpositivist historiography tracing from Hayden White through Edith Wyschogrod, F. R. Ankersmit, and others. The rationale for this comes from Ghosh's 1995 essay "The Ghosts of Mrs. Gandhi."[4] In this essay, Ghosh relates how the sectarian violence in the aftermath of Indira Gandhi's assassination was profoundly important in his development as a writer, yet he had never previously attempted to write about it. The challenge, as he articulates it, is the seeming inability of literary form to represent violence as anything other than what he describes as an "apocalyptic spectacle," one that casts violence as "primordial and inevitable, a fate to which masses of people are largely resigned" (202). Over the course of the essay, Ghosh argues that ultimately the challenge is to find a means of dispelling a sense of historical determinism—that civil violence is not an inescapable fate of postcolonial nations, defined as they are by histories of imperialism and, more recently, neoimperialism. I suggest to students that the key to understanding the nonlinear temporality of *The Shadow Lines* is the question Ghosh poses in that essay: "is it possible that the authors of [such apocalyptic] descriptions failed to find a form—or a style or a voice or a plot—that could accommodate both violence and the civilized willed response to it?" (202).

To help students explore how Ghosh attempts to create such a form in *The Shadow Lines*, I provide a minilecture on postpositivist critiques of historiography. I trace for students the initial argument of White that Western history, as it emerged as an academic discipline, privileged the category of the beautiful over the sublime, rendering the past in an ordered, meaningful teleological sequence in which causation of events can be firmly established. After establishing the basic argument, I trace two prominent strands as exemplified by the work of Wyschogrod and Ankersmit. Wyschogrod argues that the necessary response to the determinism of academic histories is to focus on what she calls the "negated possibles" of history (167). Such an alternative history or counterfactual historical speculation develops a richer phenomenological sense of the past by recovering not only events as they happened but also other potential events that seemed feasible at the time. Ankersmit, in contrast, attempts to undo the determinism of historical narratives by rehabilitating the category of experience, particularly what he describes as "sublime experience" (11). According to this idea, historiography has been so dominated by the post-Kantian privileging of language as the basis of all meaning that it becomes almost impossible to conceptualize experience outside of representation.

After presenting these alternative historiographies, I invite the class to experiment with applying theoretical frameworks to *The Shadow Lines*. First, I ask them to identify specific passages in Ghosh's novel that each of the theories helps them understand. After students have been able to identify at least some key moments, I ask them to explore how the novel's narrative is *not* exhausted by such theories. In particular, I help students explore how Ghosh emphasizes the extent to which Tridib's decision to sacrifice his life in an effort to rescue a rickshaw driver is not fully interpretable, even decades later by the people who knew and loved him best. Ghosh's emphasis on the "final redemptive mystery," however, differs from the focus on the sublime for which Ankersmit argues; in *The Shadow Lines*, this unknowable moment produces a shared intimacy between the narrator and May. In this way, the narrative answers Ghosh's earlier question of how to find forms that can accommodate both representations of violence and responses to it in ways that do not cast the former as inevitable. The inability of the narrative (and the characters who tell it) to establish the motivations that led Tridib to risk his life, perhaps even needlessly, provides Ghosh the means to focus on the sacrifice rather than trauma as the unresolved element of the past.

To conclude the final class period, I explore the implications of Ghosh's novel with respect to his assertion in interviews about the limits of the term *postcolonial* and the ways in which it restricts the imagination. In an interview with T. Vijay Kumar, Ghosh declares that his resistance to the term is motivated by the way in which it defines India as merely "a successor state to a colony" ("'Postcolonial' Describes You as a Negative" 105). If the goal of imagining precisely is ultimately about discovering historical connections rendered invisible by the shadow lines of nation, then the category of the postcolonial risks reproducing such lines by defining countries as successor states.[5] I conclude by signaling how Ghosh anticipates more recent works such as Aravind Adiga's *The White Tiger*, in which the web of global interrelations has shifted the balance of power fundamentally away from a postcolonial hermeneutic of center and periphery.

NOTES

[1] This essay uses the 2005 Mariner Books edition of *The Shadow Lines*.

[2] Jameson's argument that "[a]ll third-world texts are necessarily . . . national allegories" is premised on his assertion that *the story of the private individual destiny is always an allegory of the embattled situation of the public third-world culture and society* ("Third-World Literature" 69).

[3] My pedagogical focus is furthered by R. Radhakrishnan's distinction between the "polyvocality and heteroglossia" of Ghosh and the "metropolitan ventriloquism" of Rushdie (*Theory* 27).

[4] This essay uses the version of "The Ghosts of Mrs. Gandhi" published in *Incendiary Circumstances.*

[5] I develop more fully the role of the imagination in Ghosh's literary works in my book *Imagination and the Contemporary Novel* (126–52).

Metamorphoses and Transnational Realities in *The Circle of Reason*

Robbie B. H. Goh

Many students, though familiar with Amitav Ghosh's concern with the social conditions in India, particularly as experienced by Asian transnational workers, struggle with the surreal narrative mode and the bizarre events and physical transformations they encounter in *The Circle of Reason* (hereafter *Circle*). *Circle* is admittedly quite different in narrative temper and style from more straightforward social realist Ghosh novels such as *The Glass Palace*, *The Hungry Tide*, and the novels in the *Ibis* trilogy. The disjunction between the novel's style and readers' expectations is exacerbated if students come to *Circle* already familiar with Ghosh's nonfictional works like *The Imam and the Indian* or *Dancing in Cambodia: At Large in Burma*, where Ghosh's abiding interests in history, politics, and religion and their impact on society's abjects are laid out much more clearly and emphatically.

Teaching students about magical realism and its narrative characteristics seems to be illuminative. Ghosh himself has expressed a deep ambivalence about the label "magical realism" being applied to his work: speaking of the "restrained" tone and "much more . . . realist mode" of his novel *The Shadow Lines*, he told Frederick Luis Aldama of his disappointment at its muted reception among Western publishers seeking to find in Indian writing a replication of the commercial publishing success of "the great Latin American boom" ("Interview" 87). For Ghosh, magical realism in this light refers to the "deeply demeaning" view that "Third World" writing is "all over the top, acting wildly and so on." Yet Ghosh in the same interview acknowledges the influence of magical realist writers like Gabriel García Márquez and Salman Rushdie, and if he balks at the "over-the-top" aspects of magical realism and the hegemony of Western publishing that it embodies, he does not exactly deny the fantastical elements that also emerge in some of his writings, among which *Circle* and *The Calcutta Chromosome* would be the foremost examples. Certainly many of the features of magical realism that Wendy B. Faris lists—including elements "we cannot explain according to the laws of the universe as we know them," the questioning of "received ideas about time, space, and identity," "metafictional" elements where the novel talks about writing and storytelling, the ubiquitous appearance of "metamorphoses," a positionality "against the established order," and a Jungian "sense of collective relatedness" ("Scheherazade's Children" 167–84)—quite clearly appear in *Circle*.

I find that explaining the literary tradition of magical realism helps students make a mental shift for reading *Circle* in a way that allows them to retain a focus on Ghosh's social concerns. I tell them that we might see the novel as a social realist novel that uses some elements of magical realism to make its points about the condition of migrant laborers or the socioeconomic system in India.

Invoking magical realism allows me to direct students' attention to one of the main themes running through *Circle*: the body that is grotesquely transformed or acted upon in ways that appear to defy reason and common explanation. This common strand of bodily metamorphoses runs through texts and genres as otherwise disparate as Aristophanes's *The Birds*, Franz Kafka's *The Metamorphosis*, Eugène Ionesco's *Rhinoceros*, René Magritte's *The Son of Man*, Darren Aronofsky's *Black Swan*, Wilson Harris's *Palace of the Peacock*, and Salman Rushdie's *Midnight's Children*, to name just a few examples. It is important to note that these examples of human bodies physically transformed, grotesquely deformed, cross-species hybridized, and unnaturally bound (in a locale or to other bodies) are generally used by magical realist texts to depict the exertion of oppressive power on ordinary individuals. Thus Theo D'Haen sees magical realism as "*correcting* so-called existing reality" and "right[ing] the wrongs this 'reality' depends upon" ("Magical Realism" 195), while Stephen Slemon sees in it a characteristic "resistance toward the imperial center" (408).

As with many novels in this broad tradition, *Circle* uses surreal and often bizarre bodily conditions and transformations to make its point about real sociopolitical conditions in India and elsewhere—the "everyday problems of simple people" (49).[1] A number of characters are introduced to the reader primarily by way of exaggerated physical traits that might best be defined as grotesque deformities. Chief of these is the protagonist, Alu, whose name (meaning "potato") refers to his "extraordinary head," which is "curiously uneven, bulging all over with knots and bumps" and resembles "a huge, freshly dug, lumpy potato" (3). While much of this obsession with Alu's head comes through the perspective of Balaram and his fascination with phrenology, it is confirmed by other characters, such as Bolai-da, who gives Alu his descriptive nickname; the general population of the Ras, who judge "Alu with his potato head" to be uglier than Mast Ram; and Mrs. Verma, whose first impression of Alu is of a "strangely distended head" (203, 361). Alu's body also undergoes mysterious transformations over the course of the novel. After the tragic loss of his family in the Lalpukur explosion he develops "two boils, the size of duck's eggs . . . not ordinary boils, but suppurating craters of pus, as though his flesh had gathered itself together and tried to burst from his body" (155). Gopal's response to this mysterious ailment only emphasizes its surreal nature and the timing of its appearance: "Let them be . . . it's only Balaram trying to come back to the world" (155). By the time he journeys across India to Mahé in preparation for sailing to the Middle East, Alu has "boils erupting all over him" (157). The boils inexplicably disappear when Alu is trapped in the wreckage of the Star, "miraculously still alive" after three days without food or water (241). Another tragic event later in the novel— the police raid in al-Ghazira resulting in deaths and arrests in Alu's community— leads to another fugitive journey and another strange bodily ailment: "the thumbs had stiffened and the skin had sagged over the bones, like a shroud on a skeleton" (370). Yet when Kulfi dies and Alu (passing as her husband) has to light her funeral pyre, his thumbs mysteriously regain their function.

Alu is far from being the only character thus treated. Almost as grotesque in bodily appearance are Abusa the Frown, "with his face bent and a frown carved forever into his forehead because his mother had dreamt of barbed wire the night before" his birth (201); Mast Ram, with his snake's eyes and a face "so closely covered with pock-marks and holes it looked as though it had been dug up to lay the foundations for something better" (203); Nury, who "looked as though he had been twisted and pulled inside out . . . as though he were carrying his bile on his skin" (245); one-eyed Abu Fahl; Zindi, an "indescribably vast woman" (361); Bhudeb Roy, with his "tiny, opaque, red-flecked" eyes, his mouth a "yawning, swallowing, spittle-encrusted chasm," and the "engorged, hairy mass" of his stomach (22); and others. Many characters are afflicted with illnesses that may or may not be explicable in medical terms, as in the case of Parboti-debi's "very sickly" daughter, whose protracted illness seems to have "driven Parboti-debi . . . a little mad" (128). The girl's conception is depicted in magical realist terms, as if it had happened the night the plane crashed into the village like a "gigantic chrome-plated penis thrown down by the skies" (98). Later it is revealed that the girl's father is the weaver Shombhu Debnath; then, when child and mother are reunited with the biological father, the girl suddenly and abruptly shows "no sign of her illness" (140). Zindi's adoptive son, Boss, develops a sickness of ten days' duration while they are on the run after the al-Ghazira episode, yet the illness is never diagnosed or revealed, and in fact it may not be "anything serious" (362). Conversely, Kulfi, who shows no signs of illness or weakness earlier in the novel, abruptly develops chest pains that lead to her death just two months or so after she begins experiencing them (355).

At one level, bodily ailments and transformations reflect the harsh living and working conditions of migrant laborers. Here I invite students who are familiar with Ghosh's concern for the underclass to make connections with similar depictions in some of his other novels—the description of the hardships faced by the unsettled dwellers in the Sundarbans in *The Hungry Tide*, for example. For those unfamiliar with Ghosh's other writings, I point to Ghosh's description of himself as a "disillusioned Marxist" (Alam 140) and ask them to consider how the bodily grotesqueries and transformations in *Circle* might accord with a disillusioned Marxist's perspective of the condition of the transnational laborer. At this point the issue of exaggeration or nonrealistic caricature often arises, particularly with students unfamiliar with the lot of unskilled (and sometimes illegal) migrant workers, especially in more inhospitable socioeconomic conditions such as in the Gulf Cooperation Council (GCC) countries on which al-Ghazira is modeled. Some contextualization and statistics are very useful at this point to show that there is a reality underlying *Circle*'s seemingly unreal depictions.

I find that most literature majors (with the possible exception of those with interests in related issues in human geography, global studies, or political science) are largely unaware of the harsh and exploitative conditions of the Kafala system operating in many GCC countries, and that they benefit from some basic eye-opening statistics and background readings (Ruhs; Beydoun and Baum).

I stress that the Kafala system is notorious for allowing unscrupulous employers to exploit migrant laborers, to violate their human rights and deprive them of worker welfare and safety protections, and that Kafala-style labor systems result in the serious injury or death of many migrant workers in South Asia and other parts of the world. In the case of Bangladesh, for example (the majority of whose migrant worker population works in Kafala-style regimes in the Arab Gulf countries, Malaysia, and Singapore), in the period 2003–12, a total of 15,752 migrant labor casualties were repatriated, a figure that has only increased in recent years (Ullah et al. 46). Apart from fatalities, migrant workers (legal or otherwise) in such regimes face the possibility of sudden and often arbitrary termination of employment (such as happens to Kulfi and Professor Samuel), withholding of rightful earnings by employers or labor contractors (the fate of Mast Ram and others), endemic or epidemic sickness because of poor living conditions (the fever that breaks out in the Ras), police brutality (seen in the arrest and beating of Abusa and in the heavy-handed response to the community march to the Star), and, of course, the emotional and psychological toll of the loneliness and hardships such a life engenders. At this point students either respond incredulously (and are thus challenged to do their own basic research on such issues, after which their incredulity wanes significantly) or approach the depictions of migrant worker life in *Circle* with a whole new perspective. They are at that point more sympathetic to reading *Circle*'s depictions of grotesque physical characteristics and afflictions—boils, deformed skin, body odor, physical deterioration, frequent accidents, even death from violence or ailment—as an exaggeration-for-effect of the real, harsh conditions of life faced by migrant workers.

Of course, there is nothing literal or realist about these depictions; there is an undeniably fantastical quality in the narrative that discourages its reading in terms of strict causality or rationality. Here, once again, I find that an explanation of some of the features and narrative aims of magical realism is of great benefit. I observe to my students that many of the events in *Circle*—the mysterious waxing and waning of the functioning of Alu's thumbs, for example, or the "impossible to explain" series of misfortunes that collectively lead to Abusa's self-immolation, an act that also sets fire to "at least fifty shacks in the Ras" (206, 210, 212)—can be seen as typical of magical realism's emphasis on idiosyncratic, even bizarrely subjective perspectives. I then challenge them to consider how these magical realist features of "subjective distortions" and "grotesque shifts of perspective" might constitute a "critique of history," as Patricia Merivale says of magical realist texts like *Midnight's Children* (341)—how they can mount a challenge to the notion of a single monolithic history by recording the multiple voices of subjective responses to that history. Although there is usually some initial resistance—particularly from students who maintain objectivist notions of history—after some open discussion in class, students generally accept the idea that the novel's "subjective distortions" are a form of sociohistorical account, a chronicle of the perspectives and desires of underclass individuals.

Any discussion of the migrant lives in *Circle* should include the push factors that compel migrants to leave their home country despite the obvious risks and dangers involved. The other side of *Circle* as a "migrant lives" novel is that it is also very much a "condition of India" novel—a fact that is crucial to understanding the desperation that impels those migrant careers. Here it helps to briefly compare and contrast *Circle* with other well-known condition of India novels. I point out that *Circle* is not concerned with a detailed and direct depiction of the sociopolitical condition of India, the way that the works of writers like Rohinton Mistry, Manju Kapur, Vikas Swarup, and others are (or, for that matter, novels by Ghosh himself such as *The Hungry Tide*). The novel is less interested in laying bare the systemic corruption, misgovernance, and oppression that other anglophone Indian writers concern themselves with and more interested in the effect of those systems on individuals, portrayed through the subjective individual perception and experience of the system. In *Circle*, few specifics of the social history of India emerge, and what is foregrounded instead is affect—the influence or impact of the Indian habitus on individual characters.

This affect is perceived by characters as a hidden pressure, an invisible force whose origins are recondite but that nevertheless has concrete and traumatic consequences for individuals and communities. Jyoti Das, as the detective figure whose ostensible task is to discover the truth of the Lalpukur episode and, if necessary, to apprehend its engineers, hints at this recondite force early in the novel, when he is described as having "lost himself in that labyrinth of cause and effect" (83). Indeed, Jyoti as authority figure, as the nemesis of abject fugitives like Alu, turns out to be ironic, for he is revealed by the end of the novel to be as much of a hapless victim of the system as those he pursues. Much is gained by discussing Jyoti as Alu's doppelgänger, originally on the other side of the socioeconomic and power divide, but linked not just through the chase but also by a common process of physical transformations, malaises, and subjective experiences of shocks and afflictions. Already in the plane leaving Bombay he experiences a "light-headedness" that "had nothing to do with the altitude" (266) and appears to be a visceral response to leaving behind the pressures of life in India. In al-Ghazira he feels a mysterious lassitude, more extreme than the mere jet lag one would experience flying from India to the Middle East and accompanied by its own version of deteriorated joints corresponding to Alu's wasted thumbs: "Stretching his arm out to put the phone back, he could feel an almost painful stiffness in his joints. The crumpled sheets of his bed had left their impression on his skin over the last day and a half; his arm was marbled over with wrinkles" (320). While students always find this transformation and affliction incomprehensible on first reading, they can be helped to contextualize it through recognizing the earlier dis-ease and affective shocks Jyoti receives. In one key episode, Jyoti belatedly realizes that his superior has manipulated him to use his family connections in order to get the superior's nephew appointed as Jyoti's replacement: "Das felt as though he had been hit in the stomach. He propped himself upright with an outstretched arm, resisting the temptation to double up" (271). Jyoti's progression in the novel is undoubtedly tinged with the fantastical, in the tradition of magical realist narratives, but the fantastical is premised upon the shocking and alienating effect that India has on him.

Alu, Balaram, and the rest of their Lalpukur community also show the effects of oppressive conditions in India. The Lalpukur episode, which causes Alu to lose all the family he has and to become a fugitive from justice, is in large part the consequence of the unchecked local tyranny of Bhudeb Roy, who might well deserve to be called a "germ," according to Shombhu Debnath, or to be classified as one of the "filthy little district and mofussil politicians who have suddenly come into so much power," as Jyoti thinks (119, 124). Although his antagonists Balaram and Shombhu Debnath are no doubt guilty of escalating the conflict, there is clear provocation in Bhudeb Roy's incessant and tyrannical control of the physical and human resources of Lalpukur. The resultant explosion and Bhudeb Roy's false report that makes Alu a fugitive represent the exploitative power of inequality, which is seen as tolerated and endemic in India.

The endemic problematic is not attributable only to corrupt individuals like Jyoti's superior or Bhudeb Roy but is seen as part of a structural problem in India as a whole. The issue of transnational refugees and the economic strain they pose, the weak will of central government to control outlying areas, the culture of patronage and nepotism, and the lack of human and infrastructural development are all part of India's problem of its "Teeming Millions" and the lack of a plan to adequately provide for them (185). The intolerable hardships of the migrant laborer's life, including abuse and exploitation in regimes like al-Ghazira and Algeria, are necessitated by what the novel sees as the comprehensive socioeconomic failures that push desperate migrants out of developing countries like Bangladesh, India, and Egypt. Eva Aldea maintains that within the global order depicted by the novel, "any organization of the migrants . . . any attempt at imposing a territorial order on the chaotic world of their community, is doomed to failure" (128). Certainly it is true that a surreal fatalism surrounds all attempts at organization and reform (as it were) from below, whether it be Balaram's rural vocational institute and the war on germs in Lalpukur, the cooperative society's war on money in al-Ghazira, or even Mrs. Verma's attempt to organize a folk-art cultural event in El Oued. *Circle*'s treatment of the condition of India can thus be related to the novel's critique of a larger global capitalist order—a critique whose roots can be seen in Ghosh's "disillusioned Marxist" sensibilities.

The gradual convergence of the values and movements of pursuer and pursued, Jyoti on the one hand and Alu and gang on the other, is an important part of the novel's critique of the established order and its discourses. I find it helpful to discuss this in terms of the "sense of collective relatedness" that Faris sees as a key feature of magical realist novels ("Scheherazade's Children" 183). The sense of collective sympathies and fates is clear to students in the depiction of the migrant workers, who obviously share similar perspectives and experiences as part of a downtrodden laboring class. However, the novel goes further by bringing the erstwhile authority figure and antagonist Jyoti into alignment with the perspective and values of this community. As they come to recognize that by the end of the novel Jyoti has become an exile too, I ask students to consider the ways in which the novel's narrative form and symbolism enact a bonding or merging of perspectives, thoughts, and desires—of subjective landscapes, so to speak—between different characters. This task allows students to notice and talk about symbolic convergences, such as Zindi's response to the news of Alu being trapped in the collapse of the Star, when Zindi's face seems similarly to collapse in sympathy, the attrition in her voice resembling the attrition involved in the laborers' work of construction: "The lines and ridges on Zindi's cheeks seemed to sink deeper. Her jowls trembled and then the whole of her face collapsed inwards. She struck her forehead with the heel of her palm. Him, too! she cried, and her voice rasped like sandpaper on lead. All the others and now him!" (199).

Another starting point for a discussion of unconscious collectivity could be the theme of birds, which begins with Jyoti's artistic obsession. Later, in Algeria, the febrile imagination of his prey, Zindi, transforms him into a hybrid being, a "Bird-man," who is also associated with a vulture that the fugitives see in the sky and take as a harbinger of death. When Kulfi suddenly dies, seemingly of the excitement caused by being accosted by Jyoti, the vulture seems to literalize the conflation of the "Bird-man," the pursuing authority figure, and the harbinger of death. More to the point, there is a powerful convergence of the subjective symbolisms of Jyoti, Zindi, Kulfi, and others, the forging of a kind of fantastical collective unconscious. By the end of the novel, Jyoti, disheartened and disillusioned by his trials and experiences, has decided to abandon his job and family in India and (again like a bird) is "migrating . . . to Düsseldorf" (421). This symbolic thread not only marks Jyoti's conversion to and new sympathy with the perspective of the exiles but also suggests a deeper, preconscious affinity of essential human values—an affinity that is usefully taught in the tradition of magical realism's focus on "collective relatedness."

Behind this positing of a seemingly supernatural malignancy is the novel's bleak vision of a class of people victimized by history. Underlying the magical realist–like depiction of the "malevolent willfulness" controlling the lives and careers of the main characters is a simple realization of the hopelessness of individual action without a positive political will and socioeconomic opportunities in the regimes governing their communities. As Balaram intuits early in the novel, "nothing can change people here" (19) because of the strongly deterministic divide between the rich and powerful on the one hand and the poor and helpless on the other. Aldea maintains that "the novel can be seen as a representation of the dislocation of peoples as an effect of the struggle between precapitalist and capitalist modes of production" (127); while the powerful in the novel—Bhudeb Roy, Jyoti's superiors, al-Ghazira employers and labor contractors—are not clearly "capitalists," it is true that they exert a "dislocating" effect on the abject class. It helps at this point to mention Marx's notion of the "fantastical" relation between money and goods that seems to bypass the agency and control of the individual worker and is correlated to the laborer's being "controlled by others" in the capitalist system of production (K. Marx 77, 476). Any lingering resistance to the "fantastical" elements of the novel is usually by this time dissipated, and students are empowered to consider *Circle*'s magical realist narrative elements as a plausible and intriguing way to highlight the abstracted powerlessness of abject transnationals and to express their subjective reactions to the power systems of bureaucracy and wealth. Curriculum space permitting, this is an ideal juncture for challenging students to take this line of inquiry beyond the text—to, as it were, corroborate the novel's vision and narrative mode by considering the power relations and abject plights that are evident to the students in their own social milieus.

NOTE

[1] This essay uses the 2005 Mariner Books edition of *The Circle of Reason*.

Ghosh in the Great Game: *The Shadow Lines* as Post-1857 and Post-9/11 Reading

Hilary Thompson

Perhaps the most difficult texts to teach are the ones we love. One reason for this may be that the more we love a text, the more it becomes layered, perceived through multiple readings, leaving us almost incapable of retrieving a first reading's feeling. *The Shadow Lines* particularly embodies this challenge, as it immediately greets readers with a storyteller, an unnamed narrator, for whom an intricate web of familial relations and a detailed sense of an extended family's history are proverbial. I try to prepare students before we begin reading the book, warning them about the lack of explicit structure and signposts for important information and then asking them to consider the significance of retelling history in this way.

Still, I was surprised the last time I taught the novel when one student asked me to draw the narrator's family tree on the board. As I did so, I found myself explaining that an easy way to mentally organize the family was around two of its matriarchs, the grandmother and her sister Mayadebi. I then realized that the task the student had given me was the one I should have given the class. In a similar way, every time I've read *The Shadow Lines*, I've jotted down important dates of family events and then tried to relist them in chronological order. What I end up with chiastically connects the 1890s, the decade of a Crystal Palace exhibition in London and the purchase there of the gigantic table that will come to reside in India and to symbolize so much memory, and the 1980s, the decade of the narrator's own stay in London. In the future, I hope to assign this task to students to see what they come up with. Perhaps this active charting would allow students reading the novel for the first time to get a bit of the sensation a second-time reader would have. Perhaps it would also make reading the novel into a kind of game.

I teach *The Shadow Lines* in a course called Global Fiction and "The Great Game," where we engage with contemporary South Asian fiction and representations of geopolitics. Using nineteenth- and early-twentieth-century literature of empire as a springboard, we go on to consider recent Indian, Pakistani, and South Asian diaspora fictions of World War II, the Cold War, and the War on Terror. Following texts on the Indian Sepoy Rebellion of 1857—I have used both Arthur Conan Doyle's *The Sign of Four* and J. G. Farrell's *The Siege of Krishnapur*—and then Joseph Conrad's *The Shadow-Line*, Ghosh's novel cuts right down the middle of our reading list. After it, we turn to Mohammed Hanif, Uzma Aslam Khan, Michael Ondaatje, and Nadeem Aslam. The figuring of space as a playing field or charted map and the attempt to subject time to such territorial imagining become recurring motifs in what we read. *The Shadow Lines*'s particularly quirky approach to structural organization, whether of space, time, or causality, becomes influential for how we read subsequent texts and discuss the events they represent. This mode of organization lies behind my own syllabus structure; rather than progressing chronologically, the reading list zigzags between earlier and later texts as I try to accommodate significant intertextual ancestors alongside their present literary descendants. I've arrived at this order because I believe that *The Shadow Lines* offers us an important opportunity. In translating the combined structures of spontaneous reminiscence and extended family history into narrative form, the novel asks us to see the geopolitical from the angle of unexpected kinship. It says that events distant, obscured, or somehow misplaced live with us more than we know.

Groundwork: Farrell's Aesthetic Ambiguity and Conrad's Cartography

Farrell's *The Siege of Krishnapur* remains controversial for its portrayal of the sepoy rebellion of 1857, and this is a debate I find important to teach as I lay a foundation for a consideration of Ghosh. Two articles, John McLeod's "Exhibiting Empire in J. G. Farrell's *The Siege of Krishnapur*" and Michael L. Ross's "Passage to Krishnapur: J. G. Farrell's Comic Vision of India," map out the terms of this debate, and we read them along with Jenny Sharpe's analysis of the unsubstantiated myths of the rapes of Englishwomen in the 1857 revolt. At issue for many Farrell critics is the ultimate effect of his novel's parodic mode. While McLeod acknowledges that the novel operates within the tight constraints of the colonialist conventions it strives to mock, he nonetheless maintains that *The Siege of Krishnapur* is an ironic performance of colonialist tropes that utterly exposes their hollowness and contradictions. A send-up of supposed British bravery in the midst of siege, and of colonial culture's obsession with collecting and exhibiting prized artifacts, the novel becomes for McLeod a metafictional display of the defeat of Western hubris. As the confined colonizers watch their cherished possessions and assumptions come under fire, the novel's readers perceive the upending of colonialism's epistemological as well as ideological order. Ross, by contrast, sees Farrell's parody as fundamentally reinscribing the power dynamics it wishes to pillory. For him the novel's tightly Eurocentric focus and the lack of subjectivity, inwardness, or full human presence in the depictions of native Indians and particularly the sepoys compromise the novel's critical potential. Indeed, he claims, "the violence the author's comic treatment inflicts on the insurgent natives is in its way as damaging as the violence they visit on their smug, disdainful rulers" (77).

One scene, discussed briefly by Ross, brings the problem of Farrell's ambiguous parody into focus and sets an intriguing precedent for Ghosh. In a bizarre moment, Lucy Hughes, deemed a loose woman by the colonial community, is swarmed by insects supposedly drawn to her white muslin dress. This "cloud of cockchafers" is compared to "drifts of glistening black snow," and we are told that the insects "swarmed into the crevices and cornices of her ears, into all the narrow loops and whorls, they poured in a dark river down the back of her dress between her shoulder-blades and down the front between her breasts." Lucy is forced to tear off her clothes, because "this was no time to worry about modesty," and is transformed as a result: "there she stood, stark naked but as black as an African slave-girl" (249). For Ross this scene is evidence that, despite some critics' wish to see the besieged colonizers as cross-racialized and forced to inhabit the position of their Indian others, the episode that most fits the bill only fleetingly transforms an already morally questionable community member, playing the scene largely for comedic gains. Here I believe that debating the end result of Farrell's parody as either critique or complicity within a framework defined narrowly by the politics of identity falls short. As a countermeasure, I introduce Sharpe's discussion of the colonial myths and rumors surrounding the 1857 uprising. Sharpe describes numerous unsubstantiated and subsequently discredited reports of Englishwomen's rape and dismemberment at the hands of Indians. In particular, she notes one outlandish account in which Englishwomen supposedly had their faces blackened with suet and oil before they were made to watch the vicious murder of their children and then were subjected themselves to the violent sepoys and mobs (35). Farrell's scene of blackening and violation, especially as it involves an Englishwoman who is already far from being a communal icon of purity, seems to uphold McLeod's point: the episode uses satire to target the myth and ideology of English female purity more than it makes any sort of statement concerning racialized subjectivity.

And yet the collective, creaturely form of life that the insects embody is also clearly associated with the eventual sepoy attack. While the appearance of chapatis in the place of documents in a dispatch box hints at brewing trouble early on, one of the novel's key colonial administrative focalizers, the Collector, notices them only when his vision is "led towards them by a column of ants . . . issuing from a crevice," as they make their way to the chapatis. Since the Collector fails to make sense of the chapatis as a sign that some event is imminent, both they and the ants serve to mark something one registers without fully interpreting.[1] Later, when a coming onslaught is clear, the Collector sees it as a "ravenous monster" that lives off its own momentum: "He had come to think of the attack as a living creature which derived its nourishment from the speed of its progress" (319). When he plans to halt the sepoys by falling back through ever more barricaded rooms, they push through all of them, crunching past even their own dead and appearing behind half-open doors "like a porcupine with glistening bayonets" (323). When one dies, the next appears, looking almost indistinguishable from his predecessor. Clearly focalized through colonial eyes, the sepoys nonetheless give form to a kind of collective, swarming, nonhuman life, one that will pick up momentum in the texts of eras beyond 1857.

We discuss the attack of Farrell's sepoys as an assault not only on English interiors and the aesthetic tradition they represent, but also on English interiority, or psychological interiority as an exclusive property of the Western subject. In this case, Farrell's sepoys seem to turn the tables on a colonial mapping of psychic territory. This idea that progress through time and through psychological stages can be thought of spatially and territorially is one we carry over into a reading of Conrad's *The Shadow-Line*. An early-twentieth-century bildungsroman of a young sailor embarking on his first commission as captain, the novella seems to be all about forward motion and teleology. To come into his own as an adult and a leader, the unnamed narrator must command a ship through Eastern waters and past a supposedly haunted point in the sea where the ship's last captain died and where his body lies. Overcoming the ship's stasis, the crew's illness, the mysterious absence of medicine on board, and then a dazzling storm, the narrator eventually succeeds after his reckless start, and the world's horizons, specifically the Indian Ocean, open up to him. Yet students notice that, in the midst of charting a developmental narrative of its subject, the novella insists on splits and contrasts: the older sailor is recalling a youthful episode and commenting on his younger self, and thus readers must keep two perspectives in mind, often shuttling from one to the other as the narrator gets ahead of himself. In addition, the narrator frequently speaks of other characters as alter egos. As if to confirm that self-mastery means living as two—that is, living as though an older self were watching and counseling you—the novella ends with the young captain contemplating taking his life ever after "at half-speed" (126). Interiority here means internalizing the shadow line, the sense of a stopping point, and conquering the ravenous monster of one's own urge for excessive momentum. Thus Conrad opens up discussions of the map as allegory, specific points on it as potential signifiers, and movement across it as regulated, goal-oriented narrative.

In order to extend this discussion into postcolonial literary theory, alongside this novella I assign the first chapter of Graham Huggan's book *Interdisciplinary Measures: Literature and the Future of Postcolonial Studies*. Huggan draws from and usefully summarizes key poststructuralists—Derrida, Deleuze, and Barthes—while relating their core concepts to the postcolonial theory of Said, Spivak, and Bhabha. Underscoring the ways that colonialism and cartography have operated in tandem and thus resemble each other, he points out that maps, while purporting to be accurate mimetic representations of space, are always approximate, interested constructions—ones that enclose territories within supposedly static borders and place privileged sectors in prominent, usually central positions. He closes by exploring literary strategies for, in his chapter's title phrase, "decolonizing the map." Those who contest the narratives that allow for such seemingly stable, timeless structures might experiment instead with representing heterogeneous, interstitial, decentralized spaces or shifting grounds and borders. Huggan's arguments provide both a way to read Conrad against the grain and a helpful transition to Ghosh.

Delayed Interactions: **The Shadow Lines,** *Its Intertexts and Endpoints*

Despite our having laid this intertextual and theoretical foundation for a read-ing of the novel, classes often find *The Shadow Lines* disorienting at first. A narrator begins by informing them of dates of family members' travels, secret and widely known family sentiments, and bits of other people's life stories. Readers understandably wonder what they are meant to do with the informa-tion. The narrative's overall direction is unclear. I try to make these challenges the basis of our discussion, asking what the text makes us map and then what priorities or logic might be ordering the narrator's stories. We discuss the move from Conrad's singular line to Ghosh's plurality, exploring the manifold signifi-cances lines take on. As we go along, I treat the text as a mystery, checking in with students about which details seem to take on extra meaning, what they suspect might have happened in the narrator's family, and why those events might matter. Without assigning any psychoanalytic theory, I explain the con-cept of deferred action, whereby later events can act as triggers, forcing into full-blown significance earlier occurrences that were registered but not fully understood at the time. We begin to collect examples that might work in this way, either feelings that might have as yet unexplored causes or events ripe for later repercussions.

Pieces begin to fall into place: students foresee Tridib's death and even dimly glimpse May's probable involvement, but impossible to guess are the exact cir-cumstances. The novel's climactic pages present a peculiar challenge: on the one hand, the narrator's voice undergoes a seeming apotheosis, speaking almost authorially to deliver several thesis statements; yet, on the other, the complexity of the chain of events surrounding the genesis and growth of the fateful 1964 riots is all too easily oversimplified. I explicitly ask students to reconstruct this chain as accurately as they can and to reflect on the steps they're tempted to jump. Just as the narrator worries that the memory of the riots sweeping across the sub-continent to reach Calcutta has become lost and that these events will never be recognized as genuinely politically significant, so the unique quality of the first Kashmir demonstrations is often missed. Ghosh is at pains to describe the first protests at the theft of the Prophet's hair as syncretic, collective, and not communally violent. When I then question students as to what role national borders play in the protests' growth into riots and the riots' eventual expansion, they want at first to claim that these borders decrease the momentum. Only after returning to the text do we begin to appreciate the inverse logic that Ghosh repeatedly emphasizes. Complementary opposites spur each other on through their very symmetrical opposition, he insists, and this is true not only of the communal panic that leads Hindus to flee the riots, crossing over into India, and then inspires Muslims there to fear for their lives. It is also true of national media and national governments, which don't know how to register spontaneous, syncretic demonstrations without "a note of surprise" (221) or how to stop a riot because "the madness of a riot is a pathological inversion, but also therefore a reminder, of that indivisible sanity that binds people to each other independently of their governments" (225).[2] That Ghosh highlights this "indivisible sanity" and believes in its power, even in tragic negative form, is his great gift. The utter unexpectedness of 1964—as opposed to 1947 or any other watershed year—as the crucial point in the narrator's temporal map of himself in relation to his extended family testifies to ties barely visible.

At this point, I try to broaden the discussion and bring it closer to home. I remark on the tumultuous American events of the 1960s and the way some even felt that the country might have been on the brink of civil war. I ask students for their memories of the earliest events that affected their lives while also making them aware of national or international politics. Nearly all of them refer to the day of 9/11, and we explore those memories. In the supplementary material I've assigned—Ghosh's essay "Imperial Temptations," which discusses post-9/11 politics in the United States, and his participation in a 2012 BBC World Book Club discussion specifically focused on *The Shadow Lines* ("Amitav Ghosh—*The Shadow Lines*")—Ghosh makes two comparisons that are crucial for our course: 1857 with 9/11 and 9/11 with 1964, or with the various incidents of civil violence in the India of his youth. Living in New York City in September 2001, Ghosh claims that for him as an Indian the "attacks and their aftermath were filled with disquieting historical resonances" ("Imperial Temptations" 28). In comparing 1857 with 9/11, Ghosh focuses on three main qualities of the Indian revolt: the strong ambivalence of Indians, the violent British retaliatory tactics that amounted to a "shock and awe" strategy, and the mixed results of that terrifying British campaign (29–30). As with the contemporary mujahideen, the 1857 sepoys rose up violently against their erstwhile trainers, but their extreme methods alienated moderates in their midst. Ghosh sees today's Islamist fundamentalism as inspiring similarly divided loyalties in the Middle East. Likewise, the violence with which Britain responded in 1857 may have turned the Indian struggle for independence away from violent means toward what Ghosh calls "a more parliamentary and constitutionalist direction" (30). Yet Ghosh also stresses that to see the other side of this influence "we need only look at a list of cities where al Qaeda's fugitive leaders are said to have taken refuge: Aden, Rawalpindi, Peshawar, Quetta, Lahore, Karachi," and then points out, "The British dominated these cities for centuries, and yet the antagonism to the West that simmers in them now is greater even than it was in 1857" (30). The Pakistani writers whose novels we will go on to read echo and build on Ghosh's point, adding to nineteenth-century colonial history the twentieth-century Cold War politics that fatefully made Afghanistan and Pakistan instruments in larger conflicts. Following Ghosh, writers such as Kamila Shamsie and Uzma Aslam Khan will use multigenerational stories of family migrations to bring these points home. For Ghosh and for many South Asian writers, 1857 stretches out into a long history of 9/11, exerting its influence across an

extended kinship structure. Thus it's not surprising that, speaking more personally of his memories of the day of 9/11, Ghosh should remark, "In some peculiar
way, the sense it had for me was that the things we had lived with in the subcontinent of my childhood had suddenly come home in America, in Europe" ("Amitav
Ghosh—*The Shadow Lines*"). Intriguingly, Ghosh speaks of homecoming, but
one that seems to have taken his lifetime to occur and that comes to him in a
later home.

It takes almost the entire course of the bildungsroman for the narrator of *The
Shadow Lines* to hear the specific circumstances surrounding the death of his
ideal alter ego, Tridib. In direct contrast to this pace is the tempo in Robi's
dream memory of the riotous, fatal attacks on the rickshaw in Dhaka in 1964.
As the family car with its driver and security guard go on ahead, the rickshaw
that is carrying their granduncle and is pulled by his Muslim neighbor Khalil
begins to grow enormously out of proportion. Mobs of men rush toward it, leap-
ing on it until Robi sees "that rickshaw, reaching heavenwards, like a gigantic
anthill, and its sides are seething with hundreds of little men" (240). We see the
return of Farrell's "ravenous monster," an uprising that feeds off its own momentum and seemingly moves beyond the human, even beyond human species
life itself, as it becomes insectlike. Have we merely returned to the colonial
perspective Ross finds so problematically dehumanizing? While I have pointed
out this resonance between Farrell and Ghosh to students, their thoughts about
it remain inconclusive. On the one hand, the passage is narrated in these terms
by Robi, who has become part of the Indian Administrative Service and thus is
a kind of distant postcolonial descendant, perhaps, of Farrell's Collector. On
the other hand, the passage resonates with the imagery in the narrator's own
seemingly authorial thesis statements about civil violence.

We find a repeated recourse to natural imagery in Ghosh's descriptions of
human uprisings, and, given recent interest in Ghosh as a writer of ecocosmo-
politan fiction, I hope to pursue this point further in future classes. In his
description, for example, of the lack of documentation of the 1964 riots, the
narrator claims, "They had dropped out of memory into the crater of a volcano
of silence" (226). In the famous atlas scene, he imagines that those who once
drew borders in good faith must have assumed "the two bits of land would sail
away from each other like the shifting tectonic plates of the prehistoric Gondwa-
naland" (228). And, when the narrator describes the "particular fear" accompanying the onset of mob violence, he claims that it is "not comparable to the fear
of nature" but also that it resembles "the fear of victims of an earthquake" and
"is a fear that comes of the knowledge that normalcy is utterly contingent, that
the spaces that surround one, the streets one inhabits, can become, suddenly
and without warning, as hostile as a desert in a flash flood" (200). Perhaps we
currently discuss such a catastrophic world under the rubric of the posthuman,
the posthistorical, or the Anthropocene. But I believe that this is also the world
of *The Shadow Lines* that Ghosh sees coming home to the West with 9/11. It is
not simply the aftereffects of the world of colonial cartography broadly defined;

it is also the world of invisible kinship—stretched across vast distances and now seen to include even the planet itself—that, having lost its seeming normalcy, appears in negative form and speaks through the spontaneous hostility of familiar spaces.

NOTES

[1] While I do not assign Homi Bhabha's famous writing on this subject, I do make it available as optional reading for interested students ("By Bread Alone").

[2] This essay uses the 2005 Mariner Books edition of *The Shadow Lines*.

Narrative Form and Environmental Science: Teaching *The Hungry Tide* in the Core Curriculum

Russell A. Berman

The character of core curriculum pedagogy has evolved significantly over recent decades. Once frequently a venue for presenting great books from the Western canon, core curriculum courses now feature a more diverse and global selection of texts. In addition, learning goals have shifted away from familiarization with a particular tradition to the cultivation of broader intellectual skills, such as critical thinking and close reading. Core curriculum teaching takes most scholars out of their specific area of expertise but offers in exchange the opportunity to present the study of literature to those many undergraduates whose own interests may steer them in very different directions, especially toward the sciences.

I have taught *The Hungry Tide* in such a core curriculum context at Stanford, in the Thinking Matters program. All freshmen are required to complete at least one of these courses, selecting from a set of about eight choices offered each quarter. In contrast to many other core programs, Thinking Matters is not limited to the humanities but instead draws widely from across the whole university; the more literary courses are therefore in competition with offerings from the social and natural sciences as well as the schools of law and medicine. Each course poses a major problem or an enduring question in order to demonstrate to students how to apply university-level thinking, probing complexities, exploring ambiguities, and potentially articulating solutions. Students learn how to formulate questions productively and to engage in discussion to answer them.

Sustainability or Collapse, the course in which I have taught *The Hungry Tide*, was designed to appeal to students with environmentalist interests, addressing them from perspectives in both the humanities and the sciences. When I teach this course, I work with a colleague from geophysics, who presents scientific discussions of various topics ranging from demographic projections of population growth to climate change and energy resources, while I present on a set of cultural representations of nature and the environment from the standpoint of a literary scholar. The course seeks to deepen students' understanding of sustainability questions and to develop their capacity in the close reading of texts and cultural interpretation. Along with literary texts such as Johann Wolfgang von Goethe's *Novelle*, John Steinbeck's *The Grapes of Wrath*, and Aldo Leopold's *A Sand County Almanac*, we have analyzed films such as Nikolaus Geyrhalter's *Our Daily Bread* and Josh Fox's *Gasland*. The interdisciplinary character of the course has helped attract a diverse student population. Some participants bring an activist environmentalist agenda; others are more interested in environmental science, while a further group is attracted to the opportunity to read literature in this thematic context. Teaching to a heterogeneous student body is itself a challenge, insofar as we have to make the case to the students inclined toward the sciences that literary study brings worthwhile perspectives to the table, just as the more humanistic students have to be convinced to engage in the science. Both pedagogical projects are important in fulfilling the core course mission.

Teaching *The Hungry Tide* in this particular curricular context has therefore involved guiding students toward questions regarding the specifically literary aspects of the text as well as the several relevant thematic issues explored in it. We inquire into the specific form of the story and the way the narrative is organized, but we also explore the motivations of the protagonist, an environmental scientist, as well as the novel's evaluation of human-animal relations. A further focus point is the collision between concern with the environment and the treatment of animals on the one hand and questions of human rights and the treatment of refugee populations on the other. *The Hungry Tide* provides an opportunity to teach students how to engage with a moderately complex narrative form (with multiple plotlines and time frames) in order to build their reading skills, while also inviting them to debate the precarious environment and the treatment of refugees. This latter element, the topical character of the work, is particularly important for those students whose primary interest is science or environmental policy. It is very useful for instructors to make the argument that, while students may eventually pursue careers in specialized fields with the expertise to solve certain problems, their future success will always depend on convincing others, including the broader public, which will require narrative and language: hence the importance of their studying literature. Nonhumanities students have proved open to this line of thinking.

The initial narrative structure of *The Hungry Tide* can be challenging to the freshman reader, but this hurdle sets the stage for a discussion of the formal organization of the work. The first part of the novel, entitled "The Ebb: *Bhata*," traces the itinerary of two central figures, Kanai and Piya, from a train station in Calcutta to Lusibari in the Sundarbans, the maze of islands in the Ganges estuary. Alternating chapters address each of the characters. (As noted, the syllabus also includes *The Grapes of Wrath*, and the character of chapter alternation there lends itself neatly to a contrast with *The Hungry Tide*.) Keeping track of the two separate plotlines requires focused attention; it is useful to point this out to students. In addition to the oscillation between these two figures, however, readers soon encounter two supplementary complexities. In the present of the novel, Kanai is returning for the first time to Lusibari, where he visited his aunt and uncle decades ago. The memory of the previous visit is recounted as backstory, a counterpoint to the present trip. That backstory involves an adolescent erotic encounter with Kusum, the mother of Fokir, who plays a key role in the present. Second, Kanai returns to Lusibari at the exhortation of his aunt, Nilima, so that she can present to him a notebook written by his now deceased uncle, Nirmal. Beginning in the chapter "The Letter," passages from that notebook appear in *The Hungry Tide*, printed in italics, set apart from the primary text. The student reader therefore has to juggle the two present narratives of Kanai and Piya, Kanai's backstory, and Nirmal's interpolated text. Piya also has a backstory, though it is somewhat less integrated into the central plot trajectory than is Kanai's.

Some students, especially those less practiced in novel reading, require support in navigating through this complexity. One useful exercise involves assignments in which students focus on just one of the various moving parts in order to describe its particular sequence of events. This could involve reading and summarizing alternate chapters in order to highlight a single plotline. More challenging would be an assignment to provide contrastive readings of the different materials. At the beginning of the novel, comparative descriptions of Kanai and Piya provide an obvious opportunity to focus attention on character. As students progress toward the conclusion, the two visits to the Garjontola shrine lend themselves well to an exercise in comparative description. In the chapter "Memory," Nirmal travels there with Horen and Kusum, and we witness the sublime syncretic worship at the Bon Bibi shrine, as reported in the italicized text from the past. In contrast, in the chapter "Signs," Kanai finds himself abandoned in the jungle, facing the terror of an attack by crocodiles or tigers. The two very different experiences of the site give students a chance to explore the cultural associations of the individual figures: the intellectual Nirmal's encounter with religion (which he otherwise dismisses as "false consciousness" [84]) and the urbane and arrogant Kanai's "atavistic" (269) conflict with the lower-class Fokir.[1]

In addition to analyzing the distinct plotlines, it is equally important to help students understand how Ghosh synthesizes them. Students should explore how the novel coheres into a unified story despite the separate itineraries. One answer, which might be best provided in a lecture, requires pulling back from the microanalyses of the individual characters in order to describe the overall movement: in part one, the trips to Lusibari (with the various supplementary accounts); and in part two ("The Flood: *Jowar*"), the group excursion and the characters' separate returns to Lusibari in the context of the devastating storm. Ultimately the structure is quite constrained: to Lusibari, away, and back again, a tidal repetition, within a matter of only a few days. *The Hungry Tide* lacks the epic breadth of other novels by Ghosh, instead displaying a nearly novella-like concentration. Once students have managed to engage with the text and have grasped its narrative structure, a provocative question to ask involves the broader implication of this formal unity. Despite the separate trajectories, individual characters do find their homes, explicitly so in the case of Piya, the Indian American who grew up in Seattle but chooses to settle in the Sundarbans (329). Furthermore, the question of unity becomes thematic in subtle ways, concerning nationality and religion, each of which can serve as an engaging topic for student essays.

The Indian national question, implicit in the presence of the Bangladeshi refugees at Morichjhãpi, is named in the lyrical opening description of the Sundarbans: *"The islands are the trailing threads of India's fabric, the ragged fringe of her sari, the* āchol *that follows her, half wetted by the sea"* (6). The geography of the novel becomes a metaphor, the textile of the nation, woven into a fabric but also "the ragged edge," fraying and unraveling. How does the novel raise the question of Indian unity, and how does the formal structure echo that question? In what ways does the legacy of the Partition cast a shadow on the Indian present in *The Hungry Tide*? Exploring these topics necessarily requires that the instructor provide some background discussion of Indian history.

The Partition and its legacy are also (if not exclusively) religious questions. Thanks to growing student interest in issues of spirituality, this topic may hold particular appeal. The middle-class protagonists—Kanai and Piya, but also Nirmal and Nilima—appear impervious to, indeed sometimes contemptuous of, religion and tradition. Yet the visits to the Bon Bibi shrine are crucial events, in effect staging the postsecular critique of modernity. It is crucial to recognize how Ghosh emphasizes the syncretic character of the ritual, the Islamic influence in the context of the Hindu veneration. This spiritual hybridity at a crucial juncture in a novel concerned with "India's fabric" points to topics worthy of exploration in student research papers: educated secularism versus popular religion, Hinduism and Islam in India, orthodoxy and syncretism in cultural traditions, as well as the connection between the moments of religion in *The Hungry Tide* and the alternative world of science represented by Piya. The novel can provide opportunities for students to discuss how they themselves navigate between scientific aspirations and religious traditions.

Teaching *The Hungry Tide* is also a chance to explore questions of the environment, environmentalism, and environmental science. This topical focus proves very attractive to many students who might not otherwise be predisposed to appreciate novels. It is vital that we literary scholars seize such opportunities to demonstrate how the novel, as genre, is capacious enough to address issues important to those many students whose main area of interest is not the humanities. *The Hungry Tide* has the potential to engage the STEM student precisely because the protagonist, Piya, is a scientist and the trajectory of the novel is driven by her pursuit of her research project into the environmental adaptations of the dolphin. A focus on her can provide the springboard to essay assignments about students' own scientific interests and plans.

Understanding Piya as a scientist includes several distinct dimensions. First, students can be asked to develop a succinct account of her research project, her earlier study of the topic, and precisely what and why she tries to study in the Sundarbans. This analysis would require reading through the novel and highlighting the science-focused passages, especially her reflections on a potential "hypothesis of stunning elegance and economy" (104). STEM students are likely familiar with scientific method and hypothesis formulation, and this exercise allows them to use their disciplinary expertise from their science classes in this new humanities context. Second, students should evaluate Piya's research techniques, such as her utilization of equipment, her record keeping, and her experience with the various support personnel, including not only corrupt officials and a hostile boat crew but also the helpful and extremely knowledgeable Fokir, with whom however she shares no common language. This network of relationships makes up a complex world in which she carries out her science against resistance but also with unexpected assistance. The resistance in particular has a gendered character: Piya embodies not only the scientist but also the female scientist facing a particular set of challenges. How she addresses these challenges deserves scrutiny, especially from STEM students. Third, her scientific expertise lies in the specialized area of marine mammal behavior, and her work is driven by her concern with the dwindling population of the riverine dolphins. Her focus on the dolphin, therefore, is embedded in a larger ecological awareness, a topic addressed in the course by excerpts from Leopold's *Sand County Almanac* but also pervading the novel itself as an anxiety about environmental degradation. In Nirmal's interpolated text, we read that *"[t]he birds were vanishing, the fish were dwindling and from day to day the land was being reclaimed by the sea. What would it take to submerge the tide country? Not much—a minuscule change in the level of the sea would be enough"* (179). Species extinction and the loss of biodiversity are linked to the precarity of the ecosystem in the Sundarbans, which functions as an expansive conceptual backdrop to Piya's intense focus on the dolphin. Her specialized research depends, in other words, on a broader, encompassing concern, and this particular structure of scientific research, the connection between the narrow topic and the broad framework, represents a further topic that STEM students could connect to their own areas of interest.

While the novel affords this multidimensional reflection on the nature of science, it also invites critical thinking with regard to the project of environmentalism itself, which may challenge some of the commitments students bring to the class. Piya pays particular attention to examples of symbiosis between humans and animals (139–40), and she not only studies dolphins but also develops a positive identification with them: her occasional sightings of a mother and calf arguably sentimentalize the dolphin and certainly echo the novel's treatment of Piya's relationship to her own mother. Yet the animal world encompasses much more than Piya's friendly dolphin species (the nonthreatening cousins of the killer orcas from the Puget Sound next to Seattle, where she grew up). In the backstory account of Nirmal and Nilima's early years in Lusibari, we read that "[n]o day seemed to pass without news of someone being killed by a tiger, a snake or a crocodile" (67). Such fatalities, however, only occur because of the intrusion of human settlement into the natural habitats of these species. *The Hungry Tide* thus stages a structural conflict between the natural environment with its species diversity and the spatial requirements for human habitation, or, phrased differently, between animal rights and human needs.

This collision of contradictory values becomes explicit in the discussion of the Bengal tiger nature preserve, which poses a threat to the human population. Yet the protection of the endangered species is government policy and is supported by influential international environmentalist groups, despite the danger of the preserve to the locals. *The Hungry Tide* highlights the problem in the chapters "A Killing" and "Interrogation," when a "mob" (239) of villagers captures and brutally kills a tiger that has caused two deaths. Piya is outraged by what she perceives as a cruel act of vengeance, but Fokir prevents her from intervening. Kanai later scolds her for having expected Fokir to share her Western environmentalist values concerning animal life: "Did you think he was some kind of grass-roots ecologist? He's not. He's a fisherman—he kills animals for a living" (245). By having Kanai fault Piya for projecting her value system onto Fokir, despite their cultural differences and the immense gap in the resources available to each of them, *The Hungry Tide* challenges environmentalist readers to reflect on their own underlying assumptions and their political implications.

The villagers' slaughter of the marauding tiger and the subsequent exchange between Kanai and Piya stands in a dialectical relation to a larger historical event, the Morichjhãpi incident of May 1979, the primary focus of Nirmal's notebook. Refugees from Bangladesh settled illegally on Morichjhãpi Island in the Sundarbans, believing they would be tolerated by the state government, which instead chose to condemn them as squatters intruding in a forest preserve. On a grander scale than in the "Killing" chapter, through Nirmal's narration we confront the conflict between environmentalism and human rights. In Nirmal's account, the settlers attempt to establish an orderly society that echoes the utopian plans that had led to the establishment of Lusibari a century earlier (141). Nonetheless, the state lays siege to the island and eventually removes the settlers by force, resulting in a significant (but undetermined) number of deaths (99). Kusum, who has joined the refugees, comments to Nirmal and clarifies the underlying values conflict:

> *"This island has to be saved for its trees, it has to be saved for its animals, it is a part of a reserve forest, it belongs to a project to save tigers, which is paid for by people from all around the world." Every day, sitting here with hunger gnawing at our bellies, we would listen to these words over and over again. Who are these people, I wondered, who love animals so much that they are willing to kill us for them?* (217).

Kusum's speech in this chapter, aptly entitled "Crimes," is a high point in the critical reflection that *The Hungry Tide* brings to bear on environmentalism. The values conflict is rich and complex, a productive point of discussion when teaching the novel. Students can explore tensions between conservationism and human rights and thereby encounter complexities of which they may not have been previously aware. Is the project of protecting nature and preserving resources inimical to the immediate needs of local populations? How do we measure animal lives against human ones? How should we weight the significance of each side in the binary? Yet that binary, animals versus humans, should itself be interrogated. Biologically, humans, of course, are also animals, but to say that humans in some instances behave like animals is a profoundly pejorative characterization, as captured in the adage *homo homini lupus*, that humans treat each other like wolves, i.e., viciously. Nilima names this inversion when she chides Kanai for his perpetual womanizing: "Who can blame the tigers when predators like you pass for human beings?" (202). However, it is again Kusum's eloquence that names the beastly quality of human society in which a law of the jungle appears to prevail: "this whole world had become a place of animals, and our fault, our crime, was that we were just human beings, trying to live as human beings always have, from the water and the soil. No one could think this a crime unless they have forgotten that this is how humans have always lived—by fishing, by clearing land and by planting the soil" (217).

The passage entails complex cultural criticism with which students should engage in discussion or essays. Kusum's discourse suggests that the larger social forces—the state, the international environmental groups, and "the world"—act violently, in the manner of animals, because they have "forgotten" the core of the human condition. In that case, is there evidence that *The Hungry Tide* tries to remember what has been lost in order to pursue a just society? Does the novel have an anamnestic character? Nirmal explains that he writes his diary for the sake of memory since "[n]o one knows better than I how skillful the tide country is in silting over its past" (59).

Alternatively, Kusum's defense of the refugees could be questioned from a deep ecological point of view. Her insistence that humans continue "clearing land" and "planting the soil" might be read as a program for unlimited resource consumption: are the land and the soil to be viewed only as resources for human use? To defend the refugees by answering in the affirmative effectively negates consideration of broader ecological perspectives, such as Leopold's mandate to recognize a biotic community in which all elements of nature, humans among others, coexist. From this point of view, Piya was right to protest the killing of the tiger, and Kanai's argument that the villagers have their own distinctive cultural perspective would lose validity in the face of the assertion of the intrinsic value and hypothetical priority of animal life.

Other students may choose to research the Morichjhāpi incident itself as a microcosm of larger issues in Bengali and Indian politics. We have already seen how the novel names the Sundarbans as "the trailing threads of India's fabric," suggesting that the geography and the narrative located there also convey a national history. That history is embedded in the international border between India and Bangladesh, a legacy of the 1947 Partition, and the fundamental precondition of the refugee status of the settlers at Morichjhāpi. Activists and other politically inclined students will find intriguing essay material in the repeated discussion of the relative value of reformist initiatives on the one hand and revolutionary militancy on the other. This plays out between Nilima, who builds up a hospital to ameliorate the lives of the local inhabitants, and Nirmal, who still nurtures the revolutionary aspirations of his youth and believes he can recover them in the illegal occupation of Morichjhāpi (178–80). The choice plays out on another level as well, in the contrast between the utopian project of Sir Hamilton (42), founder of Lusibari (a project that is echoed in the refugees' idealistic self-organization), and the Bengali government that suppresses the spontaneous initiative on the island through an explicitly designated "Left Front ministry" (99). Many students today show an increased interest in political engagement, and this treatment of competing political strategies sets the stage for productive discussions about the differences between gradual improvement and revolutionary projects, and between utopianism and state authority.

Such explicitly political inquiries into the novel can lead back to some fundamental literary and aesthetic questions as they concern Nirmal, who aspired to a career as a writer before becoming a schoolmaster and who in his notebook describes himself as torn "between the quiet persistence of everyday change and the heady excitement of revolution—between prose and poetry" (180). This mapping of reform onto prose (like the novel as genre) and revolution onto poetry reveals Nirmal's own peculiar romantic Marxism, but it can also provide an opening for questions of aesthetics and politics, the intellectual constellation that occupies Nirmal and explains why he directly names a series of poets: Thakur (45) and "Blake, Mayakovsky and Jibanananda Das" (64). Students can be asked to research these poets and try to determine their significance for Nirmal. Yet the one poet who overshadows all the others is Rainer Maria Rilke: Nirmal has the habit of concluding many of his journal comments with a citation from *Duino Elegies*. The selections typically gloss the topic of the respective entry. Thus, for example, at the end of the chapter "Blown Ashore," the Rilke verse "such disinherited ones to whom neither the past nor the future belongs" refers to the refugees whom Nirmal describes as "these thousands of people who wanted nothing more than to plunge their hands once again in our soft, yielding tide country mud" (137). An exercise in close reading can involve students ferreting out each of these connections between the Rilke citations and their contexts. More generally, however, the prominence of Rilke and the allusions to the other poets provide an opportunity to raise questions about genre and the differential capacities of prose and poetry. Both on this level of formal genre reflections and in the thematic discussions of the environment, *The Hungry Tide* has the capacity to engage student readers in important discussions about form and content that can carry over into readings of other novels as well.

NOTE

[1] This essay quotes the 2005 Houghton Mifflin Harcourt edition of *The Hungry Tide*.

Teaching Humor in
a General Education Classroom
with *In an Antique Land*

Adele Holoch

How do we encounter others as scholars, as travelers, as citizens of the world? How do we approach and recognize difference across intellectual, ethnic, and cultural borders? How does laughter make difference more marked, and how can it also foster connections through and beyond that difference? These questions are central to the general education literature and core curriculum courses I teach, where I incorporate postcolonial literature and theory, together with humor theory, as foundations for exploring them. Postcolonial theory, as Robert Young writes, is concerned with "the relations between ideas and practices: relations of harmony, relations of conflict, generative relations between different peoples and their cultures" (7), and in the classroom we consider how those relations impact the individuals on either side. For the first- and second-year students who take my courses as a general education requirement, Amitav Ghosh's *In an Antique Land* offers a lively literary basis for our questions. Published in 1992, Ghosh's narrative, variously identified as travelogue, ethnography, and historiography, was inspired by an intellectually and creatively invigorating reading experience of Ghosh's own. As an undergraduate at Oxford, Ghosh became so intrigued by the contents of two letters he read in the volume *Letters of Medieval Jewish Traders* that a year later he set off for Egypt to undertake historical and ethnographic research into the world of their author, a twelfth-century merchant from Aden. Through the encounters Ghosh chronicles, together with theoretical foundations in Edward Said's *Orientalism* and Henri Bergson's and Sigmund Freud's work on humor, my classes gain new perspectives on our roles as scholars and travelers.

We begin with ideas of humor, community, and otherness, drawing on Bergson's influential paper "Laughter: An Essay on the Meaning of the Comic," which introduces the notion of humor as a social corrective. Bergson argues that laughter reinforces the boundaries of a group when the group uses it to correct the behavior of an individual who has deviated from the expectations of the collective. I also introduce Said's *Orientalism*, highlighting Said's notion of the Orient as a body of knowledge, "a 'fact' which, if it develops, changes, or otherwise transforms itself in the way that civilizations frequently do, nevertheless is fundamentally, even ontologically stable" (40). These ideas of collective identity—of communities working, through laughter, to reinforce their boundaries, and of approaching the other as an ontologically stable entity—are of particular importance in my second-year core curriculum course, a class on colonialism and Western identity focused on how the West has defined itself through encounters with the colonial other. Working from these foundations, my students and I interrogate our understanding of ourselves as a "we" encountering the text together: what collective identity (or identities) do we assume, what ideas or assumptions do we share, and how does the diversity of cultural backgrounds in the classroom, together with the other personal, academic, and professional experiences and interests that make us disparate, change or challenge that identity? How do these similarities and differences inform our responses to texts, particularly when that response is laughter? I then introduce *In an Antique Land*, and together we examine Ghosh's journeys across generic and cultural boundaries, considering how Ghosh invites us, through his humorous self-representation and his play with those boundaries, to reflect on the strength of the borders that divide us and to consider their dynamic nature as well as the perpetual instability of the communities, and individuals, within them.

We begin by discussing generic categorizations: How are ethnographies defined, and what role does the ethnographer generally play in shaping the narrative? What is a historiography? What boundaries delimit the difference between narrative nonfiction and fiction, how have those boundaries been challenged, and how might establishing such a difference impact readers' relationships with the encounters and the supposed facts the text presents? I then invite students to try categorizing Ghosh's work. If they identify it as a historiography, pointing to his lengthy intervals of research into twelfth-century Egyptian culture, I ask them to consider Ghosh's incorporation of his ethnographic experiences. How does the presence of personal narrative challenge our faith in the author as a historical researcher? If the work is, as Neelam Srivastava argues, "firmly anchored to the formal characteristics of narrative fiction" (46), what are those characteristics? How do Ghosh's allegiances to these characteristics and his identification as a writer of fiction—in one interview, Ghosh acknowledges that "[i]n the first instance I think of myself as a novelist. I don't think of myself as an academician" ("Between the Walls" 9)—shape our reception of the information he at least superficially presents as stable, fixed truth? Drawing on my students' training in the rhetorical concepts of logos, ethos, and pathos, we interrogate the credibility of Ghosh's narrative self, an interrogation he invites through his explicitly and implicitly humorous self-presentation.

Ghosh was twenty-three when he arrived in the small Egyptian village of Lataifa to begin ethnographic research toward his doctoral degree in social anthropology. One of the narrative's more broadly comic moments comes from an encounter with Jabir, a teenage relative of Ghosh's landlord, who teases him mercilessly when Ghosh is unfamiliar with the word Jabir uses for sex, concluding that Ghosh is also unfamiliar with the act itself. "He doesn't know a thing," Jabir tells a friend. "Not religion, not politics, not sex, just like a child. . . . That's why he's always asking questions" (64).[1] Jabir and his friend also tease Ghosh about his unfamiliarity with the expression "beating the ten," using gestures to give him "a fair idea of its meaning," and question him about his culture's practices of circumcision and shaving (62). Conducted among young men roughly the same age as many of my students, and concerning a topic that is at once private and common in conversation among friends, these exchanges facilitate varying degrees of intimacy with the readers in my classroom. Through their laughter—whether at Ghosh or at Jabir, whether reading on their own or recounting their impressions in our discussions—they become more conscious (sometimes uncomfortably) of their positions in relation to the characters and to one another. Are they laughing at Ghosh, rendered other by an unfamiliar expression? Are they laughing at Jabir, for coming to the conclusion he does? Writing of the humor in *In an Antique Land* in the essay "Laughing Out of Place," Christi Ann Merrill discusses Freud's "triangle of alliances," the triangulation between the individual who makes the joke, the subject of the joke, and the audience of the joke—"the third person, who has made no efforts, and bears witness to laughter" (Freud 103). As we examine the exchange with Jabir, I encourage students to consider their own position as that third person and to give that position—as Merrill writes—its "due attention . . . as interpreters" (117). Whose assumptions, if any, are mistaken, and what allegiances do they, the audience, draw upon to make that claim?

Merrill turns to Wayne Booth's *The Rhetoric of Irony* to further theorize the positionalities of the reader and the "implied author" and their alliance against a narrator whose worldview the reader rejects (112). She refers to Ghosh "as he was then," suggesting that Ghosh, the older, wiser "implied author," portrays the experiences of his younger self with a certain degree of irony. In class, I introduce definitions of irony, from Samuel Johnson's *Dictionary* entry ("a mode of speech in which the meaning is contrary to the words") to Booth's more elaborate explications. Booth argues that, while reading irony is in some ways analogous to translating, it requires more from a reader than that, engaging with readers' and ironists' shared unspoken assumptions (*Rhetoric of Irony* 33). We also consider Booth's discussion, in *The Rhetoric of Fiction*, of narrative unreliability, which Booth writes is not "ordinarily a matter of lying" but rather "most often a matter of what [Henry] James calls *inconscience*; the narrator is mistaken, or he believes himself to have qualities which the author denies him" (159). Drawing again on students' training in rhetorical concepts, I ask them to consider how Ghosh presents himself as a character, to examine what kinds of authority he gives himself or what kinds of authority we readily grant him as readers. We turn to his representations of other educated individuals in the text, such as Ustaz Mustafa, an Egyptian lawyer who speaks in literary Arabic and who professes to know all about India because "I read all about [it] when I was in college in Alexandria" (46). Despite Ustaz Mustafa's avowals of his own education, he is comically ignorant about Indian culture, declaring that "[t]here is a lot of chilli in the food and when a man dies his wife is dragged away and burnt alive" (46) and expressing his bafflement around Ghosh's religion: "What is this 'Hinduki' thing? I have heard of it before and I don't understand it. If it is not Christianity nor Judaism nor Islam what can it be?" he queries, before asking if Ghosh is like the magi and worships fire (47). As readers aligned with Ghosh as implied author, we are likely to laugh at Ustaz Mustafa's ignorance; but we may also be inclined to laugh at Ghosh's youthful narrator, who shares some likeness to Ustaz Mustafa in the sweep of his presumed knowledge.

With Ghosh's narrative figure, that sweep can be particularly evident in the conclusions he comes to about the Egyptian community he visits. At one point in the narrative, he contemplates the community's capacity to comprehend the violence that profoundly impacted him in his childhood. He recalls that, during Partition, "a mob of hundreds of men, their faces shining red in the light of the burning torches in their hands," rioted outside his family's house (208). After he reflects on that experience, he writes that the members of his Egyptian community cannot possibly understand how "theirs was a world that was far gentler, far less violent, very much more humane and innocent than mine" (210). I juxtapose that passage with an account earlier in the narrative, when Ghosh learns that a man has been murdered for refusing to move from a swing. According to "the ancient, immutable law of the Arabs," Ghosh writes, the murdered man's family can now declare a blood feud. As Jabir explains to Ghosh, under *thâr*, the law of feud, and *damm*, the law of blood, the family can kill all the male kin on the paternal side of the murderer's family in revenge. "'All that for pushing a man off a swing?' I ask, bleary-eyed," Ghosh writes (69). He adds, "I was somehow very doubtful, but for all the attention Jabir paid me, I could have been a six-year-old child" (70). While the paired passages are not overtly humorous, the commonalities they share with passages that are more broadly comic—and the reiteration of Jabir's sense that Ghosh, the ever-questioning ethnographer, is "like a child"—underscore our sense that perhaps Ghosh's narrative figure should not be taken as seriously as it would seem. Even if we do not laugh at him here—and, as I ask in class, do humor and irony in fact need to generate laughter to serve the functions we have outlined?—does their ironic juxtaposition destabilize his ideas, particularly the breadth of his conclusions about another community? Does it undermine Ghosh's credibility as an ethnographer or a historiographer? Does acknowledging the human capacity to make mistakes, to be inclined toward such broad assumptions, in fact undermine him, or does it add complexity to our understanding of the process of researching, learning about, or "knowing" another culture? Finally, and more broadly, how does bringing together these disparate passages—preserving their difference but putting them in conversation with each other—affect our understanding of them both?

I have taught at the University of Iowa and Champlain College, institutions where the student body is largely homogenous and where many students may not yet have much experience with traveling. There, students are sometimes inclined to ask: What is the purpose of intercultural encounter? If the borders between us remain so clearly demarcated, if our assumptions about one another and about other cultures seem intractable, why examine them? Why cross them and engage in these conversations? Another literary text I incorporate in my second-year Colonialism and Western Identity course, E. M. Forster's *A Passage to India*, ends with the Indian doctor Aziz and his British friend Fielding deciding that the friendship they desire cannot be sustained. In spite of their well-intentioned efforts to connect across cultural differences, the differences and divisions between them remain too great; even if India achieves nationhood and drives the British out, the earth itself will rise up and resist their alliance. Ghosh comes to a similar conclusion after a conversation with an imam escalates to an argument in which the imam declares the practice of burning the dead "a primitive and backward custom" and calls Ghosh a savage (235). The two men then engage in a shouting match over the superiority of each culture's weapons. In Ghosh's words, "the Imam and I had participated in our own final defeat, in the dissolution of the centuries of dialogue that had linked us: we had demonstrated the irreversible triumph of the language that has usurped all the others in which people once discussed their differences" (236). But when Ghosh returns home with the friend who accompanied him on his encounter, Khamees, his friend turns to him, laughing. Khamees tells Ghosh not to be upset, then teasingly promises to accompany him to India when Ghosh returns there. "But if I die there you must remember to bury me," Khamees says (237). Khamees's reference recalls the conflict; it does not erase it or gloss over the differences revealed. They remain marked, but conversation and laughter are still possible: the men remain friends.

As we conclude our discussion of *In an Antique Land*, we return to Said's *Orientalism*, where, in his introduction, the theorist calls for "the slow working together of cultures that overlap, borrow from each other, and live together" and argues that such peaceful collaboration can be accomplished through "time, patient and sceptical inquiry, supported by faith in communities of interpretation that are difficult to sustain in a world demanding instant action and reaction." For my students, I contend that this vision is what makes intercultural encounter worthwhile across the challenges of difference and division, even, and perhaps especially, when those divisions feel profound and distinct. Writing in one passage of his experiences as an outsider in an Egyptian community, Ghosh discusses how he was told not to fast during Ramadan, because he is not a Muslim. He marvels at the idea of millions of people all over the world turning to face the same point in the sky, saying the same words of prayer, and performing the same prostrations. He understands that "to belong to that immense community was a privilege which they had to re-earn every year, and the effort made them doubly conscious of the value of its boundaries" (76). Ghosh is not denying the presence of those boundaries or trying to break them down. He is a traveler within them, and his journeys there have led him to a more complex understanding of himself. That understanding is not stable. One of the beauties of Ghosh's ironic self-presentation, the play between the implied author and

Ghosh's narrative self, is that it is difficult to know what he has learned and what he is still in the process of learning. For students contemplating their own ideas of self and identity, both within and outside the contexts of the classroom, this in itself is a valuable question.

NOTE

[1] This essay uses the 1992 Granta edition of *In an Antique Land.*

Empty-Belly and Full-Stomach Environmentalism in the Introductory Literature Class: Teaching *The Hungry Tide* in the Anthropocene

Jonathan Steinwand

At my small Minnesota college, located on the border with the get-rich-quick, drilling-and-fracking-boom state of North Dakota, I have heard it stated that jobs are more important than ecosystems, that the poor cannot afford to worry about the environment, and that it is elitist for environmentalists to insist that the poor protect the environment to their own detriment. Public and academic discourse provide variations on these arguments. But the subaltern speaks in a way that we need to learn to hear. Ramachandra Guha and Joan Martínez-Alier[1] have developed a useful distinction between the full-stomach environmentalism of the rich and privileged on the one hand and the empty-belly environmentalism of the poor and disenfranchised on the other hand. Although this distinction encourages a polarization that should not go unexamined, the contrast illumines the terrain of conflict over development and conservation projects throughout the world. By attending to the way in which literature engages such crucial debates, students become aware of how the study of literature can help them gain perspective on the global issues that have vital implications for how we negotiate a socially and environmentally just future.

Guha and Martínez-Alier's distinction can be usefully applied in the introductory environmental literature class to Amitav Ghosh's *The Hungry Tide*. The class I teach is English 165: Global Literature and Environmental Justice, which introduces students from a wide range of majors to the study of literature through environmentally engaged fiction, poetry, drama, and nonfiction. (For details on the study of poetry in this course, see my article "Teaching Environmental Justice Poetry in the Anthropocene.") The course begins with a screening and discussion of James Cameron's *Avatar*, which sets a tone for subsequent reading and discussion. Students readily connect the attack on the Na'vi with the colonial exploitation of indigenous peoples. Likewise, they quickly see the parallels between the pursuit of "unobtainium" and the race for extraction of natural resources in our own history and in our present moment. I emphasize these connections through short videos (Cameron, *Message*; Survival International, "Real *Avatar*") and related readings (Survival International, "Victory"; Joni Adamson). With a little prompting, students see the problems inherent in a plot that follows the white male savior fantasy pattern.[2] Yet despite (and certainly also because of) this particular flaw in the film, *Avatar* prepares students well for subsequent works in the course. We compare the character Grace Augustine with Dr. Thomas Stockmann in Henrik Ibsen's *An Enemy of the People* and later with Piyali Roy in Ghosh's novel to see that all three of these scientists are so dedicated to their science that they follow what they learn in their fields to fight against the unyielding greed and small-mindedness of politicians and businessmen. Like Dr. Stockmann, who is labeled an enemy of the people, Jake Sully is accused of betraying his race. By the end of the course, students are in a position to consider whether Crake in Margaret Atwood's *MaddAddam* trilogy deserves our condemnation or praise for using science against humanity.[3]

By looking at Nadine Gordimer's "The Ultimate Safari" along with Rob Nixon's reading of the story in *Slow Violence and the Environmentalism of the Poor* and William Cronon's essay "The Trouble with Wilderness," students begin to consider the global politics of wildlife conservation. To enrich the discussion, we can draw on the Leonardo DiCaprio–produced[4] Netflix documentary *Virunga*, in which the mountain gorillas and a national park are imperiled by oil development, a civil war, and the violence associated with these activities (von Einseidel). And we can connect the discussion to the media frenzy over the Minnesota dentist, Dr. Walter Palmer, who spent $55,000 to track down and kill Cecil the Lion in Zimbabwe. The talk show host Jimmy Kimmel's outrage over the death is worth showing to students raised on *The Lion King* (see Bradley, for example), but the case of Cecil the Lion was also a social media phenomenon in the summer of 2015, and one valuable activity is having students track down their favorite responses to the story from the weeks following the media frenzy. National Public Radio, for example, ran a story that argued for the positive role of big-game hunting in conservation economics and politics (Northam), including a conservation organization official who distinguishes law-abiding big-game hunters from poachers—and who repeats the same decontextualized black poacher trope as perpetuated in nature shows such as *Mutual of Omaha's Wild Kingdom*. Nixon provides South African context for the history of this demonization of the local poacher:

> The colonial rescripting of wildlife scarcity as a black problem—which helped rationalize the early twentieth-century creation of national parks—depended on demonizing blacks as barbarous poachers whose relationship to wildlife was one of illegality and threat while depending, conversely, on mythologizing whites as stewards of nature whose conservationist principles evidenced a wider civilizational superiority. (*Slow Violence* 190)

Once these discussions have been introduced, students are ready to dig further into these approaches by getting to know the characters in Ghosh's novel.[5]

Cronon argues that the idea of wilderness developed out of a romanticized idea of the wild being untouched by human civilization (79). He points to eighteenth- and nineteenth-century philosophers and writers who determined that encounters with the sublime in nature provide psychological if not also spiritual re-creation of the human soul (73). Equipped with this modern approach to nature, European settlers in North America and their descendants, like Theodore Roosevelt, sought to set aside sublime landscapes as wilderness recreation areas or national wildlife sanctuaries. Often the indigenous inhabitants had to be evicted to meet the standard of this idea of wilderness. The natural biodiversity of these areas was conceived of as a national treasure; then, with the automobility of the twentieth century, these national parks, as Cronon documents, increasingly became tourist destinations (73). Guha argues that the flavor of environmentalism that develops in the global North thus results in a paradox:

> The uncertain commitment of most nature lovers to a more comprehensive environmental ideology is illustrated by the puzzle that they are willing to drive thousands of miles, using scarce oil and polluting the atmosphere, to visit national parks and sanctuaries—thus using anti-ecological means to travel to marvel at the beauty of forests, swamps, or mountains protected as specimens of a "pristine" and "untouched" nature. (367–68)[6]

The white tourists haunting the margins of Gordimer's story provide a point of departure that readies students for the empty-belly perspective. When students read "The Ultimate Safari," full-stomach environmentalism, which holds wilderness as the sanctuary where one goes to encounter the sublime for spiritual rejuvenation, is challenged by the empty-belly, first-person perspective of a war refugee, whose community has already been split for the sake of establishing Kruger National Park.

In *Varieties of Environmentalism: Essays North and South*, Guha and Martínez-Alier document how conflicts over development projects "pit 'ecosystem people'—that is, those communities which depend very heavily on the natural resources of their own locality—against 'omnivores,' individuals and groups with the social power to capture, transform and use natural resources from a much wider catchment area; sometimes, indeed, the whole world" (12). Drawing on the distinction and further discussions developing the distinction, I've worked with students to come up with a list (fig. 1).

The Hungry Tide provides the centerpiece of the course. Popular and current examples of the distinction reinforce the relevance of the point beyond the course texts, but it is through developing relationships with the characters who inhabit the Sundarbans ecosystem in Ghosh's substantial novel that the idea sinks in and students begin to listen for the voices of the subaltern. It is strategically ironic and telling, therefore, that we get only mediated access to Fokir's voice. Yet, through Fokir's actions, Kanai's translations, Horen's sense of place, Kusum's outrage (216–17), and the story of Bon Bibi, readers begin to understand the empty-belly perspective.[7] Nilima and Nirmal are our guides who mediate the empty-belly environmentalism of Fokir, Kusum, and Horen and the full-stomach perspective of Piya and Kanai.

The full-stomach perspective is exposed most clearly when Kanai and Piya discuss the tiger killing and Piya has her romanticized view of Fokir as a "grassroots ecologist" challenged (245). Kanai also pinpoints in this section the full-

Full-Stomach Environmentalism	Empty-Belly Environmentalism
Dominates the global North, though sometimes shared by elites and opportunists in the global South	More prominent in the global South, yet shared by a marginalized counterculture of poor and indigenous people in the North
Wealthy, elite, First World thinking	Poor, Third and Fourth World perspective
"Omnivores"—"industrialists, professionals, politicians, . . . government officials [and] rural elite" (Guha and Martínez-Alier 12) "living on the resources of other territories and peoples" (45)	"Ecosystem people"—"fisherfolk" (Guha and Martínez-Alier xxi), "small peasants, landless laborers, tribals, pastoralists, and artisans" (12) "living on their own resources" (45)
Mostly from cities and towns; little sense of being rooted in a place	Mostly rural but increasingly dispatched to city slums as "ecological refugees" (12)
Nature is a resource available for consumption: for recreation, retreat, pleasure, or extraction	Nature is home; creatures are relatives, fellow inhabitants populating foundational stories
Seeks to preserve wilderness and wildlife apart from civilization	Works for subsistence and survival in relation to environment
Often more attentive to the exotic and remote than the local and thus "willing to drive thousands of miles . . . to marvel at the beauty . . . of a 'pristine' and 'untouched' nature" (Ramachandra Guha 37–38)	Focused on local, small-scale projects, but aware of "conspicuously uneven development in the global-capitalist world" (Huggan and Tiffin 23)
Perpetuates "the myth of empty lands" (Nixon, "Environmentalism" 235)	Negotiates the dangers of living in the midst of nature
Motivated in part by imperialist nostalgia—the longing for that which we are destroying	Follows local traditional knowledge evolving over time
Science and technology will solve ecological problems; progressive sense of history	Follows traditional trades; circular or spiraling sense of history
Trade-off for prosperity requires environmental sacrifice zones (which should remain out of sight, out of mind; as far as is possible and NIMBY [not in my backyard])	Resilient communities organize to object to corporate and public projects that encroach without benefiting the local community
Thinks globally, acts globally—overlooks the local	Thinks locally, acts locally—less concerned about the global impacts
"always potentially vainglorious and hypocritical" (Huggan and Tiffin 2)	"often genuinely heroic and authentic" (Huggan and Tiffin 2)

Figure 1

stomach complicity in overlooking the poor who are displaced by wildlife conservation (248–49). Students can be asked to pinpoint further indications of the full-stomach perspective in these characters' sense of entitlement (8), their disproportionate wealth, their privilege of mobility, their assumptions (such as the young Kanai's expectation that the jungle would be uninhabited [15] or Piya's confidence that she is protected by her foreignness [30]), and Piya's sentimental attitudes about charismatic megafauna. The demonization of the local poacher by the Forest Department offers another example of how conservation politics disadvantage the ecosystem people (38–39). Once they finish the novel, students can also discuss how Piya and Kanai have both moderated their full-stomach perspectives.

In my essay "What the Whales Would Tell Us," I discuss Fokir's song and Kusum's outrage over the Morichjhāpi incident (192–95); some additional materials that can be used to emphasize the contemporary relevance of the Morichjhāpi massacre include the author's note to Ross Mallick's article "Refugee Resettlement in Forest Reserves," which Ghosh refers to as influential in inspiring the novel (332). I assign this article and discuss with students the creative conversation that develops between fiction and scholarship. I've found students perk up when I show a few World Wildlife Fund (WWF) Save Tigers Now advertisements and we examine the campaign's Web site together and track DiCaprio's investment and involvement in this and other projects.[7] Lest they think Morichjhāpi is merely an historical anomaly, we view the evidence provided by Canal Plus that shows the Baiga tribe recently evicted from the Kanha Tiger Reserve (Survival International, "Undercover TV"). Finally, it is worthwhile then to consider Survival International's Parks Need Peoples campaign, which seeks to

> stop ignoring the illegal eviction of tribal peoples from their ancestral homelands
>
> stop claiming tribal lands are wildernesses when they've been managed by tribal communities for millennia
>
> stop accusing tribespeople of poaching when they hunt to feed their families
>
> stop supporting logging, mining and other extractive industries—the real causes of environmental destruction ("Tribal Conservationists")

The point is not to shame the WWF or the Leonardo DiCaprio Foundation but to dig deeper into assumptions of what constitutes environmental justice for the rich and the poor in the world. We can also reflect together as a class on how easily full-stomach people can become complicit by not understanding and appreciating the local complexities of an issue.

Ghosh's short essay "A Crocodile in the Swamplands" is also useful in considering that the same government that destroyed the community of Morichjhāpi supported the Sahara group's tourist development project, which would have built an enormous five-star resort with every amenity you can think of right in the heart of the Sundarbans. Students find it refreshing to see Ghosh take a passionate stand on this issue and to learn that his writings contributed to the abandonment of the project. At the same time, discussion of the social and environmental costs of resort tourism can unsettle comfortably packaged mental images of the ideal vacation.

There is a nearly endless and ever-expanding list of cases instructors can use to illustrate full-stomach and empty-belly environmentalism. The pedagogically useful *Environmental Justice Atlas* provides a searchable map of environmental disputes around the world (Temper and Martínez-Alier). Besides reporting on spectacular disasters, however, the *EJAtlas* attends to how communities organize opposition and sometimes succeed in confronting not just spectacular violence but also the slow violence of extractive industries. Although it is far from comprehensive, the *EJAtlas* provides an effective visualization of the global implications of environmental injustice through case studies. I have students explore the map on their own or in groups and report how specific cases demonstrate and complicate the distinction between empty-belly and full-stomach appetites for environmental justice. To illustrate the limitations of such a tool, I share a map of oil spills in North Dakota with my students. And I add in local examples of the Toxic Taters antipesticide movement and the Friends of the Headwaters opposition to the Sandpiper and Line 3 Pipelines in Minnesota. Another option would be to have student groups submit contributions to the *EJAtlas*.

Ghosh presents Nilima and Nirmal as our guides for mediating the gap between full-stomach self-satisfaction and empty-belly-aching. Nilima worries about how the new nets will affect the sustainability of Sundarbans fishing over time (111–12). Her women's union develops into an organization, the Badabon Trust, that serves the needs of the empty-belly community (68–69). Though he derides some of Nilima's work as "social service" (69, 320) that perpetuates the capitalist system, Nirmal brings his knowledge of the local history, weather, and climate to help make the Badabon Trust stronger. Furthermore, his idealism in support of the empty-belly cause of the Morichjhāpi refugees leaves an impression that inspires Kanai to mediate the two perspectives through his reconstruction of the story of Nirmal's notebook.

The story of Bon Bibi provides a final example that mediates the two perspectives. In an essay called "Wild Fictions," Ghosh holds up the legend of Bon Bibi as "a parable about the destructiveness of human greed" and as a model for what contemporary fiction can accomplish to counter the slow and spectacular violence of initiatives such as Project Tiger, which are based too much on the full-stomach idea of wilderness set apart from human beings. The key point for Ghosh is that nature must "be re-imagined in such a way as to restore the human presence within it—not as predator but partner—[and] this too must first be told as a story."[8]

By the end of the course, students have debated the advantages and disadvantages of both extremes of the empty-belly and full-stomach perspectives on the environment. There are empty bellies in the North groaning with concern about environmental health when corporate and public projects disproportionately dump pollution on people of color and the economically marginalized. Environmental racism in Flint, Michigan, and the Standing Rock Indian Reservation can be detailed as recent examples in the United States. There are Asian competitors for animal products and the conflict minerals used in our cell phones to complicate any simplified version of North vs. South.[9] As Graham Huggan and Helen Tiffin point out, "the opposing terms seem at once necessary and overblown, starkly distinct yet hopelessly entangled" (2). Students leave the course with a greater awareness of this entanglement, and they listen for the subaltern voice where it was not noticed before. The poetry, fiction, drama, and creative nonfiction discussed convey the urgency, the relevance, and the rich complexity of the issues at stake on our planet today. When these discussions take hold, students leave our classes confident that literature has the capacity to enlarge our understanding as we come to imagine how people, as Ghosh puts it, "inhabit a place"[10] and organize, when necessary, to confront environmental injustice.

NOTES

[1] Although *Varieties of Environmentalism* uses the name Juan, elsewhere Martínez-Alier goes by Joan.

[2] When I saw the film for the second time in the IMAX theater in Hyderabad, India, with students studying abroad, I realized that Jake Sully fulfills the fantasy of an entitled study abroad experience—his video logs; his love affair with the chief's daughter; his immersive learning of the Omaticaya language, food, traditions, skills, and religion; and his transformation from careless outsider to respected leader. For readings that criticize or broaden the context and application of the film's postcolonial message, see Joni Adamson; Bergthaller; "Head of State"; Justice; Newitz; and Žižek.

[3] I have used the first book in the trilogy, *Oryx and Crake*, but more frequently I have students read the second novel, *The Year of the Flood*. Whichever one I use, the other is at the top of students' reading lists by the end of the course, followed by the third book, *MaddAddam*.

[4] DiCaprio is listed as one of several executive producers, but it is worth noting that he is increasingly lending his name and his fortune to global conservation projects such as this and the World Wildlife Fund's Save the Tigers project. The Leonardo DiCaprio Foundation Web site provides an impressive testimony to the financial impact the foundation is having on global conservation projects and awareness. According to the site, "in addition to founding LDF, Leonardo also serves on the board of several environmental organizations[:] World Wildlife Fund, Natural Resources Defense Council, National Geographic's Pristine Seas, Oceans 5, and the International Fund for Animal Welfare" ("About Us").

[5] Although my course does not delve too much into the issue, we should acknowledge that the fantasy of the big-game hunter took hold through literature (think Hemingway) as much as literature like *The Hungry Tide* might work against such a fantasy to provide an alternative to the human-versus-nature conflict.

[6] Ramachandra Guha's critique is primarily a critique of deep ecology and thus reduces the diversity of environmentalisms active in Europe and North America. Eliza-

beth DeLoughrey and George Handley do a good job of unpacking the controversy in a useful way ("Toward an Aesthetics" 21–25).

[7] This essay uses the 2005 Houghton Mifflin Harcourt edition of *The Hungry Tide*.

[8] In a note to this passage, Ghosh acknowledges his debt to Guha, among others.

[9] For example, the Makah whale hunt (fictionalized by Linda Hogan in *People of the Whale*) was supposedly supported in part by Japanese whaling interests (Verhovek); some African elephant and rhinoceros poaching is motivated by demand in Chinese medical practices and a black market for ivory carving (Neale and Burton); and major electronics companies, including Apple, Samsung, and Sony, depend on child labor to mine cobalt in the Congo ("Exposed").

[10] In an interview for the audiobook of *The Hungry Tide*, Ghosh argues that "fiction . . . can help people inhabit a place—to inhabit it in the fullness of their minds, to inhabit it with their imaginations, to see the ways in which lives link together, the lives of animals, the lives of trees, the lives of human beings" ("Author Talks").

The Calcutta Chromosome in a Magical Realism Course

Ben Holgate

Amitav Ghosh's third novel, *The Calcutta Chromosome*, allows an examination of how magical realism operates in a text that transgresses multiple genres while also questioning the limits of magical realism as a tool for literary analysis. In the literature classroom, teachers may also use the book for other subjects, such as postcolonialism, world literature, intertextuality, or science fiction. In classrooms more generally, however, the novel has broad appeal, as it may be approached from a wide variety of nonliterary disciplines, including history, South Asian studies, and the history of science. Indeed, *The Calcutta Chromosome* as an educational resource is not unlike the nature of Ghosh's fiction: the exploration of one topic opens up new directions of inquiry for a plethora of other topics. The novel can easily turn out to be as much a quest for students as the intricately woven plots prove to be quests for its characters.

The Calcutta Chromosome represents a departure—albeit temporary—from Ghosh's usual sweeping historical, realist narratives set in Asia. In keeping with his other works, however, it incorporates Indian history and the ramifications of British colonization of the subcontinent, blending different genres within the same text. Variously described as a thriller, a detective story, a gothic melodrama, and a work of historiography, *The Calcutta Chromosome* is most commonly referred to as a work of science fiction, a view that was reinforced after the book won the Arthur C. Clarke Award for the best science fiction novel in the United Kingdom in 1997. Few critics, however, have identified, let alone investigated, the magical realist elements in the novel. Students should be encouraged to see this not as an impediment but rather as an opportunity to make their own critical evaluations without being encumbered by preexisting commentary. As Anne Hegerfeldt says in a completely different, although directly relevant, context: "If magic realism has not been found in fiction from Britain, it is not because it is not there, but because critics have not looked for it" (4).

It is important that *The Calcutta Chromosome* is taught in the framework of contemporary literary history. Ghosh's utilization of magical realist techniques positions him as a successor to Salman Rushdie in Indian fiction written in English. Rushdie's seminal magical realist novel, *Midnight's Children* (1981), marked what might be called the start of a second wave of magical realist fiction, often from formerly colonized territories, following the flourishing of the narrative mode in Latin American fiction from the 1940s, which culminated in Gabriel García Márquez winning the Nobel Prize in Literature in 1982. But whereas Rushdie's style of magical realism, especially in his early works, is noted for its overt supernatural elements, verbal pyrotechnics, and swirling narratives, Ghosh's form of magical realism is, as Maggie Ann Bowers says, "less exuberant, and less ubiquitous" (55); it is subtle and understated, with a mosaiclike structure and a strong textual core.

Critical theory on magical realist fiction is fraught with different and often conflicting opinions about definitions of the narrative mode and what it entails. While a seminar or short course focused on a single novel should avoid getting bogged down in this long-running debate, students ought to be given some guidance on a theoretical level about magical realism so they will have a critical foundation upon which to work. It also assists group discussion of the text if the students are working from the same starting point. I have found, when teaching tutorials and seminars on magical realist novels, that few students studying magical realist texts in a formal situation for the first time have a clear critical understanding of the narrative mode, although they often have an intuitive idea of what it is, based on previous reading of magical realist fiction. There are two working definitions that I usually provide to my students to help them on their way.

Lois Parkinson Zamora and Wendy Faris argue that magical realism presents the supernatural as "an ordinary matter, an everyday occurrence," in such a way that it is "integrated into the rationality and materiality of literary realism." The magic is not quixotic but "normative and normalizing" ("Daiquiri Birds" 3). (Incidentally, it is worth pointing out to the class that the anthology *Magical Realism*, edited by Zamora and Faris, remains one of the most informative critical books on magical realist theory, even after more than two decades.) Christopher Warnes, another leading theorist of magical realism, offers a slightly different definition, asserting that magical realism is "a mode of narration that naturalises or normalises the supernatural . . . a mode in which real and fantastic, natural and supernatural, are coherently represented in a state of equivalence" (3). From these two basic definitions students can glean the fundamental elements of magical realism: the magical or the supernatural is represented as quotidian; the magical is embedded within and emanates from literary realism; and the magical and realist discourses have equal weight, with neither dominating the other. It is the first and second points that distinguish magical realism from other kinds of fiction that also employ the supernatural, such as fantasy, gothic, or horror.

Ghosh employs magical realist episodes in two other novels, *The Circle of Reason* and *Sea of Poppies*, yet the magical realist elements are only incidental to these two books, whereas in *The Calcutta Chromosome* they are integral to the narrative.[1] The central supernatural factor is the discovery by Mangala, the illiterate Indian subaltern laboratory assistant who works for the British surgeon-scientist Ronald Ross, of a "weird strain" of malaria that can transfer human personality traits from one individual to another, thereby promising reincarnation and immortality. This malarial strain involves a chromosome, dubbed the Calcutta chromosome, that exists only in nonregenerative tissue or the brain (247).[2]

Through the character of Mangala, Ghosh creates an alternative historiography of Indian indigenous scientific knowledge. The novel posits a postcolonial revision of the accepted history of science, that the real-life Ross, who was employed by the British military during the height of the British Raj, was the sole discoverer of the cause of malaria while working in India in the late 1890s. Ross won the Nobel Prize in 1902 for revealing that the female *Anopheles* mosquito transmits the disease. Instead, Ghosh's text suggests Indian indigenous science complemented and assisted British colonial science in the race to determine malaria's roots in a process of cross-cultural fertilization. In the novel, Mangala is portrayed as an uneducated "genius" who has hit a roadblock in her own scientific inquiries about malaria and so pushes an unwitting Ross in the direction she wants him to go (242–43). In other words, while Ross may believe that he is experimenting on the mosquito, it is he himself who is the experiment (78). The novel therefore infers that the accepted history of Ross's "discovery" involved a colonial appropriation of localized scientific knowledge without attribution. It is on this point that the teacher may decide to branch out into broader topics, such as postcolonialism, historiography generally, or the history of science.

The Mangala-Ross subplot creates an opportunity for the teacher to address two common characteristics of magical realist fiction. The first is that the narrative mode enables writers to introduce alternative ontologies, as well as epistemologies, by exploiting the magical discourse that is juxtaposed with a realist discourse. This is a primary reason that writers from postcolonial territories—quite often former colonies of Britain, like India, Australia, Canada, and certain African and Caribbean countries—are attracted to magical realism as a vehicle by which to challenge orthodox and often Western-derived views of the world. Magical realist fiction, as Hegerfeldt observes, "insists that the concept of reality cannot be confined to the empirically perceivable"; as such, the narrative mode "re-evaluates modes of knowledge production generally rejected within the dominant Western paradigm" by depicting as real "metaphors, stories, dreams or magical beliefs" (3).

The second common characteristic is the utilization of magical realism within historiographic metafiction. I am drawing here on Linda Hutcheon's concept of fiction that lays claim to historical events and people but also involves a "theoretical self-awareness of history and fiction as human constructs" by rethinking and reworking past forms and contents (5). The artifice of history is foregrounded in the fictional text in order to question the historical record's authenticity and reliability. As Ato Quayson says, "In magical realism, historiographic metafiction often also embraces various processes and contradictions by which the historical is established, producing . . . a structure of (absurdist) feeling with respect to history" (749). Students may be steered toward other magical realist novels that incorporate historiographic metafiction, in particular *Midnight's Children*, which imagines an alternative history to India following independence in 1947, or Toni Morrison's *Beloved*, which examines the ramifications of slavery in the years immediately after the American Civil War. In *The Calcutta Chromosome*, Ghosh's narrative conceit is that Ross never appears in the text directly but rather exists as an unseen character offstage. Instead,

Mangala and Lutchman, her fellow assistant in Ross's lab, are foregrounded in the narrative.

Teaching on the historiographic structure of the novel needs to incorporate Ghosh's ingenious architecture of intertextuality, which is such a distinctive, if not unique, feature of the book. Indeed, the structure is so intricate that *The Calcutta Chromosome* could also be taught as a primary text in a course on intertextuality. For those students unfamiliar with the literary concept, I usually point them to Julia Kristeva's definition, built on Bakhtinian theory, that the literary word is "an intersection of textual surfaces" (36) that operates as a dialogue in three dimensions in terms of the writer, the addressee (or the character), and the cultural context (either contemporary or antecedent). In Kristeva's analysis, "any text is constructed as a mosaic of quotations; any text is the absorption and transformation of another" (37).

Ghosh mines the historical colonial archives and goes a step further by creating the novel's own alternative colonial archive. The "key intertext," as Anshuman Mondal notes, is the real-life Ross's *Memoirs*, which the novel reads "against the grain in order to deconstruct and displace it" (*Amitav Ghosh* 55). Ross's autobiographical writings provide an excellent opportunity for students to undertake a close reading of a primary, historical source and compare that with Ghosh's postcolonial revisionism. What stands out in *Memoirs* is Ross's depiction of himself as an isolated hero on a quest to solve the malaria riddle, battling an ignorant and uninterested British bureaucracy. Just as important, the actual Ross acknowledges that a Lutchman worked in his lab for three years, until 1898, and laments that they never had contact afterward (360). He also says that prior to his own research some local "savants" "had *suggested* that the mosquito carries the [malaria] infection in some way" (125). The point here is that Ross, in his memoirs, pays tribute to indigenous Indian science in respect to identifying the cause of malaria, while the novel portrays the British scientist as co-opting indigenous scientific knowledge without attribution. We know that Ghosh, during his own research, had read Ross's lab notes and diaries, focusing on how "most of the connections (he [Ross] made) came from his servants" (Silva and Tickell 220). The task for students, then, is to ask why Ghosh misrepresents Ross. The answer, clearly, lies in Ghosh's desire to restore indigenous knowledge to its place in the history of science.

Ghosh, however, does not just rely on Ross's *Memoirs* but builds on the original, historical documents by inventing a variety of fictional sources, such as journal entries, diaries, scientific notes, letters, e-mails, and oral recollections, attributed to different characters. Many of these imagined texts come from the Indian character L. Murugan, a former principal archivist at the mysterious nonprofit organization LifeWatch, a global public health consultancy and epidemiological data bank based in New York (8, 34). Murugan is obsessed with Ross and takes leave of his job in the United States to travel to Calcutta to pursue his theory that Mangala was really behind Ross's malaria discovery. Murugan disappears and is thought to have committed suicide (33). However, Murugan's decayed ID card resurfaces at an indeterminate time in the early twenty-first century, prompting his former colleague, the Egyptian-born Antar, a programmer and systems analyst in New York, to embark on his own quest to determine what happened to Murugan, with the help of LifeWatch's supercomputer, Ava. Murugan's unpublished 1987 paper about a "secret history" of malaria research is one of a number of Murugan's texts that Ava reproduces (35). Magical realist fiction, as Faris says, "conjures a narrative space" that she dubs the "ineffable in-between." It is a space in which "the realistic and the magical coexist," and it is ineffable because "its perspective cannot be explained, only experienced" (*Ordinary Enchantments* 45–46). Ghosh's exploration of the space between the actual colonial archive and his imagined indigenous archive generates much of the magical realism of the novel, creating a mosaiclike structure and a strong textual core.

The Calcutta Chromosome has four major interlocking narratives that interweave their respective times and geographies. The plot is driven by Antar's quest from New York sometime in the early twenty-first century to determine what happened to Murugan. Murugan generates the main action narrative with his own quest in Calcutta in 1995 to ascertain what happened in Ross's laboratory a century before. The third narrative involves Ross's race to discover the cause of malaria in 1890s India. The fourth narrative revolves around the supernatural reincarnation quest of Mangala and Lutchman (and their twenty-first-century counterparts, Urmila and Sonali), who exist outside time and space. Thus the novel is structured around four separate yet interwoven quest narratives, three of which are embedded within particular times and geographies and one of which floats beyond temporal and terrestrial limitations. This complex mosaic enables Ghosh to transgress historical periodization, cultural barriers, and continental divides in order to question assumptions about epistemology and teleology. What is it that we know, and how do we know it? Is collective knowledge a progressive accumulation of facts and insights that moves forward in a linear fashion, or is it intuited randomly through forces beyond our limited understanding? The multiple-narrative structure of *The Calcutta Chromosome* makes the story ahistorical, allowing it to transcend horological and cultural specificity. The novel is therefore quintessentially magical realist in its disruption of time and place, but at the same time it is not bound by its cultural context. This is an important point for students to understand, because magical realism is often thought of as emanating from a specific cultural setting, a view that is largely due to the narrative mode being originally associated with Latin American fiction. Ghosh's book, however, demonstrates that the supernatural elements can also emanate from an epistemological kind of magical realism, which is often characterized by metafictional techniques.

Finally, what should also be highlighted in the classroom in regard to *The Calcutta Chromosome* is the question of how effective magical realism is as a tool for literary analysis. This is a basic issue that unfortunately often goes unremarked in critical commentary on magical realism, both by those who champion the narrative mode and by those who reject it. Students should make up their own minds, as the answer is by no means clear-cut. At issue is whether magical realism helps define the text or acts as a hindrance, preventing the critic from recognizing other elements within the text that are not magical realist and that may in fact be more representative of the author's artistic expression. Given that *The Calcutta Chromosome* ranges across a variety of genres, as outlined above, are those genres more indicative of the poetics operating within the text than magical realism is? Or is magical realism as important as the other generic forms, if not perhaps more important, in regard to describing what occurs in Ghosh's writing? If the answer is the former, the corollary is that magical realism as a tool for literary analysis may have inherent limitations.

For further reading about critical theory on magical realism, in addition to Zamora and Faris's excellent anthology I refer students to Bowers's comprehensive overview, *Magic(al) Realism*; Warnes's insightful book on the narrative mode in a postcolonial context, *Magical Realism and the Postcolonial Novel: Between Faith and Irreverence*; and Faris's excellent monograph *Ordinary Enchantments: Magical Realism and the Remystification of Narrative*. Rushdie's *Midnight's Children* is a must-read for any student interested in postcolonial magical realism, as well as a companion text for *The Calcutta Chromosome*. García Márquez's canonical magical realist novel *One Hundred Years of Solitude* is required reading for any critical study of magical realism, given that it is so influential and has become a narrative template for many subsequent magical realist texts.

NOTES

[1] In *The Circle of Reason*, a warplane crashes into the grounds of a school in Bangladesh, causing the schoolmaster's wife to become pregnant, and the ghost of a dead sheik is said to save the migrant worker Alu when a building under construction collapses on him in the Persian Gulf. In *Sea of Poppies*, the Indian poppy farmer Deeti has a supernatural vision of a British trading ship in the mid–nineteenth century, while the Indian Baboo Nob Kissin believes his body becomes inhabited by his dead aunt while on that same ship.

[2] This essay uses the 2011 John Murray edition of *The Calcutta Chromosome*.

India and Its Diaspora's "Epic Relationship": Investigating Ghosh's Epic Genealogies in a World Literature Course

Sneharika Roy

In "The Diaspora in Indian Culture," Amitav Ghosh describes "the links be-tween India and her diaspora" as an "epic relationship" (247). Ghosh's insight regarding the "epic" nature of diaspora opens exciting pedagogical possibilities in a world literature course. While his transgeneric oeuvre has already stimu-lated a host of genre-based approaches, the perspective of epic has hitherto re-ceived little attention. Yet the canonical form of the epic, with its impulse to commemorate collective experience, runs through much of his work, particu-larly the multifamily, multigenerational diasporic sagas such as *The Shadow Lines* and *The Glass Palace*. I find his most explicit engagement with epic and its conventions in *Sea of Poppies* and the opening chapter of *River of Smoke*. In both cases, a family shrine becomes a metatextual metaphor for the ekphrastic enshrinement of the Indian migrants' genealogy. This diasporic ancestry harks back to the Indian homeland and spans the Indian Ocean, which had to be crossed to reach Mauritius. A transnational and culturally inclusive conception of epic thus emerges, one that is not quite that of traditional Western or Indian epic. Investigating *Sea of Poppies* in tandem with classical Western and Indian epic can allow readers to appreciate its place within an ancient, multistranded epic tradition (diachronic perspective); it can also serve as an indication of *Sea of Poppies*'s affinities with a contemporary trend of diasporic epic narratives in world literature (synchronic standpoint).

The premise that undergirds my pedagogical strategies is the following: Ghosh's redeployment of the epic convention of genealogy is both an act of clas-sical continuity and one of postcolonial discontinuity vis-à-vis the epic genre, resulting in the emergence of a new form, the "diasporic epic." Diasporic epic is conceived as a critical reengagement with, rather than a rejection of, national epics, typified by Virgil's *Aeneid* and Vālmīki's *Rāmāyaṇa*. Aeneas's and Rama's devotion to duty makes them ideal political ancestors for their national cul-tures, thereby linking personal and national genealogies. Diasporic epic rejects this specifically nationalistic, culturally "pure," and deterministic conception of ancestral roots. It reformulates ethnocentric identity in hybrid terms of trans-national inclusiveness, personal agency, and heightened self-reflexivity.

I propose beginning with Ghosh's conception of world literature, as reflected in "The March of the Novel through History," a fine starting point for a pre-liminary interrogation of world literature in a classroom context. Instead of a hard-and-fast definition of world literature, students can find thought-provoking metaphors. The bookcases of Ghosh's Calcutta-based grandfather, of the Bur-mese writer Mya Than Tint, and of the Indonesian author Pramoedya Ananta

Toer are filled with "masterpieces" of the English language as well as translations of nonanglophone Nobel Prize winners (290–93).[1] Significantly, the bookcase symbolizes, according to Ghosh, what the Bengali writer Bankim Chandra
Chatterjee articulates as an aesthetics of production based on "[i]mitation" and
cultural "borrowing" (298). It also concretizes the notion of an ideal reader,
embodied by the "fictional bookcase": its "vastness and cosmopolitanism . . .
requires novelists"—including Ghosh himself—"to locate themselves in relation
to it" (303). It is within this context of canons, cross-cultural imitation, and cosmopolitan reader expectations that the subject of epic genealogies derives its
pedagogical value.

Having delved into Ghosh's interpretation of world literature as an expression
of dislocated writing and reading practices, I would then broach the theme
of diasporic dislocation in *Sea of Poppies*. To bring home the reality of this
phenomenon, the UK National Archives Web site entry on "Indian Indentured
Labourers" may be used. Slippery distinctions between slavery (involuntary,
indefinite period) and indentured labor (based on a fixed-term contract but still
marked by "repression and abuse") are best negotiated in class through discussion. To illustrate the continuity between the triangular trade and indentured
labor, instructors may use the genealogy of the eponymous *Ibis*: its origins can
be traced back to its role as a "blackbirder" (slave ship). Following the abolition
of the slave trade in the British empire, it is refitted as an opium vessel but also
carries indentured Indian laborers (12).[2] However, one also gets a more personal
definition of indenture and the migrant experience through the focalization of
Deeti, wife to the high-caste Rajput Hukam Singh. On being informed that
Mauritius, the final destination of the migrants, is "an island in the sea—like
Lanka," Deeti is horrified (75). Here Mauritius is associated with "Ravana and
his demon-legions," i.e., the "villain" who rules over Sri Lanka in the *Rāmāyaṇa*.
To go to Mauritius would involve severing links with family ("you would never
again enter your father's house") and crossing the "Black Water" (75). Brinda
Mehta's succinct definition of the crossing of the Black Water is a useful aid in
explaining Deeti's Hindu revulsion toward ocean travel since geographical displacement is tantamount to cultural dislocation: "According to Hindu belief, the
traversing of large expanses of water was associated with contamination and cultural defilement as the crossings led to loss of tradition, caste, class and a generally 'purified' ideal of Hinduness" (1). The River Ganga is one such source of
Hindu purity and selfhood. Hence, to "never feel the cleansing touch of the
Ganga" is to "know that you were forever an outcaste" (75).

Deeti's sense of deracination can be correlated to the migrant's experience of
"triple disruption" as described by Salman Rushdie: "he loses his place, he en-
ters into an alien language, and he finds himself surrounded by beings whose
social behaviour and codes are very unlike . . . his own." Deprived of all three,
the diasporic subject is "obliged to find new ways of describing himself, new
ways of being human" ("Günter Grass" 277–78). Rushdie's definition of diasporic experience—defining oneself in a moment of deracination (i.e., through

not the presence but the loss of place, language, and cultural moorings)—can be seen as the counterdefinition of epic, a genre of rootedness in place, language, and culture. It is at this point that the generic ramifications of epic become relevant.

Instructors may alert students to the fact that there is no single Sanskrit equivalent for the term *epic*. One generic term for the *Rāmāyaṇa* is *itihaas* ("history"), a work that narrates "the way it once was" (Pollock, "Introduction" 17). As an *itihaas*, it retraces the history of the Raghavamsa, the dynasty of Raghu, who is the ancestor of Rama. Rama was appropriated as an ancestor by Indian kings from at least the twelfth century onward (Pollock, "Rāmāyaṇa" 270–79). Illustrative medieval examples include Jayasimha Siddharaja of the Solanki dynasty in Gujarat, west India, cast as an incarnation of Rama in the historical epic *Dvyashraya Kavya* (273) and Vikramaditya VI of the Western Chalukya dynasty in Karnataka, south India, referred to as "Chalukya-Rama" (271). Another generic label used for the *Rāmāyaṇa* is *dharmashastra* (literally the "science of dharma" or "righteousness"), which "makes absolute claims for regulating the moral order" (Pollock, "Sanskrit" 60). In addition to historic and moral parameters, there are also aesthetic considerations: the *Rāmāyaṇa* is considered as the *adi-kavya* ("first kavya") or the original courtly poem.

Multiple conceptions of epic also exist in the European context. Traditionally, one distinguishes between the primary, oral epics of Homer, based on personal glory, and the secondary, literary epics modeled on Virgil's *Aeneid*, predicated on social and national ideals (Bowra 13–14). Virgilian epic's focus on duties and a life philosophy recalls that of *dharmashastra*. Its emphasis on "the greatest and noblest in man" (13) is not unlike the heroic sentiment of the *kavya*. Like the *itihaas*, the *Aeneid* is also concerned with ancestral genealogies and extending them to present rulers. Virgil harnesses genealogy to explicitly nationalistic ends by "linking his fabulous hero Aeneas to his living patron Augustus." Since his "first aim is to praise the present," he "joins it to the past and exalts it as the fulfilment of a long, divinely-ordained process" (Bowra 15). Thus Jupiter promises to bestow on Aeneas's descendants (culminating in Augustus) "an empire without end" (1.344; lines 1.314–44 may be read in class). This teleology is similar to the golden age of sociopolitical stability associated with the rule of Rama: "His people are blessed, and joyful, contented, well-fed, and righteous . . . / Just as in the Golden Age . . . Rāghava is establishing hundreds of royal lines" (Book I, Sarga 1, 71–75; excerpts from Sarga 1 may also be read collaboratively).

The instructor may then encourage students to compare this epic utopia of genealogical continuity and rootedness with the diasporic experience as described by Rushdie. The migrant's experience of being uprooted from land and culture cannot be more diametrically opposed to the epic teleology of rootedness in territorial history and ancestral genealogy. A working axis of interrogation may then be formulated: Can a migrant, deprived of roots and social norms, be the subject of epic, a form predicated on territorial identity and collectively shared values? Like Deeti, who is obliged to "find new ways of describing [herself], new ways of being human," can the epic also find new ways of defining itself, a diasporic way of being epic?

When I teach novels from Ghosh's trilogy at the American University of Paris, I explore these ideas collaboratively with students by asking them to focus on character transformations (often sites of generic transformation). Since subchapters are presented through the focalization of the main characters, it is easy to divide the work by creating groups and assigning a specific character to each group. (Recommending specific pages for each group to read facilitates the process.) Given the relationships that develop between characters, different groups could be encouraged to team up temporarily or throughout their presentations. All groups should prepare information on their character's genealogy and social trajectory—i.e., initial and transformed socioeconomic status (caste, race, religion, profession, etc.) and personality—supported by textual evidence and specific page numbers.

The groups' findings could be arranged on the board or an online blog in the following manner:

Deeti's Initial Identity	Deeti's Changed Identity
Wife of high-caste Rajput soldier (arranged marriage)	Wife of untouchable and migrant (marriage by choice)
Opium grower	Leader of the migrants on board the
Kabutri-ki-má ("mother of Kabutri")	*Ibis* and matriarch of Colver clan in Mauritius
Seemingly submissive in the Indian patriarchal system	Defies patriarchy and breaks caste taboos by choosing an untouchable as her partner
Respects caste	
Sees her fate as governed by celestial bodies like Saturn	Privileges hybridity and personal agency over karmic and colonial determinism
Relevant page nos.: _____	Relevant page nos.: _____

The process should be continued for Zachary, Nob Kissin, Kalua, Paulette, Jodhu, Ah-Fatt, even the *Ibis*. As more characters are analyzed, certain conclusions emerge. Each conclusion may be juxtaposed with and tested against the working interrogation of new ways of being epic.

From Genealogical Determinisms to Diasporic Destinies and Adoptive Ancestors

First, it becomes clear that the lives of most of the characters follow arcs of transformation from inherited caste- or race-based filiations to new affiliations based on individual choices and empathy. There is a general movement from traumatic loss, often of members of a family, to transformative self-fashioning.

For example, the caste-conscious Deeti, like all the migrants, must give up her Rajput caste-identity to escape her in-laws and cross the "contaminating" Black Water. Paulette, recycling Nob Kissin's Bhakti[3] ideas of casteless egalitarianism, explains to the migrants that "it's like taking a boat to the temple of Jagannath, in Puri. From now on, and forever afterwards, we will all be ship-siblings—*jaházbhais* [ship-brothers] and *jaházbehns* [ship-sisters]—to each other" (372). This use of familial and fraternal lexicon is deliberately echoed in the description of the new identities of prisoners like Neel and Ah-Fatt (314). Self-determined siblinghood leads us to the next idea: not only do the characters lose their initial genealogical bearings and choose their "siblings," but they also elect or invent a common ancestor. Deeti realizes that the *Ibis* is to become "the Mother-Father of her new family, a great wooden *mái-báp*, an adoptive ancestor of parents and dynasties to come" (373). There is a deliberate temporal reversal embedded in the epithet "adoptive ancestor." It anachronistically suggests that "children" (the migrants) adopt a "parent" (the *Ibis*) and not the other way around. This reversal should be highlighted—it will be crucial in the final part of the discussion.

From National to Transnational Epic

Deeti's family shrine in Mauritius (see *River of Smoke* 3–19)[4] includes characters of multiple castes (Brahmins, Rajputs, untouchables), races, and nationalities (Indians, the mixed-race American Zachary, the Bengali-speaking Frenchwoman Paulette, the Cornishman Penrose, etc.). This *smriti-mandir* (literally "memory-temple") is therefore a powerful expression of cultural inclusion and transnational mobility. It is a hybrid, democratic counterpoint to the racial purity and divine origins of the genealogies of the Solar dynasty (referenced by Neel in *Sea of Poppies* [416–17]) in the *Rāmāyaṇa* and the Roman line running from Aeneas to Augustus in the *Aeneid*. The eccentric presence of the *Ibis* in the shrine provides an oceanic counterparadigm to land- and nation-based ethnocentrisms. Its role is thus akin to that of the slave ships functioning as "cultural and political units" and "a distinct mode of cultural production" (Gilroy 17). Such celebrations of agency and elected affiliations are nonetheless counterbalanced by a Rushdean sense of disruption, powerfully evoked through moments of temporary abandonment (Neel's son) and irrevocable loss (Kabutri is effectively orphaned after her father's death and the departure of her mother, Deeti).

Sea of Poppies can thus be read as a postcolonial revision of traditional epic in a diachronic perspective. It can also be seen synchronically as part of a contemporary trend of diasporic epic. A synchronic comparative reading will serve to recapitulate the ideas explored thus far as well as broaden critical and cultural reading horizons. The topos of crossing the sea links *Sea of Poppies* specifically to epic narratives of the Middle Passage such as Derek Walcott's *Omeros*. The hallucinatory return to the African homeland experienced by Achille, a Caribbean fisherman, in chapter twenty-five of book three of *Omeros*, is a self-contained episode that offers a pertinent cross-cultural parallel. Given the difficulty of the text, different groups may be assigned different themes, such as genealogy, moments of disruption and disinheritance, the symbolism of the swift, and so on, to guide their close readings of this passage. Like the migrants who sever ties with their ancestors, Achille recognizes that he is culturally sundered from his father and, by extension, from his ancestors. This estrangement culminates in the father disinheriting his son: "And you, nameless son, are only the ghost / of a name" (138–39). Achille is orphaned. The symbolic death of the son rather than the father and the ghost's role as an agent of disaffiliation rather than of generational continuity are both provocative reversals of traditional epic.[5] However, this loss of ancestral culture and continuity is counterbalanced by an act of agency. Like the migrants who lose inherited identities and adopt the *Ibis*, a mobile ancestor of metamorphosis, Achille's tutelary goddess is the ocean-crossing swift, a syncretic symbol of Christianity and Africa, more in tune with Achille's diasporic disposition (138). Like the swift, Ghosh's *Ibis* is both a ship and a bird (see analogies with wings and a beak in *Sea of Poppies* 8–9). Both Walcott and Ghosh use birds as symbols of liberation, reinforcing a transnational, oceanic conception of identity.

It is important to resist the easy binaries that jump out at us by appreciating the extent to which Ghosh and Walcott do not reject genealogy *tout court* but distance themselves from a specific kind of genealogy. They use the genealogical lexicon of deracination and (dis)inheritance to resist the epic formulation of genealogy as a form of personal and political determinism. Instead, adoption and ancestor-descendant role reversal allow for the self-conscious rearticulation of identity and genealogy in multicultural and self-empowering terms.

New Ways of Being Epic

Finally, self-consciousness is a key point. The very incongruity of anachronistic adoptions (of a ship in *Sea of Poppies* and a swift in *Omeros*) allows diasporic epic to openly avow its status as what Rushdie calls an "artefact," an imaginative reconstruction of the past self-reflexively realigned with a contemporary vision. Through a triple dislocation, the diasporic subject gains an exacerbated awareness of the past as an artifact, as Rushdie demonstrates:

> This is what the triple disruption of reality teaches migrants: that reality is an artefact, that it does not exist until it is made, and that, like any other artefact, it can be made well or badly, and that it can also, of course, be unmade. . . . A writer who understands the artificial nature of reality is more or less obliged to enter the process of making it. ("Günter Grass" 280–81)

History too is an artifact, though traditional epic is at pains to disavow its constructed nature. Indeed, Aeneas and Rama are already "adoptive ancestors," since subsequent Roman and Indian monarchs such as Augustus and Jayasimha literally adopted them as their progenitors in order to add mythical credibility and luster to their reigns. The anachronisms involved in such ancestor adoption are naturalized as a kind of genealogical fait accompli. In the *Aeneid*, choosing an ancestor is validated through association with divinity. Thus Virgil has gods—the ultimate figures of authority whose word cannot be questioned— proclaim the genealogy of Augustus and Rome (see lines 1.314–44). In contrast, diasporic epic denaturalizes this strategic alignment of present-day figures with illustrious ancestors. It explicitly calls our attention to the artificial nature of the past, irrespective of who is "making" it—the victors or the vanquished—and to the avenues of agency opened by such an awareness of the constructed nature of history.

The students are now armed with enough material on Ghosh and the epic genre to identify the newness of diasporic epic on their own. As a final in-class activity to allow them to tie everything together, they can work in groups to craft a basic outline of an essay with a thesis articulating the specifics of Ghosh's creation of a new kind of epic genealogy. Such group work facilitates brainstorming and peer learning. Students will also have a ready-made reservoir of examples through the table of character genealogies compiled in class. A sample outline may be given for students to follow (e.g., an outline for the standard five-paragraph essay, with thesis, topic sentences with supporting evidence and analysis, and conclusion), along with bonus points for the group that expands the scope of the essay through a relevant cross-reference to Walcott, perhaps in the conclusion. The instructor can elicit thesis statements from the class or raise questions that could serve as starting points for thesis statements. The original working hypothesis, for example, can now be presented as a potential statement: "Genealogy, an epic convention based on roots, can be used more subversively for the migrant, a figure deprived of ancestral roots, through anachronistic reversals privileging agency over hereditary identities" or "A classical convention emphasizing roots can articulate a postcolonial vision valorizing hybridity and routes through tropes of adoptive ancestors." This activity has the additional advantage of shifting the focus from critical reading to critical writing, enabling students to more solidly appropriate the material discussed in class through writing. The subject of the essay outline could also be similar to that of an eventual home assignment or exam. This would allow the instructor to make his or her expectations and evaluation criteria clearer to the students in the course of collective discussion (e.g., a stronger focus on the generic parameters and less summary).

Collaboratively exploring epic genealogies in classical and diasporic epic thus has rich pedagogical potential. Students get to understand the evolution of genre in a transcultural and transhistorical perspective. They thus acquire a bird's-eye view of ancient and contemporary trends in literature. An approach counterpointing epic genealogies and adoptive ancestors also has significant political scope. Rushdie's reflections on reality making can allow students to develop a more critical stance toward the representation of genealogy and history by appreciating the extent to which biological and cultural givens become constructs, subject to personal and political agendas when transposed to discourse. As Rushdie reminds us, once characters and readers understand the artificial nature of personal and public history making, we are all "more or less obliged to enter into the process of making it." Only then can we envisage new ways of being epic and, perhaps, new ways of being human.

NOTES

¹ This essay uses the version of "The March of the Novel through History" found in Ghosh's *Imam and Indian*.

² This essay uses the 2008 John Murray edition of *Sea of Poppies*.

³ A medieval reform movement within Hinduism that emphasized personal devotion to God, irrespective of social status.

⁴ This essay uses the 2011 Hamish Hamilton–Penguin edition of *River of Smoke*.

⁵ For a detailed analysis of postcolonial reconfigurations of epic temporality, see the chapter "'History in the Future Tense': Genealogy as Prophecy" in *The Postcolonial Epic*, 2018, esp. pp. 103–09.

Teaching Ghosh in an Upper-Level, Single-Author English Course

Alan Johnson

This essay addresses the double challenge of teaching a novelist like Amitav Ghosh to students in an American university. By "double challenge" I mean, first, that where one reads and teaches a novel (or any other work of literature) is entwined with how one teaches it. These factors naturally shape how students make sense of a novel for themselves. Ghosh is an especially apt novelist to teach if one wishes to illustrate the paradox at the heart of the genre, which is its simultaneously local and global inclinations. He is also a writer who throws into relief the "critical attitude of unbelonging," to use Ankhi Mukherjee's apt phrase for postcolonial critique, that generally characterizes the work of non-Western[1] writers. The second challenge follows from this and is familiar to teachers of non-Western literature: how much context—social, historical, geographical—do I provide? Too much, and the text's literary features may disappear; too little, and students can come away with serious misconceptions about the region or the writer. The task before us, then, is to lead students to discover how novels set in regions that are, or seem to be, outside the orbit of their everyday sensibilities reflect ways of thinking about the world that are both very different from and much the same as theirs. Based on my experience teaching an upper-level English class devoted to Ghosh, this essay describes attempts to address these challenges. The first part summarizes my first class session, which introduced many of the key themes I wanted students to keep in mind as they began reading Ghosh's works. The second part presents some of the strategies I used to illustrate some of Ghosh's specific thematic concerns and to explain particular cultural references in the assigned texts.

First Day of Class: Situating Author and Reader

When I first met with my students in this class, for all of whom Ghosh and his subject matter were entirely new, I was anxious. Where to begin? How best to orient my students? I was especially interested in how they would respond to the theme of location/dislocation that animates Ghosh's (and many postcolonial) narratives—a theme that resonates on a personal level with students everywhere, given our intensely globalized and technologized world. I was eager (partly due to my own cross-cultural upbringing) to show my students that in Ghosh's novels we find an unusually eloquent illustration of the genre's inherent contradiction: namely, its foundation, as Ghosh puts it, "on a myth of parochialism" ("March" 110).[2] While my students knew this—knew that a novelist must give his or her characters "a particularized time and place" (Watt 21)—I wanted to show them why this is an especially fraught principle for an Indian writer of Ghosh's generation, which has lived through dramatic material and ideological changes.[3] But I wanted to do this without suggesting to my students that their own location was by comparison less important than Ghosh's or his characters'.[4] I also hoped to plant in their minds the idea that Ghosh, like any substantive writer, will continually position his new writings in relation to a variety of determinants: his preceding books, the genres he chooses, and fresh historical and political developments. I thus anticipated that by the time they had read several of Ghosh's works, students would see that location is more about the author's (and his characters') arrivals and departures, about displacement and migration, than about stasis. But I also hoped they would see Ghosh's remarkable "ability to look both ways" at a seemingly self-evident event or idea (Mondal, *Amitav Ghosh* 174).

Since my brainstorming notes coalesced around the theme of location, I decided to begin by asking the class to briefly describe, in writing, their upbringing. In the allotted ten minutes, they might address such questions as, What are some events you especially remember? What comes to mind when you think of home? Can you describe this home specifically—people, house, objects, town, and so on? I explained that they must be willing to share what they had written. Their varied, often entertaining responses provided lively points of discussion about how we conceive of home, and with their help I summarized some common terms, jotting these on the board. Home was, for instance, the memory of potato harvests in southern Idaho. We agreed that sentiments about home also depend on some conceptual features that are less noticeable, such as that home is, as one student observed, structured as much by absence as by presence.[5] A house has an address, but a sense of home, however much it is shaped by the memory of a physical structure, does not depend for its meaning on the structure alone. Some students, citing the *Odyssey* or *Huckleberry Finn*, noted that an abiding narrative theme has been the journey home. To push this forward a bit more, I shared with them George Lakoff's observation that we all think and talk in terms of "frames" or "schemas" (71–72), including those about home. Our culture, education, and historical moment—collectively, our location—is the lens through which we view the world, just as writers do.

But I was getting ahead of myself and sensed that it was time to turn to Ghosh. I cited a motif that appears frequently in Ghosh's writing and that I knew upper-level English majors would latch on to: books. I shared a short quotation from one of Ghosh's most revealing essays, "The March of the Novel through History," in which he ponders why the nineteenth-century Bengali prose master Bankim Chandra Chattopadhyay (in anglicized form, Chatterjee) wrote his first novel in English, and a "ponderous" style of English at that. Bankim (as he is commonly referred to) did so, Ghosh concludes, because "to locate oneself through prose, one must begin with an act of dislocation." Ghosh adds that Bankim, being surrounded by shelves of English books during this colonial period, was really writing for a mental "bookcase" as a means of preparing himself to converse with the authors whom he had read from around the globe. When he turned to Bengali for his novel writing, he excelled. But it was, Ghosh observes, the "rehearsal" of writing his English novel, the need to first "distance" himself in this way, that enabled this "first truly modern 'Indian'" novelist to "lay claim to the rhetoric of location, of place." He could in this way locate himself "in relation to" the imagined bookcase and thereby bridge the "entirely different" British and Bengali "conventions of narrative" ("March" 118).

After I read these lines aloud, I asked students what they thought Ghosh means by this mental bookshelf, suggesting they might compare it with their own. What writers populated their own history of reading, and how might they analyze this mental shelf? The responses naturally included a host of popular authors (J. K. Rowling and Judy Blume come to mind) and canonical moderns (Woolf, Conrad), as well as Homer and Shakespeare. Very few of my students, if any, had read a non-Western novel, though some had read some non-Western poetry, such as by Bashō, in translation. This led to a productive discussion about canonicity, global cultural production, and the continuing power of Western markets and languages in this production. When I asked about films, it was, not surprisingly, a different story: thanks to streaming sites, many had watched Korean, Chinese, or Hindi (Bollywood) films. This gave me an opening to address the rubric under which this course is offered in my department: "a Major Literary Figure other than Chaucer, Milton, and Shakespeare." Several students were acutely aware that such a division reflects problematic assumptions about literary value and period. Why are these particular authors ascribed their own course titles? some wondered. Why not Woolf or Morrison? Others defended the designations: there is, after all, no quarrel about Shakespeare's greatness. The discussion became animated and generated a number of astute observations about such contested issues as the politics of canon formation.

Acutely aware of our session's time constraint, I promised (rather abruptly, in retrospect) that we would revisit this important topic at various points in the term. In a bid to situate their individual predilections, I suggested that their omission of non-Western literary works was in line with that of both mainstream culture and the institution of literary studies, which until recently simply assumed the universality of Western cultures. As hard as it is to change such hierarchies, imagine, I said, the challenge facing someone like Bankim in his colonial context. As Ghosh points out, Bankim was a product of both a colonial English-language education and a Bengali cultural tradition that included hierarchies of its own. He therefore had to wage his intellectual battle on two fronts: the Europeans' "monstrous claim to omniscience" (as Bankim put it in a famous letter, written in English) as well as the arcane Sanskrit scholasticism of some of his fellow Bengalis (qtd. in "March" 116). Ghosh is thus, I emphasized, an inheritor of Bankim's courageous, ultimately successful initiative to make the modern novel his own by embracing "the very loss of a lived sense of place that makes . . . fictional representation possible" ("March" 119). Ghosh is certainly not, I reminded them, saying that his situation is identical to Bankim's; the latter had to adapt the framework of the modern European novel to his own place and time in a climate of colonial repression and censorship. Yet Ghosh shares a common sensibility with his predecessor that is vital for a full appreciation of his (Ghosh's) art and that a careful reading can detect.

As I do in all my courses, I asked my students to see if they could find parallels to this relationship in the careers of other writers. Since all of our department's students have read at least some classic American works, and since every student in this upper-division class had taken two required courses in literary analysis (at the second- and third-year levels), there were a number of informed responses. Some saw, for example, a similar "anxiety of influence" exerted by James Fenimore Cooper's *Leatherstocking* novels on later writers like Henry David Thoreau, principally in the latter's rendition of a distinctly North American natural environment. One student, ranging farther afield, pointed to the influence of William Faulkner's Oxford, Mississippi–inspired Yoknapatawpha County on Gabriel García Márquez's Macondo, Colombia, in terms of both social isolation and a distinctly New World sensibility.

Following this interlude, I returned the discussion to Ghosh. To illustrate Ghosh's inherited (yet also distinct) locational sensibility and to combine the various threads of our conversation, I turned for a moment to film, a genre I always find to be a more accessible entry point for such discussions. I cited Hollywood's well-known adaptations of canonical texts, especially those of Jane Austen and Shakespeare; histories, such as Rome's; and folktales. We briefly discussed possible reasons for the continued popularity of film adaptations of classic literary works, such as the originals' cultural as well as archetypal significance. But I reiterated my earlier point: there are rich stories available to mine from other cultural traditions that Hollywood ignores—why this comparative absence?[5] Conversely, why do Indian filmmakers adapt Shakespeare, whereas American producers never turn to, say, the classical Sanskrit playwright Kālidāsa? The class readily saw the connection to Ghosh's bookcase: in India, as in many other regions once colonized by Europe, those learning English (still the language of commerce and upward mobility there) are obliged to read the same canonical exemplars—Shakespeare, Milton, etc.—as students do in America and as Bankim did in the nineteenth century. But this does not mean, I stressed, that the cultural influence is one-way. For a long time now, cultures once constrained by European powers have been "writing back to the Empire." In fact, I argued (partly, I admit, to elicit a reaction), non-Western artists today usually have more to say than their American or English counterparts precisely because they have at hand not one but two cultural archives they can tap into.

By way of example, I observed that the Hindi filmmaker Vishal Bhardwaj can rely on his audience's knowledge of *Othello*, which he restages in rural northern India as *Omkara*. Knowing that I too could rely on my students' knowledge of Shakespeare, I showed the three-minute trailer of the 2006 film (available on *YouTube*)[6] as a way of reiterating the local-global paradox with which I began the class. I mentioned that Bhardwaj brings to Shakespearean drama not simply a national flavor but a narrower, regional one that required its Hindi-speaking actors to learn the area's Khariboli dialect.[7] Yet Bhardwaj retains the use of Urdu song lyrics (composed by the legendary Gulzar) common in mainstream films and uses Hindi film stars, no doubt with an eye on marketability. I said that this interplay between regional and mainstream (as well as global) cultural markers is especially distinctive of India, with its many languages, religions, and cultures, and was something students would notice as they read Ghosh. But I emphasized that, as we saw in our discussion about American literary influences, such an interplay features in the art of most other nations as well, including the United States. Students readily saw a comparable regional-national relation in how their own rural Idaho communities consume, for instance, some of the latest metropolitan trends in music even as they oppose the perceived erosion of local values. Studying a localized film adaptation (here I mentioned my standby example of *Clueless*, the 1995 film version of Austen's *Emma*) similarly throws into relief the kinds of questions we can bring to our reading of Ghosh's novels. Like Bhardwaj's film, I said (at the risk of pointing out the obvious), Ghosh's works highlight the importance of history, geography, and global cultural exchange in the lives of his characters. I also thought it important to add that this interplay is never between two separate cultural entities, as our common terminology implies: Western vs. non-Western, North Indian vs. South Indian. Ghosh and Bhardwaj instead throw up the irresolvable contradiction that Bankim similarly confronted, which is the desire for "universal demands of modernity" on the one hand and particular local histories and identities on the other (Khilnani 7, 159). Ghosh's notional shelf of eclectic titles depends, after all, on the locations and predilections of readers far and wide—including in small-town America.[8]

Strategies and Contexts

Example 1: *The Circle of Reason*

In part one, chapter two, of Ghosh's first novel, *The Circle of Reason*, we are given a seemingly insignificant bit of trivia from the cultural context of northern India, where the novel is set in the decades following India's 1947 independence. Balaram, a key character and the father of Alu, arguably our hero, is a devotee of reason, which explains why his talismanic possession is a biography of Pasteur. He is worried that Alu lacks the same devotion to reason and that his interest in weaving rather than the mind will ruin his future, so Balaram seeks his friend Gopal's counsel. Gopal, having "decided that Balaram needed a diversion," suggests they see the new (in 1969) Hindi film *Aradhana* (53).[9] This leads to one of many arguments about the merits and demerits of popular culture and about the book's main theme (reflected in the title), that reason is never purely objective but instead "bound up with irrationality" (Mondal, *Amitav Ghosh* 52). Near the end of this first part of the novel, significantly titled "Satwa: Reason" (the other two parts being "Rajas: Passion" and "Tamas: Death," each term a necessary part of the others in Hindu philosophy), Ghosh offers another tidbit related to the film *Aradhana*. By now, Alu has embarked on the boat *Mariamma*, bound for the East African port of al-Ghazira, which has grown wealthy on oil and where he hopes to set up his sewing business. Also on board is a young man named Rakesh, who recounts that his motivation for the journey began when, "in a small town south of Bhopal," he "heard the unmistakable throbbing of *Mere Sapnon ki Rani* spilling out" (182). The iconic song is from the same film, *Aradhana*, and thus thematically connects Rakesh with Balaram. Like Balaram, who emerges misty-eyed and smiling from what Gopal disdainfully calls a "noisy melodrama" (53), Rakesh is "transfixed, overwhelmed by reminiscence" as he listens to this exquisitely romantic song, which, "as though it were a rope around his wrists," leads him to a shop whose flashy owner says he made his money in al-Ghazira (182).

By the time my class had reached this point in *The Circle of Reason*, we were into the fourth week of the term, having begun with Ghosh's third book, *In an Antique Land*. So the students were already attuned to some of Ghosh's recurring themes, such as the fact that history and memory are always messy and that what we think of as reason is, as Balaram's case reveals, actually entangled with emotion and obsession. To show the class how a novel's passing allusion, while not essential to a meaningful understanding of the text, can amplify its themes and deepen our empathy for characters, I played a *YouTube* clip from *Aradhana* featuring the aforementioned song. Those who know the song from childhood may grow as misty-eyed as Balaram as we listen, but everyone (including my students) seems to appreciate its catchy beat and gently alluring rhythm. The scene in which the song occurs features the hero traveling by Jeep alongside a train and singing to his love, who is seated in the train and shyly enjoying the serenade. The setting, featuring the famous hill station of Darjeeling, fits the romantic tune and lyrics, with their refrain translating to "when will the queen of my dreams come?" and their revealing line "alleys of love." To illustrate to my students how a close reading of even such a seemingly esoteric allusion can reveal its value, I mentioned, first, that it's in a literal alley that Ghosh's character Rakesh finds himself when he hears the old tune and, second, that the song's nostalgic pull in fact leads him to his newfound love, the prospect of money (symbolized by the oil boomtown to which he travels). Rakesh thus succumbs not only to a song but also to its touristic setting, which neither he nor the majority of filmgoers at the time could afford to visit. The irony, then, is that Rakesh's nostalgia—which, I should add, was evident to my students even without my Bollywood gloss—reconnects him momentarily to his childhood through places he has actually visited (the city of Indore) and viewed (Darjeeling). The latter, by virtue of a song, becomes real. As for Balaram, the students could clearly see his inner conflict between reason and desire when, after seeing the film, he scolds Gopal for failing to know what "real" means (53). In other words, the novel's two brief references to the film, when seen in their cultural context, are windows onto these characters' split sentiments as well as onto Ghosh's overarching observation that mainstream history, like science, is still largely a colonial European legacy, which ignores smaller stories like those of his characters. Ironically, however, their lives prove to be less localized than the packaged narrative of Pasteur's life. I concluded this exercise in contextual reading by asking my students if they could imagine being similarly afflicted by the unexpected pull of home while in a different location, even in the United States. Some volunteered their experiences of traveling to new places, encountering a reminder of home—one example was eating a hamburger in Japan—and feeling somewhat homesick.

I then turned our discussion to the role images play in relation to the location/ dislocation theme that concerns so many writers, including Ghosh. Specifically, I asked students how the motif of weaving in *Circle* might relate either to these characters or to the novel's larger themes. I read aloud from the book's thematically important excursus on the importance of weaving that concludes the second chapter (55–58), which is communicated in a voice that slides from Balaram's to that of the omniscient narrator. World history, we are told, has been driven by the textile trade, so that "[t]he loom recognizes no continents or countries. It has tied the world together with its bloody ironies from the beginning of human time. It has never permitted the division of reason" (55). I mentioned that *text* is related to *textile*, so that Ghosh himself is weaving a story, much as Rakesh does. (I frequently mention to all my classes the value of using an online etymological dictionary to look up a text's key words. Whether or not this glance at root meanings elucidates the narrative, it always proves to be a valuable exercise for students.) This doubled reference thus underscores Ghosh's abiding interest in the irony that the imperial, exploitative development of global trade—essentially, modern history—has enabled the spread of stories (an idea found in subsequent books, such as when, in *In an Antique Land*, Ghosh announces his wish to reveal the stories that history has swept aside, like "tiny threads" that have been "woven into borders of a gigantic tapestry" [95]).[10] Rakesh, like a postcolonial version of Conrad's Marlow spinning his "yarn" on the *Nellie*, has told his shipmates (and us) his story—that is, how a song serendipitously led him to an alleyway shop and the news about al-Ghazira—on board the *Mariamma*, a name that is at once Hindu (for the goddess Durga), Christian (a form of Mary), and Muslim (also for Mary). Like the boat's name, Rakesh's weaving of a story about migration, nostalgia, and fortune seeking is emblematic of Ghosh's commemoration (not romanticization) of cultural exchange in the context of empire and commerce. I reminded my class that Rakesh is part of a wave of Indian migrants whose movement across Asia and the Middle East in search of livelihood Ghosh describes in a number of his novels. The concluding lines of that part of the novel, when Alu is gazing at the lights of al-Ghazira as the boat reaches the port, encapsulate several of these themes: "through a century and a half the same lights have shone in one part of the globe or another, wherever money" exists, luring "*Mariamma*'s avatars" with their "immense cargo of wanderers seeking their own destruction in giving flesh to the whims of capital" (189). "Whims" here signals chance rather than reason and aligns with the aforementioned feeling that wells up in Rakesh when, "even years later," his memory of first seeing *Aradhana* will work its powerful "magic" on him (182). I pointed out that this is a "magic" familiar to many diasporic Indians for whom subcontinental films provide a vicarious means of returning home—an experience that many of my students could see reflected in, to cite one example, the way that Swedish immigrants to Idaho maintained homeland rituals that continue today. We discussed the irony that this vicarious return home via film is necessarily semifictional, a mix of personal memory and the film's depiction of the home culture. I then suggested that if, as we'd discussed previously, a writer must locate him- or herself in relation to a notional, cosmopolitan bookcase in a process that involves dislocation, so must "wanderers" like Rakesh and Alu carry with them a piece of home to remind them that "foreign places are all alike in that they are not home" (266). One student, in a later assignment on *The Shadow Lines*, captured the similar predicament facing characters befuddled by redrawn borders and changed landscapes: "Ghosh provides us with two characters through which we can [view] home: The Narrator, who takes it everywhere," and "Th'amma, who can't find it anywhere." Another student commented that Ghosh accentuates "the idea that home is not a place of origin, but [one] that the characters must find."[11] During our reading of *Circle*, several students connected its thematic threads by noting that when Alu finds his father's old copy of *The Life of Pasteur* on a bookshelf in Algeria (near the end of the novel) it conveys to him the same aura of past life as the film song does for Rakesh.

Example 2: *The Hungry Tide*

This novel, which we read about two-thirds of the way into the term, was the clear favorite among my students. Based on student comments, this seems to have had something to do with the novel's relatively more linear plot, as compared with *The Circle of Reason* and *The Shadow Lines*. This affinity may also have arisen from the photos shown in class of the Sundarbans, the striking mangrove forest preserve in which the novel is set.[12] Because this unusual region has not received the treatment it deserves outside of West Bengal and India, my students said these images provided a useful reference point for them as they read the novel. Not that they found Ghosh's descriptions wanting; they remarked that they especially liked "the vividness of the setting" and Ghosh's ability to seamlessly convey the area's geography and history.

These comments reflect what I think was an important reason for the class's attraction to the novel: its evident environmentalist concern, including the plight of tigers.[13] To be sure, the students held varying views about environmental activism, but they were all drawn to the topic. Another, equally compelling reason for their interest seems to have been the novel's attention to marginal peoples, such as the fisherman Fokir and Bangladeshi refugees, whose syncretic folklore (such as that of the goddess Bon Bibi) was a catalyst for active discussion. Students also responded strongly, even emotionally, to the troubling dilemma of human versus tiger survival, particularly when they read Ghosh's descriptions of poor villagers burning a captured tiger and the massacre of refugees on the island of Morichjhāpi by officials who are ostensibly safeguarding tigers. From a pedagogical standpoint, the growing body of ecocritical interpretations of this and other non-Western novels provided me with ample instructional resources. I made some of these available to the class by uploading critical essays to our online teaching platform and posting lists of scholarly titles they could consult as needed while researching their essays.[14] I also extracted pertinent passages from a number of these essays to share with students, along with questions about the extracts. One handout, for instance, provided a brief description of the context for the Morichjhāpi incident and links to pertinent Web sites. I also quoted from Pablo Mukherjee's essay on the novel and added that he argues, in my view correctly, that environmental concerns and realities are inseparable from any serious engagement with "the conditions of migration" (148). My intent in signaling my agreement with Mukherjee was not to forestall any possible disagreements with this view, which in any case the novel clearly shares (as students discerned), but rather to model a critical engagement with the scholarly resources.

I should emphasize that, although this particular novel centers on the tension between environmental protection and minority rights, examining the novel in the context of a course devoted to Ghosh means that there are several options for putting the book in conversation with the other assigned texts. Thus my course's overriding concern with the location of Ghosh's settings and readers (i.e., my Idaho students) led us into a brief but valuable discussion about the feud between environmentalists (and the United States government) and Idaho ranchers over the reintroduction of wolves to the region. This in turn generated a fruitful discussion about how and why novelists have focused on such complex issues. I thus encouraged my students, in a version of reader response, to bring to Ghosh's novel their own related concerns, thereby reemphasizing my prefatory remarks about seeing in such visibly unfamiliar contexts reflections of some of their own concerns. At the same time, students naturally found it hard to locate any such reflection in Ghosh's descriptions of local village beliefs (which, indeed, the novel's urban characters found strange). Indeed, students recognize a strategy also observed in works by writers ranging from Chinua Achebe to Kurt Vonnegut: the strategy of simultaneously conveying a sense of estrangement and familiarity. Ghosh's distinction is to be just as invested in a global cross-cultural outlook as in a national or regional one. By "invested" I mean that his novels celebrate linguistic, cultural, and philosophical pluralism but do not thereby diminish the stakes involved in safeguarding local ways of seeing. For example, Fokir's communication through song is endangered by urban society's seemingly unstoppable encroachment. Yet it is Ghosh's novel itself, a quintessentially urban invention, that illuminates this fact.

To illustrate how heated the debates about postcolonial histories can be, I gave the students handouts pairing opposing viewpoints on a specific theme and explained that this pairing was only one example of how to approach the various tensions Ghosh exposes in all his works, from questions about national unity to those about neocolonialism. For example, brief citations from A. N. Kaul's harsh criticism of Ghosh's handling of India's nationhood in *The Shadow Lines* or Gauri Viswanathan's indictment of *In an Antique Land* for its inability to "get beyond nostalgia" ("Beyond Orientalism") appear alongside words in defense of Ghosh, such as those by John Mee, Suvir Kaul, and Anshuman Mondal. Mondal, in his monograph on Ghosh, offers a succinct consideration of Ghosh's refusal to have his novels neatly resolve the especially painful dilemmas associated with postcolonial histories. In class discussions about these novels, I occasionally returned to Ghosh's touchstone bookcase essay to remind students of what he believes is at stake in representing discrepant histories—namely that the novel is doubly paradoxical in requiring that a writer endure displacement in order to write about place and that this displacement is made possible by the harrowing dispersions of people across the planet. Thus, although students were initially perplexed by the English names of the Sundarbans' towns, such as Canning, Ghosh's recounting of colonial history and its acquisitive reach, together with the aforementioned contextual readings and images, gave them insights into the non-Western perspectives through which Ghosh wishes to "provincialize Europe."[15]

In the course of discussing Ghosh's works up through *Sea of Poppies*, students and I naturally touched on the rich variety of topics he explores. We had memorable discussions on the metaphor of the nation as family, and on arguably problematic representations of women, in *The Shadow Lines*. *The Calcutta Chromosome* instigated spirited exchanges about the viability of virtual space and parallel realities and the implications for Ghosh's more sustained treatment, in his other works, of physical space. *In an Antique Land* generated similarly fruitful comments, though ultimately no one chose to write about it, possibly because of the understandable challenge of tackling its unusually hybrid form. I had in fact assigned it first in the belief that this form would invite a wide range of critical entry points. Nonetheless, its clear elucidation of what Gaurav Desai calls the "lived experience of cosmopolitanism" (*Commerce* 20), critique of national border obsessions, and fascinating reconstruction of fragmented lives did give students a framework they could apply to the other texts. In this way, I attempted to take up Ghosh's challenge of, in Vijay Mishra's words, "a radical rethinking of the (Western) past" (xvii). However limited such an attempt may be by our disciplinary constraints, Ghosh's stories assume a life of their own that is hard to dispute.

NOTES

[1] I use the terms *Western* and *non-Western* provisionally, both in this essay and in the classroom, as crude shorthand to distinguish the perspectives of the average American

student who is unfamiliar with the regions Ghosh describes from those of a student who lives in those regions. Gradually, as my students work through Ghosh's texts, I encourage them to question these and other assumptive terms, though many readily grasp Ghosh's critique of such oppositions.

[2] This essay uses the version of "The March of the Novel through History" found in *Incendiary Circumstances.*

[3] Born in 1956, Ghosh came of age in the post-independence period, when Prime Minister Nehru's socialist and centralist vision "etched" the state "into the imagination of Indians as never before" (Khilnani 41). Today's middle-class generation is by comparison accustomed to a country that has embraced global trade. Yet Ghosh, with his itinerant background, is not a typical representative of his generation of Indians, for whom, as Vijay Mishra observes, "where you come from" is who "you are" (4).

[4] The perception among Western students that their lives are comparatively banal often depends on the misconception that the non-Western writer inhabits a more exotic and dramatic world.

[5] At least one student rightly challenged my point by mentioning such Disney films as *Aladdin* and *Mulan*. I acknowledged the examples but added that further examination would show how these tales have become distinctly American. In retrospect, I see that the questions elicited from my response—what is an original tale? what does "American" mean? and so on—would have profited from a daylong discussion. I have returned to this topic in other classes.

[6] A teaching assistant in my department recently made me aware of software like *KeepVid* that enables one to download and save open-source clips for future use.

[7] If I were to teach the class again, I would refer to Ankhi Mukherjee's enlightening discussion of Bhardwaj's three Shakespeare adaptations and the filmmaker's own comment, in an interview with Mukherjee, that "'[l]ocalism' captures the reality of that region" and "makes a fantasy believable" for his audience (Mukherjee 213).

[8] If I were to teach a version of this lesson again, I would probe the issue of contradiction further by discussing the biting criticism of *The Shadow Lines* by Indian critics, which Mondal effectively evaluates (*Amitav Ghosh* 166–73). It may also be instructive to compare Bhardwaj's adaptation of *Othello* with Mauritian-Indian playwright Dev Virahsawmy's adaptation of *The Tempest* as *Toufann* ("Storm"), which Vijay Mishra discusses. Interestingly, as Mishra notes, Virahsawmy's version exemplifies the diasporic allure of Hindi film by having a character sing the hit title song from the iconic 1971 film *Hare Rama Hare Krishna* (60–63). Intertextuality thus proliferates in such contexts.

[9] This essay uses the 2005 Mariner Books edition of *Circle of Reason.*

[10] This essay uses the 1992 Vintage Books edition of *In an Antique Land.*

[11] Another student similarly observed that the narrator of *The Shadow Lines* "feels more at home in the places of his imagination than he does in the real world."

[12] I also provided quotations from the groundbreaking work of Annu Jalais as well as information from, among other sources, Ghosh's Web site (amitavghosh.com) and UNESCO's World Heritage Centre Web site (whc.unesco.org/en/list/452).

[13] Despite a widely reported study in 2012 that younger generations are less likely to be environmentally concerned (Zafar), this has not at all been my experience. For an explanation of why such studies are flawed, see Tankersley and Foster.

[14] Examples of works that students drew upon in this regard are Malcolm Sen's "Spatial Justice: The Ecological Imperative and Postcolonial Development"; Pablo Mukherjee's "Surfing the Second Waves: Amitav Ghosh's Tide Country"; Roman Bartosch's

"A Good Dose of Formalism? Reading *The Hungry Tide*"; and Jonathan Steinwand's "What the Whales Would Tell Us." I provided, via the online platform, a list of two dozen recent critical works related to Ghosh or postcolonial and world writing. Since these were third- and fourth-year English majors, I could rely on their general knowledge of criticism and theory. I did, however, discuss specific theories associated with postcolonial, translation, and world literature studies.

[15] Like many teachers of both postcolonial literature and Ghosh, I introduced Dipesh Chakrabarty's thesis, encapsulated in this well-known phrase (and book title), through an extract from Ghosh and Chakrabarty's exchange, published in 2002 ("Correspondence").

Torrents of Tweets:
Teaching the *Ibis* Trilogy
with Digital Humanities Pedagogy

Roopika Risam

One of the primary pedagogical challenges of teaching Amitav Ghosh's *Ibis* trilogy—*Sea of Poppies, River of Smoke,* and *Flood of Fire*—is guiding students through the novels' range of characters, geographies, languages, and histories. Ghosh's engagement with the archive produces rich narratives but also a significant level of difficulty for students navigating the breadth of his writing. It is here that digital humanities pedagogy offers students ways of negotiating the challenges that the *Ibis* trilogy presents while helping them develop core twenty-first-century literacies.

Teaching with Digital Humanities

In recent years, digital humanities has received significant attention within the academy. Dubbed "the next big thing" (Pannapacker), digital humanities has been a site of departmental and institutional investment and has begun to be seen not only as an area of research but also as one of pedagogy. In his definition of digital humanities, Matthew Kirschenbaum writes:

> Whatever else it might be, then, the digital humanities today is about a scholarship (and a pedagogy) that is publicly visible in ways to which we are generally unaccustomed, a scholarship and pedagogy that are bound up with infrastructure in ways that are deeper and more explicit than we are generally accustomed to, a scholarship and pedagogy that are collaborative and depend on networks of people and that live an active 24/7 life online. (60)

Our students may be part of this digital milieu, but they often lack the tools to engage with it critically. With the advent of Web 2.0, participatory forms of culture have emerged, made possible by low barriers for civic engagement and creative expression online. In opposition to consumer culture, participatory culture positions users in the role of producers, not simply consumers of knowledge. While much has been made of the millennial digital native—a young adult reared with laptop and Internet access in hand (Prensky 1)—the concept is complicated by questions of access that reflect socioeconomic class, geography, and racialized and gendered experiences with technology (Hargittai 93). Moreover, the act of consuming technology does not necessarily produce deeper understanding of it.

Yet using digital humanities pedagogy can redress such gaps, encouraging development of the skills students need to thrive in the classroom, in the workplace, and online. This is not an attempt to teach students particular technical skills, applications, or platforms but a methodological approach that enables them to envision a relationship between themselves and knowledge production. As Tanya Clement has argued,

> Like pedagogy intended to teach students to read more critically, project-based learning in digital humanities demonstrates that when students learn how to study digital media, they are learning how to study knowledge production as it is represented in symbolic constructs that circulate within information systems that are themselves a form of knowledge production. (366)

She further proposes that digital humanities offers students new approaches to multiple literacies, including multiculturalism, multimodalities, and multimedia.

The primary twenty-first-century literacies that digital humanities pedagogy offers students the opportunity to develop are creativity and innovation, critical thinking and problem solving, communication and collaboration, and media literacy. Engaging with literary texts through digital humanities encourages students to develop new ideas, put them into practice, and communicate them to their peers. It asks them to be open to diverse perspectives and to engage them iteratively through experimentation and play. Doing so requires flexibility, outside-the-box thinking, and inventiveness, as well as awareness of the relationship between ideas and the practicality of implementation. Moreover, such practices encourage students to develop healthy attitudes toward failure, viewing it as a learning opportunity and understanding that achieving longer-term goals relies on the ability to evaluate and adjust in response to feedback and obstacles. Certainly, the teaching of literature has been linked to the task of enhancing critical thinking skills. Using digital humanities pedagogy, we are still able to develop these habits of mind, asking students to use and analyze evidence, make arguments, evaluate multiple perspectives, synthesize information, and draw conclusions. In such projects, students are required to communicate effectively across multiple contexts and for multiple purposes. Moreover, they practice collaboration and the ability to work effectively in teams. Collaboration, as Brett Hirsch argues, "introduces a new mode of work into the humanities: hacking together, not alone," with an emphasis on "collectivity and collaboration in the pursuit and creation of new knowledge" ("</Parentheses>" 16). Finally, students increase their media literacy as they explore how digital media constructs messages and how multiple publics interpret them. Indeed, as Koenraad de Smedt has argued, digital humanities is not simply "the use of machines" but "new ways of thinking" (92). Martyn Jessop further describes these ways as "the cognitive abilities of thinking both with and against the machine" (30). Such engagement equips students with critical awareness of media tools and genres.

Rather than developing such literacies through the more conventional forms employed in English classrooms—literary analysis essays and close reading—students demonstrate mastery of these skills through digital humanities pedagogy by creating alternative assignments. Mark Sample has made the case against the essay, arguing there is a disconnect between the work we ask students to do in our courses—producing genres of writing that most people will not read—and the skills students need to thrive in twenty-first-century media environments and the workplace. He argues in favor of asking students not to write but to "weave—to build, to fabricate, to design" (404). He notes, "I don't want my students to become miniature scholars. I want them to be aspiring Rauschenbergs, assembling mixed-media combines, all the while through their engagement with seemingly incongruous materials developing a critical thinking practice about the process and the product" (405). Such an approach engages students in the act of critical making, defined by Matt Ratto as using "material forms of engagement with technologies to supplement and extend critical reflection and, in doing so, to reconnect our lived experiences with technologies to social and conceptual critique" (253). Through such forms of engagement, we make students both collaborators in production and self-reflexive users of technology, rather than passive consumers. This perspective is grounded in a key construct of digital humanities: ways of knowing and theorizing emerge from hands-on engagement. This "craft knowledge" (Rockwell) is predicated on the concept that "learning how to build requires your sense of how things work" (Berens). Indeed, the goal here is not to use digital humanities for the sake of its currency within the academy or its cachet—and certainly not for the sake of teaching with technology—but for the knowledges that emerge from its practices.

In addition to cultivating twenty-first-century literacies, using digital humanities pedagogy helps students negotiate the challenges that Ghosh's writing offers. These difficulties reflect the broader difficulties facing those who teach postcolonial literature. Since the 1990s, scholars have been writing about the pedagogical implications of postcolonial literature, which requires multiple types of knowledges, tools, and approaches. Gayatri Spivak, for example, has considered the challenge of reading "culturally different" books ("How to Read" 126). Novels like those in Ghosh's *Ibis* trilogy require historical, political, and cultural knowledges with which students are not necessarily equipped. Teaching them requires helping students develop not only the requisite skills for literary interpretation but also awareness of the contexts that render the texts legible. These tasks are complicated by local aesthetics, such as the relation between English and vernacular languages, a tension that is amply present in the *Ibis* trilogy, from the Hinglish spoken by British sahibs to the Chinglish that emerged from the opium trade to the dizzying Laskari, the ship pidgin blending English, Portuguese, Tamil, Arabic, Bengali, Malay, and more.

Furthermore, postcolonial scholars have been sensitive to the colonialist dynamics of classrooms, arguing that "education is perhaps the most insidious and in some ways the most cryptic of colonialist survivals, older systems now passing, sometimes imperceptibly, into neocolonialist configurations" (Ashcroft et al. 425). Therefore, one of the challenges of postcolonial pedagogy is to decolonize the classroom, moving away from the banking method of education, in which students are conceived as vessels into which instructors deposit knowledge, in favor of active forms of learning (Freire 58). To do so is to forgo the "sage on the stage" model of instruction in favor of the instructor as the "guide on the side," whose role is, as Alison King suggests, "to facilitate students' interaction with the material and with each other in their knowledge-producing endeavor" (30). As the New London Group, an academic team that examines new literacies, suggests, digital pedagogy encourages student engagement with globalization, cultural diversity, and technology (Cazden et al.). This further promotes familiarity with interdisciplinary modes of thought, undoing rigid distinctions between literature, history, and cultures. Such an approach fits both the ethos of postcolonial studies and Ghosh's own work, which is rich in interdisciplinary allusions. Therefore, digital humanities pedagogy is useful as a strategy that asks students to think and work across the disciplines. As Jon Saklofske and his coauthors note, digital humanities is "not a discipline, not a theoretical approach, and not an end in itself of research or teaching practices" (323). Instead, "it is a means of scholarship and pedagogy that embraces the digital frame as its knowledge *environment*, inclusively and self-consciously moving beyond the exclusive and often unacknowledged hegemony of print cultural paradigms" (323–24). As Benedict Anderson has argued, the emergence of print capitalism itself shaped the imagined communities that gave rise to the modern nation-state (45). Thus, engaging with digital humanities offers students a new way of thinking through some of the core concepts that undergird modernity and alternative perspectives on how communities are formed, all of which are in the spirit of Ghosh's work. Within the broader rubric of digital humanities, there are a number of approaches that are useful for teaching the *Ibis* trilogy. In particular, textual analysis, digital writing, social media, time lines and mapping, and rewriting *Wikipedia* offer multiple ways of teaching these novels.

Digital Approaches to Teaching the **Ibis** Trilogy

While textual analysis is at the heart of methodologies commonly deployed in literature classrooms, computer-aided textual analysis offers the possibility of engaging with texts in new ways. As Stéfan Sinclair and Geoffrey Rockwell argue, tools that assist with textual analysis afford opportunities that are not practically achievable by close reading alone: searching large texts quickly, conducting complex searches, and interacting with a text through word clouds, word trends, and keywords in context (243). Sinclair and Rockwell developed the open-source textual analysis tool *Voyant* (voyant-tools.org), which provides a Web-based reading environment for electronic text. Users can upload or copy and paste a corpus, or collection of words, to the tool, which executes a number of text analysis functions: word counts, word clouds, word frequency, and contextual keywords. By enabling the stopwords list, users can eliminate words that do not contain meaningful significance (e.g., articles and prepositions) and can edit these lists to create custom ones. The challenge of using textual analysis to study the *Ibis* trilogy is that the novels are currently copyrighted. As a result, producing a corpus for these novels would require time-intensive scraping of an e-book edition or running optical character recognition (OCR) and manually rekeying a print edition. Yet using *Voyant* is an opportunity to engage students with the historical, cultural, and literary material that informs Ghosh's novels. For example, Project Gutenberg offers full-text access to forty-nine thousand public domain texts, including Herman Melville's work and a wealth of slave narratives, which are important intertexts for *Sea of Poppies*.

Another way to use textual analysis to teach the *Ibis* trilogy is to introduce students to distant reading through *Google Books Ngram Viewer* (books.google .com/ngrams). Coined by Franco Moretti, "distant reading" offers a way of understanding literature not through the close reading techniques that have been at the heart of literary scholarship but by looking for patterns that shape periods or recur in genres. As he notes, "distance . . . *is a condition of knowledge*: it allows you to focus on units that are much smaller or much larger than the text: devices, themes, tropes—or genres and systems" ("Conjectures" 57). *Google Books Ngram Viewer* charts the frequencies of words and short sentences through counts of yearly units, or n-grams, in print sources published between 1800 and 2012. While there are a number of limitations to the tool—the data set is limited to texts available in *Google Books*, critics have suggested that the OCR may not be entirely accurate, and texts may be incorrectly dated—*Google Books Ngram Viewer* offers an interesting perspective on language that augments readings of Ghosh's work. Entering a word or phrase into the search field generates a visualization of the relation between the word and the approximately 5.2 million scanned books in Google's database. A search for the term *race*, for example, shows a spike in the term's use in the mid-1800s, while use of the term *caste* increases more or less steadily between 1820 and 2012. Used in conjunction with the *Oxford English Dictionary*, *Google Books Ngram Viewer* helps students engage with the relation between language and time, including the evolution of usage and meaning. Such a tool is useful in formulating research questions that promote greater understanding of the trilogy's context: why certain words, like *race* or *caste*, seem to appear more frequently at particular historical moments; what kinds of connections exist between literature and history; whether there are correlations between related terms. Electronic versions of the novels composing the *Ibis* trilogy offer workarounds for lighter forms of textual analysis. Search functions within e-books, on *Google Books*, or through Amazon's Search Inside feature enable students to identify word frequencies and occurrences in *Sea of Poppies, River of Smoke,* and *Flood of Fire* and use this information to interpret the novels.

Most important to remember, however, is that textual analysis tools are significant not because of the technologies themselves or even because of the data they generate but because of the kinds of research questions students design to use with them—whether these are questions students are able to answer or simply new avenues of inquiry. For example, students might begin by outlining themes based on their reading experience and then use textual analysis tools to identify word- or sentence-level evidence related to the theme. Or an instructor might offer a list of significant words or motifs in the texts, ask students to explore the terms using tools, and help them use these results to identify themes in the text. They might compare the results from textual analysis tools with their own impressions of the novels or close reading they have done. These approaches engage students in the trilogy in an experimental mode as they consider their results, refine their searches, and evaluate the interpretations made possible through multiple forms of textual analysis. Moreover, in considering the limitations and materiality of the tools they are using to produce big data online—e.g., the sociocultural dimensions of the technologies and the ethics of Google, and the big data they are producing online—students also strengthen their new media literacy.

Digital writing is another area in which students can engage meaningfully with Ghosh's work. Openly available online, a range of new media composition tools allow students to create and compose multimodal texts that communicate through alphabetic, aural, visual, gestural, and other modes. Digital writing offers students a way of interfacing with the world and communicating in methods that take advantage of rich contemporary media environments. Being able to compose digitally is itself a useful skill, but it also facilitates new ways of writing about literature. Comics, digital stories, remix videos, and social media are a few ways students can use digital writing to explore the *Ibis* trilogy.

A number of online applications allow students to compose in multiple modes and to produce digital texts that demonstrate their understanding, interpretations, and adaptations of Ghosh's work. No longer the domain of children alone, comics represent information through an interdisciplinary medium that asks students to blend alphabetic and visual modes. Comics integrate multiple perspectives, providing a creative form of expression at the meeting place of the visual and the verbal. Moreover, they promote stronger literacy for English language learners. Online applications, many of which are free, make creating comics accessible for students who may not be confident in their artistic skills, as they provide backgrounds, objects, and even customizable avatars that students can design to visualize the novels.[1] Students could be asked to use a scene from one of the novels that best illustrates a theme to compose a four-panel comic that locates the theme within the scene. They could be asked to distill a single message from one of the novels in a single frame. Another possibility is to introduce students to the *Amar Chitra Katha* comics, exemplars of a quintessentially

Indian style, and ask them to collaborate as a class on an *Amar Chitra Katha–*style comic book based on one of the novels. As comics use juxtapositions, they allow students to play with meanings generated through the combinations they compose, giving them an alternative experience of how meaning is constructed that complements how they read the trilogy.

Freely available video-editing software has made digital storytelling and remix videos easier to execute and eliminates the high learning curve of digital editors like *Final Cut Pro.*[2] Digital stories and remix videos offer students a chance to demonstrate their understanding or interpretation of Ghosh's work in creative ways, showcasing their own voices. Digital stories are two- to three-minute videos in which students narrate a story over still images or videos that illustrate the story being told. A simple assignment could ask each student to create a digital story about the *Ibis* told from the perspective of one of the motley crew of characters whose destinies intersect through the ship. A collection of these digital stories would demonstrate the wealth of perspectives in the trilogy. Alternatively, they might create videos that help contextualize the novels, on topics like nineteenth-century seafaring and boats, coolie labor, the caste system, or the Opium Wars. When making remix videos, students take images, texts, sounds, and video that are already available online and combine them in new ways to share a message. Doing so, they put into practice theories of remix, mash-up, and semiotics. Remix videos challenge students to think about important issues in new ways and to identify and use existing sources to communicate a new message. An assignment for the *Ibis* trilogy could assist students with negotiating the historical context of the trilogy. For example, an instructor could ask students to browse online images and archives like *NINES* (nines .org), a compendium of nineteenth-century scholarship, and remix those sources to create companion videos for the *Ibis* trilogy. Because they comprise fragments that require interpretation to make meaning, remix videos offer students an object lesson in how Ghosh uses the fragments of the historical archive to make meaning in the *Ibis* trilogy.

Bringing social media into assignments both engages students with Ghosh's work in new ways and encourages them to see social media as a research tool for literary analysis. *Twitter* (www.twitter.com), which constrains its users to communicate in 280-character messages (tweets), presents a challenge of concision online but offers a number of ways to open up the classroom space. Cross-class or cross-institutional collaboration can be fostered through a *Twitter* hashtag. An instructor might plan to teach one of the novels from the trilogy at the same time as a colleague, compose a common hashtag for the classes, and ask students to tweet their thoughts on the novel and engage with others on the hashtag. Another option is to assign students sections of the novel to live-tweet as they read, using a class hashtag. As students read, they can tweet short summaries, thoughts, and questions. Such a task, rather than distracting students, requires them to be actively engaged in the reading process and conscious of their experience constructing meaning in the trilogy. Alternatively, students could be assigned to tweet from the perspectives of different characters, again using a common hashtag. With characters from so many backgrounds, classes, castes, races, nations, and experiences, the act of thinking through the novels from the perspectives of particular characters helps ground the students' interactions with the trilogy.

Another approach is to draw on existing social media posts to compose an argument about the trilogy. The application *Wakelet* (wakelet.com) helps students use social media to assemble a multimodal document that incorporates text, video, and links. Through a *Wakelet* assignment, students can gain greater understanding of the different forms of evidence available to them online. Ghosh himself is an active social media user, with a *Twitter* feed, a blog, and multiple Web sites and *Facebook* presences. On these platforms, there is a wealth of information that supplements reading the *Ibis* trilogy, such as tweets on topics related to the novels and blog posts that reflect on the linguistic histories informing the novels. An assignment using *Wakelet* might ask students to investigate and analyze Ghosh's social media usage, considering the perspectives it provides on the trilogy. *Wakelet* enables users to search for specific people or individual tweets, blog posts, *Facebook* posts, and Web sites and drag and drop the text, videos, images, and links into a multimodal document. Students can arrange, rearrange, and annotate the sources they add and generate their own text to guide readers through their analyses of Ghosh's social media presence. Another assignment could draw on these sources to develop a *Wakelet* collection about the trilogy's reception using tweets, *Facebook* posts, *YouTube* videos, and blog posts responding to the novels.

Another way to help students navigate the *Ibis* trilogy through social media is by using sites that generate social media posts and networks for fictional characters. Web sites like *Fakebook* (www.classtools.net/FAKEBOOK) and *Simitator* (simitator.com) allow users to compose social media posts in the voices and personae of literary characters. In developing social media presences for specific characters, the class could create a social network for the novels, visualizing relationships between characters. Social network analysis has become a matter of interest within the digital humanities, and, while the forms of analysis used in projects like *Six Degrees of Francis Bacon* (sixdegreesoffrancisbacon .com) are beyond the scope of what is practically achievable in a single class, using social media generator to re-create the social networks within the novels helps students investigate the circles in which characters travel, explore different characters' freedoms and constraints, and define limitations in characters' social connections and mobility.

Other methods of visualizing the text include creating time lines and maps. Given the complex temporal forces that shape the historical era in which the trilogy takes place, a time line assignment can help students identify historical information relevant to interpreting Ghosh's novels and cultivate their curiosity about histories and stories with which they may be unfamiliar.[3] Students might be assigned years whose events they must plot on the time line, composing a précis of each event and choosing an appropriate image to accompany each point. With the complexity of the trilogy's own temporality, students also could be assigned to collaboratively develop a time line that tracks events in the trilogy set alongside historical events, which would generate a visualization of the novels' temporal structures and aid students' interpretations of the novels in the trilogy. In the light of the geographical challenges that the trilogy poses, tracking characters moving back and forth across vast swaths of ocean, from the United States to Mauritius to India to Hong Kong and more, creating maps assists students with conceptualizing the geographies with which Ghosh engages. While Ghosh himself provides maps along with the texts, the act of identifying locations, putting down markers, composing text for these markers, and selecting images or video to accompany them gives the students hands-on experience in mapmaking and cultural mapping.[4] This is an opportune exercise for discussing critical cartography, spatial humanities, and the constructedness and fallibility of maps, as well as the connections between text, space, and place. Such mapping assignments help students see a new dimension of a series like the *Ibis* trilogy that spans multiple locations, while increasing their understanding of the world, allowing them to learn not only how to use but also how to critique geospatial technologies, and developing their critical thinking skills about geospatial data. Combining map and time line assignments goes one step further to help students think critically about geospatial data and time by exploring the relation between geography and temporality.[5]

Finally, rewriting *Wikipedia* is another method for engaging students with the *Ibis* trilogy through digital humanities pedagogy. To the chagrin of many instructors *Wikipedia* has replaced encyclopedias as the go-to source for finding information. As a result, it wields a tremendous amount of power in creating knowledge for the world. Yet it also has the power to constrain that knowledge. A critical look at *Wikipedia* reveals that coverage of the world beyond the United States and Western Europe is lacking. Even within those regions, entries related to ethnic minorities, women, queer communities, and other marginalized groups are comparatively less developed or even missing. The content that is most widely represented on *Wikipedia* reflects the interests of *Wikipedia* editors, the majority of whom are male, middle class, and white. According to the *Wikipedia* editor survey, "If there is a typical Wikipedia editor, he has a college degree, is 30 years old, is computer savvy but not necessarily a programmer, doesn't spend much time playing computer games, and lives in the U.S. or Europe" (Wikimedia Foundation). *Wikipedia*'s editing policies further limit representation on the site. *Wikipedia* uses the adage "verifiability not truth" to gauge what material should be included. Knowledge that has been published many times, even if inaccurate, is "verifiable" and therefore considered to be "reliable" regardless of content (Koh and Risam). The other troubling policy is "notability," used to decide whether a subject is worthy of inclusion. A notable source requires multiple sources that recognize its importance. As a result of these policies, *Wikipedia* reproduces regimes of knowledge and power already implicit in other forms of knowledge—like print—in which marginalized communities already struggle for access and representation (Koh and Risam).

Sending students to examine Ghosh's *Wikipedia* page and the pages for his novels demonstrates the pitfalls of this resource. Asking students to compare the coverage and depth of entries related to Ghosh's work with entries on similarly prolific and canonical contemporary authors like John Updike or Tom Wolfe facilitates their understanding of the politics of knowledge production. Finally, an assignment that asks them to rewrite *Wikipedia* offers them an authentic writing experience and the chance to intervene in issues of representation as they learn how to identify features of a genre and to write within constraints.[6] While editing *Wikipedia* has a learning curve, it is an exercise that is appropriate for the scope of a semester-long course. Students should create accounts using pseudonyms to protect their identities and begin engaging with *Wikipedia* by making small, good-faith edits—trivial corrections, like fixing typos or making minor additions on noncontroversial articles. This demonstrates to the *Wikipedia* editor community that they are not swooping in to mass-modify pages for self-serving purposes and helps establish trust and credibility should a dispute over information occur. When beginning as *Wikipedia* editors, students should consider expanding existing pages before creating new ones. For example, when comparing Ghosh's *Wikipedia* entry or those of his novels with entries related to other writers, students might note what is missing from the Ghosh sources and research the information necessary for contributing to his entries. They should observe the genre conventions of the entries, from the sections typically included in author entries to the level of detail provided about novels to the clinical tone of *Wikipedia* articles, which strive for neutrality and avoid effusive language. They should also observe *Wikipedia*'s style guide for citing peer-reviewed sources supporting their edits and provide a one- or two-sentence rationale for their changes on the "Talk" page. They should save their work frequently in order to create layers of edits that cannot be removed as easily as a single large edit. Whenever possible, they should also create links to other *Wikipedia* pages, which makes their changes harder to delete. Editing *Wikipedia* gives students both experience with the politics that shape how knowledge is produced online and the tools to intervene in it. While critical readings of *Wikipedia* will help shape students into savvy users of it, assigning students to make corrections will shape them into critical users and editors.

Within the broader rubric of digital humanities, there are a number of approaches that are useful for teaching the *Ibis* trilogy. Here I have offered examples of how to use textual analysis, digital writing, social media, maps and time lines, and rewriting *Wikipedia* to engage students with the texts while meeting the challenges of both twenty-first-century literacies and the difficulty of Ghosh's writing. A caveat, however, is that these assignments and activities must be given and assessed with care. They require the instructor to have a strong sense of the connection between each assignment and the learning objectives for the course. They engender questions about whether using technology is the best way to achieve a particular course goal, what the ethical dimensions might be of asking students to sign up for third-party services like *Google* that collect identifying information, and whether the platforms will be accessible for all students. Moreover, instructors may be reticent about assigning alternatives to close reading or essays because they are unfamiliar with how to assess them. Yet understanding how such activities align with measurable learning objectives is the key to assessment; instructors can identify criteria related to these objectives and evaluate students' progress toward meeting the course goals. As such, using digital humanities pedagogy to teach the *Ibis* trilogy is rife with affordances in the development of twenty-first-century literacies and of strategies students need to be good readers and creators of knowledge. It fosters creativity and media literacy and encourages students to develop their communication, teamwork, problem solving, and critical thinking skills—all while offering multiple points of entry for Ghosh's rich trilogy.

NOTES

[1] Among the comic generators easiest to use are *Bitmoji* (www.bitmoji.com), *Toondoo* (www.toondoo.com), *Stripgenerator* (stripgenerator.com/strip/create), *Strip Creator* (www.stripcreator.com/make.php), *Comic Life* (plasq.com), *Comic Creator* (www.readwritethink.org/files/resources/interactives/comic), and *Make Beliefs Comix* (www.makebeliefscomix.com/Comix).

[2] Some useful tools that allow students to create and disseminate videos include *WeVideo* (wevideo.com), *Magisto* (magisto.com), *Loopster* (loopster.com), *Shotclip* (shotclip.com), *YouTube* (youtube.com), and *Vimeo* (vimeo.com).

[3] Time line apps useful for such assignments are *Capzles* (capzles.com), *MyHistro* (www.myhistro.com), *Read Write Think Timeline* (www.readwritethink.org/files/resources/interactives/timeline_2), *Tiki-Toki* (www.tiki-toki.com), and *TimeGlider* (timeglider.com).

[4] Maps can be easily created using *Google Maps* (maps.google.com), *Google Earth* (earth.google.com), and the *National Geographic* map tool (mapmaker.nationalgeographic.org). Through the archival content management system *Omeka*, the *Neatline* plugin (neatline.org) is useful for making maps but requires a self-hosted *Omeka* installation.

[5] *TimeMapper* (timemapper.okfnlabs.org) is a simple way to blend time lines and maps, and the *NeatlineSimile* plugin (omeka.org/add-ons/plugins/neatlinesimile), which also requires a self-hosted *Omeka* installation, creates time lines that can be added to *Neatline* maps.

[6] Some useful resources for teaching with *Wikipedia* include the Wikipedia Education Program (outreach.wikimedia.org/wiki/Education), Wadewitz et al., and Koh and Risam.

Savvy, No Savvy:
Reading *River of Smoke* in China

Emily Stone

A sprawling novel set almost two hundred years in the past, with a sinuous narrative overflowing with temperamentally and culturally diverse characters who speak to one another entirely in a system of international English dialects seen perhaps nowhere in print outside the trilogy that contains the volume, may seem an overwhelming assignment for Chinese undergraduates. At the same time, the historical novel's setting in the Chinese city that was briefly recognized as Canton, but was long before and is again today referred to as Guangzhou; its characters' reliance on Cantonese words to communicate with one another despite their individual national origins; and the balance of the story upon waves in the opium trade that reverberated through China, the South China Sea, the British Empire, and the rest of the world also made it an obvious choice for a class titled Cross-Cultural Literature: Representations of China in the West, which I taught at Sun Yat-sen University (SYSU) in Guangzhou in the spring of 2012.

This essay discusses work my students did with Amitav Ghosh's *River of Smoke* in and outside class, with particular attention to a reading exercise that makes use of difficulty (a term I borrow from Mariolina Rizzi Salvatori and Patricia Donahue) in order to arrive at both a more confident and a more nuanced understanding of Ghosh's story. My students came from across the disciplines, and for some this was the only class in global literature or English-language literature that they would take. Reading the novel was entertaining beyond expectations for many people in the class, myself included, as a result of the collaborative nature of the project. This essay is a result of the same collaboration.

River of Smoke was one of three core texts for the class, along with Pearl Buck's *The Good Earth* and Maxine Hong Kingston's *Tripmaster Monkey*. What the novels share beyond the blanket similarity of taking China or the Chinese diaspora as their subject is a storytelling hybridity that belongs partially to the authors—Buck was one of the only ethnically non-Chinese American citizens in the twentieth century to have grown up in China and to have approached her life and her work with a largely culturally Chinese identity; Kingston often plays with a Chinatown identity that is related to but not entirely recognizable as either Chinese culture or American culture; and, in Ghosh's own words, "I'm from a family that has been displaced many times" (Teeman)— and partially to the characters and settings (*Tripmaster Monkey* takes place in and around San Francisco's Chinatown, a microcosm of a larger, hypothetically inclusive, if often uncertain and unsettled, multiethnic and multicultural America; *River of Smoke* is centered on a colonial-era combination of cosmopolitanism and lawlessness in the Pearl River Delta; *The Good Earth* is the outlier in that it addresses an insular society in an unadorned realist style). That hybridity makes the novels difficult to summarize, to distill, or, as some students put it, to "get." It also allows for, even demands, multiple readings of the same narrative depending upon the audience's particular points of connection. In a class about cultural exchange, those nuanced readings struck me as essential.

The critical framework for all of this reading was (and was limited to) the introduction to Edward Said's *Orientalism*. We spent the first weeks of the term with Said, first working on reading comprehension, then interrogating the ideas in the text, and ultimately looking for contemporary applications of those ideas (at the time, there was a great deal of popular interest, globally, in the apocalyptic treatment of the year 2012 among the ancient and contemporary Maya people, which gave us examples of hegemonic appropriation of the cultural material of a subaltern group). As a jumping-off point for reading *River of Smoke* and the other assigned literary texts, the opening pages of *Orientalism* introduce students to the general notion that otherness and foreignness are not products of a static reality but constructions that alter both the perceiver and the perceived.

The word "general" is important here. Administrators in China in the first decades of the twenty-first century have been particularly interested in American and European pedagogies that reward critical thinking over giving teachers answers that they already know. (And foreign teachers have much to contribute, but if our expertise indeed lies in such critical thinking, we would be remiss if we did not acknowledge that practices in conventional Chinese classrooms necessarily result from a nuanced set of cultural assumptions that we're unlikely to be able to fully understand.) The Cross-Cultural Literature class at SYSU was in part conceived as a simulation of the curriculum and the style of an upper-level class for English majors at an American university. The work was conducted entirely in English (I cannot read or speak Mandarin, China's official language and the language of the university, or Cantonese, the language of the region where the university is located.) This was a small seminar course with about ten students (counting auditors), half of whom were English majors at SYSU and the other half of whom came from across the disciplines. This was an ambitious project for the students to take on since English was a foreign language for all of them and the structure of the course was unfamiliar to them. Their vast knowledge of Chinese culture and history compensated for some of that uncertainty and in effect allowed them to replace one kind of expertise with another.

One way to describe this class is as a general introduction to difficult texts that worked by asking the students to pay attention to how their own experience as Chinese readers of English-language literature about China contributed to or alleviated the difficulty that was organic to the texts. The writing assignments worked toward the same end: over the term, students wrote three short "read-research-respond" papers in which they offered a preliminary personal response to a text in the first paragraph, followed by a second paragraph summarizing outside research and then a third paragraph placing the personal interest within the larger literary or critical context; the instructions for the final paper were to examine how one of the assigned novels functions in a contemporary Chinese context. The challenge of the course was to offer a survey of English-language literature about China and, at the same time, to introduce students to the conventions of writing about literature in English.

Orientalism provides students with a vocabulary and a historical precedent for ideas about otherness, hybridity, hegemony, power, and perception. Of course, Said's examples are no longer contemporary or ultimately the most relevant to the representations of China in global literature in the twenty-first century. Said's Orient is not East Asia but India and the Middle East; the hegemonic power is not American popular culture but British and French colonialism. Marking these ways in which specific terms and references deviate from what we expect them to mean was itself a lesson in critical reading that prepared the students to work with the complicated prose of the assigned novelists.

Said describes orientalism as a discourse that

> is produced and exists in an uneven exchange with various kinds of power, shaped to a degree by the exchange with power political (as with a colonial or imperial establishment), power intellectual (as with reigning sciences like comparative linguistics or anatomy, or any of the modern policy sciences), power cultural (as with orthodoxies and canons of taste, texts, values), power moral (as with ideas about what "we" do and what "they" cannot do or understand as "we" do). (20)

This is now a commonly held belief in most (or, complicatedly, certainly most Western) academic and literary communities. But, for Chinese college students (and, for that matter, American college students) who are new to literary and political theory, Said's suggestion is as revolutionary today as it was when the book was published in 1978. For that reason, starting with *Orientalism* helped my students recognize instances of mainstream postcolonial thought that they might otherwise have missed in the assigned novels as well as in the criticism of those novels (including reviews in major media) that they came across in their research.

One reviewer of Ghosh's *River of Smoke* wrote that, while "the past can sometimes feel tamed" in historical novels, with hindsight "hovering just off the page," Ghosh achieves a remarkable intimacy with the past, its characters, their ambiguities, and their arbitrary stumbles and successes, "somehow succeed[ing] in taking us back inside the chaos of when 'then' was 'now'" (Hadley). Bahram's earnestness as an entrepreneur is palpable. Neel's phenomenal adaptability is awe-inspiring. (It is difficult to ignore, however, that readers almost never have the opportunity to see the inner lives of the novel's Chinese characters.) If I can extract one more general tenet from postcolonial theory, it is that the world is more complicated than we understand it to be. Since its inception, the genre of the novel (with its elision of internal and external spaces, its panoramic description, and its capacious digressions) has shared that assumption. And Ghosh relishes just such complexity as both a thinker and a storyteller. In *River of Smoke*, the systems of power and corruption are not easily delineated. To begin, how do we categorize a work that is written in English and published in England but is a product of India? Since the characters themselves are hybrids of so many cultures, all of which have an effect on their fortunes, do we understand these people to be the manipulators or the manipulated? In a world where the British sphere of influence spreads and comes to include more and more satellite locations, how can we understand the relation of one of these locations to another? My student Xueying Li pointed to this dilemma surrounding the novel's central character in her final paper, "A Metaphor for Multiculturalism: The Characterization in *River of Smoke*":

> For contemporary Chinese readers, we are aware that the opium trade is bad and dirty, filled with violence, greed. The British government is trying to seize territory and sovereignty in the banner of openness, freedom and liberty. However, what Ghosh does in the book is not only to reveal the hypocrisy the readers can read into lines by themselves, but further offer a [much tougher] position for us to experience: you are making profits from the opium yet you are not a bad guy. Bahram is such a model.

These ambiguities of meaning are indeed written into the story. As Li explains, "By nature language can be an obstacle blocking communications as well as a bridge connecting various cultures according to the context and discourse it is in." Ghosh is interested in the languages of the high seas:

> Laskari—that motley tongue, spoken nowhere but on the water, whose words were as varied as the port's traffic, an anarchic medley of Portuguese calaluzes and Keral pattimars, Arab booms and Bengal paunchways, Malay proas and Tamil catamarans, Hindusthani pulwars and English snows—yet beneath the surface of this farrago of sound, meaning flowed as freely as the currents beneath the crowded press of boats. (*Sea of Poppies* 102)[1]

And he is interested in the language of the trade ports:

> In pidgin they reposed far greater trust, for the grammar was the same as that of Cantonese, while the words were mainly English, Portuguese and Hindusthani—and such being the case, everyone who spoke the jargon was at an equal disadvantage, which was considered a great benefit to all. (*River of Smoke* 163)[2]

These languages capture, in their sounds and implications, in their connections and missed connections, the politics of those spaces.

It is impossible to separate Ghosh's treatment of the history of the Opium Wars from the language of the novel. Noticing how narrative and form overlap, each one a metaphor for the other, can be one of the great joys of reading the books in the *Ibis* trilogy. Yet some native English speakers as well as foreign readers express frustration that they don't get *River of Smoke* on the first attempt. Both the language and the story seem impenetrable, each one stalling the other. Some readers believe they lack the expertise to comprehend the book, and second-language learners especially may throw up their hands at the experience of searching for unfamiliar words in the dictionary and not finding them there. The opportunity then is to point out this overlap between language and story as an asset of the text rather than as a defect of the reader. What appears to be impenetrable code is in fact the key to deciphering the text. Laskari and pidgin are by definition inexpert languages and evolve in real time. Coincidentally, this is the linguistic environment of the classroom too.

I took advantage of that resonant classroom space with my SYSU students and made the work of reading Ghosh collaborative. We read the text aloud, as if we were doing a dramatic performance. My students and I worked slowly and enthusiastically through passages from the text together, in much the same way that I had worked with the same population of students on dialogues from Shakespeare in another class. The results were much the same: words, phrases, and patterns of speech that initially appeared to be inscrutable became lyrical and logical in the readers' mouths. I can identify a few reasons why this works: It's easier to skim over something that you don't understand than to pronounce it word for word—reading aloud makes students accountable to one another and themselves. Pronouncing an unfamiliar word, particularly one written in dialect, is sometimes all a reader needs to do to arrive at the familiar form (*allo* for "all the" and *wanchi* for "want" pick up their natural inflections when spoken in the context of an otherwise recognizable sentence). And (in a more holistic version of those same results) reading aloud allows for meaning to emerge in context. As the emotional reality of the scene becomes clear, the words remain as unfamiliar as before but the possibilities for their meaning narrows, giving the reader and the reading more confidence. (Ghosh, like Shakespeare, combines an uncanny and ironic play with language with canny and unironic narrative; the double and triple entendres provide shape and elegance to stories that are pure joy and heartache.) In this particular instance, many of the students knew Cantonese but with varying degrees of fluency, fewer recognized Fujianese words, some knew local geography, and others had insight into the interactions between Chinese citizens and Indian visitors described in the book. This provided an opportunity not only to interpret the text but also to consider the way that local knowledge (and by extension any individualized, specialized knowledge) positions a reader in relationship to a text. This reading practice, together with the read-research-respond writing assignments, reinforced the notion (one that, if we look back to Said, has both positive and negative connotations) that meaning is participatory.

This is a lesson much better learned in practice than in theory, and my students and I spent two one-hour class sessions immersed in a ten-page passage from *River of Smoke*. The scene I chose was a conversation between the Indian opium trader Bahram Modi (also known as Barry Moddie) and the Chinese drug dealer Ah-Lau, or Allow, in chapter nine. Taking the middle of the book as our point of departure had practical as well as pedagogical benefits. Practically, scheduling constraints and language limitations made it impossible for the students to read all three assigned novels from beginning to end; instead I chose representative excerpts ranging from fifty to one hundred pages from each novel to work on together as a group and invited students to choose one of the three to finish reading independently in preparation for the final paper. Pedagogically, starting in the middle demonstrated that it is possible to understand a text in spite of challenging unknowns. *River of Smoke* in fact throws all readers into the middle: the middle of the *Ibis* trilogy narrative, the middle of an endlessly nuanced history, the middle of a cultural and linguistic interchange that the author no doubt expects to be simultaneously alien and accessible.

This in-class reading is risky, because it relies on something like an epiphany. It starts with the assumption that students are having trouble understanding the text (I asked them to struggle with it on their own for homework as preparation for a rereading in class) and anticipates a substantive change in that experience in a short period of time. The degree to which both of those things turn out to be the case is unpredictable, depending upon the particular students and the dynamics of the discussion on any given day. I suggest that teachers avoid overpreparing for this exercise, which is ultimately less about translating the text than it is about demonstrating that the text is translatable. In my case, as a non-Cantonese speaker reading the recently published novel for the first time, I could teach my students how *River of Smoke* worked only by asking them to help me understand what it meant. I can't think of a better example of differently situated knowledges and different positions vis-à-vis a text.

We started with the introduction of Ah-Lau/Allow by Bahram's purser, Vico, who explains, "Patrão, it is one Ho Sin-saang. His full name is Ho Lao-kin. . . . Maybe you knew him by a different name, patrão. These Chinese fellows are always changing their names—one minute it's Ah-something and next minute it's Sin-saang this and Sin-saang that," which I recognized as disparaging in tone, though I failed to catch the slapstick absurdity of Vico's misunderstanding (in fact one that, to that point, I had shared in my own encounters with Chinese people) until a student explained that "Sin-saang" is merely a term for "mister," while the "Ah" before a name is a form of casual address. We continued on, translating between Cantonese, pidgin (really a noun meaning "business," the novel tells us, before it was an adjective to describe the business-centered language of Canton's Fanqui Town and then a term for such languages generally), and English. Along the way, we contemplated the relation between linguistics and constructions of power. For instance, what does it say about the colonial enterprise that *gamsia*, a Fujianese word for thanks or gratitude, became the gritty *cumshaw*, meaning to tip someone or pay someone off? We found new confidence in the words we didn't know: no one in the room, neither the teacher nor the students, had any prior knowledge of the Indian words for opium that appear in the text (yet more evidence of a situated reading), but we could agree on their meaning nonetheless.

Placing the unfamiliar in the context of the familiar (with the help of Johnny Depp in *Pirates of the Caribbean*), we puzzled through the etymology of the novel's vernacular to recognize that "This-time cannot do-pidgin in Canton. . . . Mister Barry savvy, no-savvy ah?" translates to something along the lines of "You can't do business in Canton now—do you understand?" Most students still found that the expansive novel was too cumbersome to take on in a term paper, but comments on shorter assignments included "Guessing, exploring, and learning pidgin make the reading joyful" (Zeyin Liu) and "it is hard at first, especially for a nonnative reader. But when our brain [gets] used to this language, it suddenly [becomes] attractive and amusing" (Yolanda Zhang).

I developed the Cross-Cultural Literature course and this reading exercise with Chinese readers studying English as a foreign language (EFL) in mind. But my EFL exercises are always based on the belief that learning a language is intellectual work, a set of conceptual problems rather than a pursuit of mastery. The EFL classroom provides an opportunity to draw particular attention to the relation between the language and the story of any text in part because students must actively attend to the literal and figurative meaning of individual words where native speakers, assuming they are confident readers, do this automatically. Of course, many readers in their native language, perhaps especially at the undergraduate level, are overconfident and confuse an inherent understanding of a sentence or passage with an overly general reading, an oversimplified reading, or a convenient misreading. Therefore, the exercises outlined here could be equally beneficial to student readers of Ghosh who are native English speakers. The text provides several points of intersection in dialogue that might make useful jumping-off points. Baboo Nob Kissin, Bahram Modi, and Neel Rattan Halder (the former Raja of Raskhali now known as Anil Kumar Munshi) would allow students familiar with India and Indian dialects to do similar work. For students who might still recognize the speech patterns of Anglo-India, the Burnhams, who originated in *Sea of Poppies* and reappear in *Flood of Fire*, are perfect specimens. Students who are casually or formally multilingual in European languages should make use of Paulette Lambert's conversations with Zachary Reed or Fitcher Penrose, or with anyone who comes across her path for that matter. *River of Smoke*'s first chapter, set on Mauritius, takes the form of a Kreol overture in which the Gran Vakans of Deeti's Fami familiarly drop readers into the center of another world from which they must navigate their way back.

River of Smoke brings with it a three-part discovery for Chinese students (all the more exciting if it unfolds organically): that a great many of the unfamiliar and nonstandard words in the novel are deliberately so; that any reader—Eastern or Western; Indian or Chinese; speaker of Bengali or Gujarati, of Cantonese or Fujianese; teacher or student—will find that his or her access to the text is determined by a very specific linguistic and cultural position; and that it may be precisely their position as Chinese speakers that allows them to put meaning together, join text and context, and follow information to implication. Ghosh's novels, in their play with language and their fascination with vocabulary and etymology, construct a literary space in which there is no omniscient reader. Encoded in this approach is a set of instructions for the general reader, not to mention the generalist teacher: difficult texts depend upon the reader's ability and willingness to make sense of the unfamiliar in the context of the familiar. *River of Smoke* offers an alternative to the limited vocabulary of the reductive and unambiguous "global English" (or "business English," whatever ironic connection such a dialect may have to the pidgin English of this cast of characters) promoted in educational settings abroad. The *Ibis* carries a language that can construct its own world on the page while reflecting the three-dimensional one in which we live—never finished, always open to interpretation.

NOTES

I am especially grateful to my student Xueying Li, whose excellent final paper for the course led me to some of the secondary sources on Ghosh that I use here and who, along with her peers Zeyin Liu and Hang Tu, helped me to re-create some of the translations that the class originally discovered together.
[1] This essay uses the Picador 2009 edition of *Sea of Poppies*.
[2] This essay uses the Picador 2012 edition of *River of Smoke*.

NOTES ON CONTRIBUTORS

Kanika Batra is professor in the Department of English, Texas Tech University. She teaches, researches, and publishes in postcolonial, gender, and urban studies and is working on a book manuscript on postcolonial feminist and queer publications.

Russell A. Berman is Walter A. Hass Professor in the Humanities in the Departments of German Studies and Comparative Literature, Stanford University. He writes on topics in German literary and intellectual history, including Theodor Fontane and Thomas Mann, as well as on contemporary issues bearing on transatlantic relations and the Middle East. His publications include *Fiction Sets You Free* (2007), "Life after Merkel" (2016), and "Arendt's Conservatism and the Eichmann Judgment" (2017). He is the editor of *Telos*.

Ned Bertz is associate professor of history at the University of Hawaiʻi, Mānoa. He is the author of *Diaspora and Nation in the Indian Ocean: Transnational Histories of Race and Urban Space in Tanzania* (2015).

Vincent van Bever Donker is associate lecturer in English at the University of Northampton. His monograph *Recognition and Ethics in World Literature: Religion, Violence, and the Human* develops the structural and philosophical importance of recognition for engaging with both the ethical challenges and commitments of world literature. His research interests also include the secular and the sacred in African literature and the shifting forms of empire in popular science fiction.

Vedita Cowaloosur teaches in the mass communication program at Curtin Mauritius (Charles Telfair Campus). She completed her postdoctoral fellowship in the English Department at Stellenbosch University in South Africa and her PhD in English and comparative literary studies at the University of Warwick, UK. Her research interests include the politics of language in South Asian literary and popular culture as well as Indian literature in translation.

Smita Das is a postdoctoral scholar recently graduated from the University of Illinois, Chicago. Her work, which explores race, gender, and sexuality in the South Asian and African diasporas, has been published in *South Asian Review, Journal of Black Studies*, and *Interdisciplinary Journal of Portuguese Diaspora Studies*.

Gaurav Desai is professor in the Department of English, University of Michigan, Ann Arbor. He previously taught at Tulane University. He is the author of *Subject to Colonialism: African Self-Fashioning and the Colonial Library* (2001) and *Commerce with the Universe: Africa, India, and the Afrasian Imagination* (2013). He is also coeditor of *Postcolonialisms: An Anthology of Cultural Theory and Criticism* (2005) and editor of *Teaching the African Novel* (2009).

Debjani Ganguly is professor of English and director of the Institute of the Humanities and Global Cultures at the University of Virginia. She is the author of *This Thing Called the World: The Contemporary Novel as Global Form* (2016) and *Caste, Colonialism and Counter-modernity* (2005). She is currently editing a two-volume *Cambridge*

History of World Literature and working on a book project called "Techno-planetary Catastrophes: Form at the Limits of the Human."

Robbie B. H. Goh is professor of English at the National University of Singapore. Some of his more recent publications include *Protestant Christianity in the Indian Diaspora: Abjected Identities, Evangelical Relations, and Pentecostal Visions* (2018), *The Politics of English in Asia* (coedited with Lionel Wee and Lisa Lim), and articles in *Asian Studies Review, Culture and Religion,* and *Social Semiotics.*

Ambreen Hai is professor of English language and literature at Smith College, where she teaches anglophone postcolonial literature from South Asia, Africa, and the Caribbean; literature of the British Empire; literary theory; and women's and gender studies. She is the author of *Making Words Matter: The Agency of Colonial and Postcolonial Literature* and many scholarly articles on postcolonial and transnational writing.

John Hawley is professor of English at Santa Clara University and president of the South Asian Literary Association. He is the author of *Amitav Ghosh: An Introduction* (2005), coeditor of *The Postcolonial and the Global* (2007), and editor of a special issue of the *South Asian Review* on the future of South Asian studies.

Ben Holgate is a Leverhulme Early Career Fellow at Queen Mary University of London in the Department of Comparative Literature. Previously he was an associate lecturer at the University of York, UK, in the Department of English and Related Literature. Ben's first monograph, which is about magical realism as environmental discourse, will be published by Routledge in 2019.

Adele Holoch is an adjunct faculty member who teaches in the Core Division of Champlain College. Her publications and research interests consider humor as a mode of community building and resistance, focusing on satire, profanity, and the grotesque in contemporary postcolonial literature.

Alan Johnson is professor of English at Idaho State University. He is the author of a 2011 book on British-Indian literature as well as articles on such topics as Mahasweta Devi, ecocriticism, Hindi film, and the humanities.

Suchitra Mathur is professor of English at the Indian Institute of Technology, Kanpur. She works in the areas of gender studies and cultural studies, with special focus on Indian popular culture.

Arnapurna Rath is assistant professor of English in the discipline of humanities at the Indian Institute of Technology, Gandhinagar. Her research interests are in the fields of South Asian literature, Bakhtin studies, comparative literature, and digital media. Her academic writings have appeared in such journals as *Asiatic, JSL, Journal of Human Values, Church History and Religious Culture, South Asian Review, Asia Pacific Translation and Intercultural Studies,* and *Littcrit.* A compilation of her poems, *Devi: A Journey through Photo-Poetry,* was published in 2014.

Roopika Risam is assistant professor of English at Salem State University. Her research focuses on digital humanities, and her book *New Digital Worlds: Postcolonial Digital Humanities in Theory, Praxis, and Pedagogy* will be published by Northwestern University Press in 2018.

Sneharika Roy is assistant professor in the Comparative Literature and English Department at the American University of Paris and a contributor to the encyclopedic project *Dictionnaire encyclopédique des littératures de l'Inde (Encyclopaedic Dictionary of Indian Literature)*. Her book *The Postcolonial Epic: From Melville to Walcott and Ghosh* (2018) offers a fresh comparative theory of epic, bridging classical and postcolonial perspectives.

Albeena Shakil is associate professor of English at the O.P. Jindal Global University, Sonipat, India. She is a former fellow of the Indian Institute of Advanced Study, Shimla, and authored *Understanding the Novel: A Theoretical Overview* in 2015.

Yumna Siddiqi is associate professor of English at Middlebury College. Her book *Anxieties of Empire and the Fiction of Intrigue* (2008) explores the contradictions of postcolonial modernity in detection and espionage fiction at the turns of the nineteenth and twentieth centuries, and she has published articles on postcolonial literature and culture in *Cultural Critique, Victorian Literature and Culture, Renaissance Drama, Alif, South Asia Research*, and *Textual Practice*.

Jonathan Steinwand is professor of English and codirector of the environmental studies program at Concordia College in Moorhead, Minnesota, where he teaches courses on global literature and environmental justice, mentors Fulbright candidates, and serves on the President's Sustainability Council. His most recent publication is "Teaching Environmental Justice Poetry in the Anthropocene" in *The Journal of Commonwealth and Postcolonial Studies*.

Emily Stone is a lecturer in the expository writing program at New York University. Her essays and poems have appeared in literary magazines such as *Tin House, AGNI, Fourth Genre, North American Review*, and *Front Porch*; she has been listed several times among the notable authors in *The Best American Essays* and *The Best American Travel Writing*.

John J. Su is vice provost for academic affairs and professor of English at Marquette University. Su is the author of *Ethics and Nostalgia in the Contemporary Novel* (2005), *Imagination and the Contemporary Novel* (2011), and more than twenty essays and articles on global anglophone literatures.

Hilary Thompson is associate professor of English at Bowdoin College. She is the author of *Novel Creatures: Animal Life and the New Millennium* (2018). Her research focuses on contemporary global anglophone literature, particularly questions of the animal and globalization.

SURVEY PARTICIPANTS

Prantik Banerjee, *Hislop College, Nagpur, Maharashtra, India*
Kanika Batra, *Texas Tech University*
Cameron Bushnell, *Clemson University*
Madhurima Chakraborty, *Columbia College, Chicago*
Shantanu Chakravarty, *Guru Nanak Institute of Technology*
Claire Chambers, *University of York*
Sharmistha Chatterjee (Sriwastav), *Aliah University, Salt Lake, Kolkata, India*
Smita Das, *University of Illinois, Chicago*
Asis De, *Mahishadal Raj College, Vidyasagar University, Kolkata, India*
Maria-Sabina Draga Alexandru, *University of Bucharest*
Dave Gunning, *University of Birmingham*
Anna Guttman, *Lakehead University*
John C. Hawley, *Santa Clara University*
Ben Holgate, *Oxford University*
Adele Holoch, *Champlain College*
Julia Hoydis, *University of Cologne, Germany*
Nalini Iyer, *Seattle University*
Smita Jha, *Indian Institute of Technology, Roorkee*
Alan G. Johnson, *Idaho State University*
H. Kalpana, *Pondicherry University*
Rajender Kaur, *William Paterson University*
Afrinul Haque Khan, *Nirmala College, Ranchi, India*
Sharon Kinoshita, *University of California, Santa Cruz*
H. S. Komalesha, *Indian Institute of Technology, Kharagpur*
S. Somasundari Latha, *R.V. Government Arts College, Chengalpattu, Tamil Nadu, India*
Sabine Lauret, *Université de Franche-Comté, Besançon, France*
Sheetal Majithia, *New York University, Abu Dhabi*
Somdatta Mandal, *Visva-Bharati University, Santiniketan, India*
Mukti Lakhi Mangharam, *Rutgers University, New Brunswick*
Jens Martin, *University of Duisburg, Essen*
John Marx, *University of California, Davis*
Suchitra Mathur, *Indian Institute of Technology, Kanpur*
Juan Meneses, *University of North Carolina, Charlotte*
Bhanumati Mishra, *Arya Mahila P.G. College, Banaras Hindu University, India*
Anupama Mohan, *Presidency University, Kolkata, India*
Padmini Mongia, *Franklin and Marshall College*
Patrick D. Murphy, *University of Central Florida*
Gaura Narayan, *Purchase College, State University of New York*
Sowon S. Park, *Oxford University*
Chris Phillips, *Lafayette College*
Sanjukta Poddar, *St. Stephen's College, University of Delhi*
Janet M. Powers, *Gettysburg College*
P. Prathibha, *Vimala College, Thrissur, India*

Michael C. Prusse, *Zurich University of Teacher Education*
Nishi Pulugurtha, *Brahmananda Keshab Chandra College, Kolkata, India*
N. K. Rajalakshmi, *Mangalore University College, Mangalore, India*
Arnapurna Rath, *Indian Institute of Technology, Gandhinagar*
Mala Renganathan, *North-Eastern Hill University, Shillong, India*
Roopika Risam, *Salem State University*
Anjali Roy, *Indian Institute of Technology, Kharagpur*
Nilakshi Roy, *Kelkar Education Trust's V.G. Vaze College, Mulund, Mumbai, India*
Brahma Dutta Sharma, *Taiz University, Turba, Yemen*
Maya M. Sharma, *Hostos Community College, City University of New York*
Jonathan Steinwand, *Concordia College, Moorhead, Minnesota*
Emily Stone, *New York University*
John J. Su, *Marquette University*
Tamishra Swain, *Banasthali Vidyapith, Rajasthan, India*
Ashley Tellis, *O.P. Jindal Global University, India*
Hilary Thompson, *Bowdoin College*
Terri Tomsky, *University of Alberta*
Alessandro Vescovi, *Università degli Studi di Milano*
Katrina Woltmann, *University of California, San Diego*

WORKS CITED

"About Us." *Leonardo DiCaprio Foundation*, www.leonardodicaprio.org/about.

Acharjee, Suman, and Gyanabati Khuraijam. "Representation of Dismantled Identity and Colonial Politics in Amitav Ghosh's *Sea of Poppies*." *International Journal of English Language, Literature and Humanities*, vol. 2, no. 3, July 2014, pp. 59–67.

Acharya, Gunvantrai. *Dariyalal*. 1934. Thema Books, 2000.

Achebe, Chinua. *Hopes and Impediments: Selected Essays*. Doubleday, 1989.

———. *Things Fall Apart*. 1959. Doubleday/Anchor Books, 1994.

Adamson, Jane, et al., editors. *Renegotiating Ethics in Literature, Philosophy, and Theory*. Cambridge UP, 1998.

Adamson, Joni. "Indigenous Literatures, Multinaturalism, and *Avatar*: The Emergence of Indigenous Cosmopolitics." *American Literary History*, vol. 24, no. 1, Spring 2012, pp. 143–62.

Agrawal, Devyani. "Un-essentialising Marginality in *Sea of Poppies*." *Muse India*, Nov.–Dec. 2012.

Ahmad, Aijaz. *In Theory: Classes, Nations, Literatures*. Oxford UP, 1994.

———. "The Politics of Literary Postcoloniality." Mongia, pp. 276–93.

"*AHR* Roundtable: History Meets Fiction in the Indian Ocean: On Amitav Ghosh's *Ibis* Trilogy." *The American Historical Review*, vol. 121, no. 5, Dec. 2016, pp. 1521–65.

Ahuja, Neel. "Species in a Planetary Frame: Eco-cosmopolitanism, Nationalism, and *The Cove*." *Tamkang Review*, vol. 42, no. 2, June 2012, pp. 13–32.

Ain, Sandip, editor. *Amitav Ghosh's* The Shadow Lines: *A Critical Anthology*. Worldview Publications, 2011.

Alam, Fakrul. "Amitav Ghosh." *Writers of the Indian Diaspora: A Bio-bibliographical Critical Sourcebook*, edited by Emmanuel S. Nelson, Greenwood Press, 1993, pp. 137–46.

Alavi, Hamza. "The State in Post-colonial Societies: Pakistan and Bangladesh." *New Left Review*, vol. 74, July–Aug. 1972, pp. 59–81.

Aldea, Eva. *Magical Realism and Deleuze: The Indiscernibility of Difference in Postcolonial Literature*. Continuum, 2011.

Almond, Ian. "Post-colonial Melancholy: An Examination of Sadness in Amitav Ghosh's *The Shadow Lines*." *Orbis Litterarum*, vol. 59, no. 2, Apr. 2004, pp. 90–99.

Alpers, Edward A. *The Indian Ocean in World History*. Oxford UP, 2014.

Ambethkar, Raja, and K. Jaya Raj. "Restoration of Human Spirit in *The Hungry Tide* of Amitav Ghosh." *The Criterion*, vol. 3, no. 3, 2012, pp. 2–10.

Ambethkar, Raja, and K. K. Sunalini. "The Spirit of Exploration and New Ways of Perceiving Reality in *The Sea of Poppies* of Amitav Ghosh." *European Academic Research*, vol. 2, no. 11, Feb. 2015, pp. 14092–104.

Amelya, Ade, and Muhd Al-Hafizh. "The Curtailment of Human Rights in Amitav Ghosh's Novel *The Hungry Tide*." *E-Journal English Language and Literature*, vol. 1, no. 3, 2013, pp. 1–11.

Amrith, Sunil S. *Crossing the Bay of Bengal: The Furies of Nature and the Fortune of Migrants*. Harvard UP, 2013.

Anand, Divya. "Words on Water: Nature and Agency in Amitav Ghosh's *The Hungry Tide*." *Concentric: Literary and Cultural Studies*, vol. 34, no. 1, Mar. 2008, pp. 21–44.

Anderson, Benedict. *Imagined Communities: Reflections on the Origin and Spread of Nationalism*. Verso, 1983.

Anderson, Clare. "Convicts and Coolies: Rethinking Indentured Labour in the Nineteenth Century." *Slavery and Abolition*, vol. 30, no. 1, 2009, pp. 93–109.

Anjaria, Ulka, editor. *A History of the Indian Novel in English*. Cambridge UP, 2015.

Ankersmit, F. R. *Sublime Historical Experience*. Stanford UP, 2005.

Appadurai, Arjun. "Disjuncture and Difference in the Global Cultural Economy." *Modernity at Large: Cultural Dimensions of Globalization*, U of Minnesota P, 1996, pp. 27–47.

———. *Fear of Small Numbers: An Essay on the Geography of Anger*. Duke UP, 2006.

Apter, Emily. *Against World Literature: On the Politics of Untranslatability*. Verso, 2013.

Arendt, Hannah. *The Human Condition*. U of Chicago P, 1958.

Arora, Anupama. "'The Sea Is History': Opium, Colonialism, and Migration in Amitav Ghosh's *Sea of Poppies*." *ARIEL*, vol. 42, nos. 3–4, 2012, pp. 21–42.

Ashcroft, Bill, et al., editors. Part XIII Introduction. *The Post-colonial Studies Reader*, Routledge, 1995, pp. 425–27.

Atwood, Margaret. *MaddAddam*. Anchor Books, 2014.

———. *Oryx and Crake*. Anchor Books, 2004.

———. *The Year of the Flood*. Anchor Books, 2010.

Bagchi, Nivedita. "The Process of Validation in Relation to Materiality and Historical Reconstruction in Amitav Ghosh's *The Shadow Lines*." *Modern Fiction Studies*, vol. 39, no. 1, Spring 1993, pp. 187–202.

Bahadur, Gaiutra. *Coolie Woman: The Odyssey of Indenture*. U of Chicago P, 2014.

Bakhtin, M. M. "The Bildungsroman and Its Significance in the History of Realism (Toward a Historical Typology of the Novel)." *Speech Genres and Other Late Essays*, edited by Caryl Emerson and Michael Holquist, translated by Vern W. McGee, U of Texas P, 1986, pp. 10–59.

———. *The Dialogic Imagination: Four Essays*. Edited by Michael Holquist, translated by Caryl Emerson and Holquist, U of Texas P, 1982.

———. "Forms of Time and of the Chronotope in the Novel." Bakhtin, *Dialogic Imagination*, pp. 84–258.

Banerjee, Suparno. "*The Calcutta Chromosome*: A Novel of Silence, Slippage and Subversion." *Science Fiction, Imperialism and the Third World: Essays on Postcolonial Literature and Film*, edited by Ericka Hoagland and Reema Sarwal, McFarland, 2010, pp. 50–64.

Barat, Urbashi. "Exile and Memory: Re-membering Home after the Partition of Bengal." *Creativity in Exile*, edited by Michael Hanne, Rodopi, 2004, pp. 213–26.

Bartosch, Roman. "A Good Dose of Formalism? Reading *The Hungry Tide.*" *Nature, Culture and Literature*, vol. 9, no. 1, 2013, pp. 87–141.

Bassnett, Susan. *Comparative Literature: A Critical Introduction*. Blackwell, 1993.

Batra, Kanika. "City Botany: Reading Urban Ecologies in China through Amitav Ghosh's *River of Smoke.*" *Narrative*, vol. 21, no. 3, Oct. 2013, pp. 322–32.

Baucom, Ian. *Specters of the Atlantic: Finance Capital, Slavery, and the Philosophy of History*. Duke UP, 2005.

Bauman, Zygmunt. *Life in Fragments: Essays in Postmodern Morality*. Blackwell, 1995.

Baumgarten, Murray. "Love and Figure/Ground: Reading Amitav Ghosh's *Sea of Poppies.*" *Partial Answers*, vol. 12, no. 2, June 2014, pp. 375–87.

Belliappa, K. C. "Amitav Ghosh's *In an Antique Land*: An Excursion into Time Past and Time Present." *Literary Criterion*, vol. 29, no. 4, 1994, pp. 15–24.

Berens, Kathi Inman. "Building the 'About': Coding Changes How and What I Teach." *Kathi Inman Berens*, 20 July 2011, kathiiberens.com/2011/07/20/building-the -about-coding-changes-how-what-i-teach.

Bergson, Henri. *Laughter: An Essay on the Meaning of the Comic*. Translated by Cloudesley Brereton and Fred Rothwell, Macmillan, 1911.

Bergthaller, Hannes. "A Sense of No-Place: *Avatar* and the Pitfalls of Ecocentric Identification." *European Journal of English Studies*, vol. 16, no. 2, 2012, pp. 151–62.

Bertz, Ned. *Diaspora and Nation in the Indian Ocean: Transnational Histories of Race and Urban Space in Tanzania*. U of Hawai'i P, 2015.

Beydoun, Nasser M., and Jennifer Baum. *The Glass Palace: Illusions of Freedom and Democracy in Qatar*. Algora Publishing, 2012.

Bhabha, Homi K. "By Bread Alone: Signs of Violence in the Mid-Nineteenth Century." *The Location of Culture*, Routledge, 1994, pp. 198–211.

———. "Of Mimicry and Man: The Ambivalence of Colonial Discourse." *The Location of Culture*, Routledge, 1994, pp. 85–92.

Bharali, Pabitra. "Amitav Ghosh's *The Shadow Lines*: Problematics of National Identity." *IOSR Journal of Humanities and Social Science*, vol. 2, no. 2, Sept.–Oct. 2012, pp. 44–46.

Bhat, Kamalakar. "Indiscreetness of Postcolonial Identities: An Enquiry into Amitav Ghosh's Migrant Cosmopolitanism in *The Shadow Lines.*" *Cosmopolitanism in Contemporary Fiction*, edited by P. Venkatesh, Abhiruchi Prakashana, 2010, pp. 42–56.

Bhatt, Indira, and Indira Nityanandam, editors. *The Fiction of Amitav Ghosh*. Creative Fictions, 2001.

Bhattacharjee, Ratan. "Tracing the Post-modern Elements in the Novels of Amitav Ghosh." *The Criterion*, vol. 4, no. 3, June 2013, pp. 1–4.

Bhattacharya, Shayani. "The Silence of the Subaltern: The Rejection of History and Language in Amitav Ghosh's *The Calcutta Chromosome.*" *Environments in Science Fiction: Essays on Alternative Spaces*, edited by Susan M. Bernardo, McFarland, 2014, pp. 137–53. Critical Explorations in Science Fiction and Fantasy 44.

Bhautoo-Dewnarain, Nandini. "*The Glass Palace*: Reconnecting Two Diasporas." Sankaran, pp. 33–46.

Bindhu, K. Y., and Subha Sachithanand. "Unravelling the Postmodern Perspectives: Amitav Ghosh's *In an Antique Land* and *The Shadow Lines*." *Golden Research Thoughts*, vol. 4, no. 9, Mar. 2015, pp. 1–4.

Black, Shameem. "Cosmopolitanism at Home: Amitav Ghosh's *The Shadow Lines*." *The Journal of Commonwealth Literature*, vol. 41, no. 3, 2006, pp. 45–65.

———. *Fiction across Borders: Imagining the Lives of Others in Late Twentieth-Century Novels*. Columbia UP, 2009.

———. "Post-humanitarianism and the Indian Novel in English." Anjaria, pp. 296–309.

Boehmer, Elleke. *Empire, the National, and the Postcolonial, 1890–1920: Resistance in Interaction*. Oxford UP, 2005.

Booth, Wayne C. *The Company We Keep: An Ethics of Fiction*. U of California P, 1988.

———. *The Rhetoric of Fiction*. 2nd ed., U of Chicago P, 1983.

———. *A Rhetoric of Irony*. U of Chicago P, 1974.

Bose, Brinda, editor. *Amitav Ghosh: Critical Perspectives*. Pencraft International, 2003.

Bose, Sugata. *A Hundred Horizons: The Indian Ocean in the Age of Global Empire*. Harvard UP, 2006.

Bowers, Maggie Ann. *Magic(al) Realism*. Routledge, 2004.

Bowra, C. M. *From Virgil to Milton*. Macmillan, 1945.

Bradley, Bill. "Jimmy Kimmel Fights Back Tears over Cecil the Lion's Death." *Huffington Post*, 29 July 2015, www.huffingtonpost.com/entry/jimmy-kimmel -cecil-the-lion_us_55b8c1d3e4b0a13f9d1acf58.

Bragard, Véronique. *Transoceanic Dialogues: Coolitude in Caribbean and Indian Ocean Literatures*. Peter Lang, 2008.

Brennan, Timothy. *At Home in the World: Cosmopolitanism Now*. Harvard UP, 1997.

Bruschi, Isabella. "*The Calcutta Chromosome*: An Attempt at Disrupting Western Cultural Hegemony." *English Studies 2006*, edited by R. A. Henderson, Università degli Studi di Torino, 2006, pp. 35–54.

Buck, Pearl S. *The Good Earth*. 1931. Washington Square Press, 2004.

Buell, Lawrence. "What We Talk about When We Talk about Ethics." Garber et al., pp. 1–14.

Burton, Antoinette. "Amitav Ghosh's World Histories from Below." *History of the Present*, vol. 2, no. 1, Spring 2012, pp. 71–77.

Butt, Nadia. "Inventing or Recalling the Contact Zones? Transcultural Spaces in Amitav Ghosh's *The Shadow Lines*." *Postcolonial Text*, vol. 4, no. 3, 2008, pp. 1–16.

Cabaret, Florence. "Qui est le subalterne de l'histoire indienne? Ou comment le personnage participe d'une relecture historiographique dans *The Glass Palace* (2000) d'Amitav Ghosh." *L'atelier*, vol. 2, no. 1, 2010, pp. 1–19.

Cameron, James, director. *Avatar*. Twentieth Century–Fox, 2009.

———. *A Message from Pandora* Trailer. Twentieth Century–Fox, 2009. *Vimeo*, vimeo .com/14459066.

Carter, Marina. *Servants, Sirdars, and Settlers: Indians in Mauritius, 1843–1874.* Oxford UP, 1996.

———. *Voices from Indenture: Experience of Indian Migrants in the British Empire.* Leicester UP, 1996.

Carter, Marina, and Khal Torabully. *Coolitude: An Anthology of Indian Labour Diaspora.* Anthem Press, 2002.

Cave, Terence. *Recognitions: A Study in Poetics.* Clarendon Press, 1988.

Cazden, Courtney, et al. "A Pedagogy of Multiliteracies: Designing Social Futures." *Harvard Educational Review,* vol. 66, no. 1, Apr. 1996, pp. 60–93.

Chakrabarty, Dipesh. *Provincializing Europe: Postcolonial Thought and Historical Difference.* Princeton UP, 2000.

Chakraborty, Nilanjan. "Myth, Politics and Ethnography in Amitav Ghosh's *The Hungry Tide*." *International Journal of Humanities and Social Science Invention,* vol. 2, no. 2, Feb. 2013, pp. 24–48.

Chambers, Claire. "'The Absolute Essentialness of Conversations': A Discussion with Amitav Ghosh." *Journal of Postcolonial Writing,* vol. 41, no. 1, 2005, pp. 26–39.

———. "'[A]cross the Border There Existed Another Reality': Nations, Borders and Cartography in *The Shadow Lines*." Ain, pp. 19–53.

———. "Anthropology as Cultural Translation: Amitav Ghosh's *In an Antique Land*." *Postcolonial Text,* vol. 2, no. 3, 2006, postcolonial.org/index.php/pct/article /viewFile/489/320.

———. "Network of Stories: Amitav Ghosh's *The Calcutta Chromosome*." *ARIEL,* vol. 40, nos. 2–3, Apr.–July 2009, pp. 41–62.

———. "Postcolonial Science Fiction: Amitav Ghosh's *The Calcutta Chromosome*." *The Journal of Commonwealth Literature,* vol. 38, no. 1, 2003, pp. 58–72.

———."Representations of the Oil Encounter in Amitav Ghosh's *The Circle of Reason*." *The Journal of Commonwealth Literature,* vol. 41, no. 1, 2006, pp. 33–50.

Chandler, James. *England in 1819: The Politics of Literary Culture and the Case of Romantic Historicism.* U of Chicago P, 1998.

Chandra, Vikram. "Arty Goddesses." *The Hindu,* 1 Apr. 2001, www.thehindu.com /2001/04/01/stories/1301061q.htm.

———. "Arty Goddesses II." *The Hindu,* 8 Apr. 2001, www.thehindu.com/thehindu /2001/04/08/stories/1308067d.htm.

———. "The Cult of Authenticity: India's Cultural Commissars Worship 'Indianness' Instead of Art." *Boston Review,* 1 Feb. 2001, www.bostonreview.net/vikram -chandra-the-cult-of-authenticity.

Chandra, Vinita. "Suppressed Memory and Forgetting: History and Nationalism in *The Shadow Lines*." B. Bose, pp. 67–78.

Chatterjee Sriwastav, Sharmistha. "'Because Stories Are All There Are to Live In': Mixed Blessings of Memory in *The Shadow Lines*." Ain, pp. 150–62.

Chattopadhyay, Bodhisattva. "On the Mythologerm: *Kalpavigyan* and the Question of Imperial Science." *Indian Science Fiction*, special issue of *Science Fiction Studies*, vol. 43, no. 3, Nov. 2016, pp. 435–58.

Chaudhuri, Supriya. "Translating Loss: Place and Language in Amitav Ghosh and Salman Rushdie." *Études anglaises*, vol. 62, no. 3, 2009, pp. 266–79.

Chenniappan, R., and R. Saravana Suresh. "Postmodern Traits in the Novels of Amitav Ghosh." *The Criterion*, vol. 2, no. 2, June 2011, pp. 1–4.

Chew, Shirley. "Texts and Worlds in Amitav Ghosh's *In an Antique Land*." *Reconstructing the Book: Literary Texts in Transmission*, edited by Maureen Bell et al., Ashgate, 2001.

Choudhary, Suruchi Kalra, and S. D. Sharma. "Amitav Ghosh and the Expression of Subaltern History: A Study of *The Calcutta Chromosome*." *The IUP Journal of English Studies*, vol. 7, no. 4, Dec. 2012, pp. 7–18.

Choudhury, Bibhash, editor. *Amitav Ghosh: Critical Essays*. PHI Learning, 2009.

Chowdhury, Shreya Roy. "Amitav Ghosh Lands in Controversy over Israeli Literary Award." *The Times of India*, 29 Apr. 2010, timesofindia.indiatimes.com/india /Amitav-Ghosh-lands-in-controversy-over-Israeli-literary-award/articleshow /5870500.cms.

Clark, Alex. Review of *Flood of Fire*, by Amitav Ghosh. *The Guardian*, 5 June 2015, www.theguardian.com/books/2015/jun/05/flood-of-fire-amitav-ghosh-review -instalment-trilogy.

Clarke, Bruce. "'The Anthropocene'; or, Gaia Shrugs." *Journal of Contemporary Archaeology*, vol. 1, no. 1, 2014, pp. 73–132.

Clement, Tanya. "Multiliteracies in the Undergraduate Digital Humanities Curriculum: Skills, Principles, and Habits of Mind." Hirsch, *Digital Humanities*, pp. 365–88.

Cliff, Michelle. *Abeng*. Penguin, 1984.

Clifford, James. "Diasporas." *Cultural Anthropology*, vol. 9, no. 3, Aug. 1994, pp. 302–38.

Conrad, Joseph. *The Shadow-Line: A Confession*. Vintage Books, 2007.

Cooper, Frederick. "Modernity." *Colonialism in Question: Theory, Knowledge, History*, U of California P, 2005, pp. 113–52.

Cottier, Annie. "Settlers in the Sundarbans: The Poetry and Politics of Humans and Nature in Amitav Ghosh's *The Hungry Tide*." *On the Move: The Journey of Refugees in New Literatures in English*, edited by Geetha Ganapathy-Doré and Helga Ramsey-Kurz, Cambridge Scholars, 2012, pp. 125–38.

Couto, Mia. *Voices Made Night*. Heineman African Writers Series, 1986.

Cowaloosur, Vedita. "The Novels of Amitav Ghosh and the Integral Hegemony of Inglish." *English Studies in Africa*, vol. 58, no. 1, 2015, pp. 1–13.

Cronon, William. "The Trouble with Wilderness; or, Getting Back to the Wrong Nature." *Uncommon Ground: Rethinking the Human Place in Nature*, W. W. Norton, 1996, pp. 69–90.

Cunningham, Susan. "Burma's Last Royals." *Los Angeles Review of Books*, 23 Nov. 2013, lareviewofbooks.org/review/burmas-last-royals.

Dalley, Hamish. *The Postcolonial Historical Novel: Realism, Allegory, and the Representation of Contested Pasts*. Palgrave MacMillan, 2014.

Damrosch, David. "World Literature in a Postcanonical, Hypercanonical Age." *Comparative Literature in an Age of Globalization*, edited by Haun Saussy, Johns Hopkins UP, 2006, pp. 45–53.

Dangarembga, Tsitsi. *Nervous Conditions*. 1989. Seal Press, 2004.

Dar, Ab Majeed. "Postmodernism in Amitav Ghosh's Novels." *Language in India*, vol. 13, no. 7, July 2013, pp. 178–87.

Das, Rajorshi. "Reading Amitav Ghosh's *The Hungry Tide* through the History and Legacy of Morichjhāpi." *The Golden Line*, vol. 1, no. 2, 2015, pp. 40–44.

Das, Sukanta. "Morichjhāpi Revisited: Fictionalizing History in Amitav Ghosh's *The Hungry Tide*." *The Criterion*, vol. 3, no. 3, Sept. 2012, pp. 1–8.

Das, Veena. *Life and Words: Violence and the Descent into the Ordinary*. U of California P, 2007.

Davis, Kathleen. "Cross-Dressing the Rose: Sly Allegory in *Sea of Poppies*." *History of the Present*, vol. 2, no. 1, Spring 2012, pp. 86–94.

Davis, Rocío G. "To Dwell in Travel: Historical Ironies in Amitav Ghosh's *In an Antique Land*." *Missions of Interdependence: A Literary Directory*, edited by Gerhard Stilz, Rodopi, 2002, pp. 239–46.

Davis, Todd F., and Kenneth Womack, editors. *Mapping the Ethical Turn: A Reader in Ethics, Culture, and Literary Theory*. U of Virginia P, 2001.

Dayal, Samir. "The Emergence of the Fragile Subject: Amitav Ghosh's *In an Antique Land*." *Hybridity and Postcolonialism: Twentieth-Century Indian Literature*, edited by Monika Fludernik, Stauffenburg, 1998.

De, Asis. "For the Right of Belonging. Peripheral Identity in Amitav Ghosh's *The Hungry Tide*." *Langlit*, vol. 2, no. 1, Aug. 2015, pp. 95–105.

———. "Mapping the Imaginary Lines: Reading Amitav Ghosh's *The Shadow Lines* (1988) on the Silver Jubilee of Its Publication." *LangLit*, vol. 1, no. 1, Aug. 2014, pp. 485–90.

De, Meenakshi. "Postmodernist Way of Narration: Relevance of Letter Series in Amitav Ghosh's *River of Smoke*." *Labyrinth*, vol. 5, no. 2, Apr. 2014, pp. 117–21.

Dedebas, Eda. "Hybrid Nations and Narratives: The Intermingling of Multinationalism and Multiple Narratives in *The Shadow Lines* by Amitav Ghosh." *Cuadernos de Literatura Inglesa y Norteamericana*, vol. 10, nos. 1–2, 2007, pp. 83–91.

Delmas, Catherine. "Transplanting Seeds in Diasporic Literature: Michael Ondaatje's *The Cat's Table* and Amitav Ghosh's *Sea of Poppies* and *River of Smoke*." *Commonwealth Essays and Studies*, vol. 38, no. 2, Spring 2016, pp. 19–27.

DeLoughrey, Elizabeth, and George B. Handley. "Toward an Aesthetics of the Earth." DeLoughrey and Handley, *Postcolonial Ecologies*, pp. 3–39.

———, editors. *Postcolonial Ecologies: Literature of the Environment*. Oxford UP, 2011.

Dengel-Janic, Ellen. "The Precariousness of Postcolonial Geographies: Amitav Ghosh's *The Shadow Lines* and *The Hungry Tide*." *Narrating "Precariousness": Modes, Media, Ethics*, edited by Barbara Korte and Frédéric Regard, Universitätsverlag Winter, 2014, pp. 71–84. Anglistische Forschungen, Heft 437.

Depp, Johnny, performer. *Pirates of the Caribbean: The Curse of the Black Pearl*. Directed by Gore Verbinski. Walt Disney Home Entertainment, 2003.

Derrida, Jacques. "The Law of Genre." Translated by Avital Ronell. *Critical Inquiry*, vol. 7, no. 1, Autumn 1980, pp. 55–81.

Desai, Gaurav. *Commerce with the Universe: Africa, India, and the Afrasian Imagination*. Columbia UP, 2013.

———. "Old World Orders: Amitav Ghosh and the Writing of Nostalgia." *Representations*, vol. 85, no. 1, Winter 2004, pp. 125–48.

Devi, Mahasweta. "Pterodactyl, Puran Sahay, and Pirtha." *Imaginary Maps*, translated by Gayatri Spivak, Routledge, 1995, pp. 95–196.

Devi, P. Prasanna. "The Hunger Motif: A Study of Amitav Ghosh's *The Hungry Tide*." *The Criterion*, vol. 3, no. 2, June 2012, pp. 1–7.

Devy, G. N. *After Amnesia: Tradition and Change in Indian Literary Criticism*. Orient Longman, 1992.

———. *In Another Tongue: Essays on Indian English Literature*. Peter Lang, 1993.

D'Haen, Theo. "Antique Lands, New Worlds? Comparative Literature, Intertextuality, Translation." *Forum for Modern Language Studies*, vol. 43, no. 2, Jan. 2007, pp. 107–20.

———. "For 'Global Literature,' Anglo-Phone." *Anglia*, vol. 135, no. 1, 2017, pp. 35–50.

———. "Magical Realism and Postmodernism: Decentering Privileged Centers." Zamora and Faris, *Magical Realism*, pp. 191–208.

Dhar, Nandini. "Shadows of Slavery, Discourses of Choice, and Indian Indentureship in Amitav Ghosh's *Sea of Poppies*." *ARIEL*, vol. 48, no. 1, Jan. 2017, pp. 1–35.

Dkhar, Jenniefer. "A Re-reading of History in the Novels of Amitav Ghosh." *Journal of Literature, Culture and Media Studies*, vol. 4, nos. 7–8, 2012, pp. 41–56.

Dora-Laskey, Prathim-Maya. "Bodies as Borderwork: From Cartographic Distance to Cosmopolitan Concern in Bapsi Sidhwa's *Ice-Candy-Man* and Amitav Ghosh's *The Shadow Lines*." *Borders, Boundaries, and Margins*, special issue of *South Asian Review*, vol. 36, no. 3, Dec. 2015, pp. 33–49.

Durrant, Sam. *Postcolonial Narrative and the Work of Mourning: J. M. Coetzee, Wilson Harris, and Toni Morrison*. State U of New York P, 2004.

Dutta, Nirmalya. "Book Review: Amitav Ghosh's *Flood of Fire* Is a Heady Mix." *DNA*, 8 June 2015, www.dnaindia.com/lifestyle/review book-review-amitav-ghosh-s -flood-of-fire-is-a-heady-mix-2093491.

Dutta, Upasana. "Modern Directions in Travel Writing: Amitav Ghosh's *In an Antique Land* and William Dalrymple's *Nine Lives: In Search of the Sacred in Modern India*." *Coldnoon (International Journal of Travel Writing and Travelling Cultures)*, vol. 2, no. 3, July 2013, pp. 69–78.

Dutta Sharma, Brahma. "Environmentalism versus Humanism in Amitav Ghosh's *The Hungry Tide*." *The Journal of Contemporary Literature*, vol. 4, no. 2, Aug. 2012, pp. 15–22.

Eckel, Leslie Elizabeth. "Oceanic Mirrors: Atlantic Literature and the Global Chaosmos." *Atlantic Studies*, vol. 11, no. 1, 2014, pp. 128–44.

Eckstein, Lars. *Re-membering the Black Atlantic: On the Poetics and Politics of Literary Memory*. Rodopi, 2006.

Elangbam, Bondina. "Is the Homosexual an Invisible Being? 'Comrade Love' in the Select Fiction of Rohinton Mistry and Amitav Ghosh." *Gendering the Narrative:*

Indian English Fiction and Gender Discourse, edited by Nibedita Mukherjee, Cambridge Scholars, 2015, pp. 35–41.

Eleftheriou, Lyda. "Bodies like Rivers: Seeking for a Space for Body Memory in the Discourse of Trauma." *European Journal of English Studies (EJES)*, vol. 19, no. 3, Dec. 2015, pp. 315–30.

Elshtain, Jean Bethke. "Judge Not?" Pojman and Vaughn, pp. 174–83.

Eswaran, Nisha. "'A Shared Burden': Reading Chaos and/as Utopia in Amitav Ghosh's *Sea of Poppies*." *Postcolonial Text*, vol. 10, nos. 3–4, 2015, pp. 1–13.

"Exposed: Child Labor Behind Smart Phone and Electric Car Batteries." *Amnesty International*, 19 Jan. 2016, www.amnesty.org/en/latest/news/2016/01/child -labour-behind-smart-phone-and-electric-car-batteries/.

Fanon, Frantz. *Black Skin, White Masks*. Translated by Charles Lam Markmann, 1967. Pluto, 1986.

Faris, Wendy B. *Ordinary Enchantments: Magical Realism and the Remystification of Narrative*. Vanderbilt UP, 2004.

———. "Scheherazade's Children: Magical Realism and Postmodern Fiction." Zamora and Faris, *Magical Realism*, pp. 163–90.

Farrell, J. G. *The Siege of Krishnapur*. Introduced by Pankaj Mishra, 1973. New York Review of Books, 2004.

Fendt, Julia. "The Chromosome as Concept and Metaphor in Amitav Ghosh's *The Calcutta Chromosome*." *Anglia*, vol. 133, no. 1, 2015, pp. 172–86.

Fletcher, Lisa. "Reading the Postcolonial Island in Amitav Ghosh's *The Hungry Tide*." *Island Studies Journal*, vol. 6, no. 1, 2011, pp. 3–16.

Foner, Eric. *Reconstruction: America's Unfinished Revolution, 1863–1877*. Harper and Row, 1988.

Forster, E. M. *A Passage to India*. 1924. Harcourt, 1984.

Forter, Greg. "Atlantic and Other Worlds: Critique and Utopia in Postcolonial Historical Fiction." *PMLA*, vol. 131, no. 5, Oct. 2016, pp. 1328–43.

Foster, Karen. "What's Good about Generation Y?" *Greater Good Magazine*, 24 Jan. 2013, greatergood.berkeley.edu/article/item/whats_good_about _generation_y.

Freedman, Ariela. "On the Ganges Side of Modernism: Raghubir Singh, Amitav Ghosh, and the Postcolonial Modern." *Geomodernisms: Race, Modernism, Modernity*, edited by Laura Doyle and Laura Winkiel, Indiana UP, 2005, pp. 114–29.

Freire, Paolo. *Pedagogy of the Oppressed*. Translated by Myra Bergman Ramos, Seabury, 1970.

Freud, Sigmund. *Jokes and Their Relation to the Unconscious*. Edited and translated by James Strachey, W. W. Norton, 1960.

Fu, Chun. "Parting, Partition and Purloined Stories in *The Shadow Lines*." *Poetics and Partition*, special issue of *European Journal of English Studies*, vol. 19, no. 3, Dec. 2015, pp. 286–300.

Gabriel, Sharmani Patricia. "The Heteroglossia of Home: Re-routing the Boundaries of National Identity in Amitav Ghosh's *The Shadow Lines*." *Journal of Postcolonial Writing*, vol. 41, no. 1, 2005, pp. 40–53.

Gallagher, Catherine. "The Rise of Fictionality." Moretti, *Novel*, pp. 336–63.

———. "What Would Napoleon Do? Historical, Fictional and Counterfactual Characters." *New Literary History*, vol. 42, no. 2, Spring 2011, pp. 315–36.

Gandhi, Leela. "'A Choice of Histories': Ghosh vs. Hegel in *In an Antique Land.*" *New Literatures Review*, no. 40, 2003, pp. 17–32.

Gandhi, M. K. *"Hind Swaraj" and Other Writings*. Edited by Anthony J. Parel, Cambridge UP, 2009.

Gangopadhyay, Rudrani. "Finding Oneself on Board the *Ibis* in Amitav Ghosh's *Sea of Poppies.*" *Women's Studies Quarterly*, vol. 45, nos. 1–2, Spring-Summer 2017, pp. 55–64.

Ganguly, Keya. "Something like a Snake: Pedagogy and Postcolonial Literature." *College Literature*, vol. 19, no. 3 / vol. 20, no. 1, Oct. 1992–Feb. 1993, pp. 185–90.

Garber, Marjorie, et al., editors. Introduction. *The Turn to Ethics*, Routledge, 2000, pp. vii–xii.

García Márquez, Gabriel. *One Hundred Years of Solitude*. Translated by Gregory Rabassa, 1970. Pan Books, 1978.

Genette, Gérard. *The Architext: An Introduction*. Translated by Jane E. Lewin, U of California P, 1992.

Ghosh, Amitav. "Addicted to Empire." Interview with Benedicte Page, *The Bookseller*, 13 Mar. 2008, www.thebookseller.com/profile/addicted-empire.

———. "Amitav Ghosh in Interview with Neluka Silva and Alex Tickell." *Kunapipi*, vol. 19, no. 3, 1999, pp. 171–77.

———. "Amitav Ghosh—*The Shadow Lines.*" Hosted by Harriet Gilbert. World Book Club, BBC World Service, 26 May 2012, www.bbc.co.uk/programmes/p00s473j.

———. "Anthropology and Fiction: An Interview with Amitav Ghosh." By Damien Stankiewicz. *Cultural Anthropology*, vol. 27, no. 3, 2012, pp. 535–41.

———. "The Author Talks." *The Hungry Tide*, Recorded Books, 2005.

———. "Between the Walls of Archives and Horizons of Imagination: An Interview with Amitav Ghosh." By Mahmood Kooria. *Itinerario*, vol. 36, no. 3, Dec. 2012, pp. 7–18.

———. *The Calcutta Chromosome: A Novel of Fevers, Delirium, and Discovery*. Picador, 1996.

———. *The Calcutta Chromosome: A Novel of Fevers, Delirium and Discovery*. John Murray, 2011.

———. *The Circle of Reason*. Hamish Hamilton, 1986.

———. *The Circle of Reason*. Abacus, 1987.

———. *The Circle of Reason*. Mariner Books, 2005.

———. "The Conscientious Objector." *Outlook*, 19 Mar. 2001, www.outlookindia.com /article/the-conscientious-objector/211102.

———. *Countdown*. Delhi, Ravi Dayal Publisher, 1999.

———. "A Crocodile in the Swamplands." *Outlook*, 18 Oct. 2004, www.outlookindia .com/magazine/story/a-crocodile-in-the-swamplands/225423.

———. *Dancing in Cambodia: At Large in Burma*. Delhi, Ravi Dayal Publisher, 1998.

———. "The Diaspora in Indian Culture." A. Ghosh, *Imam*, pp. 243–50.

————. "Diasporic Predicaments: An Interview with Amitav Ghosh." By Chitra Sankaran. Sankaran, pp. 1–16.

————. E-mail communication. Received by Gaurav Desai and John Hawley, 25 May 2016.

————. *Flood of Fire.* Farrar, Straus and Giroux, 2015.

————. *Flood of Fire.* John Murray, 2015.

————. Foreword. B. Bose, *Amitav Ghosh*, pp. 5–6.

————. "The Ghosts of Mrs. Gandhi." *Amitav Ghosh*, 17 July 1995, www.amitavghosh.com/essays/ghost.html.

————. "The Ghosts of Mrs. Gandhi." A. Ghosh, *Incendiary Circumstances*, pp. 187–203.

————. "The Ghosts of Mrs. Gandhi." A. Ghosh, *Imam*, pp. 46–62.

————. *The Glass Palace.* HarperCollins Publishers, 2000.

————. *The Glass Palace.* Random House, 2001.

————. *The Glass Palace.* Random House, 2002.

————. *The Great Derangement: Climate Change and the Unthinkable.* U of Chicago P, 2016.

————. *The Hungry Tide.* HarperCollins Publishers, 2004.

————. *The Hungry Tide.* Delhi, Ravi Dayal Publisher, 2004.

————. *The Hungry Tide.* Houghton Mifflin Harcourt, 2005.

————. "The *Ibis* Chrestomathy." *Amitav Ghosh*, www.amitavghosh.com/chrestomathy.html.

————. *The Imam and the Indian: Prose Pieces.* Delhi, Ravi Dayal / Permanent Black, 2002.

————. "Imperial Temptations." A. Ghosh, *Incendiary Circumstances*, pp. 26–31.

————. *In an Antique Land.* Delhi, Ravi Dayal Publisher, 1992.

————. *In an Antique Land: History in the Guise of a Traveler's Tale.* Vintage Books, 1992.

————. *In an Antique Land: History in the Guise of a Traveller's Tale.* Granta, 1992.

————. *Incendiary Circumstances: A Chronicle of the Turmoil of Our Times.* Houghton Mifflin, 2005.

————. "Interview with Amitav Ghosh." By Biswarup Sen. *Persimmon: Asian Literature, Arts, and Culture*, vol. 2, no. 2, 2001, pp. 62–65.

————. "An Interview with Amitav Ghosh." By Frederick Luis Aldama. *World Literature Today*, vol. 76, no. 2, 2002, pp. 84–90.

————. "An Interview with Amitav Ghosh." By Neluka Silva and Alex Tickell. B. Bose, pp. 214–21.

————. "The March of the Novel through History: The Testimony of My Grandfather's Bookcase." A. Ghosh, *Imam*, pp. 287–304.

————. "The March of the Novel through History: The Testimony of My Grandfather's Bookcase." A. Ghosh, *Incendiary Circumstances*, pp. 103–19.

———. "The March of the Novel through History: The Testimony of My Grand-father's Bookcase." *Kunapipi*, vol. 19, no. 3, 1997, pp. 2–13.

———. "Networks and Traces: An Interview with Amitav Ghosh." Interview by Elleke Boehmer and Anshuman Mondal. *Wasafiri*, vol. 27, no. 2, 2012, pp. 30–35.

———. "Of Fanas and Forecastles: The Indian Ocean and Some Lost Languages of the Age of Sail." *Economic and Political Weekly*, vol. 43, no. 25, 21–27 June 2008, pp. 56–62. Reprinted in *Eyes across the Water: Navigating the Indian Ocean*, edited by Pamila Gupta et al., Unisa P, 2010, pp. 15–31.

———. "Petrofiction: The Oil Encounter and the Novel." A. Ghosh, *Imam*, pp. 75–89.

———. "'Postcolonial' Describes You as a Negative: An Interview with Amitav Ghosh." By T. Vijay Kumar. *Interventions*, vol. 9, no. 1, 2007, pp. 99–105.

———. *River of Smoke*. Farrar, Straus and Giroux, 2011.

———. *River of Smoke*. Hamish Hamilton–Penguin, 2011.

———. *River of Smoke*. Picador, 2012.

———. *Sea of Poppies*. Farrar, Straus and Giroux, 2008.

———. *Sea of Poppies*. John Murray, 2008.

———. *Sea of Poppies*. New Delhi, Penguin/Viking, 2008.

———. *Sea of Poppies*. Picador, 2009.

———. *The Shadow Lines*. Bloomsbury, 1988.

———. *The Shadow Lines*. Mariner Books, 2005.

———. "The Slave of MS. H.6." *Subaltern Studies: Writings on South Asian History and Society*, edited by Partha Chatterjee and Gyanendra Pandey, vol. 7, Oxford UP, 1993, pp. 159–220.

———. "The Testimony of My Grandfather's Bookcase." *Amitav Ghosh*, 1998, amitavghosh.com/essays/bookcase.html.

———. "Wild Fictions." *Outlook*, 22 Dec. 2008, amitavghosh.com/docs/Wild%20 Fictions.pdf.

Ghosh, Amitav, and Dipesh Chakrabarty. "A Correspondence on *Provincializing Europe*." *Radical History Review*, vol. 83, 2002, pp. 146–72.

Ghosh, Bishnupriya. "On Grafting the Vernacular: The Consequences of Postcolonial Spectrology." *Boundary 2*, vol. 31, no. 2, 2004, pp. 197–218.

Ghosh, Manas. "Two Histories of Partition: Amitav Ghosh's *The Shadow Lines* and Ritwik Ghatak's *Komal Gandhar*." Ain, pp. 236–46.

Ghosh, Tapan Kumar, and Prasanta Bhattacharya, editors. *In Pursuit of Amitav Ghosh: Some Recent Readings*. Orient Blackswan, 2013.

Gilbert, Helen, and Joanne Tompkins. "Introduction: Re-acting (to) Empire." *Post-colonial Drama: Theory, Practice, Politics*, Routledge, 1996, pp. 1–14.

Giles, Jana María. "Can the Sublime Be Postcolonial? Aesthetics, Politics, and Environ-ment in Amitav Ghosh's *The Hungry Tide*." *Cambridge Journal of Postcolonial Literary Inquiry*, vol. 1, no. 2, Sept. 2014, pp. 223–42.

Gilroy, Paul. *The Black Atlantic: Modernity and Double Consciousness*. 1993. Verso, 2002.

Glasgow, Melita, and Don Fletcher. "Palimpsest and Seduction: *The Glass Palace* and *White Teeth*." *Kunapipi*, vol. 27, no. 1, 2005, pp. 75–87.

Goh, Robbie B. H. "The Overseas Indian and the Political Economy of the Body in Aravind Adiga's *The White Tiger* and Amitav Ghosh's *The Hungry Tide*." *The Journal of Commonwealth Literature*, vol. 47, no. 3, 2012, pp. 341–56.

Gopinath, Praseeda. "Narrating from Below." *Contemporary Literature*, vol. 57, no. 1, Spring 2016, pp. 153–61.

Gordimer, Nadine. "The Ultimate Safari." *Jump and Other Stories*, Penguin, 1991, pp. 31–46.

Green, Nile. *Bombay Islam: The Religious Economy of the West Indian Ocean, 1840–1914*. Cambridge UP, 2011.

Grewal, Inderpal. "Amitav Ghosh: Cosmopolitanisms, Literature, Transnationalisms." *The Postcolonial and the Global*, edited by Revathi Krishnaswamy and John C. Hawley, U of Minnesota P, 2008, pp. 178–90.

Griffiths, Gareth. "Silenced Worlds: Language and Experience in Amitav Ghosh's *The Hungry Tide*." *Kunapipi*, vol. 34, no. 2, 2012, pp. 105–12.

Guejalatchoumy, K., and Marie Josephine Aruna. "Crossing Borders and Boundaries: A Reading of Amitav Ghosh's *The Glass Palace*." *International Journal on Multicultural Literature*, vol. 5, no. 2, 2015, pp. 21–27.

Guha, Ramachandra. "The Paradox of Global Environmentalism." *Current History*, vol. 99, no. 640, Nov. 2000, pp. 367–70.

Guha, Ramachandra, and Juan Martínez-Alier. *Varieties of Environmentalism: Essays North and South*. Earthscan, 1997.

Guha, Ranajit, editor. *Subaltern Studies I: Writings on South Asian History and Society*. Oxford UP, 1982.

Guilhamon, Lise. "Global Languages in the Time of the Opium Wars: The Lost Idioms of Amitav Ghosh's *Sea of Poppies*." *Commonwealth Essays and Studies*, vol. 34, no. 1, 2011, pp. 67–76.

Gunning, Dave. "History, Anthropology, Necromancy—Amitav Ghosh's *In an Antique Land*." *Postcolonial Ghosts / Fantômes postcoloniaux*, edited by Mélanie Joseph-Vilain and Judith Misrahi-Barak, Presses Universitaires de la Méditerranée, 2009, pp. 305–21.

Gupta, Rozy. "Focalization: A Study of Amitav Ghosh's *The Hungry Tide*." *The Criterion*, vol. 5, no. 3, June 2014, pp. 243–47.

Gupta, R. S., and Kapil Kapoor, editors. *English in India: Issues and Problems*. Academic Foundation, 1991.

Gurnah, Abdulrazak. *By the Sea*. Bloomsbury, 2002.

Gurr, Jens Martin. "Emplotting an Ecosystem: Amitav Ghosh's *The Hungry Tide* and the Question of Form in Ecocriticism." Volkmann et al., pp. 69–80.

Guttman, Anna. "The Jew in the Archive: Textualizations of (Jewish?) History in Contemporary South Asian Literature." *Contemporary Literature*, vol. 51, no. 3, Fall 2010, pp. 503–31.

Hadley, Tessa. "*River of Smoke* by Amitav Ghosh—Review." *The Guardian*, 10 June 2011, www.theguardian.com/books/2011/jun/11/river-smoke-amitav-ghosh-review.

Halbwachs, Maurice. "From *The Collective Memory.*" *Theories of Memory: A Reader*, edited by Michael Rossington and Anne Whitehead, Edinburgh UP, 2007, pp. 139–43.

Han, Stephanie. "Amitav Ghosh's *Sea of Poppies*: Speaking Weird English." *The Explicator*, vol. 71, no. 4, 2013, pp. 298–301.

Hanes, W. Travis, III, and Frank Sanello. *The Opium Wars: The Addiction of One Empire and the Corruption of Another.* Sourcebooks, 2002.

Hanquart-Turner, Evelyne. "The Search for Paradise: Amitav Ghosh's *The Hungry Tide.*" *Projections of Paradise: Ideal Elsewheres in Postcolonial Migrant Literature*, edited by Helga Ramsey-Kurz with Geetha Ganapathy-Doré, Rodopi, 2011, pp. 73–82.

Hargittai, Eszter. "Digital Na(t)ives? Variation in Internet Skills and Uses among Members of the 'Net Generation.'" *Sociological Inquiry*, vol. 80, no. 1, Feb. 2010, pp. 92–113.

Harpham, Geoffrey Galt. "Ethics." *Critical Terms for Literary Study*, edited by Frank Lentricchia and Thomas McLaughlin, 2nd ed., U of Chicago P, 1995, pp. 387–405.

Harrington, Louise. "An-other Space: Diasporic Responses to Partition in Bengal." *India and the Diasporic Imagination / L'Inde et l'imagination diasporique*, edited by Rita Christian and Judith Misrahi-Barak, Presses Universitaires de la Méditerranée, 2011.

Hawley, John C. *Amitav Ghosh: An Introduction.* New Delhi Foundation Books, 2005.

———. "Gateway to the Unknowable: The *Kala Pani* in Amitav Ghosh's *Sea of Poppies* and Barlen Pyamootoo's *Bénarès.*" *Postcolonial Gateways and Walls: Under Construction*, edited by Daria Tunca and Janet Wilson, Brill Rodopi, 2016, pp. 147–64. Cross/Cultures 195.

"Head of State Fights for Environment: Evo Morales 'Identifies' with *Avatar* Film." *Buenos Aires Herald*, 12 Jan. 2010, www.buenosairesherald.com/article/22287/evo-morales-identifies-withavatar-film.

Hegerfeldt, Anne C. *Lies That Tell the Truth: Magic Realism Seen through Contemporary Fiction from Britain.* Rodopi, 2005.

Heise, Ursula, et al., editors. *State of the Discipline Report: The 2014–2015 Report on the State of the Discipline of Comparative Literature.* American Comparative Literature Association, stateofthediscipline.acla.org.

Hicks, K. "The Hungry Tide." *Society and Animals*, vol. 14, no. 3, 2006, pp. 312–15.

Hirsch, Brett D., editor. *Digital Humanities Pedagogy: Practices, Principles, and Politics.* Open Book Publishers, 2012.

———. "</Parentheses>: Digital Humanities and the Place of Pedagogy." Hirsch, *Digital Humanities*, pp. 3–30.

Ho, Engseng. *The Graves of Tarim: Genealogy and Mobility across the Indian Ocean.* U of California P, 2006.

Hofmeyr, Isabel. "The Black Atlantic Meets the Indian Ocean: Forging New Paradigms of Transnationalism for the Global South—Literary and Cultural
Perspectives." *Social Dynamics: A Journal of African Studies*, vol. 33, no. 2,
2007, pp. 3–32.

Hofmeyr, Isabel, et al. "Print Cultures, Nationalisms and Publics of the Indian Ocean."
Africa: The Journal of the International African Institute, vol. 81, no. 1,
Feb. 2011, pp. 1–22.

Hogan, Linda. *People of the Whale*. W. W. Norton, 2008.

Horkheimer, Max. *The Dialectic of Enlightenment*. Translated by John Cumming,
Verso, 1997.

Huggan, Graham. "Decolonizing the Map: Postcolonialism, Poststructuralism and
the Cartographic Connection." *Interdisciplinary Measures: Literature and
the Future of Postcolonial Studies*, Liverpool UP, 2008, pp. 21–33.

———. *The Postcolonial Exotic: Marketing the Margins*. Routledge, 2011.

Huggan, Graham, and Helen Tiffin. *Postcolonial Ecocriticism: Literature, Animals,
Environment*. Routledge, 2010.

Hutcheon, Linda. *A Poetics of Postmodernism: History, Theory, Fiction*. Routledge, 1988.

Huttunen, Tuomas. "Language and Ethics in *The Hungry Tide* by Amitav Ghosh."
Sankaran, pp. 121–32.

Ibsen, Henrik. *The Enemy of the People*. Dover Publications, 1999.

"Indian Indentured Labourers." *The National Archives*, www.nationalarchives.gov.uk
/help-with-your-research/research-guides/indian-indentured-labourers.

Jaising, Shakti. "Fixity amid Flux: Aesthetics and Environmentalism in Amitav Ghosh's
The Hungry Tide." *ARIEL*, vol. 46, no. 4, Oct. 2015, pp. 63–88.

Jalais, Annu. *Forest of Tigers: People, Politics and Environment in the Sundarbans*.
Routledge, 2011.

Jamal, Mahmood, director. *Women and Islam*. Films for the Humanities and Sciences,
1993.

James, Louis, and Jan Shepherd. "Shadow Lines: Cross-Cultural Perspectives in the
Fiction of Amitav Ghosh." *Commonwealth Essays and Studies*, vol. 14, no. 1,
1991, pp. 28–32.

Jameson, Fredric. *A Singular Modernity: Essays on the Ontology of the Present*. Verso,
2002.

———. "Third-World Literature in the Era of Multinational Capitalism." *Social Text*,
no. 15, Autumn 1986, pp. 65–88.

Jayaraman, Uma. "The Masculinisation of the Native Gentleman: A Close Reading of
Neel Haldar in Amitav Ghosh's *Sea of Poppies*." *Exploring Gender in the
Literature of the Indian Diaspora*, edited by Sandhya Rao Mehta, Cambridge
Scholars, 2015, pp. 148–62.

Jessop, Martyn. "Teaching, Learning, and Research in Final Year Humanities
Computing Student Projects." *Literary and Linguistic Computing*, vol. 20,
no. 3, Sept. 2005, pp. 295–311.

Jha, Vivekanand, editor. *The Fiction of Amitav Ghosh: A Critical Commentary*.
Atlantic Publishers and Distributors, 2013.

Johnson, Samuel. "Irony." *A Dictionary of the English Language*, 1755. Longman, Rees, Orme and Co., 1837, p. 408.

Jones, Stephanie. "A Novel Genre: Polylingualism and Magical Realism in Amitav Ghosh's *The Circle of Reason.*" *Bulletin of the School of Oriental and African Studies*, vol. 66, no. 3, 2003, pp. 431–41.

Joshi, Svati, editor. *Rethinking English: Essays in Literature, Language, History.* Trianka, 1991.

Jouzaee, Saeed Abdoli, and Leila Baradaran Jamili. "Double Colonization of Indian Women in Amitav Ghosh's *Sea of Poppies.*" *Journal of Novel Applied Sciences*, vol. 3, no. 1, 2014, pp. 1524–30.

Justice, Daniel Heath. "James Cameron's *Avatar*: Missed Opportunities." *First Peoples: New Directions in Indigenous Studies*, 20 Jan. 2010, www.indianz.com /boardx/topic.asp?ARCHIVE=true&TOPIC_ID=39583 www.firstpeoplesnew directions.org/blog/?p=169.

Kabir, Ananya Jahanara. "'Handcuffed to History': Partition and the Indian Novel in English." Anjaria, pp. 119–32.

Kadam, Mansing G. "Amitav Ghosh's *The Glass Palace*: A Post-colonial Novel." *Indian Writings in English*, edited by Binod Mishra and Sanjay Kumar, Atlantic Publishers and Distributors, 2006, pp. 15–32.

Kadir, Djelal. "Comparative Literature in an Age of Terrorism." *Comparative Literature in an Age of Globalizaton*, edited by Haun Saussy, Johns Hopkins UP, 2006, pp. 68–77.

Kalpakli, Fatma. "The Representation of Women in Ghosh's *Sea of Poppies.*" *English Studies: New Perspectives*, edited by Mehmet Ali Çelikel and Baysar Taniyan, Cambridge Scholars, 2015, pp. 96–103.

Kamath, Rekha. "Memory and Discourse: On Amitav Ghosh's *In an Antique Land.*" *The Poetics of Memory*, edited by Thomas Wägenbaur, Stauffenburg, 1998, pp. 205–13.

Kapadia, Novy. "Imagination and Politics in Amitav Ghosh's *The Shadow Lines.*" *The New Indian Novel in English: A Study of the 1980s*, edited by Viney Kirpal, Allied Publishers, 1990, pp. 201–12.

Kapoor, Kapil. *Language, Linguistics, and Literature: The Indian Perspective.* Academic Foundation, 1994.

Kaul, A. N. "*The Shadow Lines.*" *Indian Literature*, vol. 33, no. 4, 1990, pp. 88–95.

Kaul, Suvir. "Separation Anxiety: Growing Up Inter/National in Amitav Ghosh's *The Shadow Lines.*" A. Ghosh, *Shadow Lines*, Oxford UP, 1995, pp. 268–86.

Kaur, Rajender. "'Home Is Where the Oracella Are': Toward a New Paradigm of Transcultural Ecocritical Engagement in Amitav Ghosh's *The Hungry Tide.*" *Interdisciplinary Studies in Literature and Environment*, vol. 14, no. 1, Summer 2007, pp. 125–41.

Kearney, Richard. *On Stories.* Routledge, 2002.

Khair, Tabish, editor. *Amitav Ghosh: A Critical Companion.* Permanent Black, 2003.

———. *Babu Fictions: Alienation in Contemporary Indian English Novels.* Oxford UP, 2001.

Khilnani, Sunil. *The Idea of India.* Farrar, Straus and Giroux, 1999.

Khuraijam, Gyanabati, and Suman Acharjee. "Nation in Question in Amitav Ghosh's *The Glass Palace.*" *The Criterion*, vol. 4, no. 3, June 2013, pp. 1–6.

Khuraijam, Gyanabati, and Yumnam Oken Singh. "Amitav Ghosh's *The Hungry Tide*: The Ebb and Flow of History." *The Criterion*, vol. 4, no. 5, Oct. 2013, pp. 1–10.

King, Alison. "From Sage on the Stage to Guide on the Side." *College Teaching*, vol. 41, no. 1, Winter 1993, pp. 30–35.

Kingston, Maxine Hong. *Tripmaster Monkey: His Fake Book.* Vintage, 1990.

Kirschenbaum, Matthew G. "What Is Digital Humanities and What's It Doing in English Departments?" *ADE Bulletin*, no. 150, 2010, pp. 55–61.

Koh, Adeline, and Roopika Risam. "The Rewriting Wikipedia Project: Why Rewrite Wikipedia?" *Postcolonial Digital Humanities*, 21 Mar. 2013, dhpoco.org/blog /2013/03/21/the-rewriting-wikipedia-project-2.

Kokila, S. "Borders and Boundaries in Amitav Ghosh's *The Shadow Lines.*" *Life Science Journal*, vol. 10, no. 3, 2013, pp. 1679–87.

Kristeva, Julia. "Word, Dialogue and Novel." *The Kristeva Reader*, edited by Toril Moi, Basil Blackwell, 1986, pp. 34–61.

Kumar, S. V. Ramesh, and Rajendra Prasad. "Voicing the Subaltern in Amitav Ghosh's Novel *The Hungry Tide.*" *International Journal of English Language, Literature and Humanities*, vol. 3, no. 5, July 2015, pp. 261–69.

Lakoff, George. "Why It Matters How We Frame the Environment." *Environmental Communication*, vol. 4, no. 1, Mar. 2010, pp. 70–81.

Lal, Vinay. "The Politics of Culture and Knowledge after Postcolonialism: Nine Theses (and a Prologue)." *Continuum*, vol. 27, no. 2, 2012, pp. 191–205.

Lambek, Michael. *Ordinary Ethics: Anthropology, Language, and Action.* Fordham UP, 2010.

Lauret, Sabine. "Excavating Memories and Unlayering History: The Archaeological Narrative in Amitav Ghosh's *The Shadow Lines.*" *Commonwealth Essays and Studies*, vol. 31, no. 2, Spring 2009, pp. 78–87.

———. "Re-mapping the Indian Ocean in Amitav Ghosh's *Sea of Poppies.*" *Commonwealth Essays and Studies*, vol. 34, no. 1, Autumn 2011, pp. 55–65.

Lazreg, Marnia. "Women and Difference: The Perils of Writing as a Woman on Women in Algeria." *Feminist Studies*, vol. 14, no. 1, Spring 1988, pp. 81–107.

Lee, Rachel C. "Parasexual Generativity and Chimeracological Entanglements in Amitav Ghosh's *The Calcutta Chromosome.*" *Scholar and Feminist*, vol. 11, no. 3, Summer 2013, sfonline.barnard.edu/life-un-ltd-feminism-bioscience-race /parasexual-generativity-and-chimeracological-entanglements-in-amitav-ghoshs -the-calcutta-chromosome/0/.

Leverton, Tara. "Gender Dysphoria and Gendered Diaspora: Love, Sex and Empire in Amitav Ghosh's *Sea of Poppies.*" *English Studies in Africa*, vol. 57, no. 2, 2014, pp. 33–44.

Lint, Brad. "Ties That Bind in Opposition: Postcolonial Dynamics of Family and Freedom in Amitav Ghosh's *The Shadow Lines*." *The Journal of Commonwealth and Postcolonial Studies*, New Series vol. 3, no. 2, Fall 2015, pp. 34–44.

Lionnet, Françoise. "Cultivating Mere Gardens? Comparative *Francophonies*, Postcolonial Studies, and Transnational Feminisms." Saussy, pp. 100–13.

———. "World Literature, Postcolonial Studies, and Coolie Odysseys: J.-M.G. Le Clézio's and Amitav Ghosh's Indian Ocean Novels." *Comparative Literature*, vol. 67, no. 3, 2015, pp. 287–311.

Lukács, Georg. *The Historical Novel*. Translated by Hannah Mitchell and Stanley Mitchell. U of Nebraska P, 1983.

———. *Studies in European Realism*. Introduced by Alfred Kazin. Universal Library, 1974.

Luo, Shao-Pin. "The Way of Words: Vernacular Cosmopolitanism in Amitav Ghosh's *Sea of Poppies*." *The Journal of Commonwealth Literature*, vol. 48, no. 3, 2013, pp. 377–92.

Maharaj, Neelam A. "Amitav Ghosh and *The Forgotten Army*." *Postcolonial Text*, vol. 2, no. 2, 2006, postcolonial.org/index.php/pct/article/view/389/817.

Majeed, Javed. "Amitav Ghosh's *In an Antique Land*: The Ethnographer-Historian and the Limits of Irony." *The Journal of Commonwealth Literature*, vol. 30, no. 2, 1995, pp. 45–55.

Majumdar, N. "Shadows of the Nation: Amitav Ghosh and the Critique of Nationalism." *ARIEL*, vol. 34, nos. 2–3, 2003, pp. 237–58.

Malathi, R. "Postmodernism in Amitav Ghosh's *The Shadow Lines*." *Language in India*, vol. 13, no. 10, Oct. 2013, pp. 279–86.

Mallick, Ross. "Refugee Resettlement in Forest Reserves: West Bengal Policy Reversal and the Marichjhapi Massacre." *The Journal of Asian Studies*, vol. 58, no. 1, Feb. 1999, pp. 104–25.

Mallot, J. Edward. "'A Land outside Space, an Expanse without Distances': Amitav Ghosh, Kamila Shamsie, and the Maps of Memory." *Lit: Literature Interpretation Theory*, vol. 18, no. 3, 2007, pp. 261–84.

Mamdani, Mahmood. "The Politics of Naming: Genocide, Civil War, Insurgency." *London Review of Books*, vol. 29, no. 5, 8 Mar. 2007, www.lrb.co.uk/v29/n05/mahmood-mamdani/the-politics-of-naming-genocide-civil-war-insurgency.

Mandagaran, Arnaud, director. *India: The Turmoils of the Century*. Filmakers Library, 1994.

Mane, S., and A. Shinde. "Communal Violence in *Ice Candy Man* and *The Shadow Lines*." *Thamatics*, vol. 6, no. 1, 2015, pp. 188–98.

Marcille, Carolyn. "Technology and Colonial Power in South Asian Postcolonial Literature and Science Fiction." 2016. Indiana U of Pennsylvania, PhD dissertation.

Markandaya, Kamala. *Nectar in a Sieve*. 1954. Penguin, 1956.

Martos Hueso, María Elena. "Amitav Ghosh's 'Imaginary Homelands': The Question of Identity in *The Shadow Lines*." *India in the World*, edited by Cristina M. Gámez-Fernández and Antonia Navarro-Tejero, Cambridge Scholars, 2011.

Marx, John. "The Historical Novel after Lukács." *Georg Lukács: The Fundamental Dissonance of Existence—Aesthetics, Politics, Literature*, edited by Timothy Bewes and Timothy Hall, Continuum, 2011, pp. 188–202.

Marx, Karl. *Capital: A Critique of Political Economy*. Edited by Frederick Engels, translated by Samuel Moore and Edward Aveling, vol. 1, International, 1967.

Marzec, Robert. "Speaking before the Environment: Modern Fiction and the Ecological." *Modern Fiction Studies*, vol. 55, no. 3, Fall 2009, pp. 419–42.

Mathur, Saloni. "Wanted Native Views: Collecting Colonial Postcards of India." *Gender, Sexuality, and Colonial Modernities*, edited by Antoinette Burton, Routledge, 1999.

Mathur, Suchitra. "Caught between the Goddess and the Cyborg: Third-World Women and the Politics of Science in Three Works of Indian Science Fiction." *The Journal of Commonwealth Literature*, vol. 39, no. 3, 2004, pp. 119–38.

Mazumdar, Tapashi. "Code-Mixing and Code-Switching in the Postmodern Novel *The Glass Palace* by Amitav Ghosh: A Sociolinguistic Study." *International Journal of Multifaceted and Multilingual Studies*, vol. 1, no. 12, Sept. 2015, pp. 1–8.

McClintock, Scott. "Travels outside the Empire: The Revision of Subaltern Historiography in Amitav Ghosh." *Topologies of Fear in Contemporary Fiction: The Anxieties of Post-nationalism and Counter Terrorism*, Palgrave Macmillan, 2015, pp. 65–84.

McLeod, John. *Beginning Postcolonialism*. 2nd ed., Manchester UP, 2010.

———. "Exhibiting Empire in J. G. Farrell's *The Siege of Krishnapur*." *The Journal of Commonwealth Literature*, vol. 29, no. 2, 1994, pp. 117–32.

Mee, Jon. "'The Burthen of the Mystery': Imagination and Difference in *The Shadow Lines*." Khair, *Amitav Ghosh*, pp. 98–108.

Mehan, Uppinder. "Postcolonial Science, Cyberpunk and *The Calcutta Chromosome*." *Intertexts*, vol. 16, no. 2, Fall 2012, pp. 1–14.

Mehta, Brinda J. "*Indianités Francophones*: Kala Pani Narratives." *L'esprit Créateur*, vol. 50, no. 2, Summer 2010, pp. 1–11.

Mehta, P. B. "Cosmopolitanism and the Circle of Reason." *Political Theory*, vol. 28, no. 5, Oct. 2000, pp. 619–39.

Merivale, Patricia. "Saleem Fathered by Oskar: *Midnight's Children*, Magic Realism, and *The Tin Drum*." Zamora and Faris, *Magical Realism*, pp. 329–46.

Merrill, Christi Ann. "Laughing out of Place: Humour Alliances and Other Postcolonial Translations in *In an Antique Land*." *Interventions*, vol. 9, no. 1, 2007, pp. 106–23.

Metcalf, Thomas R. *Imperial Connections: India in the Indian Ocean Arena, 1860–1920*. U of California P, 2007.

Meyer, Sandra. "'The Story That Gave This Land Its Life': The Translocation of Rilke's *Duino Elegies* in Amitav Ghosh's *The Hungry Tide*." *Cross/Cultures*, no. 156, 2013, pp. 147–62.

Miller, Peter N., editor. *The Sea: Thalassography and Historiography*. U of Michigan P, 2013.

Mishra, Sanjit, and Nagendra Kumar. "Shaking the Roots of Western Science in Amitav Ghosh's *The Calcutta Chromosome*." *Asiatic*, vol. 5, no. 1, 2011, pp. 78–85.

Mishra, Vijay. *The Literature of the Indian Diaspora: Theorizing the Diasporic Imaginary*. Routledge, 2007.

Mohanty, Chandra Talpade. "Cartographies of Struggle: Third World Women and the Politics of Feminism." *Third World Women and the Politics of Feminism*, edited by Chandra Talpade Mohanty et al., Indiana UP, 1991, pp. 1–47.

———. "Under Western Eyes: Feminist Scholarship and Colonial Discourses." *Boundary 2*, vols. 12/13, Spring-Autumn 1984, pp. 333–58.

Mohanty, Satya P. "Literature to Combat Cultural Chauvinism." Interview by Rashmi Dube Bhatnagar and Rajender Kaur. *Frontline*, 24 Mar.–6 Apr. 2012, pp. 85–92.

Mondal, Anshuman A. "Allegories of Identity: 'Postmodern' Anxiety and 'Postcolonial' Ambivalence in Amitav Ghosh's *In an Antique Land* and *The Shadow Lines*." *Journal of Commonwealth Literature*, vol. 38, no. 3, 2003, pp. 19–36.

———. *Amitav Ghosh: Contemporary World Writers*. Manchester UP, 2007.

Mongia, Padmini, editor. *Contemporary Postcolonial Theory: A Reader*. St. Martin's Press, 2003.

Moretti, Franco. "Conjectures on World Literature." *New Left Review*, vol. 1, Jan.–Feb. 2000, pp. 54–68.

———, editor. *The Novel: History, Geography and Culture*. Vol. 1, Princeton UP, 2006.

Morrison, Toni. *Beloved*. Alfred A. Knopf, 1987.

Mujumdar, Aparna. "Modernity's Others, or Other Modernities: South Asian Negotiations with Modernity and Amitav Ghosh's *The Glass Palace*." *South Asian Review*, vol. 33, no. 1, 2012, pp. 165–84.

Mukherjee, Ankhi. *What Is a Classic? Postcolonial Rewriting and the Invention of the Canon*. Stanford UP, 2014.

Mukherjee, Meenakshi. "The Anxiety of Indianness: Our Novels in English." *Economic and Political Weekly*, vol. 28, no. 48, 27 Nov. 1993, pp. 2607–11.

———. *Elusive Terrain: Culture and Literary Memory*. Oxford UP, 2008.

———. "Epic and Novel in India." Moretti, *Novel*, pp. 596–631.

———. "Maps and Mirrors: Co-ordinates of Meaning in *The Shadow Lines*." A. Ghosh, *Shadow Lines*, Oxford UP, 1995, pp. 255–67.

———. *The Twice Born Fiction: Themes and Techniques of the Indian Novel in English*. 1971. Pencraft International, 2005.

Mukherjee, Pablo. "Surfing the Second Waves: Amitav Ghosh's Tide Country." *New Formations*, vol. 59, 2006, pp. 144–57.

Mukherjee, Payel C. "Ratnagiri as a Place of Exile and Isolation in *The Glass Palace*." *Terrains and Tropes: Contextualizing South Asia*, 10 Nov. 2012, terrainsandtropes.wordpress.com.

Murphy, Patrick D. "Community Resilience and the Cosmopolitan Role in the Environmental Challenge-Response Novels of Ghosh, Grace, and Sinha." *Comparative Literature Studies*, vol. 50, no. 1, 2013, pp. 148–68.

Myint-U, Thant. *The Making of Modern Burma*. Cambridge UP, 2001.

Nayar, Pramod K. "The Informational Economy and Its Body in Amitav Ghosh's *The Calcutta Chromosome*." *Kunapipi*, vol. 31, no. 2, 2009, pp. 52–69.

———. "The Postcolonial Uncanny: The Politics of Dispossession in Amitav Ghosh's *The Hungry Tide*." *College Literature*, vol. 37, no. 4, Fall 2010, pp. 88–119.

Nazareth, Peter. *In a Brown Mantle*. East African Literature Bureau, 1972.

Neale, Greg, and James Burton. "Elephant and Rhino Poaching 'Is Driven by China's Economic Boom.'" *The Guardian*, 13 Aug. 2011, www.theguardian.com/world /2011/aug/14/china-boom-fuels-africa-poaching.

Nehru, Jawaharlal. *The Discovery of India*. Edited by Robert I. Crane, Anchor Books, 1960.

Nelson, Diane M. "A Social Science Fiction of Fevers, Delirium and Discovery: *The Calcutta Chromosome*, the Colonial Laboratory, and the Postcolonial New Human." *Science Fiction Studies*, vol. 30, no. 2, July 2003, pp. 246–66.

Newitz, Annalee. "When Will White People Stop Making Movies like *Avatar*?" *io9*, 18 Dec. 2009, io9.gizmodo.com/5422666/when-will-white-people-stop-making -movies-like-avatar.

Ngũgĩ wa Thiong'o. *Decolonising the Mind: The Politics of Language in African Literature*. James Currey, 1986.

Nixon, Rob. "The Anthropocene: The Promise and Pitfalls of an Epochal Idea." *Edge Effects*, 6 Nov. 2014, edgeeffects.net/anthropocene-promise-and-pitfalls.

———. "Environmentalism and Postcolonialism." *Postcolonial Studies and Beyond*, edited by Ania Loomba et al., Duke UP, 2005, pp. 233–51.

———. *Slow Violence and the Environmentalism of the Poor*. Harvard UP, 2011.

Nora, Pierre. "Between Memory and History: *Les lieux de mémoire*." *Representations*, vol. 26, Spring 1989, pp. 7–24.

Northam, Jackie. "Death of Beloved Lion Heats Up Criticism of Big Game Hunting." *National Public Radio*, 31 July 2015, www.npr.org/sections/parallels/2015/07/31 /428079500/death-of-beloved-lion-heats-up-criticism-of-big-game-hunting.

Nussbaum, Martha C. *Poetic Justice: The Literary Imagination and Public Life*. Beacon Press, 1995.

Pamuk, Orhan. "My Father's Suitcase." *PMLA*, vol. 122, no. 3, May 2007, www .mlajournals.org/doi/abs/10.1632/pmla.2007.122.3.788. Nobel Lecture 2006.

Pandey, Richa Joshi. "The Idea of the Nation State and Its Disconnect with the Subaltern in Amitav Ghosh's *The Hungry Tide*." *The Criterion*, vol. 4, no. 2, Apr. 2013, pp. 1–7.

Pannapacker, William A. "The MLA and the Digital Humanities." *The Chronicle of Higher Education*, 28 Dec. 2009, www.hastac.org/blogs/nancyholliman/2009/12 /30/mla-and-digital-humanities.

Paranjape, Makarand R. "Beyond the Subaltern Syndrome: Amitav Ghosh and the Crisis of the *Bhadrasamaj*." *The Journal of Commonwealth Literature*, vol. 47, no. 3, 2012, pp. 357–74.

Parker, David. "Introduction: The Turn to Ethics in the 1990s." Adamson et al., pp. 1–18.

Pasquino, Pasquale. "Theatrum Politicum: The Genealogy of Capital—Police and the State of Prosperity." *The Foucault Effect: Studies in Governmentality*, edited by Graham Burchell et al., U of Chicago P, 1991, pp. 105–18.

Patel, Shenaz. *Le Silence des Chagos*. Éditions de l'Olivier, 2005.

Patten, Chris. Review of *River of Smoke*, by Amitav Ghosh. *Financial Times*, 24 June 2011, www.ft.com/content/b5898cee-9b4a-11e0-a254-00144feabdc0.

Patwardhan, Anand, director. *Jang aur Aman* [*War and Peace*]. First Run / Icarus Films, 2002.

Pearson, Michael N. *The Indian Ocean*. Routledge, 2003.

Phelan, James. *Narrative as Rhetoric: Technique, Audiences, Ethics, Ideology*. Ohio State UP, 1996.

———. "Sethe's Choice: *Beloved* and the Ethics of Reading." Davis and Womack, pp. 93–109.

Phillips, Caryl. *Cambridge*. Vintage International, 1993.

Pillai, Shanthini. "Resignifying 'Coolie': Amitav Ghosh's *The Glass Palace*." Sankaran, pp. 47–64.

Pirbhai, Mariam. "The Jahaji-Bhain Principle: A Critical Survey of the Indo-Caribbean Women's Novel, 1990–2009." *The Journal of Commonwealth Literature*, vol. 45, no. 1, 2010, pp. 37–56.

Pirzadeh, Saba. "Persecution vs. Protection: Examining the Pernicious Politics of Environmental Conservation in *The Hungry Tide*." *South Asian Review*, vol. 36, no. 2, 2015, pp. 107–20.

Pojman, Louis, and Lewis Vaughn, compilers. *The Moral Life: An Introductory Reader in Ethics and Literature*. 4th ed., Oxford UP, 2011.

Pollock, Sheldon. Introduction. *The Language of the Gods in the World of Men: Sanskrit, Culture and Power in Premodern India*. U of California P, 2006, pp. 1–36.

———. "*Rāmāyaṇa* and Political Imagination in India." *The Journal of Asian Studies*, vol. 52, no. 2, May 1993, pp. 261–97.

———. "Sanskrit Literary Culture from Inside Out." *Literary Cultures in History: Reconstructions from South Asia*, U of California P, 2003, pp. 39–130.

Porter, Roy. *The Enlightenment: Britain and the Creation of the Modern World*. 2nd ed., Palgrave MacMillan, 2001.

Prabhu, Gayathri. "Retelling Nature: Realism and the Postcolonial-Environmental Imaginary in Amitav Ghosh's *The Hungry Tide*." *Transnational Literature*, vol. 7, no. 2, May 2015, pp. 1–13.

Pradeep, P., and R. Poli Reddy. "*The Shadow Lines* as a Post Modern Novel." *Journal of Literature and Art Studies*, vol. 5, no. 11, Nov. 2015, pp. 1035–41.

Prasad, Murari. "Transcending the Postcolonial: Amitav Ghosh's *In an Antique Land*." *The Literary Criterion*, vol. 42, no. 2, 2007, pp. 51–61.

Pravinchandra, Shital. "Not Just Prose: *The Calcutta Chromosome*, the South Asian Short Story and the Limitations of Postcolonial Studies." *Interventions*, vol. 16, no. 3, 2014, pp. 424–44.

Prensky, Marc. "Digital Natives, Digital Immigrants Part 1." *On the Horizon*, vol. 9, no. 5, Oct. 2001, pp. 1–6.

Prusse, Michael C. "Imaginary Pasts: Colonisation, Migration and Loss in J. G. Farrell's *The Singapore Grip* and in Amitav Ghosh's *The Glass Palace*." *Transnational Literature*, vol. 2, no. 1, Nov. 2009, pp. 1–14.

Pulugurtha, Nishi. "Refugees, Settlers and Amitav Ghosh's *The Hungry Tide*." Volkmann et al., pp. 81–89.

Quayson, Ato. "Fecundities of the Unexpected: Magical Realism, Narrative, and History." Moretti, *Novel*, pp. 726–58.

Rachels, James. "Why Morality Is Not Relative." Pojman and Vaughn, pp. 160–73.

Radhakrishnan, R. "Derivative Discourses and the Problem of Signification." *The European Legacy: Toward New Paradigms*, vol. 7, no. 6, 2002, pp. 783–95.

———. "Globalization, Desire, and the Politics of Representation." *Comparative Literature*, vol. 53, no. 4, Autumn 2001, pp. 315–32.

———. *Theory in an Uneven World*. Blackwell, 2003.

Rahim, Sameer. "A Pukka Old Pishpash." *The Telegraph*, 20 June 2008, www.telegraph .co.uk/culture/books/fictionreviews/3673625/A-pukka-old-pishpash.html.

Rainsford, Dominic, and Tim Woods, editors. *Critical Ethics: Text, Theory and Responsibility*. Macmillan, 1999.

Rajan, Gita. "Ethical Responsibility in Intersubjective Spaces: Reading Jhumpa Lahiri's *Interpreter of Maladies* and 'A Temporary Matter.'" *Transnational Asian American Literature: Sites and Transits*, edited by Shirley Geok-lin Lim et al., Temple UP, 2006, pp. 123–41.

Rajan, Rajeswari Sunder. "Dealing with Anxieties." *The Hindu*, 25 Feb. 2001, www .thehindu.com/2001/02/25/stories/1325067a.htm.

———, editor. *The Lie of the Land: English Literary Studies in India*. Oxford UP, 1992.

———. "Writing in English in India, Again." *The Hindu*, 18 Feb. 2001, www.thehindu .com/2001/02/18/stories/1318067m.htm.

Ramazani, Jahan. Introduction. *The Hybrid Muse: Postcolonial Poetry in English*, U of Chicago P, 2001, pp. 1–20.

Rao, Nagesh. "Cosmopolitanism, Class and Gender in *The Shadow Lines*." *South Asian Review*, vol. 24, no. 1, July 2003, pp. 95–115.

Rath, Arnapurna. *Knots of the Narrative: Bakhtinian Chronotopes in the Fiction of Amitav Ghosh*. Lambert Academic Publishing, 2010.

Rath, Arnapurna, and Milind Malshe. "Chronotopes of 'Places' and 'Non-Places': Ecopoetics of Amitav Ghosh's *The Hungry Tide*." *Asiatic*, vol. 4, no. 2, Dec. 2010, pp. 14–33.

Ratnaker, P. Sasi, and N. Usha Srinivas. "A Reproach of Biotic Interference in Amitav Ghosh's *The Hungry Tide*." *The Criterion*, vol. 4, no. 3, June 2013, pp. 1–15.

Ratto, Matt. "Critical Making: Conceptual and Material Studies in Technology and Social Life." *The Information Society*, vol. 27, no. 4, 2011, pp. 252–60.

Reddy, Sheela. "The Ghazipur and Patna Opium Factories Together Produced the Wealth of Britain." *Outlook*, 26 May 2008, www.outlookindia.com/magazine /story/the-ghazipur-and-patna-opium-factories-together-produced-the-wealth-of -britain/237500.

Reis, Eliana Lourenço de Lima. "A Possible Utopia: Cosmopolitanism in Contemporary Art." *Aletria: Revista de Estudos de Literatura*, vol. 21, no. 2, 2011, pp. 127–43.

Rema, V. "Post-colonial Study of Amitav Ghosh's *The Sea of Poppies.*" *International Journal of English: Literature, Language and Skills*, vol. 3, no. 2, July 2014, pp. 121–23.

Rigney, Ann. *Imperfect Histories: The Elusive Past and the Legacy of Romantic Historicism*. Cornell UP, 2001.

Rockwell, Geoffrey. "Inclusion in the Digital Humanities." *philosophi.ca*, 7 Sept. 2011, philosophi.ca/pmwiki.php/Main/InclusionInTheDigitalHumanities. Accessed 16 Jan. 2018.

Roebuck, Thomas. *A Laskari Dictionary; or, Anglo-Indian Vocabulary of Nautical Terms and Phrases in English and Hindustani*. Crosby Lockwood, 1881.

Rollason, Christopher. "Empire, Sense of Place and Cultures in Contact: George Orwell's *Burmese Days* and Amitav Ghosh's *The Glass Palace.*" *Indian Journal of Postcolonial Literatures*, vol. 9, 2009, pp. 10–21.

———. "'In Our Translated World': Transcultural Communication in Amitav Ghosh's *The Hungry Tide.*" *Atlantic Literary Review*, vol. 6, nos. 1–2, 2005, pp. 86–107.

Romanik, Barbara. "Transforming the Colonial City: Science and the Practice of Dwelling in *The Calcutta Chromosome.*" *Mosaic*, vol. 38, no. 3, Sept. 2005, pp. 41–57.

Roos, Bonnie, and Alex Hunt. "Systems and Secrecy: Postcolonial Ecocriticism and Ghosh's *The Calcutta Chromosome.*" *The Cambridge Companion to Literature and the Environment*, edited by Louise Westling, Cambridge UP, 2013, pp. 183–97.

Ross, Michael L. "Passage to Krishnapur: J. G. Farrell's Comic Vision of India." *The Journal of Commonwealth Literature*, vol. 40, no. 3, 2005, pp. 63–79.

Ross, Ronald. *Memoirs*. John Murray, 1923.

Roy, Anjali. "*Microstoria*: Indian Nationalism's 'Little Stories' in Amitav Ghosh's *The Shadow Lines.*" *The Journal of Commonwealth Literature*, vol. 35, no. 2, 2000, pp. 35–49.

———. "Ordinary People on the Move: Subaltern Cosmopolitanisms in Amitav Gosh's Writings." *Asiatic*, vol. 6, no. 1, June 2012, pp. 32–46.

Roy, Binayak. "Exploring the Orient from Within: Amitav Ghosh's *River of Smoke.*" *Postcolonial Text*, vol. 9, no. 1, 2014, pp. 1–21.

———. "Mapping the Transnation: Amitav Ghosh's *The Shadow Lines.*" *Crossroads*, no. 5, 2014, pp. 16–31.

Roy, Rituparna. *South Asian Partition Fiction in English: From Khushwant Singh to Amitav Ghosh*. Amsterdam UP, 2010.

Roy, Sneharika. *The Postcolonial Epic: From Melville to Walcott and Ghosh*. Routledge, 2018.

Ruhs, Martin. *The Price of Rights: Regulating International Labor Migration*. Princeton UP, 2013.

Rushdie, Salman. "Damme, This Is the Oriental Scene for You!" 1997. *The Development of the Novel: Literary Sources and Documents*, edited by Eleanor McNees, vol. 3, Helm Information, 2006, pp. 354–68.

———. "Günter Grass." 1984. *Imaginary Homelands: Essays and Criticism, 1981–1991*, Granta/Penguin, 1992, pp. 273–81.

———. *Midnight's Children*. Jonathan Cape, 1981.

Rushdie, Salman, and Elizabeth West, editors. *The Vintage Book of Indian Writing, 1947–1997*. Vintage Books, 1997.

Saccidānandan, K., et al., editors. *At Home in the World*. Indian Council for Cultural Relations, 2005.

Said, Edward. *Orientalism*. Vintage Books, 1978.

Saklofske, Jon, et al. "They Have Come, Why Don't We Build It? On the Digital Future of Humanities." Hirsch, *Digital Humanities*, pp. 311–30.

Salvadori, Cynthia. *We Came in Dhows*. Paperchase Kenya, 1996. 3 vols.

Salvatori, Mariolina Rizzi, and Patricia Donahue. *The Elements (and Pleasures) of Difficulty*. Pearson Longman, 2005.

Sample, Mark L. "What's Wrong with Writing Essays." *Debates in the Digital Humanities*, edited by Matthew K. Gold, U of Minnesota P, 2012, pp. 404–05.

Sankaran, Chitra, editor. *History, Narrative, and Testimony in Amitav Ghosh's Fiction*. State U of New York P, 2012.

Sarkar, Barnali. "Murderous Ritual versus Devotional Custom: The Rhetoric and Ritual of Sati and Women's Subjectivity in Amitav Ghosh's *Sea of Poppies*." *Humanities*, vol. 3, no. 3, 2014, pp. 283–98.

Sarkar, Rakes. "Marginality and Creative Energy: Reading the Prospect of Postcolonialism through the *Ibis* Trilogy." *Forum for World Literature Studies*, vol. 9, no. 1, Mar. 2017, pp. 156–63.

Saussy, Haun, editor. *Comparative Literature in an Age of Globalization*. Johns Hopkins UP, 2006.

Saxena, P. "The Mystique of Magical Realism in Amitav Ghosh's: *The Circle of Reason*." *Research Scholar*, vol. 3, no. 1, 2015, pp. 326–31.

Schine, Cathleen. "Adventures in the Opium Trade." Review of *Sea of Poppies*, by Amitav Ghosh. *The New York Review of Books*, 15 Jan. 2009.

Schulze-Engler, Frank. "Literature in the Global Ecumene of Modernity: Amitav Ghosh's *The Circle of Reason* and *In an Antique Land*." *English Literatures in International Contexts*, edited by Heinz Antor and Klaus Stierstorfer, C. Winter, 2000, pp. 373–96.

Scott, David. "The Temporality of Generations: Dialogue, Tradition, Criticism." *Interpretation and Its Rivals*, special issue of *New Literary History*, vol. 45, no. 2, Spring 2014, pp. 157–81.

Sen, Asha. "Child Narrators in *The Shadow Lines*, *Cracking India*, and *Meatless Days*." *World Literature Written in English*, vol. 37, nos. 1–2, 1998, pp. 190–206.

———. "Crossing Boundaries in Amitav Ghosh's *The Shadow Lines*." *The Journal of Commonwealth and Postcolonial Studies*, vol. 5, no. 1, Fall 1997, pp. 46–58.

Sen, Malcolm. "Spatial Justice: The Ecological Imperative and Postcolonial Development." *Journal of Postcolonial Writing*, vol. 45, no. 4, Dec. 2009, pp. 365–77.

Shah, Sudha. *The King in Exile: The Fall of the Royal Family of Burma*. HarperCollins Publishers India, 2012.

Sharma, Madhu. "Debunking the Myth of Nation: A Counter Discourse by Amitav Ghosh in *The Shadow Lines*." *International Journal of Research*, vol. 2, no. 2, 2015, pp. 337–41.

Sharpe, Jenny. "The Unspeakable Limits of Rape: Colonial Violence and Counterinsurgency." *Genders*, no. 10, Spring 1991, pp. 25–46.

Shinn, Christopher A. "On Machines and Mosquitoes: Neuroscience, Bodies, and Cyborgs in Amitav Ghosh's *The Calcutta Chromosome*." *MELUS*, vol. 33, no. 4, Winter 2008, pp. 145–66.

Shohat, Ella. "Notes on the 'Post-colonial.'" Mongia, pp. 322–34.

Siddiqi, Yumna. *Anxieties of Empire and the Fiction of Intrigue*. Columbia UP, 2008, pp. 140–66.

Simon, S. "Frontiers of Memory: The Partition of India in Amitav Ghosh's *The Shadow Lines*." *Études françaises*, vol. 34, no. 1, 1998, pp. 29–43.

Simone, AbdouMaliq. *For the City Yet to Come: Changing African Life in Four Cities*. Duke UP, 2004.

Simpson, Edward, and Kai Kresse, editors. *Struggling with History: Islam and Cosmopolitanism in the Western Indian Ocean*. Columbia UP, 2008.

Sinclair, Stéfan, and Geoffrey Rockwell. "Teaching Computer-Assisted Text Analysis: Approaches to Learning New Methodologies." Hirsch, *Digital Humanities*, pp. 241–54.

Singh, Jai. "*The Hungry Tide* as Neo-Colonial Machine." *Journal of South Asian Studies*, vol. 3, no. 3, 2015, pp. 293–305.

Singh, Jaspal K. "The Indian Diaspora in Burma and the Politics of Globalization in Amitav Ghosh's *The Glass Palace* and Mira Kamdar's *Motiba's Tattoos*." *Indian Writers: Transnationalisms and Diasporas*, edited by Jaspal K. Singh and Rajendra Chetty, Peter Lang, 2010, pp. 45–65.

Singh, Kanwarpal. "Amitav Ghosh's Vision of Man-Woman Relationship in *The Hungry Tide*." *The Criterion*, vol. 4, no. 6, Dec. 2013, pp. 294–99.

Singh, Omendra Kumar. "Reinventing Caste: Indian Diaspora in Amitav Ghosh's *Sea of Poppies*." *Asiatic*, vol. 6, no. 1, June 2012, pp. 47–62.

Singh, Sujala. "The Routes of National Identity in Amitav Ghosh's *The Shadow Lines*." *Alternative Indias: Writing, Nation and Communalism*, edited by Peter Morey and Alex Tickell, Rodopi, 2005, pp. 161–80.

———. "Who Can Save the Subaltern? Knowledge and Power in Amitav Ghosh's *The Circle of Reason*." *Critical Survey*, vol. 16, no. 2, 2004, pp. 45–58.

Singh, Sushila. "Double Self in Amitav Ghosh's *The Shadow Lines*." *Language Forum*, vol. 18, nos. 1–2, 1992, pp. 135–42.

Sirohi, Anil. "The Nation as Identity in Amitav Ghosh's Novel *The Shadow Lines*." *International Journal of Research in Economics and Social Sciences*, vol. 5, no. 3, 2015, pp. 156–62.

Skinner, John. "Embodying Voices: Language and Representation in Amitav Ghosh's *The Glass Palace*." *BELL: Belgian Essays on Language and Literature*, 2002, pp. 137–49.

Slemon, Stephen. "Magic Realism as Postcolonial Discourse." Zamora and Faris, *Magical Realism*, pp. 407–26.

Smedt, Koenraad de. "Some Reflections on Studies in Humanities Computing." *Literary and Linguistic Computing*, vol. 17, no. 1, Apr. 2002, pp. 89–101.

Smith, Eric D. "'Caught Straddling a Border': A Novelistic Reading of Amitav Ghosh's *In an Antique Land*." *Journal of Narrative Theory*, vol. 37, no. 3, Fall 2007, pp. 447–72.

Sonia, M. A. "Fragmented Identities: A Study of Amitav Ghosh's *The Glass Palace*." *Language in India*, vol. 13, no. 11, Nov. 2013, pp. 316–30.

Spivak, Gayatri Chakravorty. "Can the Subaltern Speak?" *Colonial Discourse and Post-colonial Theory: A Reader*, edited by Patrick Williams and Laura Chrisman, Columbia UP, 1994, pp. 66–111.

———. *A Critique of Postcolonial Reason: Toward a History of the Vanishing Present.* Harvard UP, 1999.

———. *Death of a Discipline.* Columbia UP, 2005. Wellek Library Lectures.

———. "How to Read a 'Culturally Different' Book." *Colonial Discourse / Postcolonial Theory*, edited by Francis Barker et al., Manchester UP, 1994, pp. 126–50.

———. "Subaltern Talk: Interview with the Editors." 29 Oct. 1993. *The Spivak Reader: Selected Works of Gayatri Chakravorty Spivak*, edited by Donna Landry and Gerald MacLean, Routledge, 1996, pp. 287–308.

———. "Three Women's Texts and a Critique of Imperialism." *"Race," Writing, and Difference*, special issue of *Critical Inquiry*, vol. 12, no. 1, Autumn 1985, pp. 243–61.

Spyra, Ania. "Is Cosmopolitanism Not for Women? Migration in Qurratulain Hyder's *Sita Betrayed* and Amitav Ghosh's *The Shadow Lines*." *Frontiers*, vol. 27, no. 2, 2006, pp. 1–26.

Sreelatha, M. "Reconstructing Identities in Amitav Ghosh's *Sea of Poppies*: A Postmodernist Perspective." *Language in India*, vol. 13, no. 10, Oct. 2013, pp. 437–50.

Srivastava, Neelam. "Amitav Ghosh's Ethnographic Fictions: Intertextual Links between *In an Antique Land* and His Doctoral Thesis." *The Journal of Commonwealth Literature*, vol. 36, no. 2, 2001, pp. 45–64.

Stasi, Paul. "Amitav Ghosh's *Sea of Poppies* and the Question of Postcolonial Modernism." *Novel*, vol. 48, no. 3, Nov. 2015, pp. 323–43.

Steinwand, Jonathan. "Teaching Environmental Justice Poetry in the Anthropocene." *The Journal of Commonwealth and Postcolonial Studies*, New Series vol. 2, no. 2, Fall 2014, pp. 47–60.

———. "What the Whales Would Tell Us." DeLoughrey and Handley, *Postcolonial Ecologies*, pp. 182–99.

Su, John J. "Amitav Ghosh and the Aesthetic Turn in Postcolonial Studies." *Journal of Modern Literature*, vol. 34, no. 3, Spring 2011, pp. 65–86.

———. *Imagination and the Contemporary Novel.* Cambridge UP, 2011.

Subrahmanyam, Sanjay. *Improvising Empire: Portuguese Trade and Settlement in the Bay of Bengal, 1500–1700.* Oxford UP, 1990.

Sukanya, N., and S. Sobana. "Displacement of Nation in the Glass Palace." *International Journal of Language and Literature*, vol. 3, no. 1, June 2015, pp. 120–23.

Sultana, Gousia. "Reflection of Postcolonialism in the Novels of Amitav Ghosh." *International Journal of the Frontiers of English Literature and the Patterns of ELT*, vol. 1, no. 1, Jan. 2013, pp. 2–5.

Sumati, Yadav. "*The Hungry Tide*: Climate Sustainability En Route from Ancient Texts to Modern Fiction to Humanity." *Caesura*, vol. 2, no. 1, 2015, pp. 31–54.

Survival International. "The Real *Avatar*: Mine—Story of a Sacred Mountain." *YouTube*, 31 Mar. 1999, youtu.be/R4tuTFZ3wXQ.

———. "Tribal Conservationists: No Tribes, No Nature, No Future." *Survival International*, www.survivalinternational.org/conservation.

———. "Undercover TV Report Exposes Mass Evictions from India's Tiger Reserves." *Survival International*, 22 July 2015, www.survivalinternational.org/news/10852.

———. "Victory: India Saves 'Avatar Tribe' from Vendanta Mine." *Survival International*, 13 Jan 2014, www.survivalinternational.org/news/9621.

Szeman, Imre. "On the Energy Humanities; or, What Can Philosophy Tell Us about Oil? (A Preliminary Sketch)." *European Union Centre of Excellence Working Papers*, no. 1, U of Alberta, Jan. 2015.

Tadie, A. "Amitav Ghosh: The Nuances of History." *Esprit*, no. 1, 2002, pp. 62–73.

Tankersley, Molly. "Average Is the New Green: How Millennials Are Redefining Environmentalism." *Huffington Post*, 16 June 2014, www.huffingtonpost.com/molly-tankersley/average-is-the-new-green-_b_5499778.html.

Teeman, Tim. "Opium Was the Single Largest Sector of the Empire's Economy." *The Times* [London], 11 June 2011, pp. 16–17.

Tejani, Bahadur. *Day after Tomorrow.* East African Literature Bureau, 1971.

Telwani, Shouket Ahmad. "Subalternity: A Question in Amitav Ghosh and Khaled Hosseini." *ThirdFront*, vol. 1, no. 1, 2013, pp. 113–27.

Temper, Leah, and Joan Martínez-Alier, directors. *Environmental Justice Atlas.* Coordinated by Daniela Del Bene, ejatlas.org.

Tharu, Susie, editor. *Subject to Change: Teaching of Literature in the Nineties.* Orient Longman, 1998.

Thieme, John. "Amitav Ghosh." *A Companion to Indian Fiction in English*, edited by Pier Paolo Piciucco, Atlantic Publishers and Distributors, 2004, pp. 251–75.

Thomas, Deborah A. "Public Bodies: Virginity Testing, Redemption Songs, and Racial Respect in Jamaica." *Journal of Latin American Anthropology*, vol. 11, no. 1, 2006, pp. 1–31.

Thomas, Julia Adeney, et al. "JAS Round Table on Amitav Ghosh, *The Great Derangement: Climate Change and the Unthinkable.*" *The Journal of Asian Studies*, vol. 75, no. 4, Nov. 2016, pp. 929–55.

Thompson, Hilary. "Before After: Amitav Ghosh's Pre-1856 Cosmopolis as Post-9/11 Lost Object." *The City since 9/11: Literature, Film, Television*, edited by Keith Wilhite, Fairleigh Dickinson UP, 2016, pp. 161–75.

Thrall, James H. "Postcolonial Science Fiction? Science, Religion and the Transformation of Genre in Amitav Ghosh's *The Calcutta Chromosome*." *Literature and Theology*, vol. 23, no. 3, Sept. 2009, pp. 289–302.

Tiffin, Helen. "Animal, Environment, and Post-colonial Future." *The Future of Postcolonial Studies*, edited by Chantal Zabus, Routledge, 2015, pp. 144–54.

Tomsky, Terri. "Amitav Ghosh's Anxious Witnessing and the Ethics of Action in *The Hungry Tide*." *The Journal of Commonwealth Literature*, vol. 44, no. 1, 2009, pp. 53–65.

Torabully, Khal. *Cale d'étoiles-Coolitude*. Azalées Éditions, 1992.

Trumpener, Katie. *Bardic Nationalism: The Romantic Novel and the British Empire*. Princeton UP, 1997.

Ullah, A. K. M. Ahsan, et al. *Migration and Worker Fatalities Abroad*. Palgrave Macmillan, 2015.

United Nations, Department of Economic and Social Affairs, Population Division. "International Migration." *United Nations*, www.un.org/en/development/desa/population/theme/international-migration.

Vālmīki. *The Rāmāyaṇa of Vālmīki: An Epic of Ancient India*. Edited by Robert P. Goldman et al., Princeton UP, 1984–2016. 7 vols.

Verhovek, Sam Howe. "Reviving Tradition, Tribe Kills a Whale." *The New York Times*, 18 May 1999, www.nytimes.com/1999/05/18/us/reviving-tradition-tribe-kills-a-whale.html.

Vescovi, Alessandro. "Amitav Ghosh in Conversation." *ARIEL*, vol. 40, no. 4, 2009, pp. 129–41.

———. "Emplotting the Postcolonial: Epistemology and Narratology in Amitav Ghosh's *The Calcutta Chromosome*." *ARIEL*, vol. 48, no. 1, Jan. 2017, pp. 37–69.

———. "Fear and Ethics in the Sundarbans: Anthropology in Amitav Ghosh's *The Hungry Tide*." *Governare la paura*, 2014, pp. 141–57.

———. "Voicing Unspoken Histories: Amitav Ghosh's *Sea of Poppies* as Research Novel." *History and Narration: Looking Back from the Twentieth Century*, edited by Marialuisa Bignami et al., Cambridge Scholars, 2011, pp. 190–209.

Vink, Markus P. M. "Indian Ocean Studies and the 'New Thalassology.'" *Journal of Global History*, vol. 2, no. 1, Mar. 2007, pp. 41–62.

Virgil. *The Aeneid*. Translated by Robert Fagles, Viking, 2006.

Viswanathan, Gauri. "Beyond Orientalism: Syncretism and the Politics of Knowledge." *Stanford Humanities Review*, vol. 5, no. 1, 1996, pp. 19–34.

———. *Masks of Conquest: Literary Study and British Rule in India*. Faber and Faber, 1989.

Volkmann, Laurenz, et al., editors. *Local Natures, Global Responsibilities: Ecocritical Perspectives on the New English Literatures*. Rodopi, 2010.

von Einsiedel, Orlando, director. *Virunga*. Roco Films Educational, 2014.

Wadewitz, Adrianne, et al. "Wiki-Hacking: Opening up the Academy with Wikipedia." *Wikipedia*, 11 June 2017, en.wikipedia.org/wiki/User:Wadewitz/TeachingEssay.

Walcott, Derek. *Omeros*. Farrar, Straus and Giroux, 1992.

———. *Selected Poems*. Farrar, Straus and Giroux, 2007.

Walker, Margaret Urban. "Moral Repair and Its Limits." Davis and Womack, pp. 110–27.

Warnes, Christopher. *Magical Realism and the Postcolonial Novel: Between Faith and Irreverence*. Palgrave Macmillan, 2009.

Wassef, Hind. "Beyond the Divide: History and National Boundaries in the Work of Amitav Ghosh." *Alif: Journal of Comparative Poetics*, no. 18, 1998, pp. 75–95.

Watt, Ian. *The Rise of the Novel: Studies in Defoe, Richardson and Fielding.* 1957. U of California P, 1971.

Weedon, Chris. "Key Issues in Postcolonial Feminism: A Western Perspective." *Gender Forum*, no. 1, 2002, pp. 43–54.

Weik, Alexa. "The Home, the Tide, and the World: Eco-cosmopolitan Encounters in Amitav Ghosh's *The Hungry Tide*." *The Journal of Commonwealth and Postcolonial Studies*, vol. 13, no. 2–vol. 14, no. 1, 2006–2007, pp. 120–41.

White, Hayden. *Metahistory: The Historical Imagination in Nineteenth-Century Europe*. Johns Hopkins UP, 1973.

White, Laura A. "Novel Vision: Seeing the Sunderbans through Amitav Ghosh's *The Hungry Tide*." *Interdisciplinary Studies in Literature and Environment*, vol. 20, no. 3, 2013, pp. 513–31.

Wikimedia Foundation. "Editor Survey 2011 / Executive Summary." *Wikimedia Meta-Wiki*, 4 Oct. 2016, meta.wikimedia.org/wiki/Editor_Survey_2011 /Executive_Summary. Accessed 16 Jan. 2018.

World Wildlife Fund. *Save Tigers Now*. www.savetigersnow.org. Accessed 16 Jan. 2018.

Wyschogrod, Edith. *An Ethics of Remembering: History, Heterology, and the Nameless Others*. U of Chicago P, 1998.

Young, Robert J. C. "Ideologies of the Postcolonial." *Interventions*, vol. 1, no. 1, 1998, pp. 4–8.

Yule, Henry, and Arthur C. Burnell. *Hobson-Jobson: A Glossary of Colloquial Anglo-Indian Words and Phrases*. John Murray, 1886.

Zafar, Aylin. "Study: For Millennials, It's Not So Easy Being Green." *Time*, 16 Mar. 2012, newsfeed.time.com/2012/03/16/study-for-millennials-its-not-so-easy -being-green.

Zagade, Sanjay Haribhau. "Issues of Identity in Amitav Ghosh's *The Hungry Tide*." *International Journal of Multifaceted and Multilingual Studies*, vol. 1, no. 1, 2014, pp. 1–8.

Zamora, Lois Parkinson, and Wendy B. Faris. "Daiquiri Birds and Flaubertian Parrot(ie)s." Zamora and Faris, *Magical Realism*, pp. 1–11.

———, editors. *Magical Realism: Theory, History, Community*. Duke UP, 1995.

Zanganeh, Lila Azam. "Excavation." *Guernica*, 15 May 2011, www.guernicamag.com /ghosh_5_15_11/.

Žižek, Slavoj. "*Avatar*: Return of the Natives." *New Statesman*, 4 Mar. 2010, www .newstatesman.com/film/2010/03/avatar-reality-love-couple-sex.

Zuidervaart, Lambert. "Theodor W. Adorno." *Stanford Encyclopedia of Philosophy*, edited by Edward N. Zalta, Winter 2011 Edition, plato.stanford.edu/archives /win2011/entries/adorno.

INDEX